Essays
from the
Lowell Conference
on
Industrial History
1982 and 1983

The Arts and Industrialism

The Industrial City

Edited by
Robert Weible

Musuem of American Textile History
North Andover, Massachusetts
1985

Essays from the
Lowell Conference on
Industrial History
1982 and 1983

CONTENTS

Page

TECHNOLOGY AND THE CITY

Introduction

The creation of Lowell National Historical Park in 1978 marked the culmination of nearly a decade of effort by the citizens of Lowell, Massachusetts, to gain national recognition of the role which their city has played in shaping and reflecting American history. Lowell had been *the* showplace of American industry during the first half of the nineteenth century and, as such, had helped pioneer the transition of the American economy and way of life from agricultural to industrial; and for a century and a half Lowell has witnessed first-hand the full legacy of the industrialization process, both its positive and negative aspects, making Lowell's history a microcosm of the entire American industrial experience.

The idea of a historical park in Lowell was innovative, to say the least, and since 1978, the development of Lowell National Historical Park has paid noteworthy dividends both locally and nationally. In Lowell, the Park has helped restore a sense of community long thought irretrievable while serving as the catalyst for some very real economic growth throughout the city. As David Sekers, the Director of Britain's Quarry Bank Mill, noted at the 1983 Lowell Conference on Industrial History: "a good museum [or national park], like any good work of art, changes the view of what you see around you." And Lowell's national park has indeed changed people's perceptions here: buildings and sites formerly considered real estate liabilities—empty mills, dilapidated boardinghouses—are now thought of as cultural and historical assets. The rate of unemployment in Lowell has dropped as rapidly as business activity and real estate values have risen.

More than just serving local economic and cultural interests, however, the transformation of Lowell from a depressed milltown into a national historical park indicates an important shift in attitude about the public interpretation of history and about Americans' sense of historical place. That is, no longer is it necessary for historic sites to simply idealize the past, no longer do they need to recount only the triumphs of selected political and social elites. We have, it seems, come to the realization that history should be interpreted more factually as a rational process and less symbolically as a series of isolated events. And we have even begun to recognize the role played by common people in the past as well as by the exceptional.

Although such insights into history may be new to the public, the historical profession has long prided itself on such basic understandings. Still, as we are only recently beginning to recognize, the historical profession has lacked audiences for its message much larger than those found on college campuses. And the profession's isolation (some would say: "self-imposed isolation") has really prevented it from being taken seriously by many and from becoming a dynamic voice in business and in the formation of public policy: hence, the declining job market for historians and the shrinking enrollments in university history programs, among other things. But with Lowell and places like it, historians of labor, business, the city, and technology have a real opportunity to see their work made available in a meaningful way to new, bigger groups of people; an opportunity to change people's appreciation for the value of history; and an opportunity to help revitalize the profession itself into a more useful art.

To those of us working in Lowell, the Lowell Conference on Industrial History seemed an ideal means for helping bridge the gap between professional historians and the public. The conference not only exposes university-based scholars to the very public work being done in Lowell, but given the fact that scholarly interpretations of industrial history are continually changing, the Lowell Conference also keeps people in Lowell current with the latest professional research in the field. In effect the Lowell Conference makes its participants all partners in the same Lowell project.

The Lowell Conference is an annual event which examines a different topic in industrial history each year. The first conference met in 1980 to address "The Social Impacts of Industrialization," with such speakers as Oscar Handlin, Stephan Thernstrom, and Thomas Dublin discussing a wide range of topics, from the effects of changing technology on the work experience to the consequences of industrialization for women. In 1981, David Montgomery, John T. Dunlop, and Robert B. Reich were included among conference participants concerned with "The Relationship of Government and Industry in the United States." Proceedings from these first two conferences were published in 1981. The present volume includes the main body of works from the next two meetings of the Lowell Conference on Industrial History, meetings which focused on "The Arts and Industrialism" in 1982 and "The Industrial City" in 1983.

*   *   *

The 1982 conference was intended to explore the ways in which the growth of an industrial society has shaped the aesthetic of the modern world and to see how the arts have in turn shaped our understanding of industrial society. The meeting began with a discussion of architecture and the industrial landscape and with Richard Candee's reexamination of the building forms adopted by the Boston Associates, the group of financiers mainly responsible for the rapid growth of the textile industry in early nineteenth century New England. John Stilgoe followed Candee's presentation with his portrait of central stations, the huge electricity-generating facilities which transformed both the urban landscape and urban way of life at the turn of the century.

Although Thomas Bender's paper from the Lowell Conference is not reprinted here, Bender examined the changing landscape in early twentieth century New York and the growth of more vertical aesthetic there. Literary interpretations of the industrial landscape became the focal point of discussion in the next conference session, as Leo Marx commented on papers by Michael Folsom, David Gross, and Cecelia Tichi. All three essays appear in this volume, with Folsom's paper examining Whittier's, Melville's, and Edward Bellamy's impressions of the early industrial city; Gross's exploring William Morris's alternative visions for industrial society and the city; and Tichi's describing industrialization in American literature during the opening decades of the twentieth century. An evening session of the conference featured Patrick Malone's slide presentation on automobile design and the culture it spawned during the 1950's.

Senator Paul Tsongas, one of the people most responsible for the cultural revitalization of Lowell, opened the second day of the '82 Lowell Conference with a call for increased government support for the arts and humanities. Tsongas noted that the likelihood of such funding in the future was jeopardized by recent increases in the defense budget.

Morning sessions of the conference concerned themselves with the portrayal of people in the visual arts during the industrial era. Patricia Hills took on the very formidable task of surveying and interpreting the depiction of working Americans in the fine and popular arts from 1800 to 1950; David Jaffee examined the portrait painters who helped build a new commercial order and "new cultural code of consumption" in the northern countryside during the first half of the nineteenth century; and William Stott discussed the "documentary" and "streamlined" styles of imagery that dominated American photography in the 1930's. All three papers are reprinted here. At the conference, too, George Basalla discussed the human image in film, and director Jan Egleson spoke about making films which deal with urban-industrial subjects.

Conference sessions in the afternoon featured a performance of industrial folk songs by Alex Demas of the Lowell National Historical Park staff and John Kasson's examination of the urban bourgeoisie's changing manners in the second half of the nineteenth century. Laurence Gross's paper, included here, looked at the proletarian novel and argued that the genre has been ignored by literary critics more because it challenges the values and status of the literary profession than because of its own artistic merit. The conference concluded with a six-member panel discussion focusing on the funding of the arts and humanities. Participants included Ann Banks of the American Writers' Congress, Patricia Hills of Boston University, Haffiz Mohamed of the Massachusetts Council on the Arts and Humanities,

Richard Rabinowitz of the American History Workshop, Barbara A. Reuter of the Philip Morris Corporation, and Congressman James M. Shannon of Massachusetts.

*   *   *

Governor Michael Dukakis opened the 1983 conference on "The Industrial City" by addressing the continuing need to preserve and understand the urban-industrial heritage. The Governor also spoke of the economic benefits of urban revitalization projects, like Lowell's, built around historical themes.

The first full session of the meeting featured Eric Lampard's paper which summarized the work Lampard has done in over thirty years of studying urbanization, a process he regards essentially as changing ecological systems and population concentrations. Because Lampard's work has played such a major role in shaping our understanding of the city, his paper served as the focal point for commentary and discussion on the teaching of urban history by Michael Frisch and Frank Walsh. The two each described the tension that exists between more conceptual approaches to the subject (like Lampard's) and other more diverse and particular techniques. A panel discussion on the preservation of the industrial city followed, with David Gillespie, Kenneth Jackson, Ian Menzies, David Sekers, and Sam Bass Warner exploring the ways in which historical industrial cities can build vital economies while at the same time serving as educational tools through historic preservation and museum programs.

The second day of the meeting began with an exploration of some of the social dimensions of the industrial city. John Bodnar's paper portrayed European immigrants to the American city less as victims of modernization than as rational people making calculated decisions about their futures; Susan Hirsch, in a paper co-authored by Janice Reiff, looked at the question of job segregation and the degree to which it has been determined by local social hierarchies, as opposed to company policy; and Frank Couvares argued that the relatively successful incorporation of working class immigrants into American society should be recognized and not dismissed or explained away. Virginia Yans-McLaughlin's commentary on the three papers, included here, placed the three papers in a useful cultural and historiographical context, and Stephan Thernstrom's remarks served as the basis for a lively audience discussion.

Sam Bass Warner presented the final paper of the day focusing on some of the cultural impacts of modern technology. Warner's study of the Boston engineering firm of Stone & Webster suggested that Americans today still tend to evaluate public utility system according to the nineteenth century standards of profit margin and technological efficiency alone, while they ignore the considerable social consequences of such systems. In her commentary, Ruth Schwartz Cowan created a piece of "counter-factual" history which reinforced Warner's point that our built environment does indeed reflect the cultural values of people like Messrs. Stone and Webster. The conference concluced with a showing of the multi-image slide show "Lowell: The Industrial Revelation," at the Lowell National Historical Park Visitor Center and a discussion of Park resources, programs, and development plans.

*   *   *

The planning of the Lowell Conference reflects the cooperation between the public and private sectors, between state and federal governments, and among individuals that has come to characterize the revitalization of Lowell. In particular, the success of the Conference is due to the very active support and sponsorship it enjoys from William T. Hogan, President of the University of Lowell; John B. Duff, Chairman, and Fred Faust, Executive Director of the Lowell Historic Preservation Commission; Marie Sweeney, President of the Lowell Museum; and John J. Burchill, Superintendent of Lowell National Historical Park. Staff members from the sponsoring organizations who have helped make the 1982 and 1983 conferences possible include Charles Carroll, Paul Coppens, Terry Daigle, Cliff Lewis, Martha Mayo, Edward Miller, Leo Panas, Catherine Quinn, the late Vincent Vinagro, Robert Wagner, and Frank Walsh from the University; Paul Marion and James St. Clair from the Preservation Commission; Lewis T. Karabatsos and A. Nancy Rourke from the Lowell Museum; and W. Lewis Barlow, Patricia Butler, Andrew Chamberlain, Denise Comito, John Debo, Lawrence Gall, Duncan Hay, Colette Joyce, Peter Promutico, Peter Richards, and Maude Salinger from the Park. The publication of this volume of conference proceedings was made possible through the support and assistance of Thomas W. Leavitt, Director of the Museum of American Textile History, and with the editorial assistance of Laura Tonelli of the Museum staff. The Conference also owes a debt of gratitude to Michael Ebner of Lake Forest College, Michael Folsom of the Charles River Museum of Industry, and Heather Huyck of the National Park Service for their assistance in planning the '82 and '83 meetings; and to Governor Michael S. Dukakis, Congressman James M. Shannon, and Senator Paul E. Tsongas for their participation in the Lowell Conference and for their continued support of the many programs that have helped restore a bright future for Lowell through the city's increased awareness of its past.

Robert Weible
Chairman, Lowell Conference on Industrial History

Part I

The Arts and Industrialism

Program

The Arts and Industrialism

April 30 - May 1, 1982

SESSION I

The Industrial Landscape in Painting and Architecture
Chair: Dwight Pitcaithley, National Park Service

Richard M. Candee, Boston University
"Architecture and Corporate Planning in the Waltham System"

John R. Stilgoe, Harvard University
"Central Stations and the Electric Vision, 1890 to 1930"

Thomas Bender, New York University
"Tall Is Beautiful: Aesthetic Tensions in Early Modern New York"

SESSION II

Literary Interpretations of the Industrial Landscape
Chair: Leo Marx, Massachusetts Institute of Technology

Michael Brewster Folsom, Charles River Museum of Industry
"The Unredeemed Landscape: Early Literary Encounters with the Industrial City"

David S. Gross, University of Oklahoma
" 'How We Live and How We Might Live': Life in the Industrial City and the Alternative Vision of William Morris"

Cecelia Tichi, Boston University
" 'Trees, Animals, Engines': Industrialization in American Literature, 1900-1925"

Comment: Leo Marx

SESSION III

Patrick M. Malone, Slater Mill Historic Site
"The Automobile Culture of the 1950's"

SESSION IV

The Human Image in Industrial America
Chair: Liana Cheney, University of Lowell

Patricia Hills, Boston University
"The Fine Arts in America: Images of Labor from 1800 to 1950"

David P. Jaffee, Harvard University
"An Artisan-Entrepreneur's Portrait of the Industrializing North, 1790-1860"

William Stott, University of Texas
"Hard Times and Happy Days: The Visual Iconography of Depression America"

SESSION V

Film and the Industrial Age
Chair: Michael Schaffer, Larson and Rosen Meeting Producers

George Basalla, University of Delaware
"The Human Image in Cinema"

Jan Egleson, filmmaker
discussion of his work

SESSION VI

Alex Demas, National Park Service
"Tunes and Tales: Industrial Folk Songs of the 19th and Early 20th Centuries"

SESSION VII

The Literature of Industrialization
Chair: Lawrence Gall, National Park Service

John F. Kasson, University of North Carolina
"The Urban Bourgeoisie and the Literature of Etiquette"

Laurence F. Gross, Museum of American Textile History
"Proletarians and Professors, or Why Sweat and Holy Water Don't Mix"

SESSION VIII

The Patronage of the Arts in an Industrial Society
Chair: Haffiz Mohamed, Massachusetts Council on the Arts and Humanities

Panel: Ann Banks, American Writers' Congress
       Patricia Hills, Boston University
       Richard Rabinowitz, American History Workshop
       Barbara A. Reuter, Philip Morris Corporation
       Hon. James M. Shannon, U.S. House of Representatives

Architecture and Corporate Planning In the Early Waltham System

RICHARD M. CANDEE

In April 1831 Christopher Colt, Agent of the Hampshire Manufacturing Company in Ware, Massachusetts, wrote to the corporation's office in Boston, "Before I give you a plan of a new factory, I shall wish to visit (with our machinist) some of the most approved factories in the country."[1] Suggesting those in Paterson, New Jersey, and Lowell he sought the wishes of his company's directors. Two weeks later, in a letter to the Treasurer in Boston, he wrote:

> Is it the wish of the company that I shall proceed to Lowell
> for information? If so, can the compy get permission to take
> a plan of their best mill? Without permission to take dimen-
> sions, it will be of little use to go.[2]

This confirms the slightly later report of the British machinist James Montgomery, who had been employed in the mills at Saco, Maine, and taken the opportunity to compare the state of British and American cotton manufacturing. Describing the American cotton factories in the late 1830's he saw three distinct divisions. The first encompassed the northern New England states, including the eastern parts of Massachusetts where the principal manufacturing centers were Lowell, Waltham, Taunton, Fall River, Springfield, and Three Rivers, as well as Dover, Great Falls, Newmarket, and Nashua in New Hampshire, and Saco, Maine.

> All the manufacturing establishments in this district
> belong to joint stock companies, and, in general, they
> follow the Lowell plans in the form and arrangement of the
> Mills, as well as in the style of their machinery.[3]

Montgomery's second or 'middle' district was southern New England. Because the American cotton industry began in this area, Montgomery found much of the machinery old, but "the best and newest mills being in or near Providence, the others generally copy their plans and style of machinery."[4] To the south of New England he found that factories "generally adopt the plans and improvements of Paterson and Matteawan, [New York]," which in turn borrowed directly from Great Britain.[5]

By dividing New England into two distinct manufacturing regions centering on Providence and Lowell, Montgomery may have influenced the later writings of the man who brought him to America, Samuel Batchelder. Batchelder's *Introduction and Early Progress of the Cotton Manufacture in the United States* seems to have established the terms used by later historians for "two different systems or *schools* of manufacturing, one of which might be denominated the *Rhode*

Island, and the other the *Waltham* system."[6]

While both Montgomery and Batchelder, who had been a mill agent at both Lowell and Saco, saw these divisions primarily in terms of technological differences, these terms have been extended to symbolize distinctions of architecture, town planning, labor and wage systems, as well as corporate organization and management. This pattern was set by Carolyn F. Ware's 1931 pioneering study, *Early New England Cotton Manufacture,* and the Rhode Island factory system's primary documents more recently published in *The New England Mill Village, 1790-1860.*[7] My own efforts to document and refine the architectural and town or village characteristics of these two systems have been published elsewhere.[8] This paper re-examines some of the conventional wisdom about the building forms adopted by the Boston Associates, that group of capitalists who established power weaving at their mills in Waltham and expanded into calico printing and a variety of textile manufactures by establishing the first American industrial city at Lowell.

Although historians may emphasize the importance of differing elements in the Waltham system, there has been widespread agreement that the significant features were:

> ample working capital was provided, and the principal processes carried on in one plant, under unified management.
> The directors were selected for their general executive ability rather than technical knowledge; the workers were recruited, and they were housed in factory dormitories.
> Each factory concentrated on producing one standard type of cloth, and their products were distributed through a single marketing agency, rather than being distributed by numerous jobbers.[9]

The introduction of large-scale financing of cotton manufacturing by wealthy Boston merchants, who had heretofore avoided investing in the textile industry, was in direct contrast to the poorly funded partnerships between mechanics and merchants throughout New England. It was the result of Francis Cabot Lowell's vision of recreating a water-powered loom like those he had seen on his tour of Great Britain in 1810-1811. By 1813 Lowell and the mechanic Paul Moody had created a working model of the loom and chartered a new company composed of a dozen friends and relatives among Boston's mercantile community. By integrating the power loom into the first mill they erected in nearby Waltham, Massachusetts, they achieved what other New England manufacturers had not: powered production of cloth from raw material to finished product.[10] The technological experiment tested at Waltham's Boston Manufacturing Company, as the new corporation was known, involved the development of its own machinery which would pick and spin the cotton into just enough yarn to be woven on the new looms.

To integrate weaving into the mills of New England required a larger somewhat different workforce than that employed by the smaller firms which had sprung up on water power sites before and during the Embargo and War of 1812. Whereas women and children, usually in family groups, had been the largest part of the cotton spinning workforce, the loom required more workers of an age, at least in their late teens, than most families could offer. Single women in their late teens and early twenties entered the Waltham mills, often in small groups of friends or relatives. It has been generally assumed, as one recent historian has stated, that "Lowell and his successors employed teenage girls, housed in boardinghouses, under the eye of respectable matrons."[11]

From the beginning the Boston Manufacturing Company employed a large number of machinists to build their own equipment. In 1816, when the Boston directors decided to enlarge their operations, they authorized the building of a second mill and a new brick machine shop. The increased size of the machine shop attracted experienced men, usually married with families.

The financial organization of the Boston Manufacturing Company, too, differed from its contemporaries. More heavily capitalized and incorporated by the state, the company was managed by its Treasurer, Patrick Tracy Jackson, and agent and superintendent Paul Moody, who worked at the Waltham site. The Treasurer was delegated broad authority, eventually making that office the central post of financial decision-making among the later Boston dominated corporations. Between Lowell's death in 1817 and 1820 the company established a policy of retaining all patent rights on improvements made by its machinist and began to sell both machinery and patent rights to others. Unlike other mills, the employees were paid cash wages biweekly rather than given credit at a company-owned store. Beginning in 1819 the Boston Manufacturing Company authorized Nathan Appleton's partnership Ward & Company as its exclusive selling agent, thus establishing the form of a single, permanent, Boston sales agency as the Waltham system's method of distribution. Appleton was one of the Boston Manufacturing Company's principle investors. In 1820 the legislature granted the company's request to increase its capital stock to $600,000 to keep the ratio of liquid capital to fixed assets adequate. When Jackson and the Lowell heirs did not increase their stock holdings, shares became available to a few new merchant importers. Together with the original stockholders, these men formed the embryo of the Boston Associates, those investors who dominated the founding and promotion of new companies based on the Waltham system.[12]

Between March 1814, when the Directors authorized Lowell and Jackson to contract for the first factory at Waltham, and the recapitalization of 1820 there was a corresponding evolution of architectural and corporate town planning. The main elements of the Boston Associate-owned corporations involved the establishment of a factory design that remained unchanged until the late 1830's and the method of housing the new factory workers, especially the 'mill girls' at Waltham. Until the past few years the investigation of these aspects of the Waltham system has been hampered by the later nineteenth century rebuilding of the original mills and enlargement of the factory site, as well as the removal and demolition of earlier factory housing.

In 1970 I identified a painting in the Lowell Historical Sociaty's collection as being a view of Waltham (Figure 1) which may be dated between 1826 and 1830 (on the basis of which early Waltham churches do and do not appear in the painting).[13] In 1978 a second painting entitled, "A View of the Waltham Mgf. Establishment" signed by Elijah Smith, Jr., and dated on the reverse of the wood panel "A.D. 1824" (Figure 2) was given to Gore Place in Waltham. Charles Hammond, Curator of Gore Place, has identified Smith as a local sign and decorative painter born in Waltham in 1788 and died there in 1828. His probate inventory documents his shop, which includes paints and painter's tools as well as a half dozen signs.[14] On this basis the larger oil on canvas has been tentatively attributed to Smith also, even though his signed painting is on wood as befits a sign painter. No signed paintings on canvas by Elijah Smith, Jr. are known.

Finally, in 1981 Michael Folsom, Director of the Charles River Museum of Industry in Waltham, found and identified a watercolor and pencil drawing (Figure 3) among a cache of important machinery drawings by Isaac E. Markham in the Sheldon Art Museum in Middlebury, Vermont. Markham was a talented mechanic from Middlebury who by 1818 had built water powered looms for a local cotton and woolen mill in which he worked as the "superintendent and draughtsman" of these machines. In 1819 he moved to Waltham as an employee of the Boston Manufacturing Company, where he was still employed in May 1821, although he returned to Middlebury by December that year.[15] Thus, Markham's sketch of the Waltham mills is the earliest known view, and it differs from the paintings by being done from a point directly in front of the mills and behind the houses which faced the mill yard.

To these three contemporary illustrations of the Waltham factories and the surrounding community, each providing a different perspective, the documentary evidence can be joined for a re-evaluation of this site. As much has been claimed for the Waltham experiment as the model for Lowell and other factory towns built by the Boston Associates, these visual representations made between 1819 and 1828 or 1830 reward careful observation. Like the documentary record, however, they need to be placed in context with architectural and industrial housing practices of other New England mill villages.

The industrial landscape of New England before Waltham was

Figure 1. Waltham, Massachusetts ca. 1826-1830, oil on canvas possibly attributed to Elijah Smith. This detail from the larger painting shows the Boston Manufacturing Company lands from across the Charles River. The first mill is next to the dam, the smaller machine shop behind it. The second factory, without cupola, adjoins it while a forger blacksmith's shop is located downstream. Across the mill yard are company built houses facing the office and storage sheds. (Lowell Historical Society; original photograph courtesy of Old Sturbridge Village, Henry Peach photographer; cropping by Blaise Davi, National Park Service.)

Figure 2. "A View of the Waltham Manufacturing Establishment", 1824, oil on panel signed by Elijah Smith (1788-1828), a local sign and decorative painter. This illustrates the mill facades from Dr. Jackson's yard and provides clearer definition of the corporate housing, including the Long Row in the far right. (photograph courtesy of Gore Place Society, Richard Cheek photographer.)

Figure 3. Pencil and wash sketch of Boston Manufacturing Company mills and houses, ca. 1820, by Isaac Markham, machinist and draftsman. This detailed sketch is the earliest known view of the company and provides exceptional new information about the company houses as well as the newly-built second factory with its wooden tower and projecting picker houses. The small shed (far right) and the simple secondary structure in the foreground appear as well in figure 2. in front of the Long Row. (photograph courtesy of The Sheldon Museum.)

one of small mill villages with factories, generally of wood, but by 1807 of stone and 1810 of brick. [16] These were nearly all two or three stories tall, usually under 100 feet in length, often sited at right angles to the main waterway, and covered with one of three roof forms. Perhaps the most common was a simple pitched roof, although by at least 1810 a clerestory or "double roof," to use James Montgomery's term for the full turn of attic windows framed into the roof, had been adopted by some factories. There is limited, but firm evidence of such a roof on at least one of Arkwright's cotton factories in England. A variation which raised the roof for narrow bands of windows between a partial run of rafters was called by one 1820's mill agent a "false" roof. [17]

After Waltham the industrial landscape of New England became one of great contrast between numerous small mill villages with wood or stone factories common to the Rhode Island system (but built throughout the region) and a handful of large, brick industrial cities and towns. The composition of the Waltham mills evolved from contemporary building practices and was formed into a factory design replicated exactly in Lowell and modified elsewhere by others who tried to imitate the Waltham system. The first Waltham mill was 90 by 40 feet, four stories tall with brick walls on a granite foundation. It had a double roof, an octagonal bell cupola centered on the ridge and a brick chimney in each gable end. In size it was not much larger than many other New England mills, although it was one story taller than the brick mill erected in Lancaster, Massachusetts, in 1810. When the Directors voted to build the first mill in 1814, in fact, they stipulated "That the manufactory be built of stone" as was common in southern New England. [18] There is no written record when Lowell or Jackson changed the design to brick, although William Pierson is likely right in suggesting that the Boston style of public and domestic building established by Charles Bulfinch may have influenced them. [19]

The second Waltham mill was voted in 1816 and "completed in the Summer of 1819." [20] It was located downstream and, like the first mill, parallel to the Charles River. It housed twice the machinery of the first mill, measured in terms of 3,584 spindles, but was only 60 feet longer, making the new mill 150 by 40 feet, four stories tall, with the same granite basement foundation and double roof. Being the second mill on the site, no bell cupola was needed to call the workers to the mills. Rather, the paintings show a deck in the middle of the ridge, just beyond the center chimney on the rear roof, and fixed ladders on the front. This was a common method of fire protection. While the first mill had a wooden water closet tower at one rear corner below the cornice line, the second mill had a larger rear watercloset tower with gabled roof joining the clerestory attic windows. Both mills were fed by a headrace or canal in front of the mills and parallel to the river.

Normally the waste from the watercloset towers was carried away by the tailrace from the wheelpit. By the 1820's the water seems to exit back into the river downstream from the second mill. There is also a miniature version of these mills, one brick story above an arched stone foundation built into the river and roofed with a similar double roof (Figure 1). This was the 1816 machine shop, which had an ell extending from its lower end with its own watercloset shed projecting over the river.

Markham's drawing confirms several important features of the facade of the second mill which can also be seen in Smith's later painting. Projecting from the central bay of the front wall is another wooden tower gabled like that behind. This is "the porch round (the) stairway" on Manufactory No. 2 that the company paid R. Smith for a ceiling in August 1817.[2] This original outside tower, which removed the stairway from valuable working space in the building and helped to prevent the spread of fire, had been developed by other New England mill owners in the previous decade. In 1807 a cotton factory in Hope, Rhode Island, was insured with a stair "projection of about twelve feet square" and a watercloset tower "on the rear about five feet square." A similar example, in Sterling, Connecticut, was insured by the same company in 1810. A Rhode Island banknote of 1819 illustrates another stair tower on a four story mill in Coventry. The Lippitt, Rhode Island, mill of about 1810 still has an outside stair tower which may survive from this period.[22]

On either side of the front tower of the second Waltham factory were small, one-story brick structures with basements exposed on the rear along the cut which held the headrace. The three paintings show these joined by enclosed wooden bridges to the second story of the mill. The brick facades have a door and two windows over a pair of cellar sash, all in mirror image. These small buildings were the picker houses for the new factory and appear to be the earliest known use of separate specially designed buildings for this possibly inflammable process. The same practice was later followed by the Merrimack Manufacturing Company in its 1820's mills at Lowell, as well as by many of the Waltham system factories.

The mill yard was enclosed on the lower end by a white picket fence and along the street in front of the mills by a board fence between the low wooden sheds and the two-story brick office or counting house with hipped roof and center chimney. Beyond the office toward the upper end of the first mill Markham's sketch shows the continuation of this fence. Within the yard are several open sheds and a small barn. On the river edge, with a deck projecting over the water, is a long one-story wooden building with six chimney stacks probably used as forges for blacksmiths in machine manufacture.

Houses built by the Boston Manufacturing Company between 1815 and 1822 were located directly opposite the factories in two parallel lines. Along the street opposite the office, through which all employees and visitors entered, stood a row of houses which alternated between one and two stories in height. Until 1815 the company appears to have owned only four houses: No. 1 was rented for $80, No. 2 was a "brick house on the road" bought from S. Ross and rented to Paul Moody, No. 3 was an "old house and land bought of D. Townsend," and No. 4 was a "New Block of two houses" or tenements which were rented for a total of $120. In November 1815 P.T. Jackson was authorized to contract for building "the next season a manufactory, a House for the superintendent, one Block of two Houses, similar to those already built for the workmen, and eight smaller houses provided it can be done as cheap...as usual." Plans for the second mill and the house for Paul Moody were to be "exhibited to the Directors" before being decided upon. The old Townsend house was apparently replaced by the "new House building for P. Moody" recorded in February 1817.[23]

The four single-story cottages with central chimneys and double rear doors alternating with the larger houses on the street in the paintings were finished by November 1817. The two-story houses with two chimneys and one-story rear ells in Markham's drawing illustrate some of the two double-houses like No. 4 built by 1817. The remaining small houses formed a connected range known as the Long Row some distance behind and parallel to these houses. As Smith's painting shows, the Long Row was later enlarged with a two-story house joined to each end and was perhaps the work billed in company ledgers as "altering houses" and "finishg three tenements" in February 1822. Each dwelling was apparently a double-house, with the possible exception of the two old houses acquired earlier.[24] By 1820, when the United States census was taken and a special census of manufactories made, the company would appear to have had some 25 living units. Several more shown in the paintings reflect an increase after that date.

The company in 1820 employed 26 men, 13 boys, and 225 women. "The whole number of persons living on the premices of the Company directly depending on their business for support is upwards of 500" exclusive of some 40 laborers and mechanics "employed in erecting new buildings."[25]

The population schedules for 1820 actually total 234 persons employed in manufacture, or nearly a tenth of the 2674 people in Waltham. Twenty-seven heads of households in the census were male employees at the time and 21 of them recorded only one person in the household engaged in factory work. In addition, there were five female heads of households currently working in the mill and two women formerly employed by the company who had several factory workers in their homes. Among the families who had more than one factory worker listed were Paul Moody and James Derby, a machinist. All of these households represent 270 people apparently dependent on the mills.

In addition, the census lists another dozen households in which there were from 2 to 15 members employed in manufacturing but whose head cannot be identified from company payrolls. These represent another 134 persons reliant upon the factories, bringing the total to the "upwards of 500" the company claimed were living on their property. The second group may include some Waltham families who had several children employed in the mills. They might also include local men and women who took in boarders. We can identify a few former workers who are listed as heads of households who did this, including six workers who lived among the six males and nine females at Rhoda Crosby's. In one documented case, that of James Derby, the company sold him a houselot in September 1820 with the stipulation that they could repurchase the land "with improvements" if he left their employ.[26] As 9 members of his household, including himself, were employed by the company (excluding his wife and another female) the house was probably run as a boarding house for male workers. Together with the other male employees listed by name in the census of 1820, they represent the total number of men working as machinists, overseers, watchman and agent.

These exceptions underscore the fact that most of the housing built by the Boston Manufacturing Company was rented to men whose family members did not work in the mills. In the few cases where more than the family head was engaged in industry, that person may have been a son, daughter, or single boarder. In this respect the Waltham mills resembled factory villages throughout New England, although many more members of the families housed in buildings owned by a Rhode Island system company might work in the mill. Only the five unmarried female employees whose names appear in the census housed several other women and girls. Unlike Rhoda Crosby, only one or two of these large households are listed as factory workers. Even if some of these females did actually work in the mills, they represent a tiny fraction of the female work force.[27]

Of the dozen households with several mill workers in them, besides those of Crosby, Derby, and current female workers, most contained less than six factory workers. Only two were larger: Andrew Palmer had 15 workers out of 16 males and three women; and Jacob Farwill had 12 workers among the 14 males and four females in his home. Both may have catered to that group of 40 laborers and mechanics hired to build the company's buildings. The other homes may have been local families with several members who worked in the mill or local residents who boarded up to a half dozen mill girls with their families.

This is a far cry from the common assumption that the Boston Manufacturing Company erected boarding houses for its single, female operatives. Rather, the majority of workers who rented part of the company's double-houses did so for their families. Some may have taken in a few boarders, but the bulk of the female workforce seems to have lived in family groups not necessarily associated with the factory. Those women who appear to have taken in up to six boarders usually did so in a houshold that contained both men and women, while the larger men's boarding houses were run by men with their own families. Other mill girls appear from the census to have lived at home or with families engaged in other economic pursuits.

This then was Waltham only a year before the new system was expanded into a number of individual firms. The Boston Manufacturing Company had earlier sold certain equipment made in their machine shop. While F.C. Lowell was alive the costs were modest, but after his death and with increasing demand, new policies and prices were devised to license the right to manufacture and use Waltham patents.[28] Such sales spawned new corporations which adopted the major elements of the Waltham system, but were owned and managed by others outside the inner circle of the Boston Associates. At the same time, a handful of Boston Manufacturing Company officers and stockholders agreed to expand into the calico printing of cotton textiles. Land was acquired in East Chelmsford, Massachusetts, and controlling interest in an existing transportation canal, owned by the Proprietors of Locks and Canals on the Merrimack River, was purchased. Appleton, Jackson, Moody, Kirk Boott, and his brother John organized a new firm, the Merrimack Manufacturing Company, and offered stockholders of the Boston Manufacturing Company stock in proportion to their holdings in the old firm. Twenty-seven shareholders exercised this option and several new stockholders subscribed who would play prominent roles in the Boston Associates efforts. The Merrimack Company was chartered in February 1822 and the first mill readied for operation by November 1823.[29]

It was in September 1821 that Nathan Appleton convinced P.T. Jackson that the time had come for large scale expansion of the Waltham experiment into the printing of calicos. Indirect confirmation of their plans can be found in the contract between the Boston Manufacturing Company and the Dover Cotton Factory signed in October 1821. This agreement granted the Dover, New Hampshire, company a license to the full use of all Waltham patents to build a cotton factory of six thousand spindles "for the period of five years" for $6,000. It was also stipulated "that these privileges not extend to the bleaching or printing cotton goods."[30]

This contract gave the Dover company the right to examine the Waltham mills and machinery and gain a complete understanding of the Waltham system. The Dover Cotton Factory was an older spinning mill operated in partnership since 1813 by Isaac Wendell and John Williams. In 1819 Williams moved to Boston, representing the firm on Long Wharf. Wendell states that they "were the first to avail ourselves of the improvements at Waltham...A company was formed, mostly of Boston gentlemen, and the Mills next followed."[31] A machine shop was built to construct the full complement of machinery to "the Waltham plan...the most perfect system of all others known in this country."[32] The first mill erected at a new site on the Cocheco River in Dover was identical to the newest Waltham mill. It was 155 by 43 feet, three stories plus attic and shared the double roof, brick walls, centered cupola, and brick stair tower in the middle of its facade. The second Dover factory, begun in 1823, was identical except it returned to the four stories of Waltham's second mill with no cupola. In 1825, as the five year contract with Waltham neared its expiration, the company was reorganized with a capitalization of one million dollars as the Dover Manufacturing Company. It began to build a huge calico printing factory and bleachery, which completed a quadrangle with the earlier factories when construction was finished three years later.[33]

About one-third of the 600 men and women on the Dover payroll in 1824-25 shared common surnames, suggestng some family relation. Some occupied the twelve one-story cottages of four rooms with rear sheds. The rest lived in new or renovated houses leased by the company as double "tenements." A large boarding house was built near the machine shop and earliest Waltham-like mills to house the machinists and construction workers. Family housing for production workers initially followed Waltham's practice. By 1825, however, there is considerable evidence of single women boarding in the double houses owned by the company and rented to those who would manage them under company rules.[34] The rules may reflect a reaction to statements that "all kinds of characters were employed at the Factory and all kinds of practices carried on at the Boarding House."[35] Those who rented houses for boarders agreed to care for the property against fire and damage; to the prohibition against gambling, card playing, drinking, or profanity; and to a ten o'clock nightly closing of the house.[36]

As part of the expansion, the Dover Manufacturing Company also began to erect commercial buildings, lay out a grid of streets and houselots on newly acquired land, and plan other activities of general real estate development. While the company had begun a factory store in 1822, the second building campaign saw the design and construction of a bank, two stores, and an office at the corner of the mill quadrangle. Across from this they erected five narrow one-story buildings for shops and offices. In 1828 B.F. Perham, a Boston civil engineer who had surveyed and mapped the grid plan in 1826, provided plans for "brick dwellings with basement stores."[37] These may be the seven buildings across Washington Street from the mills later called the Cocheco Block. Together with the continued erection of wooden boarding houses, these commercial real estate activities shifted the business center of the old town of Dover to this corner of the factory complex.

During the 1820's non-industrial commercial building became common to larger manufacturing companies formed by Boston stockholders who were *not* part of the Boston Associates. Each seems to have begun like Dover and Waltham with numerous wooden duplexes, one or two boarding houses for the machinists and others, and some variant of the Waltham factories. Unlike the mills in Lowell, these showed great variety. When Isaac Wendell was forced out of the management of the Dover Factory by the new Boston directors, he formed a new mill town at Great Falls on the nearby Salmon River, which included an iron foundry, machine shop, ten double houses for the mill workers and machinists, two large boarding houses converted from older houses with added ells for dining, a new store, and a brick "Cotton Factory the same dimenstions and on the same model" as the earliest Dover Company mill, itself based on Waltham's third mill. After Wendell's site was transformed into the Great Falls Manufacturing Company and capitalized by new Boston investors in 1824, the company erected forty double wooden houses, a row of five three-story brick boarding houses opposite their factories (Figure 4), and a "spacious and elegant hotel" by 1826.[38] The Great Falls hotel contained several stores and occupied the triangle where several new streets laid out by the company converged to form the business center of the new mill town. Over the next decade the company provided several church sites, sold lots for homes and stores, as well as a stone Agent's house on a hill above a landscaped common.

This common was "used by the inhabitants as a play ground, bleaching green, or for pasture...The Main Street, the Canal, and the Mills, all running in parallel lines with large open area between them" were part of a formal plan that would be later emulated at Manchester and Lowell.[39] Like Dover, the Great Falls Company failed and was reorganized with the majority of stock being acquired by members of the Boston Associates. In fact, Patrick Tracy Jackson became the Treasurer of the corporation in 1840 and was primarily responsible for the renovation of earlier mills, the building of a new large factory in 1845, and for the construction of a new counting house and library building in front of these mills.[40]

While Dover and Great Falls were being established, two other Waltham type towns were formed which did not eventually fall under the domination of the Boston Associates. One was the Newmarket Manufacturing Company on the Lamprey River below Dover. Here, between 1822 and 1827, a group of Salem investors, linked in marriage or business with the shipping firm of Pickman, Silsbee and Stone erected three Waltham-sized cotton factories built of native granite in-

Figure 4. Brick rows, Somersworth, N.H. ca. 1935, photographed by John Coolidge. These now-destroyed corporate houses built by the Great Falls Manufacturing Company between 1824 and 1826 are among the earliest known examples of three-story industrial housing in New England. These faced the mills across the street and power canal in a fashion typical of later industrial cities like Manchester, N.H. and Lawrence, Massachusetts. The simple fan-lighted doorways borrow from the contemporary building practices of Portsmouth, N.H. and other Piscataqua River communities (photograph courtesy of the Museum of American Textile History).

stead of brick. This project was initially managed by Stephen Hanson, a Dover Quaker who had formerly owned a small cotton spinning mill. He erected wooden houses across from the first granite mills and lured a number of mill girls from the Dover company by promising "that he was going to have some nice women from Newbury Port & Salem to keep the Boarding Houses, who knew how to cook & treat Company." If the mill girls were displeased with the boarding houses he said "we might board where we pleased."[41] Hanson's tenure at Newmarket ended by 1827, and thereafter Salem supplied the Agent and kept firm hold over the finances of the company. Unlike the stock manipulations of the Boston Associates and the reorganizations of Dover and Great Falls, two-thirds of the Newmarket stock was still held by twenty-one of the twenty-eight original stockholders or their families as late as 1873.[42]

The Ware Manufacturing Company was more typical of the attempts made by Boston merchants in the 1820's to emulate the economic organization of Waltham's factories, but with neither the capital resources or experienced management of the Boston Manufacturing Company. Like its counterparts in New Hampshire, it failed in the recession of the late 1820's, its holdings eventually being dispersed to several smaller companies. Located on some 400 acres on the Ware River in central Massachusetts and purchased in 1821 by two Boston merchants, it was a tiny hamlet consisting of a small brick spinning factory, three houses, a sawmill, and a combined grist mill and machine shop formerly built by a Worcester partnership. Two dozen investors "who all reside in Boston" were induced into expanding this site into an industrial community modeled after Waltham. By 1825 they had built an iron foundry, a machine shop, a second cotton factory 200 feet long and two stories high, and they had laid out a grid of streets on the hill above the old mill yard opposite the main commercial street. When Zachariah Allen, a successful Rhode Island manufacturer, visited Ware in 1826 there were "five hundred inhabitants where four years ago there were not twenty."[43]

It was Allen's prophetic opinion this was "all forced hot bed growth of Boston Capital" which would "be supported no longer than those who have the funds are willing to disburse them to please their fancy for manufacturing." The corporation had, for example, constructed a large new hotel "which cost above ten thousand dollars" but only rented for $600 a year. According to Allen's description, it had "several hot and cold baths constructed in a spacious style, and mahogany furniture that rivals that of the houses of the first families in the Larger Cities."[44] Near the Hotel opposite a village common was the Hampshire Manufacturers Bank, incorporated by local residents and mill managers in 1825.

Like Dover, the company initially erected a company store. Instead of the cash payments of the Waltham system, mill girls and other employees were given store credits which were deducted from quarterly wages. Factory girls were housed in the enlarged boarding house acquired with the mill. A number of new double-houses, like those in Waltham and Dover, were soon built and filled to capacity. In 1827 Sampson V.S. Wilder, the company agent, wrote to a correspondent offering to provide farm girls to the mills that "All our tenements are now full" and "many of our young ladies are obliged to sleep 3 in a bed."[45]

Wilder was a stockholder from Boston and a Christian businessman who founded the American Tract Society. He was induced to fill the vacant position of company agent with a promise by several orthodox directors that the company would help build a new church in Ware. As the majority of mill supervisors and many· of the stockholders, including Treasurer Lewis Tappan, were Unitarians, Wilder was involved in a well-documented controversy in establishing a Congregational minister at Ware.[46] Wilder's correspondence from Ware with the Boston officers reveals that, like Dover, there was a map of the community but with a duplicate in Boston to assist in locating planned improvements and to permit the Treasurer to keep insurance policies correct.

The design of Ware's new factory, like several other large mills built for mill towns in New England, did not follow the Waltham prototypes. While it did adopt the double roof and central cupola, the brick building was long and low, standing only one story tall with an exposed basement story on the lower side. At each end were smaller wings set at right angles to the 200-foot main block. Its chief mechanic, Colonel Arnold Olney, was a Rhode Island machine maker, a common characteristic among factories with machine shops formed after Waltham but financed by Boston investors outside the inner circle of the Boston Associates. Aza Arnold moved from Rhode Island to Great Falls in 1824 and Ira Gay, another machinist from that state, had charge of the Nashua, New Hampshire machine shop.[47] The Ware machine shop also contracted to build machinery for the Three Rivers Company in nearby Palmer, Massachusetts. The Three Rivers Company, funded by Bostonians who also held shares in Waltham and Lowell mills, failed and contributed to the financial problems of Ware's management. In 1829 the Ware Manufacturing Company was reorganized and a new corporation took its place. One of the first acts of its new agent was a general wage reduction, the sale of the hotel, and the lease or sale of company stores or houses.[48]

From 1822 to 1825, meanwhile, the lands which would soon become the new town of Lowell in 1826 were owned almost exclusively by the Merrimack Manufacturing Company. The Treasurer and Agent, Kirk Boott, laid out the canals, streets, buildings, and factories. In this respect the earliest years of Lowell's development was nearly identical to the industrial developments by other large corporations in Dover, Great Falls, Newmarket, and Nashua, New Hampshire, Ware and Chicopee, Massachusetts; and Saco, Maine. But by 1824 other "mill sites," land with water power to run a mill the size of the second Waltham factory, were laid out along the old Pawtucket canal. In order to capitalize the projected industrial development of these sites, the Locks and Canals Company was transformed into a holding company with an interlocking directorate with the Merrimack Company. This new structure managed all the undeveloped land, the water power system, and the machine shop. Through the sequential development of new manufacturing coporations supplied with power, buildings, and machinery by the Locks and Canals Company, Lowell became the first truly industrial city in America.

Despite later suggestions that Lowell was a planned utopian community, the limited evidence of its founding decade indicates that architectural patterns expressing the social organization of the Waltham system in an urban environment evolved slowly.[49] Site development was restrained by topography and pre-existing patterns of roads and the old canal. The Merrimack Company built a new canal, laid out Dutton and Worthen Streets parallel to it for corporate housing, and established a machine shop under Paul Moody's direction at this canal's junction with the old Pawtucket Canal. By 1825 the Merrimack Company had five mills identical to the second Waltham factory, but adopting the brick stair tower. Thirty separate buildings were erected for housing in front of the mill complex, while a stone Episcopal Church and rectory were sited across the Merrimack Canal above the junction of old and new cross roads which formed a central square. Boott also built himself a mansion in the heart of a large tract east of the mills. As early as 1823 the Merrimack Company approached the other directors of the Boston Manufacturing Company to buy the Waltham machine shop operation. A new building of the Waltham factory form was built during 1824 for the Lowell machine shop, with a cluster of housing for the machinists built on the lower end of Dutton and Worthen Streets. It is this complex which occupies the foreground of Benjamin Mather's painting (Figure 5).

A map of the whole site was drawn by a Boston civil engineer, George Baldwin, in 1825 (Figure 6). It documents the development of the hydraulic and street system, as well as the proposed sites for new factories and houses along the old canal. This is a culmination of two plans for the new mill sites drawn for the Merrimack company in January 1824, and it illustrates the first buildings erected by the Hamilton Manufacturing Company.[50] This new corporation, like the Appleton and Lowell mills founded in 1828 that occupied sites on opposite sides of this canal, designed and built their own mills and housing. What is most apparent from what is known about the architecture and corporate planning of the first Lowell companies is the adoption of the Waltham factory form as a standard factory design. Unlike the

Figure 5. View of Lowell, 1825, oil on canvas by Benjamin Mather. This detail illustrates the new machine shop and associated housing in the foreground and St. Anne's Church and the Merrimack mills in the rear. (photograph courtesy of the Lowell Art Association.)

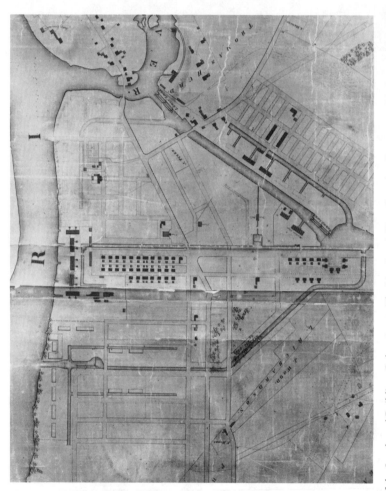

Figure 6. "A Plan of the Lands and Buildings Belonging to The Merrimack Manufacturing Company with the neighboring Farms and Roads &c at Patucket in the Town of Chelmsford" 1825, by George Baldwin. This detail shows the Merrimack mills and housing in the upper portion, machine shop and its housing below, and Hamilton Company mills and brick rows lower right. (photograph courtesy of Proprietors of Locks and Canals; Blaise Davi, National Park Service, photographer.)

Figure 7. Dutton Street, Lowell, 1849, from *The Lowell Offering* Vol. 1. The engraving shows one of the original wooden boarding houses (left) next to the single brick row on Dutton Street (center) and the larger New Block built about 1845 typical of the fully developed Lowell brick boardinghouses. The original mills at the end of the street are shown joined by a new pavillion over which the cupola has been relocated. (photograph courtesy of Lowell Historical Society.)

other northern New England mill towns which experimented in building much longer or larger factories, the designation of a mill site as the technological constant at Lowell established a single architectural form sited parallel to the power canals. As long as new canals could be built or extended, this remained the standard Lowell mill form.

The five Merrimack mills were sited in an open "U" with its yards enclosed by storehouses and an office. These mills were each designed to weave cloth for calico printing, and the printworks and bleachery were sited at the far end of the canal. While further advanced than Dover's printworks in 1825, this operation was still in its developmental stage.

Housing for the Merrimack workers was, like Waltham and Dover, primarily two-story wooden double-houses. One of these appears in a later view of Dutton Street (Figure 7), while the 1825 map indicates that there were no rear ells. Those which survived on Worthen Street had a one-story ell on each side, although it is unclear if these were original. All had privies behind each house, much in the manner of earlier Rhode Island mill villages. Near the center of the Dutton Street row, and directly behind on both sides of Worthen Street, were three longer two-story brick blocks each containing four units. Each had paired doors in the center with single doors at each corner of the main facade. Unlike their wooden neighbors, the attic was lit with four gabled dormers. When the printworks was enlarged, a connected row of one-story brick houses was built along Prince Street in 1827. The single story cottage was comparable to those in Waltham and Dover, but the type of joined urban row, called John Bull's Row, was like the industrial terraces of British manufacturing centers.[51]

While John Bull's Row was clearly built to house the families of English workers, it is less clear how many of the double and quadruple houses were also let to male workers with families. Unlike Waltham the machine shop workers and their families were accommodated in a separate row of nearly identical wooden houses built in 1824 and in another cluster of homes with Waltham-like rear ells finished by 1825. Yet, the Merrimack workforce also contained several male employees below the managerial level. The latter were housed in larger homes along Moody Street, but the remainder must have shared several of the double tenements as they did in Waltham, Dover, and other mill towns.

A plan drawn by the Merrimack Company in January 1824 shows the land opposite the mills later built for the Hamilton and Appleton companies laid out for individual wooden double-houses like those of the machinists. After the Hamilton Company was formed in 1825, however, it chose an alternative plan on longer blocks containing connected housing. Those shown on the Baldwin map are described as two brick blocks of "eight tenements in each" and nearly two-hundred feet in length. These, like the smaller blocks of Merrimack housing, retained the domestic scale of two stories and attic. Unlike the brick blocks built between 1824 and 1826 in Great Falls and their counterparts of about the same date in Newmarket, Lowell factories were slow to adopt three-story housing. The taller, connected brick blocks of corporate boarding houses do not seem to have been built in Lowell until the 1830's. Yet, once they were adopted to the increasingly urban fabric of Lowell, they became as standard as the Waltham factory design. Three-story brick boarding houses identical to those evolved in Lowell after 1830 were erected in Manchester and Lawrence in the 1840's and as far away as Lewiston, Maine in the 1850's. By the mid-1840's, in fact, the Merrimack Company replaced much of the older wooden houses on Dutton Street with a "New Block" typical of this later style (Figure 7).

A newspaper description of Lowell in 1826 mentions that "a large block for dwelling houses, stores, &c." was then "in a state of forwardness."[53] It is not clear if this was a corporate or private real estate development, but it suggests the type of commercial building which accompanied the city's rapid growth. Unlike the other single corporation mill towns of the Waltham system, there was little commercial real estate held by the manufacturing companies. The one major exception was the Merrimack House, a hotel voted by the directors of that company in 1825 and apparently erected that year at the junction of Merrimack and Dutton Streets facing the mills. It is probably more than a coincidence that the hotel at Ware was also built in 1825 and the Great Falls hotel between 1824 and 1826; the latter building was a brick round-fronted building occupying a corner location like the Merrimack House. Each of these corporations had its officers and directors among the Boston mercantile community. If one company established such an amenity for visitors and stockholders, the others would have known it quickly. Moreover, Boston's own active real estate development, especially the building of Quincy Market and its two flanking commercial brick rows between 1824 and 1826, were known in these towns.[54]

Yet, until all the potential mill sites were developed in the mid-1840's, the Locks and Canal Company retained large tracts of undeveloped land. Still, the company did not foresee the need for housing for non-industrial laborers. Just as the managers at Waltham had not counted the forty mechanics and laborers who built their buildings as employees, the Irish workers, who had no other home to return to after various building campaigns, became squatters in adjacent shanty towns. Unlike native carpenters and masons who contracted for corporate or private building, the Irish formed a new permanent underclass for which the corporations had made no provision. When the second Boston Associates multi-corporation city was begun at Manchester, New Hampshire, in the late 1830's, the building contracts of the Stark and Amoskeag companies forbade the hiring of Irish laborers or other workers.[55]

Within a decade of its founding the major features of the fully developed Waltham system had found their architectural expression at Lowell. Moreover, control of many smaller mill towns established independently on the Waltham model had been absorbed by Boston Associate investors. The design and planning of these communities has commonly been seen as part of a single fabric with Waltham and Lowell. Even though the capital was largely derived from Bostonians, however, the initial planning and building at each new site actually witnessed the experimentation with many solutions to common needs. Thus, it now appears that the mill girl boarding house system was not fully established in Waltham, for example, but in the several company towns it spawned. The failure of many of the firms which deviated from the Waltham factory type and the need to make each mill site in Lowell of equal technological value established a standard of successful industrial form for over a decade. These were of "uniform size, 150 to 160 feet long, by 45 feet wide, four stories high" until the late 1830's.[56] In 1840 James Montgomery notes, "the Mills recently built at Lowell are five stories high, with a plain roof...from which it seems probable, that though the double roof has been the plan generally adopted, it is likely to be abandoned."[57] For factories in northern New England's industrial towns and cities, this was indeed the case. After the brief period before Lowell's dominance was fully established, mill agents and lesser Boston investors like those at Ware would turn to Lowell for their models. It is this that helped make the architecture of the Waltham system communities, once a diverse amalgam of industrial and vernacular designs, increasingly similar in form and organization throughout much of the nineteenth century.

NOTES

[1] Christopher Colt to Thomas Dixon, President, April 11, 1831, Hampshire Manufacturing Co. *Letterbook* (1829-1831), Ware, Massachusetts Young Men's Library Association.

[2] Christopher Colt to James C. Dunn, Treasurer, April 26, 1831, Hampshire Manufacturing Co. *Letterbook* (1829-1831).

[3] James Montgomery, *A Practical Detail of Cotton Manfacture of the United States....* (Glasgow, 1840), p. 14.

[4] Montgomery, *Cotton Manufacture*, p. 14.

[5] Montgomery, *Cotton Manufacture*, pp. 14-15.

[6] Samuel Batchelder, *Introduction and Early Progress of the Cotton Manufacture in the United States* (Boston, 1863) p. 73.

[7] Carolyn F. Ware, *Early New England Cotton Manufacture* (Boston, 1931); Gary Kulik, Rodger Parks and Theodore Penn eds., *The New England Mill Village, 1790-1860*, Vol. 2 in Documents in American Industrial History (Cambridge, MA 1982). Also see David J. Jeremy, *Transatlantic Industrial Revolution: The Diffusion of Textile Technologies between Britain and America, 1790-1830's* (Cambridge,

MA, 1981) for the technological aspects of both systems.

8   Richard M. Candee, "New Towns of the Early New England Textile Industry," *Perspectives in Vernacular Architecture*, Camille Wells, ed. (Vernacular Architecture Forum, 1981), pp. 31-50.

9   Marvin Fisher, *Workshops in the Wilderness, The European Response to American Industrialization, 1830-1860* (New York, 1967), p. 14.

10 Jeremy, *Transatlantic Industrial Revolution*, pp. 99-101.

11 Jeremy, *Transatlantic Industrial Revolution*, p. 98.

12 Frances W. Gregory, *Nathan Appleton, Merchant and Entrepreneur, 1779-1861* (Charlottesville, VA, 1975), pp. 166-168.

13 A variation of this view from a later 19th century copy was published in Charles A. Nelson, *Waltham Past and Present and Its Industries* (Cambridge, 1879), p. 92. The churches are the 1826 Trinitarian Church, which appears in the far right of the original uncropped painting, and the new church of the Second Religious Society which was built in 1830 on the land later occupied by the common and city hall opposite the mills. The painting is on loan from the Lowell Historical Society to Old Sturbridge Village, which restored it and provided the photograph.

14 Probate Inventory, Middlesex County, Mass., First Series #20607. I am indebted to Charles Hammond of the Gore Place Society for identifying Smith and this painting, which appeared in an earlier, erroneous copy in Nelson and other local publications. Gore Place has restored this painting and provided the photograph which is published here for the first time in its original form.

15 Isaac Markham Papers, Sheldon Art Museum, Middlebury, Vt. Letter from Polly C. Darnell, Librarian of the Sheldon Art Museum, to Michael B. Folsom, June 10, 1981, citing an 1819 letter of recommendation for Markham, in Hamilton Child, *Gazetteer and Business Directory for Addison County, 1881-82.*

16 Old Sturbridge Village, Mill Village Collection. This paper incorporates the research I did at Old Sturbridge Village between 1969 and 1976, as well as subsequent research in New Hampshire. The Providence Manufacturing Company mill at Crompton, West Warwick, R.I., was built of stone in 1807 as were several others in the years immediately following. A brick mill for the firm of Poignand and Plant was the subject of a building contract, May 1, 1810. MS 25, Poignand and Plant Papers, Lancaster, Massachusetts Public Library.

17 Montgomery, *Cotton Manufacture*, p. 15; the term' "false" for what modern historians have called 'eyebrow' windows appears in a letter from John Williams to William Shimmin, Dover Manufacturing Company *Letterbook*, Vol. 1, letter 144, Dec. 1825, New Hampshire Historical Society. See Jennifer Tann, *The Development of the Factory* (London, 1970) for 1787 watercolor of Arkwright's Crawford factory and my review in *The Journal of the Society of Architectural Historians*, 31:4 (Dec. 1972), pp. 336-7.

18 Boston Manufacturing Co. *Directors Records*, Vol, 2, Baker Library Harvard Business School, 28 March 1814, p. 4.

19 William H. Pierson, Jr., *American Buildings and Their Architects, Technology and the Picturesque: The Corporate and the Early Gothic Styles* (New York, 1978), pp. 62-63.

20 U.S. Bureau of the Census, Fourth Census, 1820, Manufacturing Schedules (Record Group 29, National Archives microfilm) p. 33. According to this account of 1820, the company had since "erected Bleach works and are building a Factory" on a separate mill site, a third factory identical to the second, but possibly with a brick stair and only three stories tall with its own cupola.

21 Boston Manufacturing Co. *Ledger,* Vol. 34, (August 1817), p. 68.

22 Providence Mutual Fire Insurance Co., *Policy Book,* RI Historical Society, Vol. 1, p. 515 (policy #404, Nov. 19, 1807) and Vol. 3 (policy 1241, Dec. 11, 1810). The banknote is illustrated in Richard M. Candee, "The Early New England Textile Village in Art," *Antiques* (Dec. 1970), p. 911; the Lippitt Mill is shown in Theodore A. Sande, "The Textile Factory in Pre-Civil War Rhode Island," *Old-Time New England,* Vol.

66 (Summer-Fall 1975), p. 23.

[23] Boston Manufacturing Co. *Ledger,* Vol. 34, (Sept. 1815, March 1816, Feb. 1817), pp. 49 ff., and *Journal,* Vol. 10, Nov. 1817; *Directors Records,* Vol. 2, p. 18.

[24] Mrs. Sumner Milton, "Reminiscences of People and Houses Near Waltham Common," Waltham Historical Society Publication No. 3, *Waltham Common* (Waltham, 1926), pp. 24-26; Boston Manufacturing Co. *Ledger,* Vol. 34 (Feb. 1822).

[25] U.S. Census, 1820, Manufacturing Schedules, p. 33.

[26] Boston Manufacturing Co. *Directors Records,* Vol. 2, Sept. 7, 1820.

[27] One household, that of Sarah Hopkins, contained 2 females under 16, 17 from 16 to 26 years old, and one over 45; none were classified as being employed in industry or any other class of occupation. All statistics are drawn from the 1820 Population Schedules, U.S. Census (National Archives Record Group 29, Microfilm).

[28] Gregory, *Nathan Appleton,* pp. 156-157; Robert Varnum Spalding, *The Boston Mercantile Community and the Promotion of the Textile Industry in New England, 1813-1860* (Ph.D. Dissertation, Yale, 1963), pp. 28-29.

[29] Gregory, *Nathan Appleton,* pp. 173-181.

[30] Contract, Oct. 12, 1821, Boston Manufacturing Co., Vol. 187 (Misc. MSS).

[31] "Recollections of an old Manufacturer. From manuscript of the late Isaac Wendell" (Dover, n.d.) bound with "Historical Memoranda," Dover, N.H. Public Library.

[32] Wendell & Williams Letters (1813-1826), Isaac Wendell to Jacob Wendell (nd), Wendell Family MSS, Baker Library, Harvard Business School, Case 11.

[33] For the introduction of calico printing see Caroline Sloat, "The Dover Manufacturing Company and the Integration of English and American Calico Printing Techniques, 1825-29," *Winterthur Portfolio,* Vol. 10, pp. 31-68; Jeremy *Transatlantic Industrial Revolution,* pp. 104-117. For the construction of the calico printworks and earlier mills, see Richard M. Candee, "The 'Great Factory' at Dover, New Hampshire," *Old-Time New England,* Vol. 66 (Summer-Fall 1975), pp. 39-51.

[34] Dover Manufacturing Company, *Letterbook,* Vol. 1, New Hampshire Historical Society, pp. 50-60, provides a series of depositions which were taken in early 1825 and refer to women in boarding houses throughout. Agent John Williams' "Annual Report to the Directors," Jan. 21, 1826, states "Within the past year, six blocks of two houses each have been built for boarding our help..."

[35] Dover Manufacturing Company, *Letterbook,* Vol. 1, p. 50, Deposition #3 of Mary S. Firnald and Deborah Firnald, May 10, 1825.

[36] "Rules to be observed by those who hire houses of the Dover Manufacturing Company, for the purpose of taking boarders, or otherwise," broadside signed by John Williams, Agent from 1822-1828 (n.d.), copy in Baker Library from original in Kress Library, Harvard. Strafford Co. *Deeds,* Vol. 501:170 is a lease between the Dover Mfg. Co. and J.P. Leavitt, Nov. 4, 1829, for a men's bordinghouse.

[37] Dover Mfg. Co. *Letterbook,* Vol. III, letter #89 (Sept. 1828); II, letter #81 (Sept. 6, 1826).

[38] Great Falls Manufacturing Company, *Directors Records,* Baker Library, Harvard Business School, Vol. 1, p.5; Vol. 2, pp. 133-141, Real Estate listing "probably made" Aug. 1, 1824; *Portsmouth Journal,* August 19, 1826.

[39] Montgomery, *Cotton Manufacture, pp. 197-198.*

[40] Great Falls Manufacturing Company *Directors Records,* Vol. 2, pp. 42-43, 51-52; Richard M. Candee, *Cultural Resources Inventory, Downtown Somersworth,* Fall, 1982.

[41] Dover Manufacturing Co. *Letterbook,* Vol. 1, (March 11, 1825), pp. 51-52.

[42] Richard M. Candee, *Newmarket Revisited: Looking at the Era of Industrial Growth (1820-1920)* (Newmarket, 1979); *Fifteenth Annual Report of the Treasurer of the Newmarket Manufacturing Co.,* Sept. 4, 1873 (Boston, 1883), p. 4.

[43] "Tour to see Woolen Mills" (1826), Zachariah Allen Papers, R.I. Historical Society, Misc. MSS, p.4.

[44] Allen, "Tour...," p. 6.

45 Ware Manufacturing Co. *Letterbook*, Museum of American Textile History, letter, March 8, 1827. Records for the Ware company and its successors are split among several repositories. Old Sturbridge Village has a single *Journal* (1823); the Ware Young Men's Library Association a *Daybook* (1827-30) and a Hampshire company *Letterbook* (1829-1831) and the Museum of American Textile History a Ware Manufacturing Co. *Letterbook* (1826-1831) and related manuscripts.

46 Several of the key documents, including the 1825 map of Ware and early illustrations, have been published in Kulik, *et al, The New England Mill Village 1790-1860*, pp. 183-4, 231-252. The original map is in the collections of the Ware Historical Society.

47 Hampshire Mfg. Co. *Letterbook*, Sept. 7, 1829.

49 The terms of this debate were established by John Coolidge's classic study, *Mill and Mansion, A Study of Architecture and Society in Lowell, Massachusetts, 1820-1865*, (New York, 1942). Coolidge accepted the Waltham origins of company-owned boarding houses and the claims of utopian intentions by the founders. Thomas Dublin, *Woman at Work* (New York, 1979), is a more detailed analysis of women workers and their male counterparts for the Hamilton Company between 1826 and 1860. Spaulding's dissertation, *The Boston Mercantile Community*, offers an alternative interpretation for the utopian claims of the Lowell owners and their investment activities.

50 The two unillustrated plans are both titled "A Plan of the Land on the South Side of the Patucket Canal Belonging to the Merrimack Manufacturing Company, January 1826" and are Locks and Canals plans, shelf 106, drawings 599 and 600, now held by the University of Lowell, Lowell, Mass.

51 Coolidge, *Mill and Mansion*, pp. 33-39, figures 8-11, 18, and pp. 184, 237-239. The original negatives of Coolidge photographs, many not published, are now in the collections of the Merrimack Valley Textile Museum in North Andover, Massachusetts.

52 S.A. Drake, *History of Middlesex County, Massachusetts*, Volume 2 (Boston 1880), p. 64. The Great Falls brick rows are described in the *Portsmouth (N.H.) Journal*, August 19, 1826; Newmarket's brick blocks seem to date to 1826 and first appear on a map of Newmarket, 1832, in the collections of the Newmarket Historical Society, Newmarket, N.H.

53 *Greenfield (MA) Gazette*, May 30, 1826.

54 Candee, "The 'Great Factory' at Dover," pp. 42-43. John Williams asked the Boston Treasurer to send "a plan of the coving for stores about New Market" or Quincy Market, or have Alexander Parris, its architect, design the cornice specifically for the Dover factory. The Nashua Manufacturing Company employed the Boston architect, Ashur Benjamin, as its mill agent. His Nashua, N.H. work is summarized in Richard M. Candee, "Three Architects of Early New Hampshire Mill Towns," *Journal of the Society of Architectural Historians*, Vol. 30, No. 2 (May 1971), pp. 155-158.

55 See Coolidge, *Mill and Mansion*, p. 39, for a description of the Irish at Lowell in 1831; Amoskeag Manufacturing Company, *Building Specifications and Contract Book, Manchester Historic Association, pp. 11-41*.

56 *Handbook for the Visitor to Lowell* (Lowell, 1848), p. 11.

57 Montgomery, *Cotton Manufacture*, p. 15.

Central Stations and
The Electric Vision, 1890 to 1930

JOHN R. STILGOE

Whirring, humming, softly purring, flanked by coal piles and crowned by plumes of drifting smoke and steam, the power station thrust its way into the turn-of-the-century American imagination. In the great industrial zones ringing the nation's cities, no structure loomed more majestically or thrust its smokestacks higher. As a symbol of efficient power, the station knew no equal. As the very armature of the nation's emerging electric vision, the power station attracted the scrutiny of technical and popular writers, artists, and the general public it ceaselessly and mysteriously served. In the power station, Americans glimpsed the electric future.

Definitions

As late as the 1890's, industrialists and small boys knew chiefly the "power house." Until well into the twentieth century, the term survived to muddle discussion of the massive electricity-generating stations that replaced the old-fashioned power houses. Nevertheless, the power house remained a significant structure, for twentieth-century observers saw it as the birthplace of something more.

Originally, mills and factories drew power from water- or steam-driven wheels, usually located in cellars beneath the manufacturing floors. Hydropower technology evolved with the nineteenth century, causing entire buildings to be built over canals whose water drove turbines housed in specially designed basements. At Lowell, Massachusetts and in other industrial locations, entire complexes of factories stood surrounded and interlaced with canals of rushing water. As steam power replaced falling water as a source of continuous power, however, the difficulties and dangers of installing steam engines in each building of every factory complex caused owners and insurance companies to seek ways to isolate the furnaces, boilers, and engines from the buildings they powered. The "works engine house" evolved as a small, usually brick structure set near the center of the several buildings owned by one manufacturer. Within its walls worked at least one coal-fired steam engine coupled by immense pulleys and belts to the manufacturing machinery in adjacent buildings.[1] Such power houses, often built after the manufacturing buildings, dispatched power through a seemingly confused web of leather belts and drive shafts, cogged wheels carrying chain drives, and massive gears. Belts left the power house at almost every imaginable angle, making access to the building difficult and movement within the structure very dangerous. Such construction necessitated the employment of many men, most needed to hand shovel coal and ashes, and others to oil the assemblage of flying parts. No structure better represents the pace of nineteenth-century American industrialization, for the power houses that supplied energy to the complexes of factories Americans eventually called "works," evolved in hasty, spur-of-the-moment ways, growing ever more powerful but ever more complicated.

A works power house, therefore, smacked of both old and new simultaneously. The word "house" implies an association with an earlier, essentially agrarian time that ordered American language until the early twentieth century.[2] Words like "firehouse," "gatehouse," and "waterhouse" announced a pre-railroad era understanding of industrial structure. By 1920, particularly in the Midwest, the word "house" no longer held sway; new terms, particularly the railroad-derived "station" and the industrial-zone created "works" had reshaped old words. Such terms as "roundhouse" and "engine house" reveal the reluctance with which even railroaders departed from the agrarian vocabulary, but terms like "fire station," "waterworks," and, particularly, "power station" reflect the changed environment that changed language.

Americans understood power houses. The coal piled on one side of a works power house signified potential energy; the ashes heaped on the opposite side announced energy spent. Within, the fire raging in the firebox quite clearly heated water in the boiler, making the steam that in turn powered the reciprocating engine or engines. Reciprocating steam-powered engines struck most Americans as perfectly familiar; after all, a railroad locomotive is a "steam engine," with its great wheels and rods driven by reciprocating pistons.[3] Inside a typical works power house, visitors encountered something remarkably like a railroad locomotive, something they understood. With pistons flying, balance wheels spinning, and drive shafts revolving, the power house machinery seemed almost as magnificent as a speeding locomotive, and in time it modified American ways of speaking. The colloquialism "pull out all the stops" derives from the safety governor that spun atop most stationary engines; removing one or more of the weighted metal "stops" caused the engine to work faster and faster—removing all meant running the risk of a runaway engine, broken belts, and catastrophe. Thus even large power houses proved understandable as simple shelters for well-known types of machinery, and mass-circulation periodicals gave them little attention.

On the other hand, power houses exemplified the urban confusion of movement that alienated Henry James and so many other Americans dismayed by scurrying steetcars, drays, bicycles, and trains. The "bussing, blooming confusion" described by William James as the world of the new-born infant existed in every power house for any adult brave enough to encounter the maze of belts, drives, and other machinery. No machine better represents the accretionary process of urban development; just as cities grew, adding more and more levels, more and more avenues of traffic, more and more types of vehicles, so evolved typical power house machinery. Each new factory building, every new press or gin or grinder somehow required more belts or thicker driveshafts or even entire new steam engines. No wonder that power houses in full operation staggered visitors. So much of the created energy seemed wasted in utter confusion; firemen scrambling beneath wheels to feed fires, oilers clambering over madly speeding belts, chief engineers pulling reverse levers and bellowing over the din—power indeed, immense power, power that required the careful bolting of machines to floors and walls, but not power well harnessed.[4]

While the works power house objectified the rapid growth of nineteenth-century American industry, a growth based on seat-of-the-pants engineering, cheap labor, and a willingness to endure mechanical danger, the "power station"—by 1920 and perhaps as early as 1910—represented the promise of twentieth-century change. A power station produced electrical energy for many consumers.[5] It represented a changed attitude toward engineering and building, an affirmation of centralized power generation, and a faith in efficiency. Urged on by a natural curiosity and by magazine writers, the American public began to study and appreciate the massive structures rising in the industrial zone of every city.

Location

At first, electricity-generating companies followed power house precedent and sited their structures at the geographical centers of the districts they hoped to supply. In the late 1880's residential electric lighting seemed the greatest potential market; most factories had their own power houses that were beginning to generate electricity, and the electrically-powered trolley car had not been perfected. And "electricity" meant "direct current," simple to generate and manipulate, but difficult to transmit over long distances, indeed over a limit of perhaps ten miles. So small plants sprouted in the centers of upper-class urban neighborhoods desirous of lighting by electricity.

In 1890, an *Electrical Review* reporter summarized the brief history of the Mount Morriss Electric Light Company of New York City. The firm began making electricity in February, 1888, in a basement; five months later it built its first "station." By June of the next year its second station, capable of powering 2,500 incandescent lights and forty arc lights, had begun service. Built of "handsome brick" and in "modern design," the new structure revealed the difficulties of location that quickly plagued fledgling power companies. With its boilers and fireboxes in the basement and its first floor given over to the dynamos, the structure provided no room for coal storage; indeed coal had to be heaped in vaults beneath sidewalks.[6] Quite clearly, locating electricity stations in residential neighborhoods meant encountering difficulties ranging from smoke pollution to coal storage.

Alternating current solved the essential problem. While more difficult to produce and modulate, alternating current moves well over extremely long distances, with only a slight drop in efficiency.[7] Once engineers understood its generation, electricity firms moved quickly to better locations.

Engineering magazines devoted much attention to the proper siting of electricity stations. Writers emphasized that the stations ought to be reasonably near their markets, simply to reduce the expense of wire and cable. They stressed also the factors important in siting any business; cheapness of real estate, for example, and perhaps earlier than other industrial writers, drove home the need for acquiring enough land to permit expansion of the original station.[8] But station-siting proved a particularly vexing issue for other, more complex reasons.

Almost every station burned coal to produce steam. Water consequently acquired a two-fold importance. On the one hand, siting a power station adjacent to a navigable body of water meant having access to cheaply-freighted coal. On the other, proximity to a large body of water meant having the ability to make vast quantities of steam. The evolution of the power station is intimately connected with the development of the nation's waterfronts and riverfronts and lakefronts. Indeed, by 1930, almost every massive body of water, including such wild rivers as the Colorado and the Tennessee, struck power-industry representatives as sites for new power stations.

Alternating current created locational difficulties, too, however. Electrical engineers discovered that only very high voltage alternating current can be transmitted efficiently. For the voltage to be useful in residences and in retail establishments, it had to be "dropped" at small buildings called "sub-stations." Since sub-stations contained only switching equipment, not fireboxes and boilers, and required very little space, they could be located in residential neighborhoods with little objection.[9] Locating the main station, or "central station" as the industry called it by 1905, meant the corollary locating of sub-stations, however, for the secondary buildings proliferated in areas distant from the generating source. Locating the central station on the waterfront almost invariably meant siting sub-stations in neighborhoods far inland, often in long-established neighborhoods with high property values and no desire for industrial buildings.

With the perfection of the electric streetcar in 1888, locating power stations became even more complicated. The "trolleys" operated on direct current, and as the lines reached into suburbs and carried increasing numbers of cars, power demands taxed the original stations. For decades, many street railway companies insisted on generating their own electricity, and refused to purchase it from "electric-light companies." The independence provided insurance against rate increases, but led to the multiplication of generating stations and substations, because the trolley companies required low-voltage direct current. Every extension of trolley lines into suburbs required one or more new generating stations. Only rarely did the trolley companies have the financial resources to acquire waterfront land for their stations. Except for the giant consolidated "rapid transit" companies, electric railway companies built small stations that relied on uncertain streams, municipal water lines, or steam condensers to provide water for steam generation. Their small generating stations punctuated urban and suburban space and aroused the attention of people unfamiliar with the far-off, industrial zone central stations of the "electric company."[10] In the wee hours of the morning, long after the last trolley trip, electric locomotives pulling coal cars to power stations disturbed the slumbers of suburbanites.

One school of experts argued that central stations ought to be located in suburbs. "As to the water supply, considerable latitude is allowable, owing to the possibility of piping water from a distance," noted A.E. Dixon in a 1906 *Engineering Magazine* series on power station design. "Where water is piped from a distance, it is advisable to provide storage tanks or a reservoir close to the plant, in order to guard against breaks in the line or the occasional unavoidable cutting off of the supply while repairs are being made, or for other purposes." Coal would have to arrive at such suburban sites by rail, but the additional freight cost would be offset by the willingness of quality workers to live in an attractive location. Beyond that, Dixon remarked, "suburban locations, slightly out of the large centers of population, are desirable owing to the fact that labor troubles are not so liable to occur, and should they arise they can be handled better when located outside the lime light." One way of handling such difficulties involved the hiring of strikebreakers, and Dixon understood that "when considerable space is available around the industry on which temporary shelters can be erected," the usefulness of strikebreakers becomes ever greater.[11] According to Dixon and other writers of the 1900's, suburban locations might be more useful in the long run than waterfront or industrial-zone sites.

Locating a central station or street railway power station consequently involved analyzing many separate and yet interrelated factors ranging from the efficiency of fuel delivery to the efficiency of the work force. Of all the factors, however, that of material handling attracted the most penetratng scrutiny. By 1930, the electricity-generating industry had evolved an entire technology only tangentially related to the fine art of manufacturing electric power.

Coal

Coal and ash piles flanked almost every central station. For as long as oil remained an untested fuel, urban electricity depended on the burning of anthracite or bituminous coal. Burning coal produced the desired heat, of course, but it produced smoke and ash too. In order to produce the "cleanest" of fuels, electricity, the central station consumed the dirtiest.

At stations adjacent to tidewater, rivers, and canals, coal regularly arrived by collier or barge. Only a few central stations enjoyed the luxury of deep-water docks; such stations received coal very cheaply, because it arrived by coaster from the coal ports of Virginia. Most stations took delivery from barges pushed into position by tugboats. While cheaper than rail transport, water carriage suffered seasonal disturbances. Many rivers freeze during the coldest winter months, and floe ice sometimes chokes tidal estuaries. "The moral of this is, in selecting a waterway, choose one where the ice will be swept out by natural currents," asserted one expert. Many companies located on uncooperative waterways found it necessary to employ icebreakers or stockpile coal for the winter months or take some delivery of coal by rail.[12]

Railroads charged slightly more for delivering the same tonnage of coal, but weather interrupted the service only rarely. But "railroads are subject to interruptions from wrecks, storms, and floods, and on several occasions, in the United States during the last few years, have been so badly clogged up with freight that it has been impossible to tell how long a car or train would be on the road," Dixon notes in a passage revealing his concern for supplying absolutely uninterrupted metropolitan power. "In fact," he continues, "in some localities an embargo was placed on all except perishable freight, and even the largest industries had trouble in getting fuel enough to keep them going, even when men were sent out to trace cars in." Beyond the blockage problem, lay the likelihood of miners' strikes, and according to Dixon, "it is the practice of the railroads to seize all the coal they dare, which is on their tracks, for their own use; and while such coal is ultimately paid for, coal at such a time is the most precious jewel of the power plant." Wise electricity companies followed the lead of the Commonwealth Electric Company of Chicago. A 1901 *Western Electrician* article notes that the Company intended building a new generating station on "a large piece of ground west of the tracks of the Monon, Chicago and Eastern Illinois and other railroads." Lacking a waterfront site caused Commonwealth Electric to seek the best possible secondary location—one with a multiplicity of railroads immediately adjacent.[13]

Stockpiling proved the answer to transportation uncertainties. All but the smallest stations stood flanked by an enormous coal pile, the "reserve supply." Authorities agreed that the reserve pile, like the "working" pile, ought to be placed on the firebox side of the station, not the side of the building housing the actual generators.[14] Keeping coal near the furnaces meant reduced movement costs and also expedited the removal of ashes, which could be conveyed away from the coal piles. Great heaps of coal created management difficultues, however. Not only did the companies lose money in purchasing vast quantities of coal beyond their immediate needs, they sustained additional losses due to the deterioration of the coal itself. "Coal stored outside," according to "The Storage and Handling of Coal and Ashes in Power Plants," a 1908 *Cassier's Magazine* article by Werner Boecklin, "exposed to the usual climatic conditions, shows a tendency to 'slack,' and that heat values lost vary from 2 to 10 per cent."[15] Outdoor storage led to other difficulties too, among them being the freezing of entire piles when cold weather followed long periods of rain, and, perhaps the most frightening, the horror of spontaneous combustion. "Handling Coal for the Power House," a 1905 *Cassier's Magazine* article written by another expert, emphasized fire prevention. "Separate bins or storing compartments, with fireproof bulkheads between the different sections, are potent preservatives when a fire starts in one corner of the coal pile," notes H.S. Knowlton. "In like manner, the coal pockets are good places in which to install thermometers and automatic thermostat alarms."[16] The great reserve supplies of coal announced the decisions of dozens of companies to insure themselves against natural and man-made interruptions, whatever the cost in tied-up capital and automatic thermometers.

Maintaining a huge reserve supply of coal naturally caused many companies to acquire sites far larger than the space required for the actual power station. But the "working piles" consumed acreage too. One working pile consisted of the coal immediately off-loaded from barges or railroad hopper cars; another, usually indoors beyond the view of the public, consisted of several hundred or several thousand tons adjacent to the furnaces. Unlike the reserve pile awaiting winter freezes or summer strikes, the working piles represented coal in motion.

By 1927, American central stations consumed forty million tons of soft bituminous coal each year. L.W. Morrow's *Electric Power Stations* makes clear the extraordinary need to keep coal moving efficiently and cheaply under all circumstances. The vast appetites of central station furnaces caused electricity companies to pioneer in coal-handling technology and to support equipment manufacturers like the Brownhoist Company of Toledo. So gargantuan was much of the machinery that the public stood in awe of it, much as Theodore Dreiser reports in *A Hoosier Holiday* when he sees entire railroad cars being overturned by a great rotary coal-dumper.[17] At some central sta-

Figure 1. A New York City clamshell crane unloading coal for consumption in the central station behind (courtesy of Harvard University Library).

tions, locomotives pushed hopper cars onto immense trestles, where workmen tripped levers that caused the coal to fall from the car bottoms onto piles beneath the rails. At others, massive conveyors made of endless chains of buckets carried coal horizontally or vertically, never varying speed. But of all the machinery, the one that attracted most attention was the clamshell crane.

Clamshell cranes unloaded barges and railroad cars by dropping claw-like buckets into the coal loads, snapping shut the claws, and elevating the snatched coal; then, slowly and almost gracefully, the booms swung the buckets over working piles and the buckets opened, sending earthward immense showers of coal.[18] Cranes came in all sizes, but those serving central stations in such cities as New York towered several stories, dwarfing everything but the central stations behind them.

By 1910 the quest for efficiency had led engineers to the realization that some coal, perhaps five thousand tons, ought to be stored in the upper stories of each central station. The coal would fall in chutes past the generator rooms and engine rooms to the ground-floor furnaces, where it could be efficiently shoveled or augered into the flames. Ashes would fall from the bottom of the grates into gondola cars waiting in the basement. Central station designers contended with two great problems in realizing gravity-flow coal feeding. They had to design very strong buildings to support the coal, and they had to figure out some way to get the coal to the top of the ten- or twelve-story-tall building.

Coal hoists answered the second problem as soon as reinforced steel and concrete construction solved the first. At the Richmond station of the Philadelphia Electric Company, two hoists moved 325 tons of coal every hour to the upper level of the building. The hoists operated like clamshell cranes magnified in size. Their great buckets crashed crazily into the working piles, dropping almost like lightning bolts from dizzying heights. Then slowly, the closed buckets rose on steel cables to the top of the station, moved inside, and emptied beyond the public gaze. No urban machine, not even the rotary car dumpers at the Cahokia station of the Union Electric Light and Power Company and other stations, attracted as much attention.[19]

Hoists dominated central stations. "The majority of these plants are located on the water front and arranged to receive their fuel from boats, and from this fact the coal tower is the most conspicuous element," Dixon lamented in a discussion of station aesthetics, "in some cases to such an extent that it entirely overpowers the main building and conveys the impression that there is a coal-handling plant with a power-house annex."[20] But hoists mesmerized casual observers who watched their day-long rhythmic rise and fall from across rivers and harbors. Indeed the coal hoist clamshell bucket that slammed up and down at so many waterfront central stations eventually appeared at

Coney Island and other waterfront amusement parks. The toy clam-shell crane, worked by wheels and levers outside its glass box, sought after rings and other treasures in dozens of penny arcades. For the beachgoer, the clamshell crane represented a moment's diversion; for the electricity companies, it remained a crucial machine.

Electricity stations brought city dwellers into direct contact with mining camp families. Every municipality from the largest to the smallest enjoyed—or endured—intimate connections with "coal patch," with the hollows of Pennsylvania, West Virginia, and Tennessee. Throughout the first two decades of the twentieth century, when miners struck frequently for better wages and working conditions, the electrical station coal piles shrunk, and consumers of electricity worried about shortages. So glaringly obvious were coal piles and hoisting equipment that passenger-train riders and trolley-car riders noticed them in times of shortage, and scrutinized their shrinkage in times of labor unrest. Low-riding barges, long trains of dusty black hopper cars, and even single electrically-propelled suburban trolley coal cars spoke eloquently of the dependence of metropolitan America on rural coal towns.[21] Central station coal piles spoke loudest, however.

Ashes spoke more softly, but only slightly less insistently. Boecklin warned that "the ashes-handling problem needs fully as much consideration as that of the coal," but for decades engineers treated ash-handling as a secondary interest. Dixon explained that "as the amount of coal required is from ten to twenty times the weight of the ashes, it can be seen that it would be cheaper to cart ashes than it would be to cart coal." He argued that "it is more important to be close to the railroad or water way, so that coal can reach the plant in cars or barges, then it is to be close to the dump where the ashes can be disposed of."[22] Essentially, electricity company engineers worried chiefly about removing ashes from the ash pits beneath the stations; the remainder of the problem they only half-heartedly attacked, for good reasons.

A typical large electricity-generating station produced anywhere between ten and twenty tons of ash every hour. When the ash fell from the grates its temperature hovered around 1800 degrees Fahrenheit; in consistency it seemed a cross between rock and slag, a form called "clinker" in ash pit terms. As soon as ash handlers sprayed it with water to cool it for handling, the clinker produced what one author called "corrosive and offensive acids and gases." When the sulfur and phosporus combined with water, the resulting acids could eat through iron and steel. Engineers attempting to economize at first attempted to remove ash with the same conveying equipment that charged furnaces with coal. In about ten years they proved that ash acids would destroy the complicated hoists and conveyors, and they finally settled on the simple technique of dropping live ash into specially built hopper cars. The tiny cars, "moved by men, animals, tractors or locomotives," according to Morrow's *Electric Power Stations* could be unloaded by dumping directly into a waiting barge or into railroad cars.[23] While a few companies acquired giant water-sluicing machines to flush ashes from under grates, most attempted to perfect the gondola-hauling technique. Once safely away from machinery, coal piles, and the station itself, ashes had little interest for the central station chief engineer.

Consequently, the typical central station site appeared reasonably neat, if somewhat unbalanced. Reserve and working coal piles covered much of the site; on the remainder of the area stood the immense central station and coal-hoisting towers, and a small railroad yard for the ash cars. Careless passersby might think that coal moved in one side of the gigantic structure and electricity flowed out the other. More perceptive onlookers noticed the ash-handling equipment, the dust and steam from the ash heaps, and the billowing smoke. The conversion of coal to electricity fell short of perfect efficiency.

Electricity crackled across cities, running in the underground conduits and along steel and wooden poles. It crackled into the sprawling steetcar suburbs, powering the trolley cars that carried businessmen home to electrically-lit houses. And ashes followed, rarely to the finest suburbs, but more frequently to those lying on the outer edges of industrial zones, where land sold cheaply. "This is a valley of ashes—a fantastic farm where ashes grow like wheat into ridges and hills and grotesque gardens; where ashes take the forms of houses and chimneys and rising smoke and, finally, with a transcendent effort, of men who move dimly and already crumbling through the powdery air," writes F. Scott Fitzgerald in *The Great Gatsby*. "Occasionally a line of gray cars crawls along an invisible track, gives out a ghastly creak, and comes to rest, and immediately the ash-gray men swarm up with leaden spades and stir up an impenetrable cloud, which screens their obscure operations from your sight."[24] Fitzgerald's 1925 novel emphasizes the wonders of electricity; the gaily illuminated mansions hosting parties, the electric orange-juice maker, the blinking beacon on a dock, all are products of central-station electricity. Not all observers saw valleys of ashes, but many railroad passengers did, particularly commuters who raced twice each day across industrial zones. Every zone had at least one ash dump receiving clinker ash from central stations, lighter ashes from factories, and gritty, half-burned ashes from domestic furnaces. The electricity of the light bulb, the clothes iron, the humming trolley car seemed clean only at first glance.

Ash pits, conveyors, and cars might be half hidden, but smokestacks and smoke attracted attention constantly. Central station managers disposed of ashes continuously, sending out one or more trains each day to distant dumping grounds. They disposed of smoke, waste steam, and stack gas, too, even more continuously and expeditiously.

Figure 2. An Ohio central station equipped with concealed coal hoist, ca. 1915; note the upper track for receiving coal, the lower track for shipping ashes (courtesy of Harvard College Library).

By 1907, however, such disposal required increasing care. "Plumes of black smoke wreathing the tops of the stacks were badges of industry, and more smoke meant more work," remarked C.H. Benjamin in a *Cassier's Magazine* article entitled "Smoke Prevention in the Power House." Benjamin accurately understood the industrial zone aesthetic; "Even the advertising pictures in catalogues and periodicals were incomplete without this inky foliage, the natural accompaniment of factory chimneys."[25] But growing use of soft coal created ever darker clouds, and reformers took up the cry of smoke abatement.[26] Not until engineers learned that decreasing smoke saved money, however, did the nation's smokestacks begin to clear. Dark smoke signals incomplete combustion; railroad smoke inspectors issued demerits to locomotive firemen when engines poured forth sooty smoke not so much because the public disliked it and complained loudly, but because such smoke announced waste of fuel. Central stations, partly because they burned enormous amounts of soft coal and also because changing weather conditions required starting and stopping some boilers while running others full tilt, early displayed mechanical stoking equipment. Such equipment saved money in several ways, one of them being in reducing markedly the tonnage of coal needed to supply a given amount of heat. In the process, Benjamin gloated, engineers discovered a dramatic reduction in smoke. "It may as well be understood first as last that smoke abatement becomes a commercial reality when it saves fuel, and not till then."[27] Once central station engineers knew for a certainty that mechanical stokers would decrease coal consumption by ten to fifteen per cent, they quickly embraced smoke-abatement movements.

Smokestacks announced not only the number of great furnaces blazing far beneath the station roof—some large plants thrust more than four great chimneys into the sky—but they advertised the efficiency of the electricity-making operation. Very tall stacks created efficient drafts and elevated smoke and noxious fumes far over city streets; by the early 1930s, central station stacks usually emitted only steam and nearly transparent hot air. Unlike the stubby chimneys of industrial zone factories that spewed forth inky smoke and ashes, the jutting redbrick power station chimneys, like the great steel funnels of Atlantic liners, advertised the white-hot efficiency of the works inside the superstructure.

Design

Only a rare nineteenth-century power house received the attentions of architects, but by the late 1920's, electricity companies regularly employed such designers to help engineers make new power stations beautiful. "There is nothing that has even remotely paralleled these structures in use or design," mused Donald Des Granges in "The Designing of Power Stations," a 1929 *Architectural Forum* article.

"These modern buildings are intended to house huge machines and few people, to protect from the elements forces that are stupendous and superhuman." By the 1920's, central stations often stood 100 to 150 feet tall, exclusive of stacks and coal hoists, and stretched a thousand feet long. "There is a feeling of grandeur and of poetry and of beauty in the orderly assembly of this modern, efficient and economical equipment," he continued after describing the spatial needs of cranes and other machines, "and it acts as a stimulant and an inspiration to the designer of the structure which houses it." Other forces combined to convince electricity companies to build magnificent stations, however, the most important being the need to advertise the industry's concern for the public it served. "Like great railroad terminals," Des Granges concluded, the central stations "are being looked upon as institutions of public service" and require "a certain architectural dignity."[28] Most architects concerned themselves only with facades, however; the real design work remained the province of engineers.

Dixon, while he agrees with the editors of Street Railway Journal that many power stations resemble a "shoe box crowned with a piece of stove pipe," avoids discussing poetry and beauty.[29] Instead he makes clear the guiding principles of power station design and enumerates construction features which characterized most stations built after 1910. Two great principles guided power station designers. The first emphasized the primacy of machinery in ordering building form; as Des Granges intimates, the structural form can be created only after all of the machinery, and particularly boilers, has been chosen by the mechanical and electrical engineers. Unlike the awe-inspiring New York City railroad terminals, unlike even the great steel mils of Pittsburgh, East Chicago, and other manufacturing cities, the great central stations existed almost entirely for sheltering furnaces, boilers, generators, and switching equipment. Grand Central Terminal and the Homestead Mill Works, gigantic as they were, evolved from a need to shelter hordes of railroad passengers and steel workers; their scale is a scale suited to human crowds. Boston Edison's Edgar Station in North Weymouth, Massachusetts, and Gulf States Utilities' Neches Station in Beaumont, Texas, evolved from a requirement that immense machinery must be protected.[30] The second design principle evolved from the first. By 1910, central stations exhibited an immense faith in the future; engineers designed them to be easily expanded. The "unit system" of making each firebox, boiler, and generator a single, nearly autonomous unit, meant that power stations stretched in a series of bays, each bay housing one or more mechanical units. As electricity consumption increased, companies could add new bays at one end of the station, expanding generating capacity reasonably quickly and cheaply. Boston Edison's Edgar Station, for example, anticipated an extraordinary increase in consumption. The "proposed ultimate development" drawings created by the engineering-architectural firms show the coal-fueled station topped by four pairs of stacks and stretching along the waterfront more than a thousand feet. No wonder the old word "house" fell into disuse. A central station existed for machines, not workmen, and most unlike a house, it anticipated orderly expansion.

The principles dismayed architects. Des Granges ended his article in near confusion, knowing that "the design of the building must not interfere with the perfect coordination of turbine with condenser, of economizers and preheaters with the boilers," and with other machinery relationships. He hoped that "an attempt should be made to express strength—that is power—and where the limitations of the mechanical and structural designs are not too great, at times real beauty can be secured." But the engineering principles muted his optimism. "Yet one of the deterring factors in obtaining beauty is the piecemeal fashion in which these stations must often be built," he noted, "for the building must be chopped off at any pont which will satisfactorily house the equipment then being installed." The meteoric pace of power station machinery redesign and the ceaseless trials of new sorts of grates, hoists, and ash conveyors mocked the architects' attempts to achieve effects based on "mass, beauty of proportion, and relations of voids and solids together with texture and color."[32] Engineers insisted on doorways vastly larger than the largest known machinery, on huge areas for cranes not yet invented, on a thousand and one details that defeated architectural principles. In the years between 1890 and 1930, architectural magazines published only a handful of articles commenting on central station design.[33] Magazines like *Electrical Age, Cassier's, Electrical Review,* and *Western Electrician* published scores.

Dixon summed up the role of architects. "In power-house design, however, it is the results attained from the completed machine which must be considered, and while a good architectural effect is to be desired, the efficiency of the plant cannot be sacrificed to gain it." His lengthy analysis of the details of central station construction reveals a forward-looking attitude that belies his use of the old term "power house." Knowing that "daylight is the cheapest form of illumination and the more of it that can be admitted the better," he advocates immense windows in every bay and skylights in every other bay, "or the entire roof can be glazed." He comments on slow-burning materials, on caulking chimney ports, and on the arrangement of boiler-room walks.[34] By 1907, central station design hinged on intimate knowledge of the constituent equipment that made up the power station machine. In their enthusiasm to design structures wholly new, engineers sometimes surpassed even innovative architects.

Cement and reinforced concrete began to replace brick as the dominant material of central stations in the first decade of the twentieth

Figure 3. A Massachusetts waterfront central station equipped with multiple clamshell hoists, ca. 1919 (courtesy of Harvard University Library).

century. Central station engineers accepted the new materials faster than those employed to build factories, and by 1920, power stations announced modernity in both color and texture. "It has been well said that a concrete structure, whether built of blocks or by the more common wooden-form method, soon becomes a part of the geology of the landscape," asserted H.S. Knowlton in a 1907 article, "Reinforced Concrete in Power Station Construction," "and there is no doubt that the effect of strength and permanence which well-designed structures of this kind exhibit is one of the most important architectural advantages."[35] Beauty attracted only slight attention, however. As Knowlton and other experts pointed out in the pages of engineering magazines, concrete is nearly fireproof. Properly constructed concrete floors, according to a 1905 *Electrical Age* article, withstand "the test of fire and water better than any other kinds of floors." A "fireproof" concrete wall two inches thick could replace a four-inch-thick brick wall, and would last longer; moreover, high-voltage cables laid in concrete conduits, or buried in cement floors proved safe from fire.[36] Another advantage of reinforced concrete construction, one especially boasted of by Knowlton, "is its ability to resist the strains imposed by reciprocating or revolving machinery." Engines and generators needed absolutely solid mountings, and concrete provided bases positively stable. Indeed, only ashes defeated concrete; the strong acids ate through concrete flooring and bins almost as rapidly as they corroded steel. While Dixon remained skeptical of the long-term uses of concrete block, the electricity company engineers soon adopted reinforced concrete as the best possible material for power stations. By 1930, most stations exhibited a mixture of red brick and gray concrete; the newer the station, the greater the preponderance of gray.

As early as 1905, however, engineers had contrived their own aesthetic theory. From 'the engineering point of view, the plant is 'beautiful,' and if external appearance adds to the effect, it has only been furnished as a suitable housing for a thoroughly up-to-date installation," asserted Keppele Hall in 'A Model Power Station," an optimisic, forceful *Electrical Age* article.[37] In the eyes of the mechanical and electrical engineers who designed and operated the central stations, beauty derived from efficiency.

Efficiency

In coal-handling difficulties originated the quest for efficient operation that eventually shaped all aspects of central station design and management. "The ideal coal-handling plant is one in which no coal is wasted," warned Knowlton in 1905. "It is very common to see coal scattered about the yards and boiler rooms of power stations to the detriment of both the appearance and the economy of the outfit." Again and again, experts and editors announced the advantages of efficient coal handling. "Efficiency in Power Plants," a 1906 *Cassier's*

Magazine editorial, emphasizes that "the attainment of the highest degree of efficiency in the conduct of a commercial business based upon the conversion of fuel into power" will undoubtedly challenge engineers in subsequent years.[38] The editor stresses coal and ash feeding as the operations in most need of help, and casually introduces the subject of labor force reduction.

Central stations objectified the industrial interest in efficiency and heightened productivity that preoccupied American businessmen in the first decades of the twentieth century. The "unit system" of linking machinery, for example, enabled operating engineers to immediately isolate defective equipment without interrupting the workings of other units. Clamshell cranes and coal hoists systematized the movement of coal from barge to coal pile to upper-story holding chambers. Chain grates and coal injectors reduced coal consumption and dramatically reduced stack smoke. But every invention, every new arrangement of machinery reduced the labor force. "It is far more desirable," *Cassier's Magazine* editorialized, "for the labor to be limited to a minimum number of highly skilled men controlling inanimate mechanism than to be dependent upon a greater number of men of a lower grade."[39] Electricity companies needed little such telling.

Smoke abatement reformers inadvertently destroyed the livelihood of thousands of men. "The cost of an extra helper or two in the boiler room does not look very formidable at $1.50 per day each, but the matter appears different when these wages are capitalized," Knowlton argued as early as 1905. He concluded that "it pays to spend almost $9000 to eliminate such a man." Other engineers supported his view. "If there were no question of saving fuel or stopping smoke, the labor question alone would justify the introduction of mechanical handling in any large or medium-sized plant," Benjamin asserted two years later.[40] Clamshell cranes and automatic stokers reduced one station's force of firemen and coal passers from forty to four men. Smokeless chimneys announced more than the efficiency of combustion; they advertised an efficiency of labor use.

In 1905, W.P. Hancock, an engineer employed by the Boston Edison Electric Illuminating Company, explained labor force efficiency to the readers of *Electrical Age*. "The Organization of Working Forces in Large Power Houses" is a lengthy, comprehensive article analyzing the role of every employee within the walls and coal yard of a great central station. Hancock's guiding directive, "pay the man for what he can deliver to you in brains or manual labor equivalent," orders the entire essay. Hancock emphasizes that good wages and good working conditions attract and retain the best workers, and he devotes as much attention to manual workers as to assistant engineers. "We want men who, when occasion requires, will hand-fire 2000 pounds of coal an hour, and do so for several hours, if necessary," he remarks of firemen. "We want men who will burn coal, and not simply dispose of it; men who will use judgment in both firing and cleaning fires." Implicit in the essay is a strong faith in employing intelligent men, because only such men work efficiently. Supervisors and foremen must be "of sterling worth in the handling and judging of men," and must "realize that a fireman is a man, and, as such, is entitled to proper treatment at all times."[41] Much, much more explains Hancock's argument than moral enlightenment. An efficient, precision-operated central station employed very few men, but those men had the capacity to cripple the production of electricity by simply walking away from the complex machinery that had replaced unskilled laborers. Replacing the strikers with new hands might be possible, but not at short notice, and no electricity company could afford even a momentary failure of production.

In the late 1920's, the central station epitomized the high profits and contented work force promised by such efficiency experts as Frederick Winslow Taylor and Frank Gilbreth.[42] A few men, hand-picked for intelligence and reliability, operated the massive machines that replaced the work gangs of three decades before. One controller in the clamshell crane did the work of a hundred men; two or three firemen tending stokers and chain grates did the work of forty husky young men; one gray-headed oiler tended a half-dozen, self-oiling generators. And someplace far above the generator room sat the system operator at his panel of meters and switches, monitoring machines that seemed to run themselves.

Tension

Central stations fascinated the general public, and electricity companies encouraged the fascination. Rate-setting disputes caused the companies to engage in sophisticted public relations maneuvers, among them inviting the public to tour stations. Hancock, for example, worried about visitors spying coal dust and other filth, and insisted that cleaners played a part more important than companies recognized. Some companies tried hard to beautify station sites with trees and other plants, and most made some effort to improve structural facades. The electricity industry published booklets explaining the operation of stations and the transmission of electricity and cooperated with journalists intent on deciphering stations.[43]

Two mass-circulation periodical articles exemplify the genre. Arthur Howden Smith's " 'The Peak of the Load': What it Means to Light New York City and Transport Her Crowds" appeared in the August, 1909 issue of *Putnam's Magazine*. Four years later, Alan Sullivan's "The Power That Serves" appeared in *Harper's Monthly*. Both articles focus on the role of the operating engineer. "As a type of human efficiency consider the system operator—this modern and impassive Jove, distributing benignant thunderbolts," writes Sullivan of the man who "manipulates his hundred of thousands of horse-power with a touch of delicate finger-tips," and who has orders "to wreck any appliance up to the largest turbine rather than permit an interruption to the service."[44] Smith also honors the man who "can throw off the current from any particular station by a mere twist of the wrist or a nod to a subordinate." Like so much turn-of-the-century explication of railroad operations, which focuses on the locomotive engineer, the articles emphasize the role of one man, perhaps because only his role is intelligible. Smith and Sullivan attempt to see the central station through the eyes of the system operator, but they fail. Both journalists shift their gaze to the activities of the station itself, almost as though the station has its own intelligence.

Both writers use the same device to order their articles. A change in weather from clear skies to fog or thunderstorm gloom causes millions of people to reach for light switches. "No matter how impatiently the consumer asks, the light is there," Smith notes, "flashing up to his pressure on a switch." At the central station, however, "whistles blow shrilly, signalling to engineers scattered throughout the immense building; the telephone rings continuously; men are toying with the switches that control the untold kilowatts of power," he continues. As a single machine, as one intelligence, the equipment responds to the cloud drifting over the city. "Great fires are stoked up; boilers strain under the additional pressure placed upon them; furnace doors swing back, revealing the ravenous maws within; the whirr and thunder of machinery, the power of which is estimated in hundreds of thousands of horse-power, drowns out the rest of the world in a void of bewildering sound." A quick change in weather prompts undreamed-of mechanical complexity.

Smith concludes his article by noting that "it is not difficult to discern in 'the peak of the load' a final confirmation of the absolute triumph of civilization." While few others observers shared his sentiment, at least one, Arnold Bennett, understood the central station as a triumph of American civilization.

In his 1912 *Your United States,* Bennett describes a nighttime visit to a New York City central station. His hosts lead him along "deserted, narrow galleries, lined with thousands of small, caged 'transformers,' " up to an observation platform facing "an enormous white hall, sparsely peopled by a few colossal machines that seemed to be revolving and oscillating about their business with the fatalism of conquered and resigned leviathans." Bennett relates a variety of emotions, perhaps chiefly wonder, and notes the eeriness of it all. "Immaculately clean, inconceivably tidy, shimmering with brilliant light under its lofty and beautiful ceiling, shaking and roaring with the terrific thunder of its own vitality, this hall in which no common voice could make itself heard produced nevertheless an effect of magical stillness, silence, and solitude. We were alone in it, save that now and then in the far-distant spaces a figure might flit and disappear between the huge glinting columns of metal." Everywhere, the station seems bereft of workers, in the generating room, even in the stokehold where coal moves "scarcely touched by the hand-wielded shovel." The "solitude of machinery, attending most conscientiously and effectively to itself" made "a singularly disconcerting spectacle."[47] Bennett had wandered into the new industrial world, the throne room of the engineer.

As early as 1881, when Charles Barnard published his collection of engineer-glorifying short stories entitled *Knights of Today, or Love and Science,* every sort of engineer, including the railroad locomotive engineer, had received increasing artistic attention.[48] The electrical engineer epitomized the earth-moving, precedent-shattering role of the young American engineer, however. The rapid expansion of urban central stations forced the electrical engineer into public view as the master of the nation's most complex, most mysterious, and most labor efficient manufacturing operation. By 1929, dozens of toy companies produced toys that taught something of the wonders of electricity. The Lionel Company produced not only electric trains, but miniature power houses and operating switchboards and transformers too; other companies manufactured electric motor kits, wet-cell battery components, and "electrical novelties."[49] A career as an electrical engineer might not begin too early, thought many parents mystified by electric current but aware of its promise. Directing a central station meant directing the very essence of twentieth-century urban life; it meant controlling the metropolitan future.

Young electrical engineers brought the metropolitan electric vision to suburban and rural America. As they directed the stringing of trolley line catenary and electric wires, they promised changed lifestyles. Electricity companies advertised all the glories of the electric-powered lifestyle. To encourage businessmen to erect illuminated signs, they placed gigantic signs on the facades and chimneys of central stations and sold retail-store signs on installment plans. To encourage housewives to consume more electricity in daytime hours, they distributed nearly free clothes irons on hot summer days, when women sweltered next to the coal stoves warming old-fashioned cast-iron flatirons. To encourage manufacturers to consume more electricity, they leased motors at cut rates.[50] Central station electricity reached only short distances from cities; until the Depression spawned the Rural Electrification Agency, most American farm families did without, or relied on wind-generated power. But where the transmission lines did go, there followed metropolitan lifestyles. Where trolley companies strung wire, people achieved cheap, swift transportation; where utility companies stretched wires and cables, there families suddenly enjoyed bright lighting, washing machines, radio, and fans. And always a young "college man," a knight of today, personified the extension of metropolitan power, of "high tension" electricity.

In the central station urban Americans first glimpsed the beginning of a new era of ultra-efficient industrial production. By replacing old-style power houses with gigantic structures designed for expansion and the methodical consumption of coal—and removal of ash—engineers created places of mystery. Central stations, in their almost smokeless chimneys, tiny work forces, and brick-and-concrete walls, objectified the futuristic electrical force created within their walls. No wonder so many Americans pondered the significance of the great "electricity factories" connected to their homes by cables and wires. The central station in the years between 1890 and 1930 announced a new society shaped not by steam power, but by the refined technology of electricity.

NOTES

1   "Insurance Rates and Power House Construction," *Street Railway Review*, 4 (March 15, 1894), 149-50; Arthur Titley, "Works Engine Houses," *Cassier's Magazine*, 34 (July, 1908), 195-201; on industrial zones see John R. Stilgoe, "Moulding the Industrial Zone Aesthetic, 1880 to 1929," *Journal of American Studies*, 16 (April, 1982), 21-35.
2   John R. Stilgoe, *Common Landscape of America, 1580 to 1845* (New Haven, 1982), pp. 13-21, 158-182.
3   Walt Whitman, "To a Locomotive in Winter," *Leaves of Grass and Selected Prose*, ed. John Kouwenhoven (New York, 1950), pp. 367-368.
4   John R. Stilgoe, "Landschaft and Linearity: Two Archetypes of Landscape," *Environmental Review*, 4 (autumn, 1980), 2-17. Henry James, *The American Scene* (New York, 1907), p. 86 and *Passim;* Charles J. Kavanagh, "Some Aspects of the Power Problem for the Textile Industries," *Cassier's Magazine*, 34 (August, 1908), 371-380.
5   On the electrical industry, see Malcolm MacLaren, *The Rise of the Electrical Industry in the Nineteenth Century* (Princeton, 1943); Harold Passer, *The Electrical Manufacturers, 1875-1900* (Cambridge, Mass., 1953); Harold Sharlin, *The Making of the Electrical Age* (New York, 1964).
6   "Mount Morris Electric Light Company," *Electrical Review*, 16 (March 15, 1890), 1-3; for the pace of design change, see Joshua Weingreen, *Electric Power Plant Engineering* (New York, 1910).
7   Sharlin, pp. 193-195, 199-202; H.S. Knowlton, "The Field of Electric Alternating Current Service," *Cassier's Magazine*, 31 (February, 1907), 353-356.
8   C.L. Hubbard, "Unit Power Plant," *Brickbuilder*, 22 (March-June, 1913), 33-38, 59-62, 81-84, 109-112.
9   Thomas Edward Murray, *Electric Power Plants* (New York, 1910), 299-327.
10 Louis C. Hennick and E. Harper Charlton, *Steetcars of New Orleans* (Gretna, La., 1965), pp. 199-201; "Steam Turbine Power Plant," *Street Railway Journal,*25 (January 21, 1905), 111-112; "New Power Houses of the West Chicago Street Railway Co." *Street Railway Review,*4 (May 15, 1894), 285-289.
11 A.E. Dixon, "Planning and Construction of Power Statons," *Engineering Magazine,* 31-32 (August, 1906-March, 1907), 722-727, 909-934, 58-86, 227-247, 370-390, 551-571, 749-768, 860-873; see esp. 909-910.
12 Murray, pp. 1-138; Dixon, 912; Frederick N. Bushnell, "The Power Station," *Electrical Age,* 36 (April, 1906), 268-274.
13 Dixon, 912-914; "New Polyphase Plant of the Commonwealth Electric Company,' *Western Electrician,* 27 (July 12, 1901), 29-34.

[14] H.S. Knowlton, "Handling Coal for the Power House," *Cassier's Magazine,* 27 (April, 1905), 480-481. ·

[15] 34 (July, 1908), 235-256.

[16] Knowlton, "Handling," 481.

[17] Lester William Wallace Morrow, *Electric Power Stations* (New York, 1927), pp. 47-72; Theodore Dreiser, *A Hoosier Holiday* (New York, 1916), pp. 178-187.

[18] "Locomotive Cranes for Coal Handling," *Electrical Age,* 36 (January, 1906), 66-67.

[19] Morrow, pp. 47-72.

[20] Dixon, 860.

[21] For illustrations of "coal patches," see Edward T. Devine, "Coal," *Survey,* 51 (November 1, 1923), 128-137; Knowlton, "Handling," 481.

[22] Werner Boecklin, "The Storge and Handling of Coal and Ashes in Power Plants," *Cassier's Magazine,* 34 (July, 1908), 235-256; Dixon, 911.

[23] Morrow, pp. 66-70; Boecklin, 247-248.

[24] F. Scott Fitzgerald, *The Great Gatsby* (New York, 1925), p. 23; for an excellent analysis of the valley, seç Leo Marx, *The Machine in the Garden: Technology and the Pastoral Ideal in America* (New York, 1964), pp. 356-365.

[25] 31 (February, 1907), 339-352; see esp. 339.

[26] On smoke abatement, see J.B.C. Kershaw, "Smoke Abatement," *Cassier's Magazine,* 29 (June 26, 1909), 335-341.

[27] C.H. Benjamin, "Smoke Prevention in the Power House," *Cassier's Magazine,* 31 (February, 1907), 339-352.

[28] 51 (September, 1929), 361-372.

[29] Dixon, 860.

[30] For illustrations, see Des Granges.

[31] Dixon, 860-861; Hubbard, *passim;* Des Granges, 361-362.

[32] Des Granges, 372.

[33] See, for example, Bigelow Wadsworth, "Chauney Street Station," *American Architect,* 117 (May 26, 1920), pp. 647-650; Gilbert P. Hall, "Study for a Power House," *American Architect,* 136 (August 5, 1929), 183; "Buildings of the Murphy Power Co.," *American Architect and Building News,* 92 (October 12, 1907), 128.

[34] Dixon, 864-865; S.M. Bushnell, "Architect and the Central Station," *Cassier's Magazine,* 31 (January, 1907), 261-264; see also, "Electric Power Stations in New York," *Engineering Magazine,* 18 (February, 1900), 773-774.

[35] H.S. Knowlton, "Reinforced Concrete in Power Station Construction," *Cassier's Magazine,* 31 (April, 1907), 486-506.

[36] Eugene B. Clark, "Cement in Central Station Design," *Electrical Age,* 34 (May, 1905), 375-378.

[37] 35 (December, 1905), 401-411; see esp. 401.

[38] Knowlton, "Handling," 481; for the editorial, see 34 (June, 1908), x (of the advertising section, which is paged differently).

[39] "Efficiency," x.

[40] Knowlton, "Handling," 480; Benjamin, 342.

[41] W.P. Hancock, "The Organization of Working Forces in Large Power Houses," *Electrical Age,* 34 (June, 1905), 407-412.

[42] Frederick Winslow Taylor, *Shop Management* (New York, 1900) and *Principles of Scientific Management* (New York, 1911); Frank Bunker Gilbreth, *Motion Study* (New York, 1911).

[43] R.L. Goodale, "Getting New Business and Holding the Old as Applied to Electric Central Stations," *Cassier's Mgazine,* 31 (November, 1906), 58-62; Des Granges, 372; Long Island Lighting Company, *The Story of Our Twenty-Five Years of Service to Long Island, 1911-1936* (New York, 1936).

[45] 6 (August, 1909), 519-526; see also, "New York Edison Power Station," *Scientific American,* 87 (September 6, 1902), 147, 152.

[46] Smith, 524; see also P. Dawson, "Modern Electric Power Stations," *Cassier's Magazine,* 19 (January, 1901), 211-214 and George Buchanan Fife, "A Fantasy of City Lights," *Harper's Weekly,* 57 (February 8, 1913), 9-10.

[47] Arnold Bennett, *Your United States* (New York, 1912), pp. 79-83. For an illustration of a dynamo room, see "The Philadelphia Edison Station," *Electrical Review*, 16 (March 29, 1890), 2-3.

[48] (New York, 1881).

[49] Lionel Company, *Catalogue for 1929* (New York, 1928), esp. p. 44. On children, see C. Barnard, "Goodbye 3876," *Saint Nicholas*, 34 (February, 1907), 324-329.

[50] La Rue Vredenburgh, "Sign and Decorative Lighting," *Electrical Age*, 34 (June, 1905), 418-425; H.W. Hillman, "Electricity in the Home," *Cassier's Magazine*, 31 (November, 1906), 25-35; Goodale, 59-61; Frederick H. Kimball, "The Widening Use of Small Electric Motors," *Cassier's Mgazine*, 27 (February, March, 1905), 291-302, 363-371.

The Unredeemed Landscape: Industrial America In The Imagination Of Whittier, Bellamy, and Sinclair

MICHAEL BREWSTER FOLSOM

I will begin by trying to make clear what I am *not* talking about in this brief paper. I am not talking about the American literary response to industrialization. I am talking about three isolated texts dating from 1844 to 1905 in which writers of the second rank described the newly perceived landscape of the industrial city.* I am particularly interested in the ways writers have dealt with urban manufacturers, the built environment of industrial America, and its peoples—in order to learn something about what happens when cultural tradition is confronted with disconcerting new realities. I am concerned both with the ways the literary imagination can illuminate the meaning of our industrial world, and with the ways literature can reveal its own limitations in the attempt to deal with subject matter beyond its conventional range.

The texts I do look at are isolated, not a representative sampling of a larger body. You will have a hard time finding three others to compare with them in all of nineteenth-century writing. Throughout the great period of the transformation of the United States from an agrarian democracy to a continental industrial power, American letters virtually ignored the actual locus of the power which created that change. The built environment of the industrial region was not a stage upon which the conventional literary imagination could easily set its works.

The attempts of those few who did represent the industrial landscape indicate why the attempts were so few and why, indeed, that landscape figured so little in their own work. It is also useful to look at these texts because they differ from the texts commonly considered to reflect nineteenth-century writers' responses to industrialization. Our writers have typically worked and lived quite distant from the landscapes of industrial labor. These writers' treatments of the consequences of industrial labor are commonly oblique, figurative, tangential—based largely on the intrusions of elements of industry into the non-industrial world. The steam locomotive is the most familiar instance. My point is emphasized by the fact that, to encounter the industrial city directly and explicitly, the three writers discussed here had to move self-consciously and geographically from their familiar

---

*Three texts are appended in the notes at the end of the text.

world to a place that was as unaccustomed to themselves as to their assumed readers.

The sensibilities and temperments of John Greenleaf Whittier, Edward Bellamy, and Upton Sinclair are plainly distinct from each other, but their treatments of the industrial landscape have much in common. Each writer was driven by extraordinary ethical or ideological motives to view a district of urban manufactures. Their renderings of that district are all deeply colored by those motives. Whittier, Bellamy, and Sinclair were notable in American letters for their vigorous social activism, and each moved to the industrial city, however briefly, in reality or imagination for purposes of social reform. Their representations of that city are rhetorically extravagant and overwrought with emotion or at least with sentiment. Their judgments on the meaning of the new industrial city are strong, but, either explicitly or implicitly, all three writers contradict their own primary judgments with other judgments equally strong. And these contradictions are, indeed, what is most interesting and significant about these representations of the world of manufactures. For each writer in his own way, the industrial city seemed a compelling force for the enhancement of life, and at the same time, a fact or portent of unreedemable evil.

Whittier's essay, "The City of a Day," was first published in 1844 in a reform newspaper he edited briefly in Lowell, Massachusetts. It was collected the following year with several topical essays in a small volume he called *A Stranger in Lowell.'* In this essay Whittier antedated by almost fifty years the presumed "discovery" of the industrial city in American literature. Its opening paragraph is a rhetorical *tour de force* built up out of a series of attempts to render the new knowable by comparing it figuratively to images drawn from imaginative convention. The sequence of these comparisons is, in itself, the paragraph's most salient characteristic.

Whittier enters the subject by comparing the city of Lowell to the most outlandish and alien in received literature, the palaces that spring up in the desert of the *Arabian Nights*. Though alien, this figure is benign, merely romatic, piquant. The "chaos of brick masonry and painted shingles" in Lowell is "marvelous," "miraculous," "a work of wizardry," "wonderful." For the rest of the paragraph Whittier's frame of reference is religious, mostly Christian. Work here is the "patron saint," the mills are "temples" "huger than the Milan Cathederal." Comparisons to pagan buildings of worship, the mosque and pagoda, sustain the suggestions that the place of manufactures is truly alien, but Christian imagery comes to predominate. The "gospel" of industry is preached here, "its mighty sermons uttered by steam and water-power." Whittier hears "organ-swell," sees "scattered leaves of an evangel" and thousands of priests and priestesses "ministering around their spinning jenny and power-loom altars."

What started out as phantasmagorical has become mighty serious by the end of the paragraph. In the subsequent paragraph Whittier considers the Christianization of industrial technology at its extreme in the thought of Adolph Etzler, the utopian he had met and whose book *Paradise in the Reach of All Men* had recently been reviewed by Thoreau.[2] Now the notion that mechanism might lead to salvation seems plainly absurd to the pious Whittier. To refute Etzler, he contrasts the evidence of the Lowell mills to the theories of the visionary. What Whittier had just compared to a "palace" and a "cathederal," he now calls a "prison":

> Looking down as I now do upon these huge, brick workshops, I have thought of poor Etzler, and wondered whether he would admit, were he with me, that his mechanical forces have here found their proper employment of Millenium making, grinding on, each in his iron harness, invisible, yet shaking, by his regulated and repressed power, his huge prison-house from basement to cap-stone, is it true the Genii of Mechanism are really at work here, raising us, by wheel and pulley, steam and water power, slowly up that inclined plane, from whose top stretches the broad table-land of Promise?

Whittier went on to make his view of the mills of Lowell even more dour and absolute. He revised the conclusion of the first paragraph to pick up on his earlier association with the devil and death:

> After all, it may be well questioned whether this gospel according to Poor Richard's Almanac, is precisely calculated for the redemption of humanity. Labor, graduated to man's simple wants, necessities, and unperverted tastes, is doubtless well; but all beyond this is wearieness of flesh and spirit. Every web which falls from these restless looms has a history more or less connected with sin and suffering beginning with slavery and ending with overwork and premature death.

Having concluded that the millscape of Lowell, miraculous though it may appear to the stranger, is more or less a "prison," "a world of sin and suffering," "slavery and premature death," what is Whittier to propose? He offers nothing. He simply drops his critique of the industrial city. The rest of his essay and the rest of his writings on Lowell are light-hearted and matter-of-fact. The very next sentence is, "Many of the streets of Lowell present a lively and neat aspect," and so forth. His other essays on Lowell emphasize the quaint and the picturesque.

Edward Bellamy and Upton Sinclair, in contrast, believed they had alternatives to the chaos and misery they found in industrial America. Their visions of a better future had something in common with Adolph Etzler's half-cracked schemes. They wanted to perfect the power and organization of industry, and they looked at the urban landscape of their own times to stimulate the imagination to form alternatives, though in imaginative ways, alternatives that were very different from each other.

Bellamy's brief visit to the industrial district in nineteenth century South Boston occurs late in *Looking Backward*.[3] The draft of a scheme for a "Cooperative Commonwealth" has been fully elaborated. The visit is fraught with a variety of emotions, disappointment the first among them, for it seems utopia had been a dream, and the narrator has reawakened to his old reality. (The reader does not yet know that this return to old Boston is the dream.) What Bellamy's pale surrogate, Julian West, discovers in the territory of capitalist manufactures is insanity and anarchy. Bellamy had compared Boston's Washington Street, where manufactured goods are retailed, to "a lane in Bedlam." The South Boston factory district now seen is "a spectacle as much more melancholy than Bedlam as production is a more vital function than is distribution." The comparison is especially interesting because the productive function is essentially ignored in Bellamy's utopia. The characters we meet in his future are consumers, not producers. Julian West's guide through the future is a medical doctor, not an industrial worker. Bellamy offers us no alternative ideal industrial landscape to which we might compare the shapes of South Boston. Still, Bellamy brings his reader to the industrial district favorably disposed to the notion of industry. Indeed, all social life in his Commonwealth is organized around the principle of an "industrial army," and within the actual productive unit of nineteenth century Boston all seems orderly, rational, and efficient:

> Within each one of these factories the strictest organization
> of industry was insisted upon. The separate gangs worked
> on under single central authority. No interference and no
> duplication of work were permitted. Each had his alloted
> task and none were idle.

Bellamy saw no slavery or overwork or exploitation under industrial capitalism. What Bellamy identified as the problem was the inefficiency of competition, and this he described in the strongest and most anxious terms. His industrial landscape is the landscape of the battlefield:

> The roar and rattle of wheels and hammers resounding
> from every side was not the hum of a peaceful industry but
> the clangor of swords wielded by foremen. These mills and
> shops were so many forts, each under its own flag, its guns
> trained on the mills and shops about it, and its sappers busy
> below undermining them.

Bellamy's comparison of industrial capitalism to warfare, however, is quite restricted. On the one hand he strongly favored military organization, and on the other hand he did not mean to suggest that industry was in itself to be associated with death. The only direct victims of the quasi-military struggle between capitalist enterprises were each other. The rest of society was an indirect victim, only because competitive industries could not produce enough to meet human needs.

This competition based on the "mad wasting of human labor," as he put it, results in a social evil so appalling in Bellamy's view, that he distances it as far as he can from what he considers the American and, indeed, the human norm. Julian West turns to the residential streets of industrial Boston where he sees "in direst shape the want that waste had bred." The tenements are "rookeries," the breeding places of gregarious animals. They smell like "the between decks of a slave ship." The streets are like those of a "moslem town" (no *Arabian Nights* for Bellamy), infested, as he says, with "swarms" of children who are not even heathens, but brutalized, the lowest kind of beasts, "mongrel curs." Where Whittier had drawn upon the foreign to suggest the exotic quality of the industrial landscape in America, Bellamy drew upon such alien comparisons to indicate what he considered the depravity of those who peopled that landscape.

For Upton Sinclair, these districts were no less wonderous than Whittier found them and no less fetid than Bellamy imagined them. Like Whittier and Bellamy, Sinclair considered the world of industry fundamentally alien to the American reader. It is almost entirely an enclave of immigrants, his characters the most newly arrived among them. For Whittier, too, sixty years earlier, a distinguishing characteristic of industrial Lowell was its immigrant populations. He devotes another essay in the same work to describing the picturesque "foreign colonies" of the place. Like Bellamy, Sinclair had a program for an alternative industrial society, but Sinclair also had what few American writers have ever boasted: a downright appreciation of the power of industrial America at its most crass and foul.

Sinclair's introduction to the industrial Chicago of *The Jungle* is mediated through the presumed experience of aliens, the Lithuanian families of Jurgis and Ona Rudkus.[4] And we have to struggle a bit to determine just what Sinclair would have us think of the world he imagines. He is much more literal and matter-of-fact than Whittier and Bellamy, though his characterizations of the landscape are strong: "deafing confusion," "ugly," "dirty," "dingy," "desolate," "hideous," and "bare." Chicago is a "great sore of a city," sprawling itself over the surface of te prairie. Yet Sinclair repeatedly qualifies such negative terms with the suggestion that the very worst of industrial realities might be perceived with indifference or even with favor.

Sinclair introduces his immigrants and his readers to the sensuous experience of the stockyards with patience and painstaking detail: lingering over its smell first, then over the smoking chimneys (the dominant feature of the landscape), and last over the sounds of the herds of animals awaiting slaughter. To "some".the smell is "sickening," but most perceptions are less definite. It is "curious," "rich," "strange," "pungent," "raw and crude," "sensual," "strong," "an intoxicant." Sinclair's strangers were "not at all sure that it was unpleasant." They were "divided in their opinions." Above all they were "lost in wonder."

The description of chimneys and their smoke dominating the landscape is similarly strong and ambiguous. Likewise the lowing and grunting of cattle and swine, another "strange thing," "a thing elemental," a "vague disturbance, a trouble," "like the murmering of the bees in the spring, the whispering of the forest," "the rumblings of a world in motion."

Sinclair describes the process of "making" the land upon which the houses of Packing Town are built—digging clay pits for bricks, filling the pits with garbage, and then building homes upon the land-fill. Although this process seemed to Jurgis and Ona a "felicitious arrangement characteristic of an enterprising country like America," Sinclair makes clear that this is the perception of greenhorns. But he, too, was beguiled by the ingenuity of industrial capitalism. His enthusiasm for machinery was boundless. His description of the mechanical process by which carcasses are disassembled in American packing houses might have been written by the advertising department of Swift or Armour. And Sinclair's conclusion of his initial tour around Packing Town is almost lyrical. His strangers in Chicago "...stood there while the sun went down upon the scene, and the sky in the west turned blood-red, and the tops of the houses shone like fire." The smoke was "a study in colors now." "All the sordid suggestions of the place were gone—in the twilight it was a vision of power"; "—it seemed a tale of wonder, with its tale of human energy," "of opportunity and freedom, of life and love and joy." The chapter concludes triumphantly with Jurgis's determination: "Tomorrow I shall go there and get a job!"

All the filth and degredation in the territory of industrial capitalism is washed clean by the promise of a "good job," even a job butchering hogs or shoveling guts. And what is wrong with industrial capitalism in Sinclair's vision is simply that it doesn't make good on that promise. The rest of the novel, of course, is a tale of sin and suffering, worse than slavery, and of many early deaths caused by the greed and callousness of those who own and run industrial America, but that strong ambivalence remains. The wretched landscape was the creation of powers Sinclair deeply respected, or was in awe of. Like Bellamy and Whittier, he could not encompass the burgeoning facts of industrial capitalism with a single vision, a single conception.

From these strenuous imaginative efforts to make meaning out of manufactures we might take counsel. We here [at this conference] represent the leadership of the intellectual and historiographical attempt of late twentieth-century America to come to terms with its industrial origins. As Whittier, Bellamy, and Sinclair reveal, intractable contradictions are designed into the fabric of industrial capitalism, and we must embrace these contradictions in our analysis. Like Whittier, Bellamy, and Sinclair, we often find that our perceptions of the industrial landscape run athwart each other. The critic of industrial capitalism discovers much to admire in its ingenuity, in the grand scale of its shapes, and the lavish benefits of its works, however compromised. Even the most complacent and apologetic among us acknowledges the suffering of multitudes, the women and men and children who built the landscape we study. We find ourselves features of that landscape, beneficiaries of that system, complicit with the people whose lives we interpret.

Like Whittier, Bellamy, and Sinclair we strive to attract an audience, and we search for ways to render our materials comprehensively in terms that will gain the assent of that audience, as well as illuminate its understanding. Who, indeed, would come to Lowell to view piles of decrepit brick and be hectored about sin and suffering and early death? Who would stoop to persuade the modern stranger in Lowell that these mills were once magic palaces of exotic delight?

Well, then, if the landscape of our industrial past was neither of these things, what was it? It certainly was not a tepid compromise, a kind of a good thing with some unfortunate difficulties thrown in! What these brief passages of imagination I have discussed suggest, to me at least, is that our industrial heritage is both—in extremis—excruciating and ecstatic. Only if we embrace this contradiction, can we hope to build an analytical framework to explain what the nation has become, how we got here, and where we are going.

NOTES

[1] John Greenleaf Whittier, *A Stranger in Lowell* (Lowell, Mass., 1845) pp. 9-12.
     This, then, is Lowell—a city, springing up, like the enchanted palaces of the Arabian tales, as it were in a single night—stretching far and wide its chaos of brick masonry and painted shingles, filling the angle of the confluence of the Concord and the Merrimack with the sights and sounds of trade and industry! Marvellously here has Art wrought its modern miracles. I can scarcely realize the fact, that a few years ago these rivers, now tamed and subdued to the purposes of man, and charmed into slavish subjection to the Wizard of Mechanism, rolled unchecked towards the ocean the waters of the Winnipiseogee, and the rock-rimmed springs of the White Mountains, and rippled down their falls in the wild freedom of Nature. A stranger, in view of all this wonderful change, feels himself as it were thrust forward into a new century; he seems treading on the outer circle of the millennium of steam engines and cotton mills. Work is here the Patron Saint. Every thing bears his image and superscription. Here is no place for that respectable class of citizens called gentlemen, and their

much vilified brethren, familiarly known as loafers. Over the gateways of this New World Manchester, glares the inscription, "WORK, OR DIE!" Here

"Every worm beneath the moon
Draws different threads, and late or soon,
Spins, toiling out his own cocoon."

The founders of this city, good Christian men, probably never dreamed of the anti-Yankee sentiment of Charles Lamb:—

"Who first invented Work; and thereby bound
The holiday rejoicing spirit down
To the never-ceasing importunity
Of business in the green fields and the town?—
Sabbathless Satan: he who his unglad
Task ever plies midst rotatory burnings,
For wrath divine has made him like a wheel
In that Red Realm from whence are no returnings!"

Rather, of course, would they adopt Carlyle's definition of "Divine labor—noble, ever fruitful—the grand, sole Miracle of Man." For this is indeed a city consecrated to the Spirit of Thrift—dedicated, every square rod of it, to the Divinity of Work. The Gospel of Industry preached daily and hourly from some thirty temples; each huger than the Milan Cathedral or the temple of Jeddo, the Mosque of St. Sophia or the Chinese Pagoda of a hundred bells; its mighty sermons uttered by steam and water power; its music the everlasting jar of Mechanism, and the organ-swell of many waters; scattering the cotton and woollen leaves of its Evangel from the wings of steamboats and rail-cars throughout the land; its thousand priests, and its thousands of priestesses, ministering around their spinning-jenny and power-loom altars, or whitening the long unshaded streets in the level light of sunset! It is truly, as Carlyle says, a miracle, neither more nor less.

As has been truly said, there is a transcendentalism in mechanics as well as ethics. A few years ago, while traveling in Pennsylvania, I encountered a small, dusky-browed German of the name of Etzler. He was possessed with the belief, that the world was to be restored to its Paradisiacal state by the sole agency of mechanics; and that he had himself discovered the means of bringing about this very desirable consummation. His whole mental atmosphere was thronged with spectral enginery—wheel within wheel—plans of hugest mechanism—Brobdignagian steam engines—Niagaras of water-power—wind-mills, with "sail-broad vans," like those of Satan in chaos,—by whose power application every valley was to be exalted, and every hill laid low—old forests seized by their shaggy tops and uprooted—old morasses drained—the tropics made cool—the eternal ices melted around the poles—the ocean itself covered with artificial islands—blossoming gardens of the Blessed, rocking gently on the bosom of the deep. Give him "three hundred thousand dollars, and ten years time," and he would undertake to do the work. Wrong, pain and sin, being in his view but the results of our physical necessities, ill-gratified desires, and natural yearnings for a better state, were to vanish before the Millennium of Mechanism. "It would be," said he, "as ridiculous then to dispute and quarrel about the means of life, as it would be now about water to drink by the side of mighty rivers, or about permission to breathe the common air." To his mind the great Forces of Nature took the shape of mighty and benignant spirits, sent hitherward to be the servants of man in restoring to him his lost Paradise; waiting but for his word of command to apply their giant energies to the task, but as yet struggling blindly and aimlessly, giving ever and anon gentle hints, in the way of earthquake, fire and flood, that they are weary of idleness, and would fain be set at work. Looking down, as I now do, upon these huge, brick work-shops, I have thought of poor Etzler, and wondered whether he would admit, were he with me, that his mechanical Forces have here found their proper employment of Millennium making. Grinding on, each in his iron harness, invisible, yet shaking, by his regulated and repressed power, his huge prison-house from basement to cap-stone, is it true that the Genii of Mechanism are really at work here, raising us, by wheel and pully, steam and water power, slowly up that inclined plane, from whose top stretches the broad table-land of Promise?

In the 1892 edition of Whittier's prose works (*The Prose Works of John Greenleaf Whittier,* Boston, Vol. 1, pp. 352-353), the last sentence of this paragraph was an additional passage significantly sharpening Whittier's critical view of the factory city:

After all, it may well be questioned whether this gospel according to Poor Richard's Almanac, is precisely calculated for the redemption of humanity. Labor, graduated to man's simple wants, necessities, and unperverted tastes, is doubtless well; but all beyond this is weariness of flesh and spirit. Every web which falls from these restless looms has a history more or less connected with sin and suffering beginning with slavery and ending with overwork and premature death.

2 Whittier appears to have read Thoreau's review of Etzler, for he echoes Thoreau in the first sentence of the second paragraph of his essay: "It has been truly said, there is a transcendentalism in mechanics...." Thoreau had used the phrase, "transcendentalism in mechanics," in his review: "Paradies (To Be) Regained," *United States Magazine and Democratic Review,* volume 13 (November, 1843,) pp. 451-463.

3 Edward Bellamy, *Looking Backward, 2000-1887,* ed. John L. Thomas (Cambridge, Mass.: Harvard University Press, 1967), pp.300-302, 305. First edition, Boston, Mass. 1888.

Some time after this it was that I drifted over into South Boston and found myself among the manufacturing establishments. I had been in this quarter of the city a hundred times before, just as I had been on Washington Street, but here, as well as there, I now first perceived the true significance of what I witnessed. Formerly I had taken pride in the fact that, by actual count, Boston had some four thousand independent manufacturing establishments; but in this very multiplicity and independence I recognized now the secret of the insignificant total product of their industry.

If Washington Street had been like a lane in Bedlam, this was a spectacle as much more melancholy as production is a more vital function than distribution. For not only were these four thousand establishments not working in concert, and for that reason alone operating at prodigious disadvantage, but, as if this did not involve a sufficiently disastrous loss of power, they were using their utmost skill to frustrate one another's effort, praying by night and working by day for the destruction of one another's enterprises.

The roar and rattle of wheels and hammers resounding from every side was not the hum of a peaceful industry, but the clangor of swords wielded by foremen. These mills and shops were so many forts, each under its own flag, its guns trained on the mills and shops about it, and its sappers busy below, undermining them.

Within each one of these forts the strictest organization of industry was insisted on; the separate gangs worked under a single central authority. No interference and no duplicating of work were permitted. Each had his allotted task, and none were idle. By what hiatus in the logical faculty, by what lost link of reasoning, account, then, for the failure to recognize the necessity of applying the same principle to the organization of the national industries as a whole, to see that if lack of organization could impair the efficiency of a shop, it must have effects as much more disastrous in disabling the industries of the nation at large as the latter are vaster in volume and more complex in the relationship of their parts.

People would be prompt enough to ridicule an army in which there were neither companions, battalions, regiments, brigades, divisions, or army corps,—no unit of organization in fact, larger than the corporal's squad, with no officer higher than a corporal, and all the corporals equal in authority. And yet just such an army were the manufacturing industries of nineteenth century Boston, an army of four thousand independent squads led by four thousand independent corporals, each with a separate plan of campaign.

Knots of idle men were to be seen here and there on every side, some idle because they could find no work at any price, others because they could not get what they thought a fair price.

*   *   *

It was now toward nightfall, and the streets were thronged with the workers from the stores, the shops, and mills. Carried along with the stronger part of the current, I found myself, as it began to grow dark, in the midst of a scene of squalor and human degradation such as only the South Cove tenement district could present. I had seen the mad wasting of human labor; here I saw in direst shape the want that waste had bred.

From the black doorways and windows of the rookeries on every side came gusts of fetid air. The streets and alleys reeked with the effluvia of a slave ship's between-decks. As I passed I had glimpses within of pale babies gasping out their lives amid sultry stenches, of hopeless-faced women deformed by hardship, retaining of womanhood no trait save weakness, while from the windows leered girls with brows of brass. Like the starving bands of mongrel curs that infest the streets of Moslem towns, swarms of half-clad brutalized children filled the air with shrieks and curses as they fought and tumbled among the garbage that littered the court-yards.

There was nothing in all this that was new to me. Often had I passed through this part of the city and witnessed its sights with feelings of disgust mingled with a certain philosophical wonder at the extremities mortals will endure and still cling to life. But not alone as regarded the economical follies of this age, but equally as touched its moral abominations, scales had fallen from my eyes since that vision of another century. No more did I look upon the woeful dwellers in this Inferno with a callous curiosity as creatures scarcely human. I saw in them my brothers and sisters, my parents, my children, flesh of my flesh, blood of my blood. The festering mass of human wretchedness about me offended not now my senses merely, but pierced my heart like a knife, so that I could not repress signs and groans. I not only saw but felt in my body all that I saw.

4   Upton Sinclair, *The Jungle* (Cambridge, Mass.: Robert Bentley, 1972; reprint of the 1946 Viking Press edition, with Sinclair's introduction), pp. 24-26, 28-30. First published in serial form in *The Appeal to Reason,* Girard, Kansar, in 1905.

It was in the stockyards that Jonas' friend had gotten rich, and so to Chicago the party was bound. They knew that one word, Chicago—and that was all they needed to know, at least, until they reached the city. Then, tumbled out of the cars without ceremony, they were no better off than before; they stood staring down the vista of Dearborn Street, with its big black buildings towering in the distance, unable to realize that they had arrived, and why, when they said "Chicago," people no longer pointed in some direction, but instead looked perplexed, or laughed, or went on without paying any attention. They were pitiable in their helplessness; above all things they stood in deadly terror of any sort of person in official uniform, and so whenever they saw a policeman they would cross the street and hurry by. For the whole of the first day they wandered about in the midst of deafening confusion, utterly lost; and it was only at night that, cowering in the doorway of a house, they were finally discovered and taken by a policeman to the station. In the morning an interpreter was found, and they were taken and put upon a car, and taught a new word—"stockyards." Their delight at discovering that they were to get out of this adventure without losing another share of their possessions it would not be possible to describe.

They sat and stared out of the window. They were on a street which seemed to run on forever, mile after mile—thirty-four of them, if they had known it—and each side of it one uninterrupted row of wretched little two-story frame buildings. Down every side street they could see, it was the same—never a hill and never a hollow, but always the same endless vista of ugly and dirty little wooden buildings. Here and there would be a bridge crossing a filthy creek, with hard-baked mud shores and dingy sheds and docks along it; here and there would be a railroad crossing, with a tangle of switches, and locomotives puffing, and rattling freight cars filing by' here and there would be a great factory, a dingy building with innumerable windows in it, and immense volumes of smoke pouring from the chimneys, darkening the air above and making filthy the earth beneath. But after each of these interruptions, the desolate procession would begin again—the procession of dreary little buildings.

A full hour before the party reached the city they had begun to note the perplexing changes in the atmosphere. It grew darker all the time, and upon the earth the grass seemed to grow less green. Every minute, as the train sped on, the colors of things became dingier; the fields were grown parched and yellow, the landscape hideous and bare. And along with the thickening smoke they began to notice another circumstance, a strange, pungent odor. They were not sure that it was unpleasant, this odor; some might have called it sickening, but their taste in odors was not developed, and they were only sure that it was curious. Now, sitting in the trolley car, they realized that they were on their way to the home of it—that they had traveled all the way from Lithuania to it. It was now no longer something far off and faint, that you caught in whiffs; you could literally taste it, as well as smell it—you could take hold of it, almost, and examine it at your leisure. They were divided in their opinions about it. It was an elemental odor, raw and crude; it was rich, almost rancid, sensual, and strong. There were some who drank it in as if it were an intoxicant; there were others who put their handkerchiefs to their faces. The new emigrants were still tasting it, lost in wonder, when suddenly the car came to a halt, and the door was flung open, and a voice shouted—"Stockyards!"

They were left standing upon the corner, staring; down a side street were two rows of brick houses, and between them a vista; half a dozen chimneys, tall as the tallest of buildings, touching the very sky—and leaping from them half a dozen columns of smoke, thick, oily, and black as night. It might have come from the center of the world, this smoke, where the fires of the ages still smolder. It came as if self-impelled, driving all before it, a perpetual explosion. It was inexhaustible; one stared, waiting to see it stop, but still the great streams rolled out. They spread in vast clouds overhead, writhing, curling; then, uniting in one giant river, they streamed away down the sky, stretching a black pall as far as the eye could reach.

Then the party became aware of another strange thing. This, too, like the odor, was a thing elemental; it was a sound, a sound made up of ten thousand little sounds. You scarcely noticed it at first—it sunk into your consciousness, a vague disturbance, a trouble. It was like the murmuring of the bees in the spring, the whisperings of the forest; it suggested endless activity, the rumblings of a world in motion. It was only by an effort that one could realize that it was made by animals, that it was the distant lowing of ten thousand cattle, the distant grunting of ten thousand swine.

*   *

Later that afternoon he and Ona went out to take a walk and look about them, to see more of this district which was to be their home. In back of the yards the dreary two-story frame houses were scattered farther apart, and there were great spaces bare—that seemingly had been overlooked by the great sore of a city as it spread itself over the surface of the prairie. These bare places were grown up with dingy, yellow weeds, hiding innumerable tomato cans; innumerable children played upon them, chasing one another here and there, screaming and fighting. The most uncanny thing about this neighborhood was the number of children; you thought there must be a school just out, and it was only after long acquaintance that you were able to realize that there was no school, but that these were the children of the neighborhood—that there were so many children to the block in Packingtown that nowhere on its streets could a horse and buggy move faster than a walk!

It could not move faster anyhow, on account of the state of the streets. Those through which Jurgis and Ona were walking resembled streets less than they did a miniature topographical map. The roadway was commonly several feet lower than the level of the houses, which were sometimes joined by high board walks; there were no pavements—there were mountains and valleys and rivers, gullies and ditches, and great hollows full of stinking green water. In these pools thd children played, and rolled about in the mud of the streets; here and there one noticed them digging in it, after trophies which they had stumbled on. One wondered about this, as also about the swarms of flies which hung about the scene, literally blackening the air, and the strange, fetid odor which assailed one's nostrils, a ghastly odor, of all the dead things of the universe. It impelled the visitor to questions—and then the residents would explain, quietly, that all this was "made" land, and that it had been "made" by using it as a dumping ground for the city garbage. After a few years the unpleasant effect of this would pass away, it was said: but meantime, in hot weather—and especially when it rained—the flies were apt to be annoying. Was it not unhealthful? the stranger would ask, and the residents would answer, "Perhaps; but there is no telling."

A little way farther on, and Jurgis and Ona, staring open-eyed and wondering, came to the place where this "made" ground was in process of making. Here was a great hole, perhaps two city blocks square, and with long files of garbage wagons creeping into it. The place had an odor for which there are no polite words; and it was sprinkled over with children, who raked in it from dawn till dark. Sometimes visitors from the packing houses would wander out to see this "dump," and they would stand by and debate as to whether the children were eating the food they got, or merely collecting it for the chickens at home. Apparently none of them ever went down to find out.

Beyond this dump there stood a great brickyard, with smoking chimneys. First they took out the soil to make bricks, and then they filled it up again with garbage, which seemed to Jurgis and Ona a felicitous arrangement, characteristic of an enterprising country like America. A little way beyond was another great hole, which they had emptied and not yet filled up. This held water, and all summer it stood there, with the near-by soil draining into it, festering and stewing in the sun; and then, when winter came, somebody cut the ice on it, and sold it to the people of the city. This, too, seemed to the newcomers an economical arrangement; for they did not read the newspapers, and their heads were not full of troublesome thoughts about "germs."

They stood there while the sun went down upon the scene, and the sky in the west turned blood-red, and the tops of the houses shone like fire. Jurgis and Ona were not thinking of the sunset, however—their backs were turned to it, and all their thoughts were of Packingtown, which they could see so plainly in the distance. The line of the buildings stood clear-cut and black against the sky; here and there out of the mass rose the great chimneys, with the river of smoke streaming away to the end of the world. It was a study in colors now, this smoke; in the sunset light it was black and brown and gray and purple. All the sordid suggestions of the place were gone—in the twilight it was a vision of power. To the two who stood watching while the darkness swallowed it up, it seemed a dream of wonder, with its tale of human energy, of things being done, of employment for thousands upon thousands of men, of opportunity and freedom, of life and love and joy. When they came away, arm in arm, Jurgis was saying, "Tomorrow I shall go there and get a job!"

"How We Live and How We Might Live": Life in the Industrial City and the Alternative Vision of William Morris

DAVID S. GROSS

"I love the great despisers, for they are the great adorers, and arrows of longing for the other shore."

—*Nietzsche*

"...the world has long been dreaming of something that it can acquire if only it becomes conscious of it."

—*Marx*

William Morris' many and varied writings comprise a complex and wide-ranging response to life under industrialism, but most important is his visionary hope for a better world. That positive vision, though, grows out of his passionately negative response to the inner and outer landscapes of industrial capitalism, a response which was very similar to that of the great Romantics of the beginning of the century and of men like Carlyle, Ruskin, and Arnold of the generation just before his.[1] The difference between Morris' view and most of those others came about through his adherence to socialism. Instead of retreating to ironic resignation, despair, or ivory tower aestheticism, Morris wedded his Romantic indignation at the moral and aesthetic squalor he saw around him to a powerful view of what life could be like were our circumstances to be fundamentally altered.

Not only is such utopian desire of central significance in Morris' work, its active presence or its absence in culture as a whole is extremely important, as I shall argue here. But the significance of the utopian has been neglected in both political and cultural theory. Within Marxism as without, such visionary aspirations came to be systematically undervalued, viewed as impractical and thus without significance. Continuing to privilege what Blake had long before described as the "mind-forg'd manacles" of rationalist, narrowly empiricist thought and practice, such writers as Engels—whose 1880 pamphlet distinguishing between utopian and "scientific" socialism had tremendous influence—and Lenin systematically favored a narrow scientism, mechanical materialism, and economism in their thought and practice.

When E.P. Thompson republished his biography of Morris in 1976, twenty-one years after its initial appearance, he added a fascinating

"Postscript: 1976" of some fifty pages, in which he discussed the development of his own thought in that period in the context of the response of other writers to his book and to Morris.[2] There he argues that Morris' utopian vision is the most significant part of his work. Thompson feels that Morris' arguments about how we live as opposed to how we might live constitute a powerful view with much to offer Marxism and the Left, both theoretically and as a crucial component in any aspirations and strategy for social and political change. Without the living presence of utopian aspirations, any social movement—and, I would argue, any historical judgements or interpretations—tends towards the coldly efficient, static 'pragmatic," objective position denounced by Blake as "'single-vision.'"[3]

In his discussion of the nature and significance of the utopian, Thompson cites Miguel Abensour's assertion that Morris' key task is to "teach desire to desire, to desire better, to desire more, and above all to desire in a different way."[4] Such utopian practice can achieve things impossible outside it. And such practice is especially crucial within a mass culture which so *mis*educates our desires toward commodity fetishism. Even direct opposition to the existing order within that all too pragmatic, positivist tradition finds expression in theories devoid of vision, passion, or imagination: the assumptions of which can lend support to the sort of world the theories attempt to oppose.

What Morris is attempting in all his works, like Blake before him, is exactly what Fredric Jameson as termed "the vocation of the perceptual, its Utopian mision as the libidinal transformation of an increasingly dessicated and repressive reality."[5] The desires such practice seeks to awaken exist at the deepest level of the unconscious, and their parallels with and connections to sexual desire are many. When Morris attempts a summary of his ideal in *News from Nowhere,* he puts it this way: "The spirit of the new days, of our days, was to be delight in the life of the world; intense and overweening love of the very skin and surface of the earth on which man dwells, such as a lover has in the fair flesh of the woman he loves...."[6]

Elsewhere the goals is defined otherwise, in terms of pleasurable, worthwhile work and enjoyable rest, in healthy and reasonable proportions. It may be, as Thompson seems to feel in the book on Morris, that this utopian vision is the most important, terribly neglected component in any plan to alter our present course and save the planet. For in my experience, ironic resignation, defeatist cynicism, apathetic and pessimistic indifference constitute the greatest obstacle to meaningful change, whether in middle-class students and professors or proletarian laborers. It is a necessary though not sufficient task to awaken those hopes that lie hidden in everyone that things might really be different, better than they are.

It is the unique *quality* of Morris' vision, then, that is most important: his attempt to situate his audience in a place where they can reconceive human possibilities. This quality distinguishes vision from ordinary dream. And as part of the indictment of what Morris calls "things as they are," it is his vision of a more perfect, more satisfying human community which has led to the dismissal of his writings as dated or silly. They are not dated—and I hope this paper will demonstrate this point—and they are left unread at the cost of exhilarating hope. Consequently, if I seem to cite Morris as much as I discuss his work in the following pages, I do so in order to show how important his work is, how urgently contemporary his vision.

It is of course also the case that visionary dreams are of little significance without effective action. Blake certainly never urged us to ignore the findings of rational thought and the practical use of science and its laws. Morris, Marx, and Blake agree on the need for both Reason *and* Energy, to use Blake's terms, in constructive dialectical tension. "Without Contraries is no progression," says Blake in *The Marriage of Heaven and Hell*. The problem has been that positivist, empiricist, "objective" Reason, isolated and seen as sufficient wisdom, has had such hegemony in the capitalist world, and through Engels and Lenin in the Marxist view as well, that the utopian needs to be reasserted, to restore a balanced holistic vision.

Marx and Morris disavow idle utopian speculation in much the same terms. Marx's ringing statement that "Up to now philosophers have interpreted the world in various ways; the point, instead, is to change it"[7] is perhaps the most succinct statement of the Marxist insistence on the necessary linking of theory and practice. Morris says that "considering the present condition of the world" the crucial task "is not so much prophecy as action."[8] In the same lecture in which his utopian content is most present, Morris specifically disavows "elaborate utopian schemes."[9] Morris always gives primary significance to the evidence of his senses and of his empathetic imagination in perceiving what is wrong with his world and what needs changing. His writing always grows out of such reactions and out of his historical sense of how and why such a world has come about. He combines his insistence that it ought to be changed with powerful arguments that the evidence of those same senses, and his moral and aesthetic imagination and desire, tell him that it can be changed, that we do have the capacity to make and live in a better world.

If Morris shared with Marx an aversion to idle speculation, Marx shared with him and with Blake a sense of the crucial necessity of dreaming of a better world. To educate desire, so that people imagine the world as other, better than it is, is what Marx called bringing the world's dream to consciousness. Blake called it the Four-fold vision, which includes full awareness and pleasure in the body and its senses and the exercise of our visionary and prophetic imagination. Morris felt that the prime function of art and ideas was to awaken desires stunted by an impoverished culture and degraded civilization so that a good and pleasurable world to live in would be seen as a necessity and a right.

> Yet is must be remembered that civilization has reduced the workman to such a skinny and pitiful existence, that he scarcely knows how to frame a desire for any life much better than that which he now endures perforce. It is the province of art to set the true ideal of a full and reasonable life before him, a life to which the perception and creation of beauty, the enjoyment of real pleasure that is, shall be felt to be as necessary to man as his daily bread....[10]

It should be noted that such visionary hopes had not always been present in Morris' work. During more than two decades in the 1850's through the seventies, Morris was an escapist Romantic poet, deeply involved in the nostalgic Medievalism of his PreRaphaelite friends. During that period—despite its luxuriant decoration and richly embroidered imagery and action—his poetry, as E.P. Thompson argues, was basically a poetry of despair.[11] Repelled by industrial society, Morris saw no way of using his writing to help change it. He saw art only as refuge or escape. In striking contrast to his later urgings, he called on the readers of *The Earthly Paradise*—the long poem which made him famous in 1868—to

> Forget six counties overhung with smoke,
> Forget the snorting steam and piston stroke,
> Forget the spreading of the hideous town;
> Think rather of the pack-horse on the down,
> And dream of London, small and white and clean,
> The clear Thames bordered by its gardens green;[12]

The critique of the effects of industrialism will remain and intensify, as will his desire that we dream of a better world. But at this point the dream is pure escape from the present rather than a vision of a better future, and Morris sees his personal situation as an artist as ineffectual and sad: "the idle singer of an empty day."[13]

In 1882 in his forty-ninth year, Morris joined the socialist Democratic Federation and began a new life as a spokesman and leader of the most militant socialism of his day in England, a role which was to last until his death in 1896. As his understanding of history, economics, and the significance of his earlier perceptions deepened, he wrote his finest works. Some of the best non-fiction prose in the English language is contained in his lectures on the arts and architecture, on the causes of the misery and poverty, on the stunted lives and blighted landscapes he saw around him, and on his brilliantly argued vision that this need not be so. "Useful Work versus Useless Toil," "A Factory as it Might Be," and the speech from which I have borrowed my title are all very important works of criticism and vision. And his utopian prose romances, especially *News from Nowhere*, are among the very best works of their kind.

The industrial landscape and the response of the artist to it is a frequent subject in Morris' account of what it is like to live and work in monopoly capitalist society and of what we must find a way to change. Like our ecologists who he so directly anticipates, Morris attacks repeatedly the air and water pollution he saw as the direct result of technological production for profit:

> Is money to be gathered? cut down the pleasant trees among the houses, pull down the ancient and venerable buildings for the money that a few square yards of London dirt will fetch, blacken rivers, hide the sun and poison the air with smoke and worse, and it's nobody's business to see it or mend it: that is all that modern commerce, the countinghouse forgetful of the workshop, will do for us herein.[14]

"Whole counties of England, and the heavens that hang over them," he says, "have disappeared beneath a crust of unutterable grime."[15] Elsewhere, he asks rhetorically, using questions to provoke open, heuristic thought much as Blake so frequently had done: "Why should one third of England be so stifled and poisoned with smoke that over the greater part of Yorkshire (for instance) the general idea must be that sheep are naturally black? and why must Yorkshire and Lancashire rivers run mere filth and dye?"[16]

Often his writing on such subjects leads him to an important observation which becomes central to his thinking: the way in which habituation to a degraded environment breeds acceptance of it, extinguishes desire for anything else—as in this account of "the outward effects which betoken this rule of the wretched anarchy of commercial war":

> Think of the spreading sore of London swallowing up with its loathsomeness field and wood and heath without mercy and without hope, mocking our feeble efforts to deal even with its minor evils of smoke-laden sky and befouled river: the black horror and reckless squalor of our manufacturing districts, so dreadful to the senses which are unused to them that it is ominous for the future of the race that any man can live among it in tolerable cheerfulness....[17]

In one of his most sweeping statements on the question, he asserts that civilization "has covered the merry green fields with the hovels of slaves, and blighted the flowers and trees with poisonous gases, and turned the rivers into sewers; til over many parts of Britain the common people have forgotten what a field or a flower is like, and their idea of beauty is a gas-poisoned gin palace or a tawdry theater."[18]

Another major concern is with urban architecture, with the degraded structures in which we live and work and the conditions of life therein, especially in London. Again and again his indignation flares as he speaks of what Cobbett had called "the Great Wen," that swollen abscess of the modern city. A man of the middle ages, he says, would have had a hard time imagining "a whole county or more covered over with hideous hovels, big middle-sized and little, which should one day be called London," a scene "forever bearing witness against man that he had deliberately chosen ugliness instead of beauty, and to live where he is strongest amidst squalor or blank emptiness."[19]

The use of the historical perspective here is important. Morris frequently uses history in this way, to awaken our sense of the crucial fact that life has not always been as it is now. Such awareness is critical in countering that ahistorical quality in single vision or one-dimensional thought, that "common sense" assumption that things have always been and will always be pretty much as they are now. To counter that sense, to awaken a historical perspective from which alone can a different, better future appear possible, is one of Morris' primary goals. Thus where in the passage just cited he looks at the capital of nineteenth-century industrial society from the past, he looks back at it from an imagined better future both in his utopian novel and in the one lecture where he speaks at length about his vision of the future. In *News from Nowhere* a twenty-first century historian looks back on the time

> when if you mounted a good horse and rode straight away from my door here at a round trot for an hour and a half, you would still be in the thick of London, and the greater part of that would be "slums," as they were called; that is to say, places of torture for innocent men and women; or worse, stews for rearing and breeding men and women in such degradation that that torture should seem to them mere ordinary and natural life.

He next describes a spring ceremony

> on the site of some of the worst of the old slums.... On that occasion the custom is for the prettiest girls to sing some of the old revolutionary songs, and those which were the groans of the discontent, once so hopeless, on the very spot where those terrible crimes of class-murder were committed day by day for so many years.

Morris describes the woman:

> standing amongst the happy people, on some mound where of old time stood the wretched apology for a house, a den in which men and women lived packed amongst the filth like pilchards in a cask; lived in such a way that they could only have endured it, as I said just now, by being degraded out of humanity....[20]

In the Society of the Future Lecture, Morris looks back from the imagined future and describes the breaking up of "the huge manufacturing districts" so that nature may "heal the horrible scars that man's
headless greed and stupid terror have made: for it will no longer be a
matter of dire necessity that cotton cloth should be made a fraction of
a farthing cheaper this year than last."

> And of course mere cheating and flunkey centres like the
> horible muck-heap in which we dwell (London, to wit)
> could be got rid of easier still; and a few pleasant villages on
> the side of the Thames might mark the place of that
> preposterous piece of folly once called London.[21]

Usually though, Morriss' indictments of the ugly and miserable surroundings of life he saw came as part of larger concerns: concerns
with what it feels like as a living individual to experience the reality of
industrial society, and with the causes and solutions for the problems
he pointed out. Again and again he indicts commercial competitive
capitalism and the profit motive as the prime cause of the problem:
"This doctrine of the sole aim of manufacture (or indeed of life itself)
being the profit of the capitalist ... is held, I say, by almost everyone ....
It is this superstition of commerce being an end in itself, of man made
for commerce not commerce for man of which art has sickened...."

> It is my business here tonight to foster your discontent with
> that anarchy and its visible results; for indeed I think it
> would be an insult to you to suppose that you are con-
> tented with things as they are; contented to see all beauty
> vanish from our beautiful city, for instance; ... contented
> with the ugliness and baseness which everywhere sur-
> rounds the life of civilized man; contented, lastly, to be liv-
> ing above that unutterable and sickening misery of which a
> few details are once again reaching us as if from some dis-
> tant unhappy country, of which we could hardly expect to
> hear, but which I tell you is the necessary foundation on
> which our society, our anarchy, rests.[22]

Elsewhere Morris connects again conditions of work, living conditions, and the relations of production made necessary by capitalists'
need to turn a profit:

> For all our crowded towns and bewildering factories are
> simply the outcome of the profit system. Capitalistic
> manufacture, capitalistic land-owning, and capitalistic ex-
> change force men into big cities in order to manipulate
> them in the interests of capital; the same tyranny contracts
> the due space of the factory so much that (for instance) the
> interior of a great weaving-shed is almost as ridiculous a
> spectacle as it is a horrible one. There is no other necessity
> for all this, save the necessity for grinding profits out of

men's lives, and of producing cheap goods for the use (and subjection) of the slaves who grind.[23]

Again, elsewhere:

It is profit which draws men into enormous unmanageable aggregations called towns, for instance; profit which crowds them up when they are there into quarters without gardens or open spaces; profit which won't take the most ordinary precautions against wrapping a whole district in a cloud of sulpherous smoke; which condemns all but the rich to live in houses idiotically cramped and confined at best, and at the worst in houses for whose wretchedness there is no name.[24]

A major concern for Morris in this regard is the effect all this has on the sensibilities of the people. "How can I ask working men passing up and down these hideous streets day to day to care about beauty?"[25] The system in which we live so distorts our sensibilities that we try to *like* the ugly, reified world, not to see it for what it is.

Civilization renders these arts ["architecture and the kindred arts"] impossible, because its politics and ethics force us to live in a grimy disorderly uncomfortable world, a world that offends the senses at every turn: that necessity reacts on the senses again, and forces us unconsciously to blunt their keenness. A man who notices the external forms of things much nowadays must suffer in South Lancashire or London, must live in a state of perpetual combat and anger; and he really must try to blunt his sensibility, or he will go mad, or kill some obnoxious person and be hanged for it....[26]

The result of this process is a widespread blindness, a complacency and resignation in the face of things which should not be accepted. Thus it takes an artist like Morris to reawaken our senses to reality. (A recent critic who disapproves of Morris' socialism and finds his reactions "extreme," diagnoses him as suffering from "hyperesthesia!"[27]) In a brilliant extended metaphor he tries to make us see this abuse of the planet for the folly it really is:

The misery and squalor which we people of civilization bear with so much complacency as a necessary part of the manufacturing system, is just as necessary to the community at large as a proportionate amount of filth would be in the house of a private rich men. If such a man were to allow the cinders to be raked all over his drawing-room, and a privy to be established in each corner of his dining-room, if he habitually made a dust and refuse heap of his once beautiful garden, never washed his sheets or changed his tablecloth, and made his family sleep five to a bed, he would surely find himself in the claws of a commision *de lunatico*. But such acts of miserly folly are just what our present society is doing daily under the compulsion of a supposed necessity, which is nothing short of madness.[28]

What Morris is discussing here and elsewhere is a crucial component of what Blake called "mind-forg'd manacles" and Antonio Gramsci called "hegemony." Both Blake and Gramsci are describing the cultural forms and forces whereby most people learn to act against their deeper interests and desires and accept or support the status quo, on the assumption that it is impossible to change, or that change will inevitably make things worse. Such forms of thought and perception dull sensibilities, confuse us about what is reasonable or possible. They lead people to assume that the world they live in is inevitable or even that they like it:

a huge mass of men living under a system of society so intricate as to look on the surface like a mere chance-hap muddle of many millions of necessitous people, oppressed indeed, and sorely, not by obvious individual violence and ill-will, but by an economic system so far reacing, so deeply seated, that it may well seem like the operation of a natural law to men so uneducated that they have not even escaped the reflexion of the so-called education of their masters ... : an intellectual slavery which is a necessary accompaniment of their material slavery.[29]

Morris understands that the effects of such hegemony over the opinions, attitudes and assumptions of most people is such that only a fundamental change, at the root, can have significant effect. Thus he separated himself from the timid "socialists" of this day with their reformist illusions. He openly advocated revolution, the radical altering of the political, social, and economic bases of society, seeing such changes—at the roots—as alone capable of accomplishing a significant break with the existing repressive orders, modes of life and forms of thought. He specifically rejects the superficial or hypocritical approaches of philanthropist reformers or moralists: "The palliatives over which many worthy people are busying themselves now are useless: because they are but unorganized partial revolts against a vast wide-spread grasping organization which will, with the unconscious instinct of a plant, meet every attempt at bettering the condition of the people with an attack on a fresh side." Any reform measures, he asserts, will be met by "the revival of grovelling superstitions, preachments of thrift to lack-alls, of temperance to the wretched."[30]

In the area of city planning, Morris attacks with great prescience the sterile blocks of flats, the ancestors of the "projects," which were some peoples' solution to the workers' wretched housing, only beginning to appear in his day:

those huge masses of brick and mortar which are rising up
in various parts of the town to compete for the workman's
scanty shillings against the closeness, squalor and huddled
makeshift of the ordinary landlord; bare, sunless, and grim
bastilles are these, and look like embodied night-mares of
the hopeless thrift of the wage-slave.[31]

Not only against what was, and against reformist complicity, Morris
had no truck with the regimented, mechanical, and uniform state
socialism envisioned by some in a socialist future. He wrote *News
from Nowhere* in part as a reaction against Bellamy's *Looking
Backward.* He dubbed Bellamy's regimented labor battalions and
sterile, mechanistic conveniences "a cockney paradise," and remarked that "if they brigaded *me* into a regiment of workers, I'd just
lie on my back and kick."[32]

Morris saw the mechanical, uniform blueprints for the future of men
like Fourier and Bellamy as a disastrously wrong direction. That
tendency represents an intrusion into liberatory, anti-authoritarian
thought of essentially bourgeois, capitalist notions: the spirit of wholly
quantified values. Such a spirit was denounced by Blake and also by
Shelley, who spoke of "an excess of the calculating faculty." As Paul
Breines has recently defined the conflict, "the Enlightenment-
Utilitarian root (faith in mechanistically oriented scientific thought, industrial technology, and even the Victorian work-ethic) blossomed,
snuffing out its Romantic counterpart. A variant of bourgeois ideas
came to prevail among the idealogues of the Marxist movement."[33]

Whenever Morris evokes the regimented barracks-style housing and
the rigid forms of social life in the imagined socialist futures of Fourier
and Bellamy, it is always in order to separate his vision from theirs. In
one lecture, while trying to educate his listeners' desires for a better
future in his usual open, heuristic manner, he stops and says:

Do you think by chance that I mean a row of yellow-brick,
blue-slated houses, or a phalangstere like an improved
Peabody lodging house; and the dinner-bell ringing one into a row of white basins of broth with a piece of bread cut
nice and square by each, with boiler-made tea and ill-boiled
rice-pudding to follow? No; that's the philanthropist's ideal,
not mine....[34]

And when he visits the good society of the future in *News from
Nowhere,* Morris asks his historian friend why people are still living in
households, rather than "more in public":

"Phalangsteries, eh?" said he. "Well, we live as we like, and
we like to live as a rule with certain house-mates that we
have got used to. Remember, again, that poverty is extinct,
and that the Fourierist phalangsteries and all their kind, as
was but natural at the time, implied nothing but a refuge

from mere destitution. Such a way of life as that could only
have been conceived of by people surrounded by the worst
form of poverty."[35]

Morris is again expressing a crucial insight here: that the ability to imagine a better future, and the specific forms such visions acquire, is
crippled and stunted by what we see and experience in this
world—what we are led to believe is good or possible under the influence of the forms, values, and practices of the existing culture. In
the name of being practical, realistic, efficient, and so forth, a process
of renunciation takes place even among those opposed to the existing
order, with the result that the moral revulsion and angry rebellion
against the conditions of life under capitalism is lost. Morris wanted his
dream to free human beings, not to enclose them in a rigid and stultify-
ing conception. As Eli Zaretsky has put it: "The dream becomes for
Morris a rumination upon history, a critical reflection on the present,
an open-ended vision of the future and, above all, a means of
liberating the imagination toward purposefull and creative rather than
archaic or regressive ends."[36]

Despite Morris' aversion to forecasting the specific shapes of a
socialist future, to subjecting to theoretical and visual closure a desire
and vision he wishes to remain open and heuristic, expanding rather
than constricting consciousness, he did occasionally offer thoughts on
how life might be better arranged. His most consistent emphasis in
such passages is on the necessity for useful and enjoyable work. His
arguments there are very close to Marx' and deserve very serious attention, but they lie outside the scope of this paper. When he
discusses the "landscape" as it should be, the visual field and the
moral and aesthetic impressions such surroundings must make on
those who live among them, he insists most on its importance and on
our right that it be good and pleasurable; and he urges us to desire it
and insist upon it.[37]

He naturally insists that the workplace itself be pleasant and
healthful, and he envisions considerable decentralization of both production and social arrangements. His ideas on city planning have had
considerable influence and even some practical application in the
"green belt" and "garden city" movements of this century. In "A Factory As It Might Be" Morris spins out a fairly elaborate plan for
beautiful gardens and landscaping around and among the pleasant new
factories, the gardens to be tended by the workers/
producers/manufacturers themselves. "One's imagination is inclined
fairly to run riot over the picture of beauty and pleasure offered by the
thought of skilful co-operative gardening for beauty's sake...."[38] He
then provides a wonderful, consciousness-raising answer to a skeptical response to his vision:

Impossible! I hear an anti-Socialist say. My friend, please to

remember that most factories sustain today large and handsome gardens, and not seldom parks and woods of many
acres in extent; with due appurtenances of highly paid Scottish gardeners, wood reeves, bailiffs, gamekeepers and the
like, the whole being managed in the most wasteful way
conceivable; *only* the said gardens, etc., are, say, twenty
miles away from the factory, *out of the smoke,* and are kept
up for *one member of the factory only,* the sleeping partner....[39]

Most often, though, like Marx and Blake, Morris' utopian vision is
not invested in such specific plans for the future. He wishes instead to
educate our aspirations, to quicken our moral revulsion and rebellion
against the existing order—as the American Wobblies put it, "to fan
the flames of discontent." Morris seeks to awaken in us the dream that
Ernst Bloch, Jung, Marcuse and others believe to be present in us all,
the dream of a full and happy life for individual human beings, within
a free, fair, and open human community, in organic harmony with the
natural world. Blake said simply: "I feel that a Man may be happy in
This World. And I know that This World Is a World of Imagintion &
Vision."[40] The same sort of conviction fuels all of Morris' work.

When I was a boy growing up on the banks of the Penobscot near
Bangor—that majestic river, venerated by the Indians who named
themselves after it, and by Thoreau, who travelled up it to Mount
Katahdin—the river had become the same sort of stinking, foul, and
nearly lifeless open sewer Morris decried in his country's rivers. Only
eels could live in it, feeding on the untreated sewage and industrial
waste. The practice of sending the first salmon caught in the river at
Bangor every year to the U.S. President had to be abandoned when I
was in high school, when no salmon could even make it up to the head
of the tide. Last summer there were more than a thousand salmon
caught in the Bangor Salmon Pool. The river now runs clean and clear.
No one would have thought it possible twenty years ago, but it was
possible, and it happened.

In one of his earliest lectures Morris describes his vision whereby
"art will make our streets as beautiful as the woods, as elevating as the
mountain-sides, ... [and] as nothing of beauty and splendour that
man's mind and hand may compass shall be wanting from our public
buildings, so in no private dwelling will there be any signs of waste,
pomp or insolence, and every man will have his share of the *best.*" He
immediately goes on to say:

It is a dream, you may say, of what has never been and will
never be; true, it has never been, and therefore, since the
world is alive and moving yet, my hope is the greater that it
one day will be: true it is a dream; but dreams have before
now come about of things so good and necessary to us, that

we scarcely think of them more than of the daylight, though once people had to live without them, without even the hope of them.[41]

Twenty-three years later in 1890 he would end *News from Nowhere*: "Yes, surely! and if others can see it as I have seen then it may be called a vision rather than a dream."[42]

NOTES

[1] Raymond Williams, in *Culture and Society: 1780-1950* (London: Chatto & Windus, 1958), was the first to understand the works of these writers as a response to industrial capitalism. Leo Marx, in *The Machine in the Garden* (New York: Oxford University Press, 1964), drew our attention to their counterparts in the American tradition. Needless to say, I am indebted to such seminal studies. Williams' work in particular first drew my attention to Morris and has continued to influence my view of his work.

[2] Edward P. Thompson, *William Morris: Romantic to Revolutionary* (New York: Pantheon Books, 1976), pp. 763-816.

[3] I use the word "utopian" in this essay in the sense in which it was defined and articulated by Ernst Bloch. I know his *On Karl Marx*, trans. John Maxwell (New York: Herder and Herder, 1971) and *A Philosophy of the Future*, trans. John Cumming (New York: Herder and Herder, 1970); it is obvious from Fredric Jameson's account in *Marxism and Form: Twentieth-Century Dialectical Theories of Literature* (Princeton: Princeton University Press, 1971), "Ernst Bloch and the Future," pp. 116-59, that *Hope the Principle* (1959) is also of central significance. In this country the term has been given significant amplification and application by the *Social Text* group, especially by Jameson in *The Political Unconscious: Narrative as a Socially Symbolic Act* (Ithaca: Cornell University Press, 1981).

[4] M.H. Abensour, *Le Formes de l'Utopie Socialiste-Communiste*, these pour le Doctorat d'Etat en Science Politique, Paris, 1973, p. 330, cited in Thompson, *William Morris*, p. 791.

[5] Jameson, *Political Unconscious*, p. 237.

[6] Morris, *News from Nowhere*, (1890), *Three Works* (New York: International Publishers, 1968), p. 317.

[7] Karl Marx, "Theses on Feuerback," *The Marx-Engels Reader,* ed. Robert Tucker, second edition (New York: Norton, 1978), p. 145.

[8] William Morris, "The Society of the Future" (1887), *Political Writings*, ed. A.L. Morton (New York: International Publishers, 1973), p. 189.

[9] Morris, "Society of the Future," p. 188.

[10] Morris, "How I Became a Socialist," (1894), *Political Writings*, pp. 245-46.

[11] Thompson, *William Morris*, pp. 110-50.

[12] William Morris, *The Earthly Paradise*, *Collected Works* (New York: Russell & Russell, 1966), III, p. 3.

[13] Morris, *Earthly Paradise*, p. 1.

[14] Morris, "The Lesser Arts," (1877), *Political Writings*, p. 53.

[15] Morris, "Art Under Plutocracy," (1884), *Political Writings*, p. 64.

[16] Morris, "Philanthropists," (1884), May Morris, *William Morris: Artist Writer Socialist* (New York: Russell & Russell, 1966), II, p. 129.

[17] Morris, "Art and Socialism," (1884) *Political Writings*, pp. 125-26.

[18] Morris, "Society of the Future," p. 193.

[19] Morris, "Lesser Arts," p. 39.

[20] William Morris, *News from Nowhere*, (1890), pp. 247-48.

[21] Morris, "Society of the Future," pp. 196-97.

22 Morris, "Art Under Plutocracy," pp. 74-5.
23 Morris, "Useful Work versus Useless Toil," (1884), *Political Writings,* p. 103.
24 Morris, "How We Live and How We Might Live," (1884), *Political Writings,* pp. 153-54.
25 Morris, "The Lesser Arts," p. 44.
26 Morris, "Society of the Future," pp. 200-01.
27 Roderick Marshall, *William Morris and his Earthly Paradises* (Tisbury, Wiltshire, Great Britain: Compton Press, 1979), p. xvii.
28 Morris, "A Factory As It Might Be," (1885), May Morris, II, p. 133.
29 Morris, "Communism," (1893), *Political Writings,* p. 232.
30 Morris, "Art and Socialism," p. 126.
31 Morris, "Philanthropists," p. 127.
32 Thompson, William Morris, pp. 692-93.
33 Paul Breines, "Marxism, Romanticism, and the Case of Georg Lukacs: Notes on Some Recent Sources and Situations," *Studies in Romanticism,* 16 (Fall, 1977), p. 477.
34 Morris, "Society of the Future," p. 194.
35 Morris, *News from Nowhere,* p. 246.
36 Eli Zaretsky, "River of Fire: On the Reissue of E.P. Thompson's *William Morris: Romantic to Revolutionary,"* *Studies in Romanticism,* 16 (Fall, 1977), p. 599.
37 Morris' ideas on this subject are scattered throughout his lectures and in *News from Nowhere,* perhaps most centrally in "A Factory As It Might Be," May Morris, II, pp. 130-40.
38 Morris, "A Factory As It Might Be,' p. 131.
39 *Ibid.,* pp. 131-32.
40 William Blake, letter to Trusler, Aug. 23, 1779, *Poetry and Prose,* ed. David Erdman (Garden City, N.Y.: Doubleday & Company, 1970), pp. 676-77.
41 Morris, "The Lesser Arts," pp. 55-6.
42 Morris, *News from Nowhere,* p. 401.

"Trees, Animals, Engines": Industrialization in American Literature, 1900-1925

CECELIA TICHI

At the turn of the nineteenth century American literature began to exhibit a new anxiety, manifest at first in themes responding with both alarm and exhilaration at rapid social change, but appearing also as an uneasiness about the placidity of classic literary form. If life became industrialized, efficient, angular, mechanized, how should literary works reflect this process, not only in their overt concerns but in their very appearance on the page? In the anxiety of the time an improbable pair of writers, Henry James and Upton Sinclair, became the spokesmen in a heated debate on the relation of literature to this new industrial state. Unknown to each other, the psychological realist entered into debate with the muckraking journalist. Essentially, Sinclair argued that literature had failed the industrial culture. James took the opposing side by insisting that industrialization had failed literature.

James made his argument in *The American Scene* (1907), a work of combined travel literature and social criticism. In 1904, at the age of 61, James returned to an America he had left twenty years earlier. He found it transformed—all for the worse. His native Manhattan was now "a chaos of confusion and change." It had become a nation-city of skyscrapers, foreigners, "crude democracy of trade," and, above all, of monstrous machine-age energy. The Brooklyn Bridge seemed to him malignant in fact and symbol. "One has the sense," James wrote, "that the monster grows and grows, flinging abroad its loose limbs ... all under the sky and over the sea, becoming thus that of some colossal set of clockworks, some steel-souled machine-room of brandished arms and hammering fists and opening and closing jaws." James, whose great last novels (*The Ambassadors, The Wings of the Dove, The Golden Bowl*) were all in print, found himself literally at a loss. This "heaped industrial battlefield" which manifested just one value—power—is, he says, "indescribable." For the steam-driven river ferries, James tries out an image of "electric bobbins" before confiding parenthetically, "I scarce know what to call them." There is no coyness in his tone, but the admission that his literary powers may not be adequate to this new industrialized world so alien to his experience.[1]

Distinct literary values exist, to be sure, in *The American Scene,* but they are embodied not surprisingly in sites of pre-industrial America. One is Harvard Yard, the cloister inviting reflection and contemplation, and the other is the city of eighteenth-century Philadelphia with its "ordered charm and perfect peace," a society in which "every individual is many times over cousin, uncle, aunt, niece." These two scenes—the cloister and the clubroom of kindred souls—represent the literary America which James believes to be disappearing amid the snapping jaws of machine technology. It is not surprising to find him indict the skyscraper as a structure of glassy "flash." It lacks the "quiet interspaces," the "Quiet tones" and "blest breathing spaces." Impersonal, it wants the cloistered respite which invites that personal reflection conducive to the literary experience of writer and reader alike. And literature, by James's definition, is personal, reflective, linear, and Anglo-American. It is being destroyed by the "industrial battlefield" whose "immense momentum" has already, says James, outdistanced "any possibility of poetic, of dramatic capture."[2]

While Henry James thought industrialization deadly to the literary experience, the muck-raking journalist Upton Sinclair argued the reverse position. In *The Jungle* (1906), he accused literature of failing to reflect the contemporary industrial culture. His expose of murderous labor practices and of scandalous meat processing in the Chicago stockyards contains within a kind of position paper on literary criticism. Sinclair is especially critical of the genteel tradition of poetry which has excluded the realities of industrial life. The "anguish" of Packingtown life is, he writes, "a kind of anguish that poets have not commonly dealt with; its very words are not admitted into the vocabulary of poets—the details of it cannot be told in polite society at all." Sinclair, of course, proceeds on a correction course to tell all, in detail, to polite society. His best-known, often reprinted account of the slaughter of hogs shows his insistence that a middle class audience stupefied by the genteel literature (and by the culture's newest euphemisms, advertising slogans) look closely at what horrors are to be found beneath "the wonderful efficiency of ... pork-making by machinery, pork-making by applied mathematics."[3]

In fact the slaughter of the hogs is but Sinclair's metaphor for the slaughter of immigrant humanity in the industrial "village" of Packingtown. The hogs, "separate creatures," "kick in frenzy, wail in agony." Trusting, they come innocent to the slaughter. And theirs is the "hog squeal of the universe," says Sinclair, acknowledging that he now puts symbol and simile into the service of [socialist] philosophy. He insists that literature expand in scope and subject for reformist purposes. His proper audience is the powerful middle class able to effect the reforms necessary in industrial American society. His audience is, literally, the visitors' gallery of respectable ladies and gentlemen for whom the sight of mass slaughter is "too much." "The men would look at each other, laughing nervously, and the women would stand with hands clenched, and the blood rushing to their faces"—which is precisely Sinclair's intended impact upon his readers. In anger and anguish they—that is, *we*—are to proceed with social reform in the best tradition of the Progressive movement. Then at last literature, at least fiction, will be adequate to American industrial life.

Their arguments show Sinclair and James to be at an impasse. And in thematic discourse American writers were loathe to break it or to circumvent it. Instead, one by one, the writers concerned with literature and the industrial scene chose sides with Sinclair or with James. Had literature, as Sinclair argued, failed to be adequate to industrialization? The muckrakers, reformers that they were, thought so: Ray Stannard Baker, Lincoln Steffens, Ida Tarbell, and Ernest Poole. Some writers of the naturalistic school also thought so, though for reasons of esthetics. Theodore Dreiser and Robert Herrick insisted that fiction now, remedially, represent industrial Chicago, while in *The Octopus* Frank Norris made agricultural industrialization, or agri-business, a large part of his epic of California's San Joaquin Valley.[4]

As for James' side of the argument, that industrialization has destroyed literature and "outdistanced any possibility of poetic, of dramatic capture," a roll call of writers took that side. The romantic F. Scott Fitzgerald loathed the industrial "Valley of Ashes," just as the novelist Nathanael West detested the inauthenticity of its products. A number of writers, moreover, allied themselves with James in saying that industry had ruined nature and the craftsman's ways so consonant with it. The lament on the destruction of literary and other crafts is to be found in the work of Sherwood Anderson, Waldo Frank, Walter Lippmann, William Faulkner, and Edmund Wilson.[5]

All disagreement, however, stopped at the one premise which these writers held in common. Their positions vis-a-vis literature and machine-age technology were, it is true, irreconcilable. But they all accepted as a given—more precisely, as a fact—that humane life and the industrial scene were separate, mutually exclusive, and antagonistic. By consensus they affirmed that humanity and industry (with all attendant technologies) existed only on opposing sides of some moral and material barrier.

These and other writers were confronted, nevertheless, by the new ubiquity of machine-age technology in everyday life. For by the turn of the new century machine technology had, so to speak, jumped the nineteenth-century railroad tracks and burst the factory walls. The American public, including its writers, was now enmeshed in the technological revolution revealed in one New York diarist's inventory of "principal wonders, comparing these days [of the mid 1920's] with the simple old fashioned living of my [post-Civil War] childhood: elevated railways, subway railways, electric trollies, elevators, Brooklyn Bridges, Hudson Rivers tunnels, electric lights, telephones, heating by steam and hot water furnaces, wireless telegraphy, radio, air ships and planes, submarine boats, Rontgan X Rays [sic], phonographs, automobiles, radium faced clocks to see in the dark, steel trestle construction for tall buildings ... all of these unknown in my childhood, and undreamed of." As the diarist makes clear, the fantastic kinds of technologies once prophesied in Edward Bellamy's popular novel, *Looking Backward: 2000-1887* (1887), were rapidly taking their place in everyday life. And writers committed to a literature of socio-cultural, documentary reality could not avert their attention from them. As self-proclaimed realists, moreover, they were not at all inclined to imitate their Romantic predecessors by conveying their point of view in indirect, often organic, literary symbols. (It is revealing that Willa Cather, in her first major novel, *Alexander's Bridge* (1912), represented th psyche symbolically as a technological artifact, the engineer's cantilever bridge.)

In this new machine age one realist-naturalist writer, Robert Herrick, exemplifies the tension between presupposed "humane" values and the new technologies which seemed to threaten them. Herrick called the novel *Together* (1908) his "colossus of marriage" because of his difficulties pursuing, in fiction, a sustained critical expose of that hallowed institution. Numerous passages in *Together* reveal Herrick's up-to-the-minute awareness that industry and technology were making their impress in the conversational idiom, which in turn revealed new social values. One woman taunts her lover for his reputation as "a calculating machine—one of those things they have in banks to do arithmetic stunts." And a railroad executive in a dark business suit is "an Industrial Flywheel of society."[7]

Herrick's critique of industrial America, moreover, surfaces in a cluster of figures drawn from familiar contemporary technologies. His dialogue is riddled with electrical-mechanical figures when his most engaging woman character, the wife of a railroad executive, consults family and physicians about her psychological difficulties. The woman worries whether 'we are just machines, with the need to be oiled now and then," and is skeptical when the nerve doctor promises to be "your temporary dynamo." But she listens closely when her brother warns about exertion ("You may shift the batteries, Belle, but you are burning up the wires, all the same"). And she confesses to her physician, "I never thought before what it means to be tired. I have worked the machine foolishly. But one must travel fast—be geared up, as you say—or fall behind and become dull and uninteresting."[8]

Herrick purposely uses figures which double back on themselves to express his alarm at the presumed emotional and physical consequences of this new fast-paced style of American life. Not surprisingly, he sends his exhausted matron into the country, which is to say into pre-industrial America, to a sanitorium directed by a doctor who is himself an urban emigre. The true healer at the sanitorium, however, is not the surgeon-director but the blacksmith. For this symbol of pre-industrial America embodies spiritual and neural health and has the power to confer it upon others in his proximity. The smith, whose forge and house are principle buildings of the sanitorium, is the man "of VISION, of something inward and sustaining ... something that expressed itself in the slow speech, the peaceful manner." At suppertime the blacksmith's "ripest wisdom" emerges, and, relaxed, he looks at his wife and finds the world good.

Herrick's blacksmith exists as a totemic figure in this realistic, representational novel. In the 1910's the novelist virtually exhumes Longfellow's village blacksmith and makes his forge a shrine of miracles from a vanished, pre-industrial America. Modern urbanites, their nerves so many burned-out wires, can visit the forge and somehow be neurologically restored and spiritually revived. The urbanite then re-enters modern America informed by the "haven of peace" as the smith waves his benedictory goodbye with a glowing bar of steel.[9] In this novel the matron returns to the city to find her estranged husband, renew the marriage, and ultimately move West with him in a pioneering spirit to found a new railroad—and thus by an implication Herrick failed to see, to begin again the very cycle of industrialization which keeps people "geared up" and overloads the electrical circuits.

It is clear that in *Together* Herrick defined and grappled with cultural problems he suspected evaded solution. He believed, on the one hand, that humane life, ineffably "inward and sustaining," exists only in that pre-industrial America of the farmer and the artisan. Yet he acknowledges that that America has vanished, for the stock ticker now penetrates the forested mountains which in this century, the novel argues, are but pleasant views seen by urbanites through plate glass. The figures of electrical and mechanical power, moreover, suggest that speed and movement are becoming, in and of themselves, new values in contemporary America. As one character remarks, "The merest backwoodsman in Iowa is living faster in a sense than Cicero or [Daniel] Webster." One may visit pre-industrial America in a theme park of a sanitorium, but one lives fast and powerfully in a world of dynamos and gears. Contemporary pioneering, the novel tells us, is technological-industrial, and when characters converse, their figures of thought come from the new environment in which machine technology takes the prominent place.

As this glance at *Together* suggests, the industrialization of American literature in this century took covert forms, and was often manifest in writings whose explicit messages are anti-technological. In their larger argument, to be sure, writers held fast to the premise that humanity and industry werre separate entities locked virtually in a life-and-death struggle. Yet the texture of their prose tells another story. For writings which date from the turn of the century show that "the machine culture," to use Thorstein Veblen's phrase, had pervaded the literary imagination so thoroughly that machine-based figures of thought appear frequently and abruptly in literary texts.[10] Jack London's *Call of the Wild* (1903) is a good case in point. London's dog-protagonist, Buck, reared in civilization, answers the wilderness call to the Northern "uncharted vastness' which London portrays all at once as edenic, pastoral, and primitive. This dog has the wild nobility of London's beloved free-spirit, the wolf, for Buck is at the "high tide of his life, overspilling with vigor and virility." Into these organic phrases, however, London suddenly interjects an image direct from machine technology when we hear that every part of the dog, "brain and body, nerve tissue and fibre, was keyed to the most exquisite pitch," that "between all the parts there was a perfect equilibrium or adjustment." As a result of this perfect synchrony of machine parts, the animal responds to stimuli with "lightning-like rapidity." Electrically charged, the dog's muscles snap into play "like steel springs." Giving no sign whatever that these figures are different from those of the natural world, London moves immediately to say that the dog is lithe as wild cats and covert as the snake.[11]

London virtually repeats the pattern in a subsequent obversive work, *White Fang* (1906), which chronicles the wild wolf-dog's gradual accommodation to civilization. White Fank, like Buck, is a consummately efficient fighter whose sensate calculations are "automatic," his parts being in "better adjustment" than those of the other dogs. "Body and brain," says London, "his was a more perfect mechanism." Following these phrases, however, London hastens on to describe summer in the Rocky Mountains, as if unaware of his incongruity, the very incongruity which Mark Twain deliberately exploited for humor in "The Damned Human Race," in which the Machine is tried in a court of law along with its putative peers, the animals. London's evidently unconscious borrowing from (and inadvertent tribute to) machine technology is especially ironic and revealing in the light of his repudiation of industrial society, succinctly expressed in his well-known parody of Milton's Satan: "Better to reign among booze-fighters a prince, than to toil twelve hours a day at a machine at ten cents an hour."[12]

London is by no means singular. The same covert assimilation of industrial technology into American literature is to be found in writings of the naturalist Frank Norris, for instance in *The Octopus,* a novel plotted on the hostility between California ranchers and the corporate railroad whose tentacles reach out to strangle everything in its compass. Essentially Norris portrays two worlds in the novel, one romantic and mystical, and the other reflective of brutal socio-cultural, economic realities. The novelist-poet's self-appointed task, exactly at the turn of the century, is somehow to fuse the two worlds in order to create a modern American epic. In *The Octopus* Norris's ranchers, agribusiness corporate men, farm vast tracts of wheat with the aid of farm machinery, the telephone, telegraph, tickertape (connecting them with markets in Liverpool), and ranch hands who, at plowing time, form a military echelon in machine-like discipline. One of the ranchers is a civil engineer, and another thinks of the ranch as a machine ultimately to automated. In the meantime, because "the machine would not yet run of itself, he must still feel his hand upon the lever."[13]

Norris intermingles these many technological motifs with those of the Homeric epic. But until the conclusion he keeps machine-age referents essentially separate from the romantic, mystical passages on spirituality immanent in the California landscape. In the course of *The Octopus* readers expect that in all particulars Norris will preserve the boundary between the romantic, mystical landscape and the modern machine culture. Yet Norris, like Jack London, allows a miscellany of machine figures to obtrude, apparently without consciousness of the incongruity of the images in their contexts. In an early scene, for instance, Norris's aspirant poet, Presley, climbs a Homeric Pisgah of a California mountaintop, about to recognize in the titanic struggle in the wheatlands of the San Joaquin Valley the true, epic subject for his poem. Before Presley can have his epiphany, however, he must first calm himself and enter a receptive frame of mind. But what language does Norris use for the transition?—that of a machine coming to a stop. "By degrees the sense of his own personality became blunted, the little wheels and cogs of thought moving slower and slower." Then, "the animal in him stretched itself, purring."[14] Though it is a peculiar metamorphosis from machine to cat, Norris gives no sign of recognition of the sudden shift.

Elsewhere Norris similarly invades the mystical, romantic realm of *The Octopus,* this time in an effort to invoke the pain felt by his quintessential mystic, the character Vanomee who by temperament and intuition is the true poet of the land but is consumed with grief over the death of his murdered lover. Evidently Norris's drive to express the unabated, inordinate pain moves him to write that "under the moon's white eye ... these hours [of memory] came to [Vanomee], his grief recoiling on him like the recoil of a vast and terrible engine."[15]

Yet once again Norris reveals how fully he has assimilated figures of machine technology into his thought. The scene is a barn dance attended by virtually the entire populace of the Valley. Turmoil erupts with the arrival of a messenger whose wire announces the railroad's public sale of the very acreage the ranchers have been working and improving on lease options. Abruptly the scene of festivity turns into one of tumult. To describe it, Norris first uses figures from the natural sublime. The scene is a "whirlwind," and the peoples' shouts reverberate "as the plunge of a cataract" sounding "the thunder of the outbreak of revolt ... the blind fury of insurrection." In Hobbesian (and perhaps Hambletonian) terms attractive to the naturalist writer, Norris calls the crowd a "great beast," a "brute, many tongued, red-eyed, baring its teeth, unsheathing its claws." But the diction of intensifying, monstrous energy evidently left Norris unsatisfied, and in machine technology he sought one further phrase expressive of an exponential increase in power. Without preparation Norris writes that the "brute" mob "imposes its will with the abrupt, resistless pressure of the relaxed piston," a piston "inexorable, knowing no pity." Norris's transition to the industrial from the organic is instantaneous, and in subsequent phrasing, equally without modulation as he verbally decrescendos to a crowd merely "roaring."[16]

Norris's indiscriminate mingling of industrial and organic figures continues with his sequel to *The Octopus*. *The Pit* is set in Chicago and concerns the stock manipulations of Curtis Jadwin, the wheat financier who drives out in his "double-seated buggy" drawn by horses that always attract the attention of men who understand good stock. The team goes, "heads up, the check rein swinging loose, ears all alert, eyes all alight, the breath deep, strong, and slow, *and the stride machine-like, even as the swing of a metronome*" [italics added].[17] In this passage, of course, the synchrony and rhythm of the machine is the standard against which the movement of the horses can be measured. The equine ideal is not organic, but mechanical. Norris, as usual, exhibits no self-consciousness of his craft or of the underlying assumptions of his language.

Pistons, cogs, wheels, steel springs, recoiling engines, a metronome—what are we, as readers, to make of this literary odd lot of machine parts? It is tempting at first to find nothing new in these tailings from a Newtonian universe. (Moreover, did not Ralph Waldo Emerson himself deliberately invoke figures direct from the New England textile industry?) It may even seem picayune of a reader virtually to tweezer these images from texts which otherwise yield rich patterns of figures far more consenting to literary interpretation. Why not be satisfied, for instance, to verify the Darwinian world of Theodore Dreiser from his complementary animal figures? When Dreiser's financial titan, Frank Cowperwood, is described as leonine, wolfish, and like a "sort of bounding collie," why should readers take notice of the remark that "Cowperwood's brain had been reciprocating like a well-oiled engine"? When Edith Wharton, in *The House of Mirth* (1905), exploits the tension between aesthetics and commerce, why ought readers to notice that the desperate Lily Bart, ever a figure of "loveliness in distress," suddenly invokes phrases from a world utterly foreign to her experience. "I can hardly be said to have an independent existence," says this fragile flower, Lily. "I was just a screw or a cog in the great machine I called life." And further, when the romantic F. Scott Fitzgerald turns an automobile into a symbolic garden and writes seriously of Jay Gatsby's "tuning fork struck upon a star," why should readers pause to notice that his West Egg is of "spectroscopic brilliance"? Or, for that matter, why heed Sinclair Lewis, a writer so consistently scornful of American technology throughout *Babbitt,* when, in *Dodsworth,* he dispenses with irony to say that "it was raining, and the street looked like the inside of a polished steel cylinder."[18]

Most of these technological-industrial figures are striking precisely because they are desultory and seem, for the most part, to enter the texts without authors' awareness that they are unusual—or that they create problems. For abruptly they do change the narrative tone. Or they insinuate a new realm of imaginative possibility, but fail to develop it in clusters of compatible imagery. Appearing infrequently in lengthy novels, these figures seem aberrant, as if indicative of authors' momentary inattention or of their failure finally to edit their own work.

And yet this evident lack of self-consciousness of the part of these American writers provides an important clue to the basis for a changing sensibility in twentieth-century American literature. For it is clear that in the literary strategies of Norris, London, Dreiser, etc., there is nothing of the metaphysical poets' quest to yoke disparate images for poetic wit. The authorial self-consciousness of Donne's lovers-as-compasses forms no part of the imagination of these American authors. Nor (closer to home) do they seem to have been moved to use technological images, as Whitman did, to enhance themes of democracy and national vitality. Nor is it useful to repeat old charges of "clumsiness" in the craftsmanship, for instance, of Dreiser or London.

The crux of this issue lies precisely in this lack of authorial self-consciousness vis-a-vis the writer and the technological image. In fact the abruptness, the very instantaneous appearance of the technological figures in these earlier twentieth-century writings suggests that for the authors it has begun to be natural (or at least unexceptional) to move back and forth from organic to technological figures even as they may argue, in theme, that industrialization is antithetical to humane freedom. This enmeshment of images really signals a new sensibility in the twentieth century. For the mixing of American flora and fauna with pistons, gears, engines, etc., indicates that the cognitive boundary between industrialization and the natural world, be it pastoral, primitive, agrarian, or edenic, is disappearing. It suggests a new, machine-age sensibility to which William Carlos Williams gave expression when, in 1927, he wrote of contemporary life, "there are no sagas—only trees now, animals, engines. There's that."[19]

It is especially instructive to see, in a writer only of commercial and not literary-critical success the extent to which these industrial figures can pervade the fictional narrative by 1910. Edna Ferber's early novels make an excellent case study. As a newspaper reporter on local Midwestern papers and then on the *Chicago Tribune* (all in the 1910's), Ferber had a shrewd sense of the timely, the practical, the middle-class slant on her subjects. Although she is best remembered for such later fiction as *Show-Boat, Saratoga Trunk*, and *Giant*, three of Ferber's earlier, so-called "Emma McChesney" novels interest us here. Under the improbable titles of *Roast Beef, Medium; Personality Plus;* and *Emma McChesney & Co.* Ferber created a popular new heroine. She is the redoubtable divorcee, "Mrs. Mac," a travelling saleswoman guiding her son through the perils of young manhood as she outwits all her business competitors. Of interest here, of course, is the range of industrial figures to be found in these early Ferber novels. For instance, when Mrs. Mac's son interviews for a job in advertising, he feels coming from his prospective employer "a warning sent just in time from that wireless station located in his subconscious mind." Soon we hear the potential employer speak in similar figures: "Let me tell you something, young 'un. I've got what you might call a thirty-horse-power mind. I keep it running on high all the time, with the muffler cut out, and you can hear me coming for miles." Somewhat further on, the young man pays tribute to his mother's (Mrs. Mac's) skill in childbearing. "If I've got this far," he says, "It's all because of you. I've been thinking all along that I was the original self-starter, when you've really had to get out and crank me every few miles."

Not all of these figures come from automotive sources. Nor are they characteristic of masculine dialogue only. A stenographer compliments Mrs. Mac (and herself) in these terms: "some people are just bound to—well, to manufacture, because they just can't help it. Dynamos—that's what the technical book would call 'em. You're one—a great big one. I'm one. Just a little tiny one. But it's sparking away there all the time." Not only characters, but business days, are described in figures from industry. "A blight seemed to have fallen on Emma McChesney's bright little office," writes Ferber. "The machinery of her day, ordinarily as noiseless and well ordered as a thing on ball bearings, now rasped, creaked, jerked, stood still, jolted on again."[20]

In Ferber we have an impressive lot of figures from industry, from rolling stock to the automobile to the dynamo. These figures serve the fictional techniques of characterization, of description, of evocation of mood. In these novels no character scoffs to hear such terms used. Nor does Ferber apologize for them. Not once do these images come set inside the apologetic punctuation of quotation marks. As a journalist and commercial writer with her eye on the marketplace, Edna Ferber would be unlikely to take any stylistic risks that might alienate her audience. Her use of figures from American industry suggests a welcoming of such language as acceptable expression by the mid-1910's. Ferber's (and Frank Norris's and Jack London's) readiness to use such figures from American industry suggests how thoroughly assimilated industrialization was becoming in mainstream American culture. The larger argument on the destructiveness of industry would continue in *belles lettres,* but in the texture of the language itself—in the figures of thought and of common usage—the barrier between humane life and industrialization was crumbling.

In the 1920's two writers, John Dos Passos and William Carlos Williams, seized the opportunities this new sensibility afforded them. Williams, in scores of short lyric poems in the early 1920's, shows a new holistic world view which encompasses industrial artifacts as well as flowers. "The province of the poem is the world," Williams wrote. He demonstrated the point in poetry that makes no *a priori* distinction in value between the world of nature and that of the built environment. From the late 1910's his poems and prose became tracked with the welcome artifacts of an industrial culture: neon signs, a subway route map, a gas tank, a jack-hammer, a junked automobile. Williams drew images from industry, as in the steel roses of "The Rose Is Obsolete" (*Spring and All,* 1923), and flower petals that are bridge spans ("The Flower"). It is not surprising that this poet who celebrated broken glass and a hot water heater attempted a twentieth-century American epic based upon a New Jersey industrial city and named explicitly for it: *Paterson.* When in *Paterson* he spoke of thoughts as having "the grace and detail of/ a dynamo," when he spoke of "the ugly legs of the young girls,/ pistons too powerful for delicacy!," when he wrote of "churches and factories" as equals, he was fully exploiting, without fear or suspicion, the figures of thought in common usage since the 1910's.[21]

Williams's confrere in fiction, John Dos Passos, similarly enmeshes industrial technology with the natural world in order to represent the modern American sensibility and thus to invigorate fiction itself. In *Manhattan Transfer* (1925) Dos Passos delights to invert nature and technology. The New York harbor looks like "zinc," its wheeling gulls of "light tinfoil," its rivers "sleek as a bluesteel gun barrel." Dos Passos easily reverses the movement to awaken readers to the organic possibilities in industrial technology. The Manhattan arclights look like "shrunken grapes swaying in the wind," and its bridges have "girdered thighs," while "glowworm trains shuttle in the gloaming," and the telephone reaches out "shivering beady tentacles of sound." In Central Park at night "limosines, roadsters, touringcars, sedans, slither along the roadway with snaky glint of lights running in two smooth continuous streams." And in a novel in which tall-building construction is the city's very life, Dos Passos observes "the birchlike cluster of downtown buildings [that] shimmered up the rose morning like a sound of horns through a chocolatebrown haze."[22]

Dos Passos, like Williams, was entirely conscious of his craft, which devolved from the new technological sensibility. It is perhaps useful to be reminded that these two writers, like Herrick and the realists-naturalists, took a critical and analytic stance toward their culture. They understood, for instance, how the obsessive drive for wealth and high status were damaging to individuals, who forfeited their lives in quest of them. But by the early 1920's the totemic blacksmith of pre-industrial America formed no part of their imagination of contemporary American culture, neither as a symbol by which to attack its new machine ethos, nor as a totemic solution to its current problems. Later, in 1930, the poet Hart Crane seemed to have Dos Passos and Williams in mind when he urged modern writers to surrender "to the sensations of urban life" so that poetry—and by extension all literature—could "absorb or acclimatize the machine ... as naturally as trees, cattle, galleons, and all other poetic associations of the past."[23] It seems accurate to conclude that American literature had been moving in that direction since the turn of the century.

Footnotes

1   Henry James, *The American Scene,* ed. Leon Edel (1907; rpt. Bloomington and London, 1968), pp. 83-84, 1, 75.
2   *Ibid.,* pp. 57-59, 275-279, 83.
3   Upton Sinclair, *The Jungle* (1906; rpt. New York: New American Library, 1980), pp. 38-46.
4   See Ray Stannard Baker, *The New Industrial Unrest* (Garden City, New York: Doubleday, Page, 1920); Joseph Lincoln Steffens, *The Shame of the Cities* (New York: McClure, Phillips, 1904); Ida Tarbel, *The History of the Standard Oil Company* (New York: Macmillan, 1904); Ernest Poole, *The Harbor* (New York: Macmillan, 1915); Theodore Dreiser, *Sister Carrie* (1900; rpt. New York: Modern Library, 1932) and *The Color of a Great City* (Garden City, New York: Doubleday, 1932); Frank Norris, *The Pit* (1903; rpt. ed. James D. Hart, Columbus, Ohio: Merrill, 1970) and *The Octopus* (Garden City, New York: Doubleday, 1901).
5   See F. Scott Fitzgerald, *The Great Gatsby* (New York: Scribner's, 1925); Sherwood Anderson, *Poor White* (New York: Boni and Liveright, 1920); Waldo Frank, *The Re-Discovery of America* (New York: Scribner's, 1929); Walter Lippmann, *Drift and Mastery* (New York: Mitchell Kennerly, 1914); William Faulkner, *Light in August* (New York: Random House, 1932); Edmund Wilson, *The Great American Earthquake* (New York: Farrar, Straus and Giroux, 1979).
6   This passage is quoted from a family diary of the grandfather of Ms. Penelope Staples, a doctoral candidate in the Department of English, Boston University. The diary is dated November, 1927.
7   Robert Herrick, *Together* (New York: Grosset and Dunlap, 1908), pp. 216, 84.
8   *Ibid.,* pp. 232, 234, 375, 243.
9   *Ibid.,* pp. 446-447, 491.
10 Thorstein Veblen, *The Engineers and the Price System* (New York: Huebsch, 1921); *The Theory of Business Enterprise* (New York: Scribner's, 1904); *The Instinct of Workmanship* (New York: Macmillan, 1914).
11 Jack London, *The Call of the Wild* (1903; rpt. New York: Penguin, 1981), pp. 130-131.

[12] Jack London, *White Fang* (1906; rpt. New York: Penguin, 1981), pp. 303-304. London's parody of Milton is quoted in Fred Lewis Pattee, *The New American Literature 1890-1929* (New York: Century, 1930), p. 125.

[13] Frank Norris, *The Octopus* (1901; rpt. New York: New American Library, 1972), p. 48.

[14] *Ibid.*, p. 37.

[15] *Ibid.*, p. 99.

[16] *Ibid.*, pp. 199-200.

[17] Frank Norris, *The Pit*, p. 153.

[18] Theodore Dreiser, *The Titan* (New York: John Lane, 1914), pp. 432, 343, 532; Edith Wharton, *The House of Mirth* (1905; rpt. New York: New American Library), pp. 319-320; F. Scott Fitzgerald, *The Great Gatsby*, p. 25; Sinclair Lewis, Dodsworth (1929; rpt. New York: New American Library, 1972), p. 224.

[19] William Carlos Williams, "Notes in Diary Form," in *Selected Essays* (1954; rpt. New York: New Directions, 1969), p. 68.

[20] Edna Ferber, *Personality Plus* (New York: Frederick A. Stokes, 1914), pp. 21, 35-36, 154; *Emma McChesney & Co.* (New York: Frederick A. Stokes, 1915), pp. 135, 143-144.

[21] William Carlos Williams, *Paterson* (1946-1963; rpt. New York: New Directions, 1969), pp. 27, 44, 56. See also the poems "The House," "View of a Lake," "Overture to a Dance of Locomotives," "At the Faucet of June," "Rapid Transit," in *The Collected Earlier Poems* (New York: New Directions, 1966), pp. 70, 96-97, 194-195, 251, 282.

[22] John Dos Passos, *Manhattan Transfer* (1925; rpt. Boston: Houghton Mifflin, 1953), pp. 251, 125, 164, 244, 259, 317, 355, 371.

[23] Hart Crane, "Modern Poetry," in *The Complete Poems and Selected Letters of Hart Crane*, ed. Brom Weber (New York: Doubleday, 1966), pp. 261-262.

Proletarians and Professors, or Why Sweat and Holy Water Don't Mix

LAURENCE F. GROSS

Writing about the proletarian novel forces one to confront a number of problems not generally facing literary critics. Ordinarily, critic and audience share certain assumptions about literature. They agree sufficiently on the purpose and subject matter of both literature and criticism, the definitions of genres, and such.

Proletarian novels are seen to fit into traditional literature the same way a speaker in denim fits in here amidst the three-piece suits: not at all. But in both cases, it's intentional. Why don't these books fit? Because they are about unsettling things—poor people, even physical discomfort and suffering — all well and good if it's asceticism, but not much fun if its enforced. They are about divisions in a society which isn't supposed to have any, about anger, frustration, and resentment directed at the power structure of which literature (publishers, sellers, critics, writers) is a part.

The proletarian novel lacks a clear and agreed upon definition. It does not work toward the same ends as those novels generally treated by academic critics. Instead, it is a genre notable for the extent to which it is ignored. The fact is, however, that literature is too important to be left to entrenched critics and scholars to define or regulate.

The basis for the proletarian novel is an author's assumption that all is not for the best in society, that the lot of the working people is significant, that the shortcomings of society are important, that they deserve, even demand, attention, are subject to change, and that the proper function of literature is to discuss these subjects and pursue these ends:

> E.L. Doctorow, asked if he wrote political novels, answered "No." "I think they're 'life' novels. I don't distinguish political existence from existence. To leave out the political aspects, the political nature, of our lives is to leave out part of the truth. So everything I write is political, and so is everything everybody else writes."[1]

Modern novelists are, almost by definition, alienated from humanity, from life. The proletarian novelist is alienated, too, from the society which tries to destroy human bonds, to conform life to the needs of industrial capitalism. He/she discusses issues in society rather than outside it in either time or place, as has become the accepted habit. She/he is concerned with the earthly fates of the mass of people and depicts those factors which affect their lives. These writers deal with the typical, the earthly, and oppose false and artificial views of reality.

They are committed to the laboring class, regardless of whether or not they are members of it. They do not ignore the elite, but deal with the consequences of its philosophy and conduct rather than concentrating on the interactions of its members.

Proletarian novels focus on the experiences of the lower class, those who experience the failures and cruelties of the capitalist system; they emphasize those aspects of society which directly affect these people's lives. They assume a degree of human worth which requires attention to the sources of human misery, sources which they refuse to dismiss, ahistorically, as an aspect of "human nature" or "the human condition."

Interestingly enough, these writers alone in the United States in the twentieth century have dealt with issues of industrialization, including pollution, squalor, ugliness, prejudice within the working class, ethnicity, and other topics of concern now outside literary circles. They are about money, the lack of it, a topic rarely touched by other writers. They break rules and discuss such unmentionables as part of their adherence to a larger morality than the artificial moralism of genteel fiction.

In recent years (at least since World War II but in a tradition dating from about 1895), critics have rejected literature which did not lend itself to discussion in terms of neoprotestant theology, mystical psychology, biblical symbolism, or strictly formal considerations of style and metaphor. They have considered it sufficient grounds for rejection that proletarian novelists did not shape their work according to the dictates of the critical fraternity.

The shared problems of the working class in the United States, however, have been affecting increasing numbers of industrial workers since early in the nineteenth century. Many highly respected authors, among them Herman Melville, Mark Twain, William Dean Howells, Walt Whitman, Hamlin Garland, and Stephen Crane, have been attentive to the situation of industrial labor and to the nature of the society established on its efforts. For them, the quality of the daily life of their fellow citizens was a significant topic. Despite the efforts of critics to maintain literature as the province of genteel authors working to elevate the moral tone of their readers, these writers would insist on the primacy of questions of social values. In fact, any separation between high art and popular art comes comparatively recently. These issues were not current for Homer, Cervantes, or Shakespeare. Not until Henry James and T.S. Eliot, alienated from the country's claimed values of liberty, equality, and democracy, was literature made exclusively a defender of a hierarchical society, of the exploitation of the great majority of society by the favored few, a conspiracy between artist and critic to exclude the great unwashed. In this century, the question is not whether or not the nature of the lives Americans lead as part of an industrial system is a fit subject for literature, but how such a central concern has come to be ignored.

The explanation for the lack of discussion of fundamental questions about the nature of society is quite clear. Karl Marx described the overwhelming ability of the powers-that-be to control intellectual expression:

> In every epoch the ideas of the ruling class are the ruling ideas, that is, the class that is the ruling material power of society is at the same time its ruling intellectual power. The class having the means of material production has also control over the means of intellectual production. The ruling ideas are nothing more than the ideal expression of the dominant material relationships grasped as ideas, hence of the relationships which make the one class the ruling one and therefore the ideas of its domination. The individuals who comprise the ruling class possess among other things consciousness and thought. Insofar as they rule as a class and determine the extent of a historical epoch, it is self-evident that they do it in its entire range. Among other things they rule also as thinkers and producers of ideas and regulate the production and distribution of the ideas of their age. Their ideas are the ruling ideas of the epoch. For example, in an age and in a country where royal power, aristocracy, and bourgeoisie are contending for domination and where control is shared, the doctrine of the separation of powers proves to be the dominant idea and is expressed as an "eternal law."[2]

Throughout much of the nineteenth century, industrialists had not dominated the country's intellectual life. Although during this transitional period their ability to define issues and impose their point of view grew continually, a routine identification of society's goals and values with their own was not possible, and a debate over the merits of industrial capitalism in the United States continued, particularly in literature.

Despite the efforts of a few utopian novelists and the social realism of Rebecca Harding Davis, Crane, Garland, and Upton Sinclair, the writers who received popular acclaim were of the type of Richard Harding Davis and Owen Wister, of the Teddy Roosevelt school of politics, or James and Eliot, who regularly found in religion, in England, or in pedantry reasons to avoid discussion of the relationship between the aristocratic society they so admired and the working class which enabled it to exist.

The economic and political turmoil of the Thirties, however, created an opening in the facade of elitist literary dominance, an opening into which proletarian novels poured. Until cut off by World War II and The Cold War, a significant group of writers promoted a revolt against economic and literary "laws" which both condemned people to the ravages of oppressive exploitation and demanded that literature ignore their fate.

Just as the first American novelists worked without a native literary tradition, so these proletarian novelists had to create a form for which there were few immediate precedents in this country. In addition, the values of industrial capitalism had possessed none of the dominance of intellectual life in the earlier period which they had by now obtained. In light of the difficulties inherent in attacking a system through publishing, a branch of the society's structure, their output is all the more impressive.

Dozens of proletarian novels appeared during the Depression as if in response to the call of John Reed in *The Masses,* slightly earlier, for "Poems, stories, and drawings, rejected by the capitalist press on account of their excellence."[3] Their approaches to and treatments of the problems confronting Americans are as varied as is their quality. As a group they form a significant body of literature, valuable for its insight into the nature of society and its effect on people's lives.

Representative examples include: Albert Halper's *Union Square,* Jack Conroy's *The Disinherited,* Michael Gold's *Jews Without Money,* William Attaway's *Blood on the Forge,* Pietro DiDonato's *Christ in Concrete,* and Ruth MacKenney's *Jake Home.* The books were selected for the variety of their subjects and techniques. Their authors are now little known and the books rarely discussed. They were not picked as the best of the lot, and many others equally deserving of serious attention await attention. In this abbreviated treatment of the genre, I will comment only briefly on each one.

Halper, in *Union Square,* presents a microcosm of U.S. society during the Depression. It is the 'generality' of his view, as opposed to uniqueness of individual characters, that makes the book interesting, and the same quality keeps the book from becoming dated as long as the nature of society has not changed significantly.

The society Halper describes is not a pleasant one. There is no community, no cooperation. Too close to soap opera for the critics, perhaps, there is a poignancy about these lost lives which belies the formulaic nature of the plot.

The effects of the Depression grow as the novel progresses:

> Merchants slashed their prices for the trade, workers took cuts in wages to hold onto their jobs, girls without families who had to meet their room rent or get thrown out upon the street stayed a little later in the offices if the bosses demanded it, stayed to take "dictation" and swallowed hard, and made no outcry, there in the darkness, when the boss clicked the lights out.[4]

The Depression doesn't alter the nature of the situation, it only makes it more apparent. Competition permeates society, even down to those foraging for firewood or picking through rotten vegetables for edible pieces. The only alternative is to seek charity, and "lines of the living dead" are reduced to doing so with humility and meekness.[5] Civic and religious leaders bemoan the conditions, but nothing is done to alter them.

Jack Conroy's *The Disinherited* opens with a characterization of the coal-mining town of the central character's, and author's, youth: "Cold and white like the belly of some deep-sea monster incongruously cast out of the depths, the [mine] dump dominated Monkey Nest camp like an Old World cathedral towering over peasants' huts."[6] The description sums up the significance of the mine which would claim Larry Donovan's father and three brothers, and from which he would flee for years. Other miners "escape" only to die in World War I, a war Donovan learns is a source of great profit for the contractor for whom he then works.

Monkey Nest never improves. Offers of charity are so restricted as to be insulting, practically penal. The employing class accepts no responsibility for the results of its operations and feels no need to aid those who suffer from them. Mining condemns the miner instead of rewarding him, makes him as unfit for life as are the blind burros from the mine for conditions on the surface.

Donovan leaves Monkey Nest and moves through a wide range of jobs, from railroad yard to rubber factory, assembly line to ditch digging. Through a decade or so of this life he learns that assembly lines double in speed in a year's time and that machines are rapidly eliminating jobs in mines, factories, and construction. Even the unions are seen to betray the worker in exchange for the comfort of their leadership, destroying the one source of hope which sustains the worker. As a result, "the cruel competition for bare existence made rats of them [the disenherited]. They pecked eagerly for small favors like expectant sparrows following a well-fed horse."[7] The workers' oppression creates in them the lowest level of feelings, and Donovan's travels teach him it is no accident:

> But I never really escaped by quitting and changing jobs. All the factories had the same conveyors, the same scientific methods for extracting the last ounce of energy. The same neon tubes pulsing with blue fire and the same automatons toiling frantically beneath the ghastly rays that etched dark shadows under their eyes and blackened their lips to resemble those of a cadaver.[8]

Donovan realizes that the personal humiliation he experiences is part of a conscious plan to maximize the exploitation of the working class in the name of "scientific management."

Jews Without Money, sticking to a few blocks of New York's East Side immigrant community, displays an urban vitality very different from Conroy's expansive novel. Gold's autobiographical account recreates the pageant of the slum: "It was an immense sea of excitement. It never slept. It roared like a sea. It exploded like fireworks."[9] A mixture of nationalities, united only by poverty, the immigrant community was not boring but offered few other positive attributes.

The social and economic forces operating in the ghetto, where people are driven by poverty and hunger and must act out of desperation, are somehow not the universal "laws" said to govern society: "I never heard of a millionaire's daughter who became a fifty-cent whore or who was 'ruined' by dance halls."[10] The economic "laws" may operate with inexorable effect, but despite their Darwinian justification of the status quo, the rich stand safely outside the jungle they create.

Insanity, it seems, is as good a course as any in this realm of inescapable destitution. At bottom, there is always the painful fact of poverty: "We were poor, and you [Americans] punished us harshly for this worst of sins."[11] In the words of the narrator's father, "It is better to be dead in this country than not to have money."[12] It is perhaps another reflection of this attitude which has led critics to so carefully ignore this book and others of the same type. Poverty is acceptable as long as it is voiceless, but let it speak, and it must be quickly dismissed and repudiated before it establishes a right to be heard in the larger society.

William Attaway's *Blood on the Forge* stays far away from the urban scene. It describes three black sharecropper brothers, Melody, Chinatown, and Big Mat, as they move from the agrarian South to an isolated steel mill in the Monongahela Valley. The South seen here is neither the romanticized scene of *Gone With the Wind,* another Thirties novel, nor the realm of the decadent gentility William Faulkner was describing at the same time. Attaway presents responses to the South of the black sharecropper, a land of oppression and subservience, of fear and hunger.

When they arrive at the shacktown at the steel mill, the men are appalled by their new home; smoke obscures the sun, ashes and soot cover the ground, garbage and pollution have replaced living things throughout the area. Bad enough in themselves, the conditions horrify these men: *"We have been tricked away from our poor, good as-bad-ground-and bad-white-men-will-let-'em-be-hills. What men in their right minds would leave off tending green growing things to tend iron monsters?"* (Attaway's emphasis).[13] Their pre-industrial backgrounds leave them totally unprepared for the setting or the work. Melody can find no music here, nor can others maintain the hopes, dreams, or even superstitions of a rural past. The very money they make loses its meaning where it's unrelated to land, houses, or mules.

By way of contrast, the Slavs working there have come from industrial backgrounds, bringing cultural memories adapted to the mills, and through the strength of family and tradition are able to adapt to these conditions, to make homes and futures there. Coming thousands of miles to a new land and a strange language, these industrial foreigners are far better prepared for the mills than the pre-industrial blacks who have been moved from Kentucky to Pennsylvania.

Despite the mill's many horrors, including terrible rates of accident and death, there are reasons for the blacks to stay:

> For a man who had so lately worked from dawn to dark in the fields, twelve hours and the long shift [twenty-four hours, once a week] were not killing. For a man who had ended each year in debt any wage at all was a wonderful thing. For a man who had known no personal liberties even the iron hand of the mills was an advancement. In his own way he felt these things. As yet he could not see beyond them.[14]

But for all workers, the degree of exploitation and oppression in the mills rapidly becomes clear: "Like spiral worms, all their egos had curled under the pressure from the giants around them. Sooner or later it came to all the green men: "What are we in relation to the machines of hugh strength?"[15] Nor is it simply a matter of scale which oppresses them. It is continually apparent that the workers are of no importance in relation to steel, that management grants no stature to the labor force.

Pietro DiDonato's *Christ in Concrete* also treats the adaptation of pre-industrial workers to modern requirements. Italian masons in New York City are his subjects, and the similarity between their position and that of Attaway's black characters suggests the pervasiveness of the problem faced by successive groups of people drawn into the country's ever-growing industrial plant.

The contrast between the respect and dignity deserved by those who are "in blood and stone creating World"[16] and the situation in which they find themselves is also emphasized in DiDonato's Italianate account:

> With the beginning of each job men, though knowing one another and having raised Job for years, wed themselves to Job with the same new ceremony, the same new energy and fear, the same fierce silence and loss of consciousness, and the perpetual sense of wrongness...[,] struggling to fulfill a destiny of never-ending debt...They were the bodies to whom he [Paul] would be joined in bondage to Job. Job would be a brick labyrinth that would suck him in deeper and deeper, and there would be no going back. Life would never be a dear music, a festival, a gift of nature. Life would be the torque of Wall's battle that distorted straight

limbs beneath weight in heat and rain and cold.

On the other hand, there is the group by and for whom the system operates. When lawyers, businessmen, and the court conspire to blame Paul's father for the building's collapse rather than pay even the piddling compensation of the period, Paul wonders, "Where did these men come from? Who are they? Where and how do they live? For whom do they weep, and to whom do they pray?" Paul's natural reaction to the accepted dishonesty reminds the reader of the distance between capitalist morality and that otherwise considered civilized. The Italians' background again leaves them disoriented, so much so that Paul assumes they are in error: "O God above, what world and country are we in? We didn't mean to be wrong,"[17] The alienation of capital and labor creates separate worlds, and insures that labor's is wrong.

In *Jake Home* Ruth MacKenney returns the native born worker to prominence; Jake is, like Conroy's Larry Donovan, a child of a coal mining town: "Jake Home was born January 21, 1901, in Luyskill, Pennsylvania, one of the lost places of this earth...People whom life had condemned to Luyskill knew it only as black and hungry, cold, wet, forever hopeless."[18] Hunger is their constant companion and Jake learns early to curse those responsible.

Later, Jake, self-educated and intelligent, but with an intellectual background notable for its gaps, reads James Joyce's *Ulysses;* MacKenney describes not only the source of Jake's strengths and drive, but also the separation between proletarian and elitist schools of writing:

"He [Joyce] is one of these the world-is-all-washed-up-let's-go-hang-ourselves boys!"..."Workers, ordinary people, they aren't weary of the world. They may be weary of hard luck. Sure, they hang themselves, often enough. Real hangings, not in books. If the wife gets cancer and you can't afford to buy her morphine; or the kid has a club foot and you don't have the dough for an operation, or maybe: if you scalded yourself in your mother's wash-tub and got a purple blotch over your puss, and the girls throw up when they see you, and it's been too long since the accident for any doctor to patch you up, even if you had the dough...well, a working man has reason enough to hang himself. But it's not the same. Besides, the ordinary working stiff, he leaves the rope alone. He maybe despairs; maybe loses hope; maybe suffers. But he has a strong feeling for living. I believe it's a class feeling. I've seen it all my life."[19]

There is no anti-intellectualism here, and Milton and Shakespear are cited as authors who did not hide a poverty of thought behind an abundance of style. There is, rather, an admiration for the strength the working class exhibits amid adversity.

Taken together, the six novels represent a literature unlike the books generally analyzed and taught. They attack, in a consumer medium, what are generally claimed as values shared by all members of society. As a group, they describe the vast majority of the members of society who are systematically exploited by a favored few, a few who are traditionally seen as both subject and audience for literature. They show the destruction of personal relationships by the economic system and the reduction of people to the status of machines or automatons. They detail suffering on such a pervasive scale that one wonders how other writers can ignore it. The numbers and significance, in human terms, of the narrow segment of society which profits from the oppression are indicated by the miniscule role they play in these books. These novels also express the underlying solidarity of the working class and its awesome potential power, while recognizing the difficulty of mobilizing this strength against its rightful targets or enemies.

The proletarian novelist looks closely at the life of the period and offers insight into it which historians may only come to appreciate years later. The strength and unity of the immigrant family which is so central to *Christ in Concrete,* for example, is a fact presently being treated by historians of ethnicity, labor, and the family. Similarly, the perpetual adjustment of preindustrial laborers to industrial situations is a recurrent theme in these books which has recently become the subject of articles in revisionist labor history.

Another often shared aspect of these books, the accounts in several of brutal police oppression of the rights of free assembly and free speech, brings us to the question of the need for this essay, the refusal of critics to treat these novels. There is clearly something wrong in a society where policemen beat and trample with their horses on men, women, and children in peaceful assembly. The appalling working conditions the books describe, the speed-ups, the rates of death and accidents, the general degree of callous exploitation, are also well documented, have been for years, and have been treated in literature for well over a hundred years. Why, then, are novels which concern themselves with the meanings of these events, and others similarly contrasting with the ideals of a "free people," dismissed by academics as unimportant? Is it not true, in fact, that the lack of attention is part of what the novels are about, the division of society, the alienation of its parts from one another, the enforced silence of the oppressed?

Academics, and critics generally, are obviously dependent upon society for their support, their income. More specifically, they are dependent on that portion of society which controls the universities and the publishing trade, the elite group which benefits from the exploitation these authors protest. Richard Ohmann describes this situation in *English in America:*

Society needs help from schools to justify its present divisions, including much inequality. There is pressure—indirect but heavy—on teachers of literature to join in this effort. The ruling classes want a culture, including a literature and a criticism, that supports the social order and discourages rebellion, while it sanctions all kinds of nonthreatening nonconformity.[20]

It may not be coincidential, therefore, that the criticism which has become dominant since the Depression, since World War II and the advent of the Cold War, the "New Criticism," has ordained that art, or literture, be apolitical, even ahistorical, that it stand outside society, separate from questions of politics or economics, outside of time, in service to "higher goals."

To be ahistorical and apolitical, is, admittedly, the refuse to concern oneself with the forces which lead to the existence of art and the relationship between art and society which makes art important. It is to accept, as establishment professionals of all disciplines do, the division of knowledge into such small compartments that relationships between facts, between disciplines, even between the concerns of academe and society, can be ignored. For literary critics this means the acceptance of the reduction of their sphere to the study of genre, style, and metaphor, to descriptive, even statistical approaches; in essence, to preliminary enterprises. The avoidance of syntheses and relationships, of factors relating to life in society, is comparable to the antiquarian's approach to history as a collection of facts isolated from modern concerns.

The critics' desire to make a career, a profession, of their work reinforces their desire to restrict their study to safe areas, those not threatening to the ruling class, and spurs them to make it esoteric, as well. If literary criticism is to be a profession, and it is not to deal with concerns of general import, then literature must be made inaccessible to the ordinary reader. They want, in Everett Knight's words, "To teach the student to appreciate what to the mind of the layman is utterly unappreciable".[21] Literature, therefore, must be discussed in terms meaningful only to those other professionals for whom literature is to be written and by whom it is to be discussed. The result of this approach is to make the difficulty of comprehension a measure of a writer's (or critic's) quality and stature. One writes, therefore, to be not understood.

The result of these two factors, the drive for safety and the desire for professionalism, is to reject the proletarian novel for every aspect of its very nature. It concerns itself with the relationship between capital and labor, breaking the most fearsome taboo. It suggests or implies the need for fundamental change in the social structure—doubly taboo, since it represents dangerous ground and would even threaten the position of the critics themselves.

The subject represents all that the critics' efforts have cut themselves off from. Proletarian novelists insist on dealing with the experience of labor, the felt aspects of life, rather than the celebrations of the idle. Perhaps the critics know too little of labor, have experienced too little, to understand Attaway's steel mills or DiDonato's masons. Perhaps not. There is a hesitancy about turning from the concerns of Kierkegaard to those of, say, Roman Catholic or Baptist laborers. In any case, there is a decision to restrict the effort to thinking about thinking, to examining certain ideas capable of study in safety and isolation. For even if the professionals are too far from the work force to understand the bitter jokes about the incompetence of the managerial forces and their relative unimportance, the quality of these novels makes their content accessible to those who do not share their experience.

The proletarian novelists lacked native traditions, often were not steeped in formal education, and in their ignorance, turned to the most important issues of their society. They described the lives they observed with compassion and alarm. Their own careers were generally short, cut off by the blind patriotism of World War II and the Cold War.

Their approaches range from Halper's cynical irony to DiDonato's visceral outrage, from Attaway's psychological portraits to MacKinney's epic of life and love on the far left. Their insights, and their vitality, are unparalleled in the works of those writers favored by establishment scholars.

These novels deal with the most fundamental questions of value in our society and are ignored, not in spite of the seriousness of their concerns, but because of it. And as a result of the rulers' ability to control literature in particular and intellectual life in general, their insights into the nature and effects of industrial capitalism are denied to those now enduring the oppression these books describe and to students of literature and society who could appreciate their qualities if the critics permitted.

One wonders whether to call it tragedy, irony, or both. There is an irony in the fact that while we witness the reification of art, the making into a commodity of literature, which Frederic Jameson describes, these novels offer something of an escape from this killing trend. He writes, "An authentic cultural creation is dependent for its existence on authentic collective life, on the vitality of the 'organic' social group in whatever form.[22] The exclusion from full membership in society of the poor, the black, the female, the ethnic, the leftists, in all sorts of combination, permits them something of the collective life from which art springs.

The tragedy is that, in the words of Meridel LeSueur's main character in *The Girl*: "Memory is all we got. We got to remember. Remember everything."[23] Reification, the turning of art into commodity, destroys the traditional tools of collective memory, and in association with an amenable critical fraternity, denies to the working class the affecting memories suggested by these books. Their lives of toil without accomplishment, of sacrifice without meaning or reward, are lived as in a vacuum, without the memory which would then help make sense of it, a memory, of course, which might spark dissension in this, the best of all possible worlds.

NOTES

1   Quoted by Nathan Cobb, "Yes, there's a Doctorow in the house," *The Boston Globe,* March 30, 1982, p. 42.
2   Loyd D. Easton and Kurt H. Quddot, translators and editors, *Writings of the Young Marx on Philosophy & Society* (Garden City, N.J.: Doubleday, Anchor, 1967), p. 438.
3   Quoted by, Howard Zinn, "Rediscovering John Reed, *The Boston Globe,* January, 6, 1982.
4   Albert Halper, *Union Square* (New York: Viking Press, 1933), p. 266.
5   *Ibid.,* p. 106.
6   Jack Conroy, *The Disinherited* (1933; rept. New York: Hill and Wang, 1963), p. 9.
7   *Ibid.,* p. 236.
8   *Ibid.,* p. 216.
9   Michael Gold, *Jews Without Money* (New York: H. Liveright, 1930), p. 8.
10 *Ibid.,* pp. 33-34.
11 *Ibid.,* p. 244.
12 *Ibid.,* p. 301.
13 William Attaway, *Blood on the Forge* (Toronto: Doubleday, 1941), p. 51.
14 *Ibid.,* p. 208.
15 *Ibid.,* p. 66.
16 Pietro Di Donato, *Christ in Concrete* (Indianapolis, N.Y.: Bobbs-Merrill, 1939), pp. 188-9.
17 *Ibid.,* pp. 176-7.
18 Ruth McKenney, *Jake Home* (New York: Harcourt, Brace, and Co., 1943) p. 3.
19 *Ibid.,* pp. 309-10.
20 Richard Malin Ohmann, *English in America: A Radical View of the Profession* (New York: Oxford University Press, 1976), p. 25.
21 Everett Knight, *A Theory of the Classical Novel* (London: Routledge and Paul, 1969, i.e. 1970), p. 18.
22 Frederic Jameson, "Reification and Utopia in Mass Culture," *Social Text* I (Winter, 1979), p. 140.
23 Meridel Le Sueur, *The Girl* (Cambridge, Mass.: West End Press, 1978), p. 148.

The Fine Arts in America: Images of Labor from 1800 to 1950

PATRICIA HILLS

Images of labor in the fine arts in America—at least those images which are bought by collectors, treasured by museums, and reproduced in art books—are not simply records of the bodily motions and environment of the worker. They are documents of culture—documents of the attitudes and beliefs which the artist and/or his patrons held about work, about the working classes, and about America. During the nineteenth century these attitudes conformed to those of a small minority of Americans, specifically white, middle-class, propertied males whose families had lived in New England, New York, or the Middle Atlantic and North Central states for several generations.[1] It was this very audience which encouraged the development of the fine arts in America—the "fine arts" being defined as the important architecture commissioned by civic institutions or by private wealth and the painting and sculpture sold in art galleries and shown at the prestigious exhibitions of the National Academy of Design in New York, the Pennsylvaia Academy of the Fine Arts in Philadelphia, the Boston Athenaeum, and the large international expositions.

Throughout the nineteenth century, as in the two earlier centuries, most American artists did not challenge the attitudes of this ruling elite. They did, after all, want to sell their work or see it reproduced as fine engravings and lithographs and then circulated for their own increasing fame and fortune. Artists were seemingly unaware of how much they were lead by, and reflected, the attitudes of the American monied classes. Therefore, it comes as a refreshing surprise when we read one reviewer, writing in *The Crayon* in 1859, who is conscious and tacitly critical of the artists' mandate to conform:

> Exhibitions do not display the merits of particular works of Art and the progress of individual artists so much as they do the nature of public taste, or rather the character of artistic thought which the public chooses to manifest through its encouragement of Art.... It is a mistake to suppose that artists are free to paint what pleases them best.... The Truth is, that artists are compelled to meet the public by consulting its likes and dislikes.[2]

The "public" meant those who went to exhibitions, who wrote and read about art, and above all, who bought paintings. And "consulting its likes and dislikes" meant, to the successful artist, absorbing the attitudes and tastes of that public and converting the underlying value system into artistic imagery.

Some early images, such as the watercolors of Philadelphia tradesmen done about 1811-13 by Pavel Petrovitch Svinin (The Metropolitan Museum of Art, New York) or the watercolors of New York tradesmen done in the 1840's by Nicolino Calyo (Museum of the City of New York) seem relatively value-free. But a close study of nineteenth-century American genre paintings of people at work done by our more ambitious artists reveals that the majority embody the values and attitudes of the Northern entrepreneurial class—attitudes which were anti-aristocratic, middle-class democratic, and often self-righteously "American," as noted by Alexis de Tocqueville's observations on our middle classes, *Democracy in America,* which appeared in English editions in the late 1830's.[3] And, of course, this entrepreneurial class believed in the work ethic, maintaining that work was good for character, for the benefit of the family, and for the nation. The work ethic is no better illustrated than in the popular engravings done by Oliver Pelton in the 1840's from broadsides illustrating Benjamin Franklin's *Poor Richard's Almanack.* One Pelton engraving of a blacksmith's shop [Fig. 1] has inscribed around the circumference of the image the following mottoes: "He that hath a trade hath an estate"; "At the workingman's house hunger looks in, but dares not enter"; and, at the bottom, "Industry pays debts, while despair increaseth them." The image includes two carpenters building a house, a blacksmith at the forge with his wife hammering a horseshoe, and, in the background, beehives, a symbol of busy work. The mottoes come from Franklin's almanac, issued annually from 1733 to 1758 in the pre-industrial period when work among free whites took the form of small-time commodity production and trade carried on mainly in the context of the family or small village community.

In the 1840's the nature and place of work was changing rapidly; the old ways of communal production, artisanry, and trade broke down as thousands of men and women entered the mills and factories of the Northeast. We then entered a new period, the period of rising industrial capitalism which lasted until the early 1890's.[4] Simultaneously fine arts genre painting—defined as "pictures of typical everyday life" —developed in America.[5] Contrary to our expectation that art mirrors life, the genre painting produced in the era after 1840 did not do justice to the social history. It did not reflect the tensions of the altered social structure and the increasingly alienated labor force. Quite the reverse, the genre painting often denied and concealed those very realities, as painters, in the service of their patrons, reached back for themes and images from the pre-industrial area.

$$* \qquad * \qquad * \qquad *$$

American genre painting of labor themes in the 1825-75 period can be divided into three categories: communal farm production, ar-

Fig. 1. Engraving by Oliver Pelton from Broadside illustrating *Poor Richard's Almanack* (Print No. 234a) "Industry," 1840's. Benjamin Franklin Collection, Yale University Library.

Fig. 2. Eastman Johnson, *Corn Husking*, 1860. Everson Museum of Art, Syracuse, New York.

tisanry, and trade. Each of these categories of labor images functioned as an ideological mask concealing the realities of rising industrial capitalism. Indeed, it is tempting to postulate that the history of culture is the record of such acts of concealment.

First, those paintings celebrating the communal aspects of rural "American" work include Alvin R. Fisher's *The Corn Husking Frolic* of 1828-29 (Museum of Fine Arts, Boston), Jerome B. Thompson's *Apple Gathering* of 1856 (The Brooklyn Museum), and Eastman Johnson's *Corn Husking* of 1860 (Everson Museum of Art, Syracuse) [Fig. 2], which was popularized through a Currier and Ives engraving. When praising Johnson for *The Cranberry Harvest* of 1880 (Timkin Gallery, San Diego), one writer wistfully lamented. "He is a chronicler of a phase of our national life which is fast passing away."[6] Another contemporary praised Johnson's American optimism which "preaches no ugly gospel of discontent, as does so much of the contemporary French and Flemish art of this genre."[7] Because work in the American Northeast was then dominated more and more by ruthless factory owners and city businessmen, an inevitable nostalgia, a cultural primitivism, developed for these images of rustic, cooperative work.[8]

A second major theme concerns craft and artisanry. William Sidney Mount's *Farmer Whetting His Scythe* of 1848 (Suffolk Museum & Carriage House, Stony Brook), celebrates the value of craft—the pride with which the farmer cares for his tools. In William Burr's *The Scissors Grinder* of 1856 (Coe Kerr Gallery) a young boy gazes in admiration at the older man's skill. In Charles Caleb Ward's *Force and Skill* of 1869 (Currier Gallery of Art, Manchester, N.H.) [Fig. 3], two children emulate their elders. One boy turns the grindstone, while the other holds steady the knife being sharpened. The message is explicit: there is no status division between physical and mental labor—at least none on the farm. Such rural scenes of classlessness and of unalienated labor were soothing balm to harried businessmen confronting an increasingly demanding labor force. Moreover, the realities of developing capitalism, with the worker becoming a mere extension of the machine he operated, increasingly denied the possibility of craftsmanship.

A third theme within the general category of workers is the entrepreneurial practice itself, the subject of Asher B. Durand's *The Peddler Displaying His Wares* of 1836 (The New-York Historical Society) and John W. Ehninger's *Yankee Peddler* of 1853 (The Newark Museum) [Fig. 4]. To the city businessman, the Yankee peddler was a relic of the pre-industrial era, one who had plied his trade in the context of the family and a cohesive community. He embraced those virtues of shrewdness and salesmanship that had been necessary for the economic development of the United States. The women, too, played their roles as responsive and necessary consumers. Ehninger's picture invites an analysis more detailed than what is possible in this brief

Fig. 3. Chalres Caleb Ward, *Force and Skill*, 1869. Currier Gallery of Art, Manchester, New Hampshire.

Fig. 4. John Whetton Ehninger, *Yankee Peddler*, 1853. Collection of The Newark Museum.

Fig. 5. John G. Brown, *A Tough Story*, 1886. North Carolina Museum of Art.

survey. For instance, the American flag marks it as a specifically American scene and the title locates it in the Northeast, far away from slave/slaveholder relationships. The superiority of the North, a major theme of Harriet Beecher Stowe's *Uncle Tom's Cabin* then being avidly read, was also a sub-theme of many paintings of the time. But with all the various interpretations which can be brought to Ehninger's painting, one conclusion we can draw, relevant to the issue of labor, is that the ideology of simple commodity exchange shown here masks the new reality of the labor contract. In this new epoch of capitalism the most important buying and selling in the North involved the labor power of the worker.

Eastman Johnson had a special instinct for the popular subject, and a close study of his work in the context of social history invariably reveals the nature of mid-century American culture. After the Civil War he celebrated the new freedom of the negro in *Fiddling His Way*, 1866 (Chrysler Museum of Art, Norfolk), sent to the Paris Exposition of 1867 to hang in the American section. In this work a black man performs for a rustic family as a way to earn his living. To be economically independent and resourceful is implied in the title and was at the heart of the entrepreneurial ethos, which some hoped in 1867 might be extended to the blacks. But the dream of economic equality for the former slaves was soon shattered by the realities of reconstruction.

Hard work, luck, and pluck were the formula for white, male entrepreneurial success in the Horatio Alger stories of the post-Civil War era. In Alger's first novel, *Ragged Dick,* the hero's benefactor, Mr. Whitney, encourages the young bootblack to cultivate thrift and hard work: "I hope, my lad... you will prosper and rise in the world. You know in this free country poverty is no bar to a man's achievement."[9]

J.G. Brown's paintings of matchsellers, flower girls, and happy bootblacks, the last represented in *A Tough Story*, 1886 (North Carolina Museum of Art) [Fig. 5] were the visual counterpart of Alger's stories. Rarely are we shown the pathos of child beggary, as in so many European paintings. Brown's paintings reassured his patrons that life was happy, that the American dream was true, that young beggar children were about to come into good fortune. Brown convinced at least one writer, Estelle M. Hurll, who prefaced her praises of the artist's paintings, in her book *Child Life in Art* (1894), with the following remarks:

> The American street boy is a distinct type: his ambition is to
> rise in the world. Wealth, fame, and power may be his, if he
> will but labor to attain them, and to this end he throws himself ardently into the building of a career.... His duties done,
> he is a gentleman of leisure.... Possessed of a lively imagination and a keen sense of humor, he is never at a loss for a
> source of fun.[10]

The stark reality and hardships of child laborers remained for the photographers—Jacob Riis and Lewis Hine—to record at the turn of the century.

         *   *   *

The subjects in the paintings discussed so far are small farmers, craftsmen, and tradesmen. Very few images of actual industrial workers appeared in the fine arts in the early part of the century. Bass Otis's *Interior of a Smithy* of about 1815 (Pennsylvania Academy of the Fine Arts, Philadelphia) [Fig. 6] represents an industrial work place, but the figures are incidental, inserted to give perspective and scale to the vast interior. As a document it compares with the lithographs and wood engravings of the period used in books to illustrate the skilled trades or in journal articles to describe new inventions.[11]

John Ferguson Weir's *The Gun Foundry* of 1864-66 (Putnam County Historical Society, Cold Spring, New York) [Fig. 7] was probably the first ambitious effort by an American artist to paint an industrial scene, although scenes were then being painted in England and on the Continent.[12] Weir chose a site close to his family's home—the West Point Iron and Cannon Foundry at Cold Spring, New York, where munitions were produced for the northern armies during the Civil War. At this moment a Parrott gun is being cast.[13] Weir later wrote of his work on the painting:

> I began to arrange the composition of "The Gun Foundry" in a large charcoal cartoon; assembling the masses, the big round furnace-stack and the cranes and rafters of the dusky place, with the foundrymen all in busy action absorbed in the work; the interior lit up by a glow of a great cauldron of molten-iron swung by a heavy crane to be tipped while the ropy metal was poured into the moulding-flask—which stood on end in a deep pit where a gun was to be cast.... I thus secured an initial arrangement which required nearly two years to realize in the finished painting, with the workmen of the place for models in further visits to the foundry.[14]

In Weir's dramatically lit painting the cavernous interior of furnaces and machinery dominates the workers heroically engaged in controlling the swinging cauldron. When exhibited at the National Academy of Design in 1866, many critics declared it one of the year's outstanding canvases. The work was purchased by Robert Parker Parrott, superintendent of the foundry and inventor of the Parrott gun. Parrott was so pleased by the painting's critical acclaim that he raised his original offer of $2,000 to $5,250. In the picture Parrott, his wife, the former superintendent Gouvenour Kemble, and Kemble's sister make up the group of visitors to the foundry.[15] They seem particularly insignificant as they witness this awesome scene of industrial power, yet

Fig. 6. Bass Otis, *Interior of a Smithy*, 1815. Pennsylvania Academy of the Fine Arts, Gift of the Artist.

Fig. 7. John Ferguson Weir, *The Gun Foundry*, 1866. Collection: Putnam County Historical Society.

as small as Parrott is in Weir's composition, he still controls the opera-. tion.

Weir painted another scene of the foundry in 1867 entitled *Forging the Shaft: A Welding Heat,* which represented the forging of a propeller shaft for an ocean liner. Some critics saw the painting as a metaphor for the rebuilding of post-Civil War America. The work was purchased by H.W. Derby, a New York publisher, for $4,000.[16] To Weir, the painting suggested a sublimely poetic image, and on one romantically stormy night he composed a Poe-like description of it, which goes in part:

> ...smiths do swing these great hung masses,
> glowing hot with flaming gas's—
> from the furnace to the anvil—
> to the anvil 'neath the hammer—
> Then in anger it sputters—
> as it's hammered into shape—
> like a thing of life it mutters—groan and sputters,
> sputters flaming drops of sweat.[17]

If Weir's two works aspired to the awesome sublime, then Winslow Homer's *Morning Bell* of about 1873 (Yale University Art Gallery) [Fig. 8] flirts with a pastoral mood. The historian of American art Barbara Novak described these women as milkmaids in her book *American Painting of the Nineteenth Century* (1969). A closer examination reveals that these maids are factory women trudging along the ramp to the mill at the left, from which sounds the morning bell. The rustic setting and the title suggest to us the beginning of a pleasant day, but from contemporary accounts, the New England factory system was hardly idyllic. The lone woman proceeds up the ramp at a slow, steady pace, while her companions hang behind. Even the dog, its head down and its tail drooping, reinforces the somber joylessness inherent in the subject.

If one has no knowledge of social history, women's history, or labor history one might readily misinterpret this scene. One of the problems (some might say "joys") of a painting's appeal to our sensuous responses is that when we come under its spell, we suspend our historical understanding of the social and political content of art. The combinations of color and form manipulated by the artist delight the connoisseur in us and thereby veil the content. We see, as Novak points out, the "rather startling diagonal ramp... [which] suggests Homer's familiarity with the Japanese predilection for abrupt diagonal perspectives," and "Homer's treatment of sunlight dotting the flowers and rocks in the foreground."[18]

The sensuousness of oil painting is less overt in black and white illustrations. For example, when we compare the wood engraving, also called *The Morning Bell,* reproduced in *Harper's Weekly* of December

13, 1873 [Fig.9], we see a depressing image. In that black and white illustration the women drag themselves to work accompanied by a man and a boy; one woman turns her head to confront us with the reality of her situation.[19]

Again, the relationship of picture to audience is important. The oil version of *The Morning Bell* would have been destined for a collector wanting picturesqueness; but the illustration was aimed at a popular audience looking for information. That audience got that information not only in the illustration but also in the unsigned, accompanying poem inspired by it, a poem important enough as a cultural document to be published here in full:

The Morning Bell

Not the late bell which rouses from sweet dreams
    Some fair young sleeper in her downy bed,
And bids her rise to spend the new-born day
    'Neath folly's rule, by fashion's sceptre led;

Not the sweet bell which in the church tower hangs,
    And calls with silvery tongue the hour of prayer—
Not that; for in response to its dear tones
    The weary ones would find their rest from care.

Ah, no! 'tis but the heavy factory bell,
    Which takes its tone from factory noise and din,
And wearily responding to its call,
    Beyond a day of hardship must begin!

And slowly in the well-worn, toilsome path
    Go those whose paths seem ever cast in shade,
While others reap the sunshine of their toil:
    By these the factory bell must be obeyed.

And so the morning bell rings ever on,
    And so the weary feet obey its call,
Till o'er the earth silence at least shall come,
    And death bring peace and rest alike to all.

Although the poem contrasts the mill workers with others who "reap the sunshine of their toil," there is no suggestion of a social change that might alter these circumstances. Typical of the nineteenth-century attitudes of liberal art patrons is the sentiment expressed in the final two lines assuring us that in death comes equality.[20]

        *   *   *

In the last two decades of the nineteenth-century several artists began to focus on the urban proletariat with an unsentimental compassion for their circumstances. The industrial proletariat became a viable subject not because the patrons of art wanted it—the men who had the

Fig. 8. Winslow Homer, *The Morning Bell*, circa 1873. Collection: Yale University Art Gallery, Bequest of Stephen Carlton Clark, B.A. 1903.

Fig. 9. Winslow Homer, *The Morning Bell*, wood engraving for *Harper's Weekly* (December 13, 1873). Collection: Yale University Art Gallery.

money to buy art and to preserve it—but because artists were drawn to ideas of socialism.

After the revolutions in Europe of 1848 a number of socialists, mostly German, came to the United States. But politically radical ideas spread slowly among English-speaking American artists and writers, and not until 1882 did an English edition of Karl Marx and Frederick Engels' *The Communist Manifesto* appear. Eleanor Marx and Edward Aveling in the second edition of *The Working-Class Movement in America,* published in 1891, complained that there was no *Uncle Tom's Cabin* of wage slavery.[21] Although this statement was not altogether true, certainly there were no major novels critical of the capitalist system on' the order of Zola's *Germinal* (1885). And there were no grand salon paintings showing workers oppressed by the capitalist system equivalent to those such as Mihaly von Munkaczy's *Arrest of the Night Tramps,* 1872 (Hungarian National Gallery, Budapest); Hubert von Herkomer's *Eventide in the Westminster General,* 1878 (Walker Art Gallery, Liverpool); or Luke Fildes' *Applicants for Admission to a Casual Ward* (Royal Holloway College, University of London), which was exhibitd at the Centennial Exposition in Philadelphia in 1876.[22]

When we investigate the American easel paintings of industrial workers done in the final decades of the nineteenth century, we discover that the artists who painted them had a connection to the socialist movement. In 1880 Thomas Anshutz visited Wheeling, West Virginia, and sketched workers in the local iron factory. *Ironworkers —Noontime* (The Fine Arts Museums of San Francisco) [Fig. 10], the result of these studies, captures a number of men standing in various poses, with many stripped to the waist, under the glare of the noonday sun. Modern day art historians have tended to discuss the formal aspects of the painting—but a nineteenth-century audience would have seen among the grown men four young boys washing by the water pump and scampering behind the central figures. In 1880 the official statistics for gainfully employed children between the ages of ten to fifteen was set at 1,118,535; by 1900, the number had risen to 1,750,178.[23] While 'the urban middle classes—the subjects of the American painters William Merrit Chase, Edmund Tarbell, and Childe Hassam—were getting richer, the poor got poorer. Weekly wages decreased during the 1870's, particularly after the depression of 1873; and in most poor, working families even the children had to work. The biographers of Anshutz have confirmed but have been vague about the specifics of Anshutz's involvement with socialism, although it is clear that he endorsed the Socialist Party ticket in 1908.[24] Given the times, the very fact that Anshutz painted *Ironworkers* suggests a predisposition to socialism as early as the 1880's. Anshutz was unable to sell the painting until 1883, when the prominent collector and dealer Thomas B. Clarke purchased the painting.[25]

Fig. 10 Thomas Anshutz, *Ironworkers—Noontime*, 1880-81. The Fine Arts Museums of San Francisco, Gift of Mr. and Mrs. John D. Rockefeller 3rd.

Robert Koehler's parents emigrated from Germany to Milwaukee in 1854 when Robert was less than four years old. His family was sympathetic to socialist ideas and when he returned to Germany for his art training, he was caught up in the movement. In 1885, he showed *The Socialist* at the National Academy of Design—a picture depicting a fiery orator vehemently gesticulating to make a political point. The following year he exhibited *The Strike* [Fig. 11] at the National Academy of Design. The *New York Times* reviewer described the work at length, admiring the realism but critical of the moralizing:

> Mr. Koehler has done well to show the earnest group of sweating workmen, quite possibly with justice on their side, but ready, some of them, to take the law in their own hands.... He has contrasted with them fairly well the prim capitalist. But in trying to rouse our sympathies with a beggar woman his moral gets heavy.... All the same, "The Strike" is the most significant work of this Spring exhibition.[26]

The painting, with all its didacticism, seems to be one of the first to depict not just the dignity of labor (a concept developed during the rise of the bourgeoisie) but also the class struggle of a group of workers against the industrialist. Koehler shows many degrees of commitment from militant anger to puzzled questioning among workers and their wives, with the firmly committed strikers arguing to achieve solidarity.[27]

Harper's Weekly reproduced *The Strike* as a centerfold in its issue of May 1, 1886, the day that labor leaders across the country designated to agitate openly for the eight-hour day. On May Day a general strike began; the climax came on May 3 at the McCormick-Harvester works, when the police rushed a crowd of locked-out workers, killing one and mortally wounding four or five others. The following day a protest rally held at Haymarket Square was sabotaged when someone threw a bomb at an advancing squadron of police sent in to break up the final group of demonstrators. When seven policemen were killed and others injured, the police retaliated and consequently killed four in the crowd. In the weeks following, anarchist leaders were rounded up and put on trial. A general anti-red hysteria swept Chicago and all labor leaders were considered anarchists.[28] The pictures in the popular establishment press seem to be unanimously anti-labor. Thomas Nast showed the anarchists as bloodthirsty crazed men in his *Harper's Weekly* illustrations.

During the Progressive Era, after the turn of the century, liberal reformers paid more attention to the conditions under which the working class lived and worked. A gradual change of consciousness affected the patrons of art, and many began to appreciate images of industrial workers, particularly those shown in harmonious relationship with management and the machinery of industry. Not surprisingly, a

Fig. 11. Robert Koehler, *The Strike*, 1886. Collection Lee Baxandall.

number of artists began receiving commissions from municipal and state governments to paint murals of workers characteristic of the local industries. Of course, strikes were not deemed appropriate for such public murals. Edwin Austin Abbey designed the 22 by 38 foot mural *The Spirit of Vulcan, the Genius of the Workers in Iron and Steel,* executed between 1904 and 1908, for the State Capitol rotunda in Harrisburg, Pennsylvania. Vulcan, the Roman god of workers and industry, looks down over a group of broad-shouldered men, stripped to the waist, and toiling in the heat of the furnaces. A few years later in 1911, Everett Shinn painted a 22 by 45 foot mural for the City Hall Council Chambers of Trenton, New Jersey, representing steel production and pottery making, two of the major industries of the Trenton area.[29]. Indeed, the harmoniousness of labor and capital has become a major theme in the post-entrepreneurial era.

It becomes more and more evident as the decades passed into the twentieth century that the image of labor most truthful to the point of view and real-life conditions of the laboring classes came from those artists who, if they did not embrace socialism, at least rejected the values and attitudes of the wealthy classes. In other words, these artists rejected as false the notion that the virtuous and communal life could only be found on the farm; second, they found the idealization of craft irrelevant in an age of mechanization; and third, they questioned whether the entrepreneurial spirit as transformed by capitalism would make a better life for all.

Although ideas about social revolution may have been too strong for American artists, many of whom still hoped to sell their paintings to wealthy patrons, the ideas and values of the progressive movement which emphasized reforms had a strong, positive appeal. At that time only the most blatant social Darwinist, greedy capitalist, flighty society debutante, or highly paid artist refused to recognize the need for reforms in housing and working conditions. Most artists and photographers, like the other urban intelligentsia of the time, shared the general criticisms.

The photographers lead the way in the production of new images and the development of new themes. Jacob Riis, one reformer working as a journalist, took up the camera in order to illustrate more faithfully his articles about the actual conditions in the slums [see Fig. 12]. When artists translated the photographs into drawings for Riis's installments in *Scribner's*, the images of slum life acquired a picturesqueness contradicting the reality. But by 1890, when many of the articles were collected into the book *How the Other Half Lives,* technology had advanced to the point where the photographs themselves could be published. Those half-tone photographs with their fidelity to sordid detail confirmed Riis's scathing prose.

Lewis Hine, a teacher at the Ethical Culture School, took up the camera in the early years of the 1900's in order to teach his students about the ethnic pluralism of America. Hine left that job in order to work for the National Child Labor Committee and spent a couple of years photographing the squalid conditions under which children and youth worked. He wrote descriptions of each photograph which accompanied the pictures when they were set up at public exhibitions sponsored by the NCLC. The legend on *Child Mill Worker: South Carolina Mill* of 1908 [Fig. 13] reads as follows:

Sadie Pfeifer an undernourished (poor white), 48 inches high, one of many young workers in a Carolina mill. She has worked in this mill half a year. Photo study by Lewis W. Hine for the National Child Labor Committee.[30]

She is one of the most poignant figures of turn-of-the-century American imagery, and the picture is in marked contrast to Barfoot's lithograph *Spinning* for Darton's *Progress of Cotton* (Yale University Art Gallery) [Fig. 14]. In Hine's work we become aware of the human toll of factory toil. With her arms outstretched the figure forms a triangle—the apex of which is her hauntingly beautiful face. One hand rests on the cotton ring spinning frame—that side is in shadow. Her other hand rests on the window sill. This window illuminates her face, but also symbolizes the freedom to leave the factory, attend school, and live a better life. Caught between the drudgery of poorly paid factory work and the possibility of developing herself, she looks to us to choose her future. Hine's preoccupation in this and other photographs was a "sharpening of vision"; his goal, and his morality, was to "change what needed to be changed."[31]

The painters most closely allied with the spirit of the progressive reform movement were the artist-reporters from Philadelphia—Everett Shinn, George Luks, William Glackens, and John Sloan—who followed the advice of Robert Henri and followed him to New York in the early twentieth century. Like Henri, they undertook to show the "spirit of the people"—the *joie de vivre* of working class life—rather than labor *per se*. However, Henri's *Working Man* of 1910 (John D. Rockefeller 3rd Collection) and George Luks' *The Miner* (National Gallery of Art) show the dignity and pride of working-class men. Such paintings were considered very radical compared with the genteel paintings of William Merritt Chase, Edmund Tarbell, and Frank Benson. When the young realists Sloan, Luks, Glackens, and Shinn exhibited with Henri in the famous exhibition "The Eight," held at the Macbeth Gallery in 1908, they were referred to in the press as the "black revolutionaries."

The most talented of the group was John Sloan, who celebrated the camaraderie of the working classes at their leisure, such as *Picnic Grounds* of 1906-07 (Whitney Museum of American Art) and *South Beach Bathers* of 1908 (Walker Art Center, Minneapolis). His paintings, however, rarely show paid labor, with an exception being his *Scrub Women, Astor Library* of 1910 (Munson-Williams-Proctor In-

Fig. 12. Jacob A. Riis, *Iroquois Indians at 511 Broome Street*, early 1890's. Photograph. Museum of the City of New York, Jacob A. Riis Collection.

Fig. 13. Lewis Hine, *Child Mill Worker, South Carolina, Mill*, 1908. Photograph. Collection of Naomi and Walter Rosenblum.

stitute, Utica, New York) [Fig. 15]. Although Sloan was a Socialist Party member from abut 1908 to around 1916, even running for office on the Socialist Party ticket, he felt strongly that he should not put "propaganda" into his art.[32]

Sloan, however, felt no hesitation about drawing vivid graphic cartoons for *The Call*, a Socialist newspaper, and *The Masses*, the radical monthly edited by Max Eastman. Sloan was, in fact, the unpaid art editor of *The Masses* from about 1913 through 1915, after which his involvement waned. Sloan submitted a drawing (Sloan Archives, Delaware Art Museum) to *The Call*, where it was published on March 26, 1911, the day after the tragic fire at the Triangle Shirtwaist Company took the lives of 154 women. The employers had bolted the second door at the factory loft in lower Manhattan, the only exit not consumed by advancing flames. When the women found they could not escape, many panicked and jumped seven or eight stories to their deaths. Sloan was outraged.

An equally powerful image is Sloan's cover for *The Masses* of June 1914, [Fig. 16] illustrating Max Eastman's "Class War in Colorado," an account of the Ludlow Massacre when Rockefeller agents set torches to the tents of striking miners' families whose homes had been repossessed by Rockefeller's mining company during a prolonged strike. In Sloan's illustration the miner fights back with a smoking gun in his hand while his other arm holds his still smoldering child, with charred arms, a motif also seen in the Triangle fire illustration. Such an image of a worker fighting back was most unusual for the times; however, we must remember that the patrons were the radical magazine editors and their subscribers. For the July 1914 cover of *The Masses* Sloan represented John D. Rockefeller, Jr., trying to wash the blood from his hands as workers attempt to crash down the bolted door behind him.

By far, the largest group of paintings depicting labor come from the Depression Era—the 1930's. Both the bad economic situation and the growth of the Left were conditions favoring the development of labor themes. The range of subject matter in the murals, easel paintings, and sculpture stretched across all forms of employment—mining, steel and automotive, construction, transportation, farming, textiles, and domestic and service work. The point of view was at times harmonious with Roosevelt's New Deal policies, particularly in the murals,[33] but there was also a radicalized worker's point of view revealed in many easel paintings, prints, and illustrations. Thus, strikes, battles with the police, and unemployment became frequent subjects for socially concerned artists. Not all paintings with a worker's viewpoint were grim; many artists chose to paint the happier aspects of workers' lives—the camaraderie of men and women, black and white, united and equal in their struggles to create a better life.[34]

An important element in this expansion of subject matter was a change of patronage from private wealth to the public domain. Be-

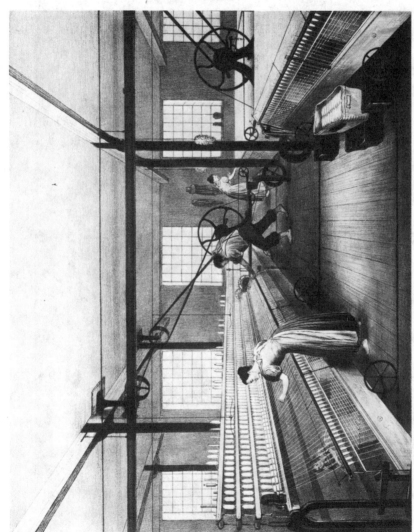

Fig. 14. Barfoot for Darton's *Progress of Cotton: #6, Spinning.* Collection: Yale University Art Gallery, Mabel Brady Garvan Collection.

Fig. 15. John Sloan, *Scrubwomen, Astor Library*, 1910. Munson-Williams-Proctor Institute, Utica, New York.

Fig. 16. John Sloan, *Class War in Colorado,* cover illustration for *The Masses,* June 1914. Delaware Art Museum, John Sloan Collection.

ginning in 1933 with the New Deal, government agencies were established to give relief to workers, including the fine and performing artists.[35] First there was the Public Works of Art Project set up in December 1933. During its seven-month existence the PWAP employed 3,749 artists across the country. Also set up was the Treasury Section of Painting and Sculpture which awarded commissions on the basis of competitions, not need, for murals and sculptures placed in post offices across the country and in federal buildings in Washington, D.C., (Some 1,400 murals were created). Finally, the Works Progress Administration set up Federal Project No. 1, which consisted of four cultural projects—Art, Music, Theater, and Writers. At the height of its operation in 1936, the Federal Art Project employed over 5,000 artists and art teachers.[36]

The murals commissioned by the Treasury Section for federal buildings, including post offices, and by the FAP for municipal buildings, including schools, hospitals, and airports, were a particularly notable achievement. Given the source of funding and the social climate of the time, it is not surprising that the content of the murals is the productivity of Americans from colonial to modern times, with regional boosterism often implicit. A mood of optimism pervades most of these murals. Small-time commodity production, craft and artisanry, and individual entrepreneurialism were themes recognized as more appropriate for the historical murals. For contemporary murals modern farming was the subject of many post office murals in small rural communities. In the bigger cities contemporary scenes focussed on modern cooperative, industrial work, such as William Gropper's mural *Construction of the Dam* of 1937 [see Fig. 17].[37] Such scenes can be found in the easel paintings and graphics as well. Charles Keller was then a young student at the Art Students' League. He was encouraged to go out and sketch workers; the result was a series of lithographs, such as *Tunnel Heading (6th Avenue Subway)* of 1939 [Fig. 18], printed under the supervision of Harry Sternberg.

Productivity meant technological progress, and progressives were optimistic this would translate into human progress. Charles Alston's two murals for Harlem Hospital represented progress in medicine. *Magic,* depicting the older traditional and tribal ways, contrasted with *Modern Medicine,* showing the modern hospital where doctors, nurses, and technicians work together to advance medical science. But because Alston, a black artist, included blacks in his two murals he was criticized by bureaucrats, and the commission was temporarily held up.[38].

For public murals (paid for by the Government) subject matter which contradicted the themes of productivity and progress were discouraged. Local business and mining interests criticized Fletcher Martin when he designed a panel for the Post Office at Kellogg, Idaho. His

Fig. 17. William Gropper, *Construction of the Dam*, 1937. Oil study for mural. National Museum of American Art, Smithsonian Institution, Transfer from the U.S. Department of the Interior, National Park Service.

Fig. 18. Charles Keller, *Tunnel Heading (6th Avenue Subway),* 1939. Lithograph. Collection the Artist.

study, *Mine Disaster*, [Fig. 19], showed two miners removing a third injured miner from a mine shaft. Martin was obliged to substitute a more innocuous image of a prospector,[39] the Western counterpart to the Eastern entrepreneurial peddler.

In general, the easel painters employed by the WPA/FAP had fewer worries about censorship. The paintings they submitted to the local FAP offices were not destined for the homes of the wealthy; but, rather, would be placed in schools, hospitals, public buildings, and of-fices where people with attitudes and values like themselves would be able to view them. Moreover, FAP painters now had the economic security to paint additional pictures beyond their required quotas— paintings which they sent off to exhibitions for viewing by both an art and a general public. Never before *or since* in the history of American art have so many talented artists felt freed from the pressures to paint what an elite patronage demanded. These issues—the economic security of the artist, the patronage, and the destination of the art-work—should be no more overlooked in the 1930's than in the earlier periods.

A critical realism developed—first called "revolutionary art" in the 1929-35-period, because artists did not want to settle for a mere por-trayal of the common man but hoped in their art to promote class struggle. In terms of art, these painters were inspired by Goya, Daumier, and the paintings of the Mexican muralists: Diego Rivera, Jose Clemente Orozco, and David Siqueiros, all of whom lived in the United States for extended periods during the 1930's and who had successfully incorporated their revolutionary ideas into their art. Poli-tically, the American artists were drawn to the ideas of the Communist Party, vigorously discussed in the meetings of the John Reed Clubs. Some joined the Party while others were simply sympathetic to the goal of a better and egalitarian world. (Reginald Marsh, for example, was a liberal whose paintings of strike situations, workers, and dere-licts brought him close to the temper of the more politically orthodox painters.) Later the term "social art" was used, particularly in the years after 1935, when the Communist Party entered the Popular Front period, and when talk of revolution was replaced by the urgent appeal to fight fascism.[40]

Whatever the strategies of the Communist Party, most socially con-cerned artists throughout the 1930's persisted in painting pictures which reflected their own views of American society. Some of these artists stressed the deleterious effects of capitalism, such as unemploy-ment and homelessness. Unemployment, visualized as the endless waiting of people in agencies or on park benches, was the subject of O. Louis Guglielmi's *Relief Blues* of 1937 (National Museum of American Art) [Fig. 20], Isaac Soyer's *Employment Agency* of 1937 (Whitney Museum of American Art) [Fig. 21], and Raphael Soyer's *Study for the Unemployed* (Boston University) [Fig. 22].

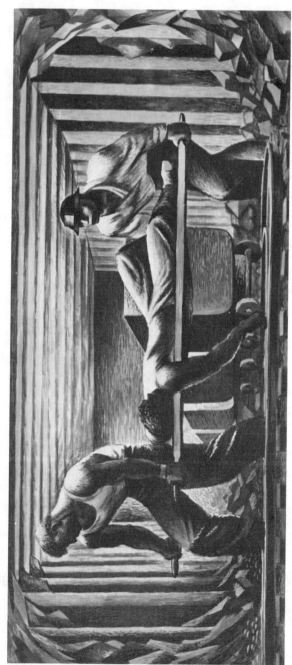

Fig. 19. Fletcher Martin, *Mine Rescue* (Study for Kellogg, Idaho, Post Office), 1939. The Art Gallery, University of Maryland, College Park, Maryland.

Fig. 20. O. Louis Guglielmi, *Relief Blues*, 1937. National Museum of American Art, Smithsonian Institution, Washington, DC, Transfer from the Museum of Modern Art.

While many of these paintings showed the alienation or helplessness of workers, others showed the tensions of class antagonisms.[41] The theme of strike violence became as common as the strikes themselves in the mid-1930's. In Guglielmi's *American Dream* of 1935 (Private Collection) one worker lies sprawled on the ground with his sign "Workers of the World Unite" next to him. In Henry Billings's *The Arrest* of 1936 (D. Wigmore Fine Art, Inc.) a female picket resists arrest by two poliemen. Alice Neel witnessed an attack by mounted policemen on Uneeda Bisquit workers in her New York City neighborhood and painted *Uneeda Bisquit Strike* in 1936. In William Gropper's *Youngstown Strike* of about 1937 (Gropper Estate), a group of workers stand together when attacked by the police. The theme of collective worker unity was also the message of Philip Evergood's *American Tragedy* of 1937 (Private Collection) [Fig. 23], based on news photos of the "Memorial Day Massacre" of 1937, when police fired on a crowd of striking workers at the South Chicago plant of Republic Steel. Evergood's painting goes beyond Sloan's *Masses* cover of the Ludlow miner; a militant Hispanic woman joins center stage with the fighting man, making explicit the multiracial unity of the workers.[42].

A less violent image of factory life is Evergood's *Through the Mill* of 1940 (Whitney Museum of American Art), where the artist used the strategy of contrast, heightening the contradictions between the grim lives of the workers at the mill and their modest housing with the grand mansion on the hill belonging to the factory owner. As someone close to the Communist Party, Evergood believed that capitalism had failed, and he painted some very gruesome anti-capitalist paintings. But he also maintained an optimism about the future possibilities of life.

Pictures of the future possibilities invariably included images of multi-racial camaraderie. In 1979 Joseph Hirsch recalled with special fondness that forty years previous his 1937 painting *Two Men* (The Museum of Modern Art), showing a black man vigorously discussing some issues while a white man listens, had been voted the most popular at the 1939 New York World's Fair.[43] Mervin Jules' *The Common Man* (Hirshhorn Museum and Sculpture Garden, Smithsonian Institution) [Fig. 24] also draws on this theme, and Evergood's *The Future Belongs to Them* of 1938-53 (Private Collection) depicts black and white women and men sharing their children with one another.

The boldest image of all is Evergood's *New Birth, New Struggle* of 1947 [Fig. 25] which deals positively with miscegenation. The white woman has given birth to the tan-skinned baby while her proud husband, the black man, beams. The two white, fellow workers dressed in their workers' clothes and hard hats reach out in joy toward the newborn babe. Here is no nostalgia for the past, no heroicizing of the

Fig. 21. Isaac Soyer, *Employment Agency*, 1937. Collection of Whitney Museum of American Art.

Fig. 22. Raphael Soyer, *Study for the Unemployed,* late 1930's. Boston University, Department of Special Collections.

individual, but a vision of a multiracial future when the most important production engaging human beings is the creation of their own progeny.

After the war, the mood changed. America entered the period of the Cold War, and social realists of leftist tendencies were red-baited and subjected to McCarthyite harrassment. It is no coincidence that during a period of government witchhunts many artists turned away from realistic renderings of society.[44] Moreover, the dealers and critics promoted abstract and non-objective art, and soon this new abstraction dominated the art world. Themes of work almost disappeared. Many of the remaining realist artists turned to the psychological anxieties of ordinary people, such as we find in the paintings of George Tooker.[45]

Fortunately the tradition of labor images did not altogether die. From the 1950's to the present (or until their own death dates) a number of older artists including Raphael Soyer, Joseph Hirsch, Anton Refregier, Ben Shahn, Philip Reisman, Jack Levine, Jacob Lawrence, William Gropper, Charles White, Stanley Meltzoff, and many others have continued to paint pictures in which "ordinary people" and workers are represented. Many of their patrons come from the tradition of the old Left. Younger artists such Harvey Dinnerstein and Jack Beal have also frequently returned to images of workers.[46] In sculpture Edward Kienholz's environments, George Segal's life-sized plaster figures, and Duane Hanson's meticulously detailed, polychromed polyvinyl figures are almost always working-class subjects. Because of the stereotyping inherent in Hanson's figures, and the way they almost force an audience into feelings of superiority, Hanson's figures are less than satisfying as images of labor.

In more recent years the anti-war movement has inspired artists to paint pictures of protest, but because working-class issues are not primary to the movement, there are few images of workers. The civil rights movement and the anti-racist campaigns elicited more paintings of workers—particularly black workers—from such New York artists as Benny Andrews and Faith Ringgold. In Boston, Arnold Trachtman did a number of paintings based on the riots which erupted when racists attempted to disrupt the desegregation of Boston schools.

The reason so few "fine arts" easel paintings are done of workers today revolves around the old question of patronage. Although adventurous dealers and innovative museum curators may exhibit such paintings and social-issue exhibitions might welcome them,[47] rarely are worker-related paintings bought by museums, private collectors, and by the newest entrant into the patronage system—the private corporation. The people who might be interested—the workers, union officials, students, and intelligentsia—cannot afford the prices which artists set on oil and acrylic paintings. If they can afford art at all, this

Fig. 23. Philip Evergood, *American Tragedy*, 1937. Private Collection.

Fig. 24. Mervin Jules, *The Common Man*, early 1940's. Hirshhorn Museum and Sculpture Garden, Smithsonian Institution.

sympathetic patronage group buys the posters, prints, and photographs within their means—or they encourage the street muralists responsive to community aspirations. We thus return as always to the issue of patronage, which is at the heart of cultural studies, and that familiar adage: "He who pays the piper calls the tune."

NOTES

I expanded the paper delivered at the 1982 Lowell Conference into a long essay translated into German and published as "Zwischen Realismus und Balsam fur die Gemuter gehetzter Geschaftsleute: Anmerkungen zu Arbeitsdarstellungen in die bildenden Kunst der USA seit 1800," in Philip S. Foner and Reinhard Schultz, eds. *Das Andere Amerika: Geschichte, Kunst und Kultur der amerikanischen Arbeiterbewegung* (Berlin: Neuen Gesellschaft fur Bildende Kunst, 1983), pp. 348-378. The present paper refines the argument presented in the German version expanding some sections and reducing others.

I want to thank the Charles Warren Center for Studies in American History, Harvard University, where I was a fellow during 1982-83, for providing me with research facilities.

[1]   Because of slavery it is not surprising to find few paintings of labor themes done by and for southerners.
[2]   Anonymous, *The Crayon* (June 1859), p. 189, quoted in Patricia Hills, *The Genre Painting of Eastman Johnson: The Sources and Development of His Style and Themes,* (New York: Garland Publishing Co., 1977), p. 57.
[3]   There was, or course, the aristocratic element, the landed gentry within the ruling elite of America, but such patrons tended to buy not genre paintings but, rather, history painting, portraits, still life, and, particularly in the post-Civil War era, foreign art.
[4]   Herbert G. Gutman, in *Work, Culture, and Society in Industrializing America: Essays in American Working-Class and Social History* (New York: Vintage, 1977), p. 13, maintains: "In the half-century after 1843 industrial development radically transformed the earlier American social structure, and during this... [period] a profound tension existed between the older American preindustrial social stucture and the modernizing institutions that accompanied the development of industrial capitalism. After 1893 the United States ranked as a mature industrial society."
[5]   Many of the paintings discussed here are reproduced in Patricia Hills, *The Painters' America: Rural and Urban Life, 1810-1910* (New York: Praeger Publishers, 1974). See also Foner and Schultz, *Das Andere Amerika;* Hermann Warner Williams, Jr., *Mirror to the American Past: A Survey of American Genre Painting: 1750-1900* (Greenwich, CT: New York Graphic Society Ltd., 1972); and Smithsonian Institution, Traveling Exhibition Service, *The Working American* (Washington, DC: Smithsonian Institution, 1979) [exhibition organized by Abigail Booth Gerdts, with introduction by Patricia Hills]. My thesis in *The Painters' America,* p. 137, is that genre painting "represented neither conditions nor events, neither the typical nor the specific, but an artful blend of fact and fantasy, of realities and dreams. The genre painting that has survived and has been treasured reassured its select audience of a continuity between the past and the present. But the paintings did not simply serve their patrons as a nostalgic respite from the pressures of the day. Widely exhibited and reproduced, many also contributed to and perpetuated nationalistic and elitist attitudes which are with us still."

Fig. 25. Philip Evergood, *New Birth, New Struggle*, 1947. Private Collection

6 Lizzie W. Champney, "The Summer Haunts of American Artists," *The Century Magazine* 30 (September 1885)), p. 854, quoted in Hills, *Genre Painting of Eastman Johnson, p. 144.*

7 William Walton, "Eastman Johnson, Painter," *Scribner's Magazine* 40 (1906), p. 270, quoted in Hills, *Genre Painting of Eastman Johnson,* p. 150.

8 The author is presently expanding a paper, "Images of Rural America in the Work of Eastman Johnson, Winslow Homer, and Their Contemporaries," presented in November 1982 at the Joslyn Art Museum, Omaha, and which will be published in their collection of essays, edited by Hollister Sturgis *The Rural Vision: France and America in the Late-Nineteenth Century.*

9 Horatio Alger, Jr., *Ragged Dick and Mark, the Match Boy* (New York: Collier Books, 1962 [reprint]), p. 108, quoted in Hills, *The Painter's America, p. 115.*

10 Estelle M. Hurll, *Child Life in Art* (Boston: L.C. Page & Company, 1894), p. 106.

11 The present discussion on Otis, Weir, and Homer has been expanded from the author's introduction, "The Working American," in Smithsonian Institution Traveling Exhibition Service, *The Working American.*

12 See F.D. Klingender, *Art and the Industrial Revolution,* ed. and rev. by Arthur Elton (New York: Schocken Books, 1970) [first published in 1947].

13 See Betsy Fahlman, "John Ferguson Weir: Painter of Romantic and Industrial Icons," *Archives of American Art Journal* 20, No. 2 (1980), p. 2.

14 Quoted in The Metropolitan Museum of Art, *19th-Century America: Paintings and Sculpture,* introduction by John K. Howat and John Wilmerding (New York: The Metropolitan Museum of Art, 1970), Entry 133.

15 See Fahlman, "John Ferguson Weir," pp. 4 and 5. I want to remind the reader of the significance of the $5,250 figure. According to the Bureau of the Census, *Historical Statistics of the United States, Colonial Times to 1970* (Washington, DC: U.S. Government Printing Office, 1975), Part 1, p. 165, a blacksmith in 1866 received a daily wage of $2.74; the annual earnings of non-farm employees for 1866 was $489.

16 Fahlman, "John Ferguson Weir," p. 6.

17 John F. Weir Papers, Archives of American Art, Roll 529, frame 937, quoted in Lois Dinnerstein, "The Iron Worker and King Solomon: Some Images of Labor in American Art," *Arts Magazine* 54 (September 1979), p. 115; and in Marianne Doezema, *American Realism and the Industrial Age* (Cleveland: The Cleveland Museum of Art, 1980), p. 16, and Fahlman, "John Ferguson Weir," pp. 5-6.

18 Barbara Novak, *American Painting of the Nineteenth Century* (New York: Praeger Publishers, 1969), p. 167.

19 Another image by Homer of mill workers, *New England Factory Life—"Bell Time,"* was reproduced in *Harper's Weekly,* July 25, 1868.
    For a recent account of mill work and mil life, see Steve Dunwell, *The Run of the Mill: A Pictorial Narrative of the Expansion, Dominion, Decline and Enduring Impact of the New England Textile Industry* (Boston: David R. Godine, 1978).

20 Two years earlier, in 1871, Elizabeth Stuart Phelps wrote *The Silent Partner,* a novel about a mill girl and her lady benefactor, which drew on records of the Massachusetts Bureau of Statistics about mill life. It, too, combined realism with sentimentalism, ending on a religious note.

21 Walter B. Rideout, *The Radical Novel in the United States: 1900-1954* (Cambridge, MA: Harvard University Press, 1956), pp. 9-10.

22 For these reproductions and other relevant works see Edward Lucie-Smith and Celestine Dars, *War and Struggle: The Painter as Witness, 1870-1914* (London: Paddington Press, 1977).

23 Fred A. Shannon, *The Centennial Years: A Political and Economic History of America from the Late 1870s to the Early 1890s,* ed. Robert Huhn Jones (Garden City, Long Island: Anchor Books, 1969), p. 203.

24 See John Sloan's diary entry of December 25, 1908, in *John Sloan's New York Scene,* ed. Bruce St. John (New York: Harper & Row, 1965), p. 273.

25 Sandra Denney Heard, *Thomas P. Anshutz, 1851-1912* (Philadelphia: Pennsylvania Academy of the Fine Arts, 1973), p. 8.
26 *The New York Times*, April 4, 1886, p. 4. Lee Baxandall, the present owner of *The Strike,* rescued the painting from oblivion. I am grateful to him for first bringing the work to my attention and for giving me copies of his research materials, which I quoted in *The Painters' America,* p. 123, as well as in *The Working American,* p. 9.
27 An important painter of labor themes contemporary with Koehler and Anshutz was Charles Frederick Ulrich, but many of his paintings were of European workers.
28 See Shannon, *Centennial Years,* p. 238.
29 Abbey's and Shinn's murals were previously discussed in *The Working American.*
30 Caption accompanying photograph reprinted in Washburn Gallery, *Lewis H. Hine,* catalogue for exhibition held at the Washburn Gallery, 820 Madison Avenue, New York, from October 23 to November 16, 1974.
31 See Walter Rosenblum, Naomi Rosenblum, Alan Trachtenberg and Israel Marvin, *America & Lewis Hine: Photographs 1904-1940* (New York: The Brooklyn Museum in association with Aperture, 1977).
32 See Patricia Hills, "John Sloan's Images of Working-Class Women: A Case Study of the Roles and Inter-Relationships of Politics, Personality, and Patrons in the Development of Sloan's Art, 1905-1916," *Prospects* 5 (1980), pp. 157-96, where the illustrations discussed here are reproduced.
33 See Karal Ann Marling, "A Note on New Deal Iconography: Futurology and the Historical Myth," *Prospects* 4 (1979), pp. 420-40.
34 For a survey of such paintings, see Patricia Hills, *Social Concern and Urban Realism: American Painting of the 1930s* (Boston: Boston University Art Gallery in conjunction with the National Union of Hospital and Health Care Employees and The American Federation of Arts, 1983); for an anthology of relevant readings see David Shapiro, ed., *Social Realism: Art as a Weapon* (New York: Frederick Ungar, 1973).
35 The chronology and statistics stated here are from Francis V. O'Connor, *Federal Support for the Visual Arts: The New Deal and Now* (Greenwich, CT: New York Graphic Society, 1969), and Marlene Park and Gerald E. Markowitz, *New Deal for Art* (Hamilton, NY: Gallery Association of New York State, Inc., 1977).
36 During its entire existence the WPA/FAP alone produced some 2,500 murals, over 17,000 sculptures, 108,000 paintings, 200,000 prints from 11,000 designs, 2 million silkscreen posters from 35,000 designs, and more than 22,000 plates for the Index of American Design. About two million children were taught in WPA classes. The 5,000 figure for artists and art teachers is also impressive, considering that there were (according to the Bureau of the Census, *Historical Statistics,* Part 1, p. 140) only about 57,000 artists and art teachers in the country in 1930, and only 66,000 in 1940.
37 For a discussion of conflicts among the artists, their patrons (Edward Bruce and his staff at the Treasury Section), and their audience (the small-town politicians and citizens), see Karal Ann Marling, *Wall-to-Wall America: A Cultural History of Post-Office Murals in the Great Depression* (Minneapolis: University of Minnesota Press, 1982), which contains a bibliography of recent regional mural surveys. I was fortunate to read the latest manuscript by Gerald Markowitz and Marlene Park, *The World's Largest Art Gallery,* to be published by Temple University Press, which charts the frequent themes and their regional differences.
38 See Greta Berman, "The Walls of Harlem," *Arts Magazine* 52 (October 1977) pp. 122-26. See also Berman's *The Lost Years: Mural Painting in New York Under the Works Progress Administration's Federal Art Project: 1935 to 1943* (New York: Garland Publishing Co., 1978).
39 See Marling, *Wall-to-Wall America,* pp. 174-82.
40 See Hills, *Social Concern,* pp. 9-25.
41 Paintings such as these are reproduced in Foner and Schultz, *Das Andere Amerika.*
42 See Patricia Hills, "Philip Evergood's *American Tragedy:* The Poetics of Ugliness, the Politics of Anger," *Arts Magazine* 54 (February 1980), pp. 138-43.

[43] Interview with author, September 22, 1979.

[44] See David and Cecile Shapiro, "Abstract Expressionism: The Politics of Apolitical Painting," *Prospects* 3 (1977), pp. 175-214.

[45] For figurative and realist painting done in the post-World War II period, see Patricia Hills and Roberta K. Tarbell, *The Figurative Tradition and the Whitney Museum of American Art* (New York: Whitney Museum of American Art, 1980), and Greta Berman and Jeffrey Wechsler, Realism and Realities: The Other Side of American Painting, 1940-1960 (Rutgers, NJ: Rutgers University Art Gallery, 1982).
Rutgers University Art Gallery, 1982).

[46] Beal has done four mural panels for the U.S. Department of Labor building in Washington, DC.

[47] Moe Foner has initiated several exhibitions, which toured nationally as part of the Bread and Roses Cultural Project of the National Union of Hospital and Health Care Employees, including *The Working American, Images of Labor,* and *Social Concern and Urban Realism.* For *Images of Labor,* he commissioned contemporary artists to submit art work for reproduction in the catalogue of the same title. Foner, during his tenure as Executive Secretary of District 1199, the National Union of Hospital and Health Care Employees, also let outside groups hold exhibitiions at Gallery 1199.

An Artisan-Entrepreneur's Portrait of the Industrializing North, 1790-1860

DAVID P. JAFFEE

Our image of the transformation of the rural North in the ante-bellum years has long been dominated by the clattering of textile mills and the wail of the iron horse, a tale in which the powerful new industrial order swept all in its way. While the endpoints of farm and factory remain familiar signposts, it is harder to see the human experience of industrialization, the way in which the residents of the rural North created a culture of commerce at the village crossroads. Few individuals involved in that process realized that they were participants in the Industrial Revolution.

The life and work of the rural portraitists provide a unique perspective on the process of commercialization in the countryside. They follow in their careers the path of many of the village artisans who emerged from a provincial agrarian economy. These self-taught craftsmen explored numerous opportunities on the roads of the North and picked up their artistic training along the way, from the pages of design books or from their brief encounters with portraitists "of the primitive sort." A large group of portrait-makers combed the countryside and created countless images ranging from stark black and white silhouettes to colorful full length oil paintings. These artisan-entrepreneurs shared the credit for the mass production of objects for the home. They eased the rapid manufacture of likenesses with stylized designs which standardized their product but distinguished their subjects by including personal items. They adopted these labor-saving techniques and used various machines to answer their rural audience's enthusiasm for new cultural commodities. Itinerant portrait-makers traveled the backroads of the rural North because that was where a ready market existed for their services. They created their likenesses of artisans, innkeepers, and improving farmers, because those were the people who shared with the portraitist the era's and the region's desire for symbols of middle class identity.[1]

If to academic onlookers the results looked "cheap and slight," these cultural pioneers constructed from a country schooling and some urban models a village vernacular that suited their training and talents and met their clients' needs and expectations. Decorative display predominated over subtle shading in all forms of rural design. The artisan's informal apprenticeship as a sign and house painter lingered on in the portraitist's reliance upon repetition and two-dimensional depth. But experimentation and innovation were not foreign matters to "the primitive sort." On their travels they incorporated stylistic innovations in their works until a vast rural market existed for products which ranged from mass-produced cheap paper silhouettes to stylized oil canvases. By following these enterprising entrepreneurs we can glimpse into the complex process of individual and cultural change, of how the portrait-maker found his way in the bustling commercialism of the nineteenth century countryside.[2] Artisan and audience joined together at the village center to forge not a new industrial order, but an emerging culture of commerce. Enterprising entrepreneurs welcomed the new opportunities made available by the intensification of craft production in the villages of the North. Progress towards becoming professional artists made some portrait-makers in the rural regions of America stand out in bold relief from the other village entrepreneurs peddling their products on the same terrain. Some even embraced the daguerreotype after its invention in 1839 without imagining the drastic effects which this industrial apparatus would ultimately have on the familiar way of life which these itinerants enjoyed. All these portraitists ironically participated in forwarding changes in the image industry that eventually would make their presence expendable in the villages of the rural North. But in the meantime they brought an era of mass production and consumption to the farmhouse door and diffused a taste for the wide range of newly available cultural commodities.

II

The provincial limner of the eighteenth century led a more circumscribed career in the rural villages than his nineteenth-century counterpart. The portrait-maker made his appearance in the village scene, and a local product, such as Winthrop Chandler, stayed close to home and kept busy painting his family and town notables to go along with his decorative work. Chandler (1747-1790), a valued member of the village community, offered his sign, carriage, and house painting skills to rural neighbors whose farming life he shared. He spent most of his life around Woodstock, Connecticut, venturing off only for a few years for his formal training. When Winthrop came of age his prosperous brother-in-law, who served as his guardian, apprenticed him to learn portrait painting in Boston. Chandler returned to Woodstock, Connecticut, in 1770 to paint his first commissions, the striking pair of portraits of the Reverend Ebenezer Devotion and his wife Martha, who decided to honor Ebenezer's fifty-sixth birthday with these commemorative likenesses. The clergyman's family stood at the top of village society, and Chandler's work displays a strong modeling of the sitter's features, while the clergyman shares his solidity with the mahogany table on which he rests. His ample library, with the titles and bindings meticulously detailed, display in this Puritan culture and testified to his status as a learned professional and significant member of the community.[3] Chandler was a versatile artisan in an isolated agricultural village, called upon to paint portraits, landscapes, and houses, as well as to serve as occasional gilder, carver, illustrator, and draftsman. When Chandler died in 1790 the *Massachusetts Spy* noted his valued station in the locality, an honor which rested more on his skills in brightening the exterior walls of Woodstock homes than in providing "lifenesses on canvas" for the interiors:

> Died at Woodstock, Connecticut, Winthrop Chandler of this town, a man whose native genius had been serviceable to the community in which he resided. In profession he was a house painter, but many likenesses on canvas shew he could guide the pencil of a limner[4]

A handful of provincial limners satisfied the demands for portrait-painting in New England society. Winthrop Chandler served the thin crust of the local aristocracy in the locale around his birth-place by providing them with welcome and "correct" images which followed the outlines of the academic art of the period. Chandler, village craftsman, profiled his neighbors with bold line and colorful design—the stock tools of trade of the provincial artisan—and added individualizing details such as books, furniture, and clothes. The portrait-maker, emerging out of the craft traditions of the agrarian economy, added a new visual dimension to the Puritan calling. The next generation of artisan-entrepreneurs would continue Winthrop Chandler's quest to satisfy rural tastes with an artisan's training.

A different experience awaited the generation that came of age after the War for Independence. Pioneers founded communities where access to market and an interest in luxury existed from the very start of settlement. During an era of developing tastes, peddlers brought together producer and consumer in this area of distant villages. Those discontented with the family farm found ample opportunities as itinerant artisans on the roads of the region. Entrepreneurially oriented individuals painted a variety of objects in their efforts to stay afloat amidst the bewildering array of possibilities which awaited the refugee from the farm. Many painted an occasional likeness during their peripatetic days, and a few could claim the title of artist at the end of their progress in the rural regions of the North.

Chester Harding, soon to be one of America's most celebrated portraits painters, recalled in his *Egotistography* that in his childhood his family moved from Massachusetts to the western part of New York, "then an unbroken wilderness." When Chester reached nineteen he thought that "there must be an easier way of getting a living" than clearing the "heavily timbered forest." The right opportunity seemed to present itself when a local mechanic invented a spinning-head and offered Harding the rights to sell the patent in Connecticut. So, "I jumped into my wagon, whipped up my horse, and was soon out of sight of what, at that moment, seemed all the world to me." Leaving home, Harding supported himself during the next few years by relying on the wide range of rural crafts and commerce which existed along the country backroads; he peddled clocks, established a chair manufactory, and tried tavern keeping.[5]

None of these ventures proved very lucrative or held Harding's attention for very long. He served a stint as a house painter in Pittsburgh but in the ensuing slow season he painted signs instead, a skill allied with gilding, an art which he had picked up during his earlier days as a chair-maker. Next he fell in with a portrait-maker named Nelson, "one of the Primitive sort." The artist-artisan of "the primitive sort" existed in great numbers by the nineteenth century. He often entered the revered world of art with little of the rigorous apprenticeship of his provincial predecessors or the august solemnity of his academic peers. Another frontier peddler of notions and profiles, James Guild, recalled his first portrait commission on his journey towards becoming a professional artist:

> Now I went to canadagua. Here I went into a painters shop, one who painted likenesses, and my profiles looked so mean when I saw them I asked him what he would show me one day for, how to distinguish the coulers & he said $5, and I consented to it and then I went to Bloomfield and took a picture of Mr. goodwins painting for a sample on my way. I put up at a tavern and told a Young Lady if she would wash my shirt, I would draw her likeness. Now then I was to exert my skill in painting. I operated once on her but it looked so like a rech I throwed it away and tried again. The poor girl sat niped up so prim and look so smileing it makes me smile when I think of while I was daubing on paint on a piece of paper it could not be caled painting, for it looked more like a strangle cat than it did like her. However I told her it looked like her and she believed it.[6]

Enthusiasm rather than experience served to encourage this generation of pioneer portrait-makers. There existed "a decided disposition for painting in this Country," John Neal, America's first art critic, wrote in 1829,"you can hardly open the door of a best room anywhere, without surprizing or being surprized by the picture of somebody plastered to the wall, and staring at you with both eyes and a bunch of flowers." This multitude of portraits "wretched as they are" flourished "in every village of our country," not as articles for the rich but for everybody, serving as familiar household furniture, embellishing the home. The artist and audience shared together in their "discovery of a new sense." Oftentimes these early efforts "could not be caled painting," as James Guild wrote, "looking more like a strangle cat," so he left his customer with "a profile if not a likeness." Like many others this ambitious fellow catalyzed the rural folk's passion for self-culture, quickly picked up a diverse training in the course of his travels, and diffused a taste for improving traits and consumer goods to his rural neighbors, who were unable to judge fully the merits of these cultural entrepreneurs and their products. For the rural North was still a world of scarcity—of images and commodities—and the ordinary villager, while eager to acquire items previously only available to the town elite, held few among their number expert enough to criticize "the primitive sort" or to afford "the better sort."[7]

III

As the demand for portraits grew at an increasingly wide range of social levels, itinerant artists began to appear throughout the United States. In the 1820's and 1830's, portraitists of every description and level of skill produced images at every price. If their first efforts represented mere copies of "the primitive sort," at least these cultural pioneers' likenesses created a desire for their offerings over a wide expanse of territory. But stylistic developments also had a place in the rural portrait-makers' repertoire. Innovation in rural design occurred within the confines of the villager's purse and the painter's promise. Some artists produced profiles that were crudely composed with the aid of mechanical devices. These mass-produced images appealed to the lower ends of the rural market and were promoted with immense zeal and imagination. Other artisans offered more elaborate representations which were based upon some urban training and an acquaintance with academic models. These portraitists had greater freedom to display their sitters' features and surroundings by the use of stylized designs and conventional details. The portrait-makers met the demands placed upon them by time and price in these higher priced "correct likenesses" with their standardized features while they satisfied the desires of an emerging rural bourgeoisie for more elaborate family icons of their newly won status.

Either way these innovations in mass production made availble to rural residents a greater number of portraits. This cycle of consumption was part of a general "cultural revolution" in which rural residents experienced a remarkable expansion in the number of ideas and items which made their way to the farmhouse door. Entrepreneurs sought a wider market to offer their cheap but elegant copies of objects, previously unavailable to rural householders. The most successful artisan-entrepreneurs to tap this market were the locals. They were the village artisans who mass produced luxury items, such as the Willard Brothers' banjo clocks, at a reasonable price, and village entrepreneurs who promoted an eclectic design, such as Lambert Hitchcock's painted chairs, fashioned from current urban styles and old rural standards. The chair-maker replaced carving with color in decorating country chairs and followed the portraitist in speeding up production. Carpets, clocks, and chairs, along with walls, floors, and doors, all bore these traces of the itinerant artisan's touch. Paint appeared on every conceivable surface of the rural household in this era. Stencils and design manuals may have offered the tools to imitate the imported elegance of Europe, but the rural folk designed on their own terms in their portraits, landscapes, and decorative efforts.[8]

In this Village Enlightenment an anonymous rural *Encyclopedie* came off the presses in Concord, New Hampshire, in 1825. Entitled *A Select Collection of Valuable and Curious Arts, and Interesting Experiments which are Well Explained, and Warranted Genuine, and May be Prepared, Safely and at Little Expense,* this work covered a wide range of topics in the arts, manufactures, and science, in which a country craftsman would be interested. Its author, Rufus Porter, painter and promoter, represents in his far-reaching travels and speculations only the most extreme example of the artisan-entrepreneur's critical role in accelerating change in the countryside. Porter published *Scientific American,* along with a series of other journals, pamphlets, and instruction manuals; he painted sleighs, houses, signs, and landscape frescoes; and he continued the profitable portrait-making which sustained his less successful ventures. He counted a camera obscura among his inventions, some a bit more fanciful, like a "horseless carriage" and an airship. Porter always remained the inveterate itinerant and kept alive his early interest in mechanics along with his entrepreneurial activities. But for Porter, like the readers of his *Select Collection,* the "arts," "experiments," and "expense" were not odd words incongruously collected into a title. This artist-inventor was the rural counterport to Robert Fulton, promoter of the steamboat, and Samuel F.B. Morse, creator of the telegraph, individuals who moved easily between the worlds of art and science, finding the spatial and mechanical imaginations to be compatible fields of vision for their creative and entrepreneurial efforts.[9]

But Porter, the portrait-maker, found his greatest success on the road, strolling into villages with his brightly decorated camera box and hawking his handbill of reasonably priced portraits (see Illustration of Porter's handbill). The artisan-entrepreneur sketched his subjects with the aid of a camera obscura, a dark box fitted with a lens and mirror to throw the sitter's image onto a sheet of paper. Porter mounted his invention on a handcart festooned with flags and was accompanied by a relative, a lad named Joe. The two traveled from village to village, offering the public a full range of "correct likenesses," produced with Porter's mechanical aids and guaranteed

Fig. 1. Rufus Porter, *Handbill* ca. 1818-1820. American Antiquarian Society, Worcester, Massachusetts.

to provide satisfaction. He advertised his profiles at twenty cents apiece, producing perhaps twenty silhouettes in an evening by the use of a profile machine for the features (see the handbill for an illustration of a silhouette) or the popular side view, where "full colours" were added to the stark profile although the construction of the ears and clothes was skimpy, or his most detailed full view where the camera obscura reduced his artistic labors to a mere fifteen minutes. Porter created a standardized product with the aid of his mechanical inventions and labor-saving techniques, and the rural client got just as much "art" as he or she was willing to pay for.[10]

Porter, as a publicist for ideas of rural design, offered his readers both recreation and "improvement in useful knowledge." He transmitted, by his recipes, the rules necessary to paint landscapes on walls or change the color of animals. These were no idle speculations of academicians but specific rules of thumb garnered from Porter's experience and reading. In his work—writing and painting—Porter placed repetition and rule at the very heart of the country vernacular. He made sure-footed suggestions for bringing down into every American home the "embellishments" which John Neal thought would eventually improve American art. Porter and his "professed artists" emphasized color and line, both capable of precise measurement in careful proportions. These farm house frescoes had no room for the romantic shadowing or sublime scenery of the cosmopolitan set . Indeed "improving" villagers wanted working farms and practical details on their walls. Mechanisms guided the craftsmen of domestic objects; stencils enabled the landscape painter to cover his client's wall quickly with gorgeous designs, and lathes allowed artisans to produce an ever-greater quantity of chairs and clocks in their shops. Enterprising artists such as Porter, by their experiments with machines and mass-production of images, followed this same process of the replication of consumer goods.[11] Rural residents eagerly stocked their households with these luxuries and took enormous satisfaction in their ability to acquire items previously limited to kings and aristocrats. Well before steam power and railroads brought factory-made goods to every farmer's door, enterprising artisan-entrepreneurs were producing commodities with a standardized look at an affordable price for village residents.

If mass-produced images such as Porter's appealed to the lower ends of the rural market, a growing group of villagers, artisan-entrepreneurs like the portraitist, found new images produced by artists with some urban influence and a knowledge of academic models. These innovative itinerants translated that training into the production of more elaborate likenesses and enjoyed great success on the roads of the rural North. A few, like Erastus Salisbury Field, pushed the possibilities of rural design to their furthest form without losing sight of their village origins or audience. Field's lengthy career spanned nearly half a century and ranged over diverse states. He passed through several significant stylistic stages while remaining within the confines of his status as a rural portraitist. He moved from farm to metropolis and back again, and finally matured into the painter of a richly embellished but still standardized product—the most "correct likeness" one could buy in rural America.[12]

Field's talents had been discovered early in his sketches of relatives made during his childhood on the family farm in Leverett, Massachusetts. His parents encouraged these efforts by providing him with paints to experiment on scraps of cardboard and then by sending him to New York to study in 1825 with Samuel Morse. The sudden death of Morse's wife ended Erastus's brief period of formal study and he returned to Leverett where he painted the portrait of his grandmother, Elizabeth Ashley, that same year. Field used in his first known portrait a somber palette like Winthrop Chandler's to capture the old Puritan in the last year of her life. He quickly left his birthplace to test his commercial prowess. Itinerant portrait-makers relied upon the connections of kin and word of mouth to establish their reputations. Field next appeared in Hudson, New York, writing to his father that his great aunt who lived there was helping him "in the prospect of retaining business." But he boasted that his artistic prowess accounted for his excellent prospects, since those who had seen his portraits "think that they are good likenesses." "I like it here very much so far and have got acquainted," the itinerant reported, and would return home only when trade slackened, "I think I shall tarry here as long as I can obtain business."

Erastus Field was destined to leave far behind his early and crude efforts at painting his hometown kin. He developed in the 1830's an imaginative solution to the problem of producing a portrait of the rural bourgeoisie which met both their general expectations of elegance at a low price and his particular needs for volume by the use of stock poses. Field evolved a formula that individualized his sitters and emphasized their status by a display of their personal possessions. Field opened the decade with a portrait of his brother stiffly seated on a hard wooden chair. His country gentlemen later took up grander poses amidst more lavish surroundings. Field always added some small personal details of the sitter to their general outlines, which he quickly sketched in by a large dark frock which occupied much of the commissioned space. By 1835 he could depict Eleazer Bullard (see Illustration Two) in measured tones, subtly suggesting his knuckles by dabs of paint applied with the same stippling technique as the modeling of the face. Bullard's features were personalized by his ruddy complexion and unshaven cheeks and he was provided with even more props and more dramatic juxtaposition of light and dark tones. Field's new command of draftsmanship and color suited his audience's desire to

Fig. 2. Erastus Salisbury Field, *Eleazar Bullard* &1835). Abby Aldrich Rockefeller Folk Art Center.

signal their arrival into an era of prosperity. The lightening of his palette and the quick outlining of his brush revealed them amidst a wealth of consumer goods and sentimental domestic scenes.[14]

In 1839 Field joined together these aesthetic and economic motifs in his masterpiece, one of the great images of nineteenth-century American life, Joseh Moore and his family (see Illustration Three). In that same year Field had moved with his family to the home of his wife's parents in the village of Ware, Massachusetts. Living across the street with his wife, two children and two orphans was Joseph Moore from Windham, Maine, hatmaker in winter, itinerant dentist in summer, and professor of religion all year round. Moore's wife was Almira Gallond, sister of Louisa and Clarissa Cook, sitters for Field, and the orphans were children of Louisa Cook. Field had painted in his travels all three Gallond sisters in three separate locales of New England. Far-flung families often provided the ties for the portraitist's commissions, but in 1839 Field gathered together the Moore and Cook clans: remembering his sitters' previous poses, he inserted them into this larger study exactly as depicted in their individual portraits. No one figure or piece dominates; the eye jumps from the black and white clad subjects to the numerous and profusely painted possessions. The Moores' furnishings arrest our attention with their exuberant colors and prominent position, competing with the children that Field carefully balanced around the adults. The tilted perspective and bright colors of the carpet draw our attention downward from the symmetrical windows which frame the top of the picture. Field successfully juggles all these items around the stencilled furniture—chairs, stands, and mirror—completing his study of the country style of the Moores' decor.[15]

Decorative display took precedence over geometric perspective in rural portraiture. Porter's flat but faithful likenesses gave rural residents less finished but still elegant items to adorn their walls. While the academic artist valued profound psychological insight and varieties of shadows and shading, the rural portrait-maker aimed at a plain style in which simplicity and often stark linearity went along with broad expanses of color and texture. His artisan's training in house and sign painting lingered in his reliance upon repetition and two-dimensionality. A master such as Field was able to achieve enormous success within the confines of those rural rules of design. Just when Field recorded his celebration of the itinerant artisan's achievement—his striking portrait of a rural craftsman and his mobile family—a new era was beginning. It was also in the momentous year of 1839 that Samuel Morse returned from Paris with Daguerre's invention.

IV

The year 1839 marked a great divide in portrait-making. Daguerre's invention of photography allowed some artisan-entrepreneurs to consolidate the changes in production and consumption which they had initiated during their itinerant days. In portrait-making, as in a host of other crafts, the new industrial order had rural origins. The industrialization of image-making by daguerreotypists followed upon the craftsmen's commercialization of the countryside. The manufacturers of the 1840's were often successful artisans who consolidated the labor-saving techniques and consumption patterns which their village colleagues had evolved over the course of their careers. From the capitalists' factory came forth the standardized products previously fashioned by craftsmen with the aid of their mechnical inventions and itinerant promotions.[16] The portraitist was not alone in facing the competition of images streaming forth from the presses of Currier & Ives or "the daguerreotype factory." A whole generation of artisan-entrepreneurs had promoted this process of cultural change. The rural artist who began his career painting a few stolid Puritan faces offered a new sentimentalized image of playful children to those Victorians who still desired family mementoes in oil. The rest of the rural audience, once introduced to the wonders of personal likenesses, demanded greater realism at even more affordable prices, eventually driving out the itinerant portrait-maker who tried to compete with the daguerreotypist.

A few hardy souls such as Robert Peckham lived through this entire process. Peckham's career represented both a typical and unique artisan-entrepreneur's confrontation with the commercial opportunities of the rural North and the changing ways of its new industrial order. This long-time resident of a village in central Massachusetts demonstrated over the course of his career the vast changes that had occurred in rural New England since the era of that earlier village craftsman and provincial painter, Winthrop Chandler. Peckham departed quickly from his first efforts in the 1820's: flat but wondrous portraits of his kinsmen's children. Like Erastus Field he matured during the next decade into the painter of substantial family records which displayed the wealth and position of the new commercial class forming in these villages. At the turning point of that process, the commercialization of the countryside, Peckham, along with many artisan-entrepreneurs in other crafts, faced threats raised by their very success. Robert Peckham passed through the popular phase of rural portraiture and with his gifts as a mature artist mixed the stylized and realistic modes in his rural designs. He was able to cross the great divide of technology and the photograph, which industrialized portraiture, and enter into the services of a new village aristocracy. But

Fig. 3. Erastus Salisbury Field, *Joseph Moore and his Family* 1839. Museum of Fine Arts, Boston, Massachusetts.

Winthrop Chandler's agrarian order had become an industrial one, and the new manufacturing magnates of central Massachusetts sat for him in place of the stern Devotions.[17]

Robert Peckham (1785-1865), portrait-maker, had strong roots in the village and craft traditions of New England. He began within the artisan fold, painting signs and carriages. Peckham remained in Westminster, Massachusetts, for fifty years but traveled some distance during his career, painting full oil portraits of families scattered around central Massachusetts and moving from stylized and two-dimensional images to more realistic and three-dimensional efforts.[18] In 1821 Peckham was painting two dimensional likenesses of the children of his brother-in-law, Oliver Adams, where the wooden poses match the furniture and toys. Their flat features and the sparse detail identify him firmly as a country limner. Peckham had matured by 1831 into an artist capable of rendering group portraits, such as *The Children of Oliver Adams* (1831). Here Peckham pays greater attention to detail. The children's frocks are carefully painted, and the composition is graceful, with the figures grouped in the center, comfortably flanked by the window on the left and the Family Record on the right. In this "Family Record" Peckham and his kinsman, Oliver Adams, were able to display their new gifts. The painter achieved a greater command of perspective and detail that allowed him to include the hotel-keeper's growing possessions: the children's colorful clothing, the wooden trunk and cradle, and the bright ingrain carpet. Peckham had found his metier in the 1830's by painting vibrant portraits of the children of the rising commercial class.[19]

The availability and portability of the photograph extended even more the "craze" for portrait-making that was sweeping the North, but the change in technology caused some shifts in personnel and perception. Robert Peckham confronted these great changes occurring in the rural North. His portraits from the 1840's all depict the children of the newly established manufacturing magnates of central Massachusetts. Peckham became a commissioned artist producing a few lavish canvases in the academic fashion for his rich clients. He assembled a new image of children and consumption. The cavorting youth of the industrialists were featured without their parents in rooms filled with toys, carpets, tables, and chairs, the very products that spilled from their father's factories.[20] The artisan-entrepreneur no longer visited the villages of the North to offer his wide range of likenesses to a popular market. Peckham traveled some distance from his original wooden Adams children and even farther from Chandler's stern Devotions. He featured a new three-dimensionality in *The Hobby Horse* (1850), as painter and patron tried to bury their rural upbringing. This massive canvas was dominated by its centerpiece, a toy produced by the Crandall clan (see Illustration Four). The Crandalls were a

Fig. 4. Robert Peckham, *The Hobby Horse* ca. 1850. National Gallery of Art.

Rhode Island family of farmer-craftsmen whose successful design and production of toys in their rural home and shop led to their removal in the 1840's to Brooklyn, New York. They built there one of the largest toy factories in the United States, and they were the first producers in America of this elegant rocking horse, copies from a German hand model that were mass-produced in their metropolitan operation.[21]

Robert Peckham surmounted the challenges which faced the village portrait-maker after his craft's industrialization. He abandoned Porter's itinerant travels and loud promotions and left the popular market to the newest entrepreneurs—the daguerreotypists. Instead he developed further along the path set by Erastus Field and celebrated the changing social configuration in the countryside. He painted even more lavish portraits of the most successful artisan-entrepreneurs with such realism and depth that his village origins were barely visible. By taking the life of Robert Peckham as our "text," we can see in his career the critical place of the artisan-entrepreneur in the transition from craft to industry in rural America. Peckham and his fellow portraitists, the farm generation growing up after the War for Independence, had provincial origins as village craftsmen, pioneered efforts at painting family members, matured within the rural idiom, and finally confronted the popular taste for portrait-making which they had fostered during their decades of painting the village scene.

V

Artisan-entrepreneurs were the movers and shakers in rural industrialization. Portrait-makers had taken the lead in promoting a desire for personal likenesses and infusing a taste for scarce commodities in the countryside. These country craftsmen, by drawing on their training as artisans and developing standardized products, pioneered the manufacture of mass consumer goods in the villages of the North. They brought simple inventions to save time into their shops and sought out wider markets for their wares, using the power sources and organization of labor at hand. These village craftsmen were no isolated set of "folk" artists, bereft of communal traditions, but rather aspiring entrepreneurs who led the charge for consumption in the countryside.[22]

This critical change—the commercialization of the countryside—took place when the village scene was the active site of innovation and enterprise. Adding the evidence from our second set of "texts," the portraits, we can see how this process of commercialization occurred in the rural North. Rural Americans in the nineteenth century sought their family portaits, whether they were Field's Moores or Peckham's Crandalls, to confirm their status in the village community and to consolidate their position as a new bourgeoisie. The minister and merchants of provincial America were joined by the growing middle class forming in the nineteenth century. Artisans came to sit for the portraitist along with innkeepers and improving farmers, all key participants in the greater commercial activity that occurred within the village and that connected the town to the regional market. Many more faces were recorded in an increasing variety of poses with softer tones.

But neither the progress of our rural portraitists nor the process of commercialization was straightforward. Itinerant artisans such as Chester Harding fled the farm, only to pick up a profusion of skills on their picaresque travels. Enterprising peddlers such as Rufus Porter promoted a variety of arts, crafts, and manufactures to rural residents. If these portraitists' progress through the countryside led them to assume both greater professional status and an increasing artistic ability, that position never precluded decorating a sign or leaving a landscape on a wall. The "self-taught" artisan voraciously devoured design books on the road and eagerly sought personal instruction in the cities. These artisan-entrepreneurs introduced innovations in craft production and consumption and grafted these changes onto the older agrarian base until a new industrial order took shape in the rural North.

The relationship between individual and social change is always a complex one and, during this era of maturing careers and developing tastes, a particularly difficult problem to untangle. Enterprising rural residents at this critical juncture encountered a lack of clearly defined career paths along with a wealth of diverse commercial opportunities. When observed at close range these entrepreneurs' innovative techniques were often the result of a chance encounter on the road or a determined effort to earn a livelihood, rather than part of a sustained design to fashion a new industrial system. But viewed with the broadest perspective, these portait-makers forged a new culture of commerce, providing the link between provincial farmers and future manufacturers and consumers. These artisan-entrepreneurs prepared the way for the mass production and consumption of household commodities. This generation experienced a unique passage; born into surroundings of scarcity, they left as their legacy households of abundance. Peddlers and promoters worked hard and long hours plying their trade in the hinterlands of nineteenth-century America. Only after the effects of industrialization had irrevocably swept away the village culture which nurtured their efforts did these portraitists assume the present aura which romanticizes their lives and works.

Erastus Salisbury Field died in the opening year of the twentieth century, and a local journal celebrated his achievement in an article entitled "Old Folks of the Country":

Although Mr. Field was an all-around painter of the old school the work which had been most highly appreciated is

that of portrait-painting—his likenesses of people of past
generation are as nearly correct as can well be made in oil,
and give to posterity faithful ideas of the personal appearance of their ancestors.[23]

Field and "the Primitive sort" of portrait-makers had constructed a
new commercial order and sanctioned a new cultural code of consumption that changed the face of rural America.

NOTES

I would like to thank Fred Anderson, Joyce Appleby, Christopher Clark, Thomas
Dublin, Gary Gerstle, Mark Hirsch, Christopher Jedrey, Gary Kulik, Michael Owen
Jones, Roy Rosenzweig, and Helena Wall for their comments on an earlier version of this
paper which was presented at the American Historical Association meetings in Los
Angeles in December 1981.

See my essay " 'One of the Primitive Sort': The Portrait-Makers of the Rural North,
1769-1860," in Jonathan Prude and Steven Hahn, eds., *Rural America, 1780-1900:
Essays in Social History* (Chapel Hill, forthcoming) for more discussion of rural portraitists.

[1] The literature on early industrialization has been most recently surveyed by Thomas
C. Cochran, *Frontiers of Change* (New York, 1981), with an exhaustive
bibliography. In our understanding of this process we still rely upon the textile
paradigm and the factory experience. For some alternative models, see Peter
Kriedte, Hans Medick, Jurgen Schlumbohm, eds., *Industrialization before Industrialization*, trans. by Beate Schempp (Cambridge, 1981), which advances the
"protoindustrialization" thesis with European materials; the essay by Thomas
Dublin on rural outwork in *Rural America* and his collection of letters portraying the
rural backgrounds of New England textile workers in *From Farm to Factory* (New
York, 1981); and Christopher Clark, "Household, Market and Capital: The Process of
Economic Change in the Connecticut Valley of Massachusetts, 1800-1860," (unpublished Ph.D. Dissertation, Harvard University, 1982).

[2] I found contemporary folklorists most useful for making one's way past the work of
romantic antiquers; Kenneth Ames, *Beyond Necessity: Art in the Folk Tradition*
(New York, 1976) is the place to begin, along with the Winterthur Conference papers
edited by Ian Quimby and Scott Swank, *Perspectives on American Folk Art* (New
York, 1980). See also several contributors' work for case studies on craftsmen in
their context: Michael Owen Jones, *The Handmade Object* (Berkeley, 1976) and
John Vlach, *Charlestown Blacksmith* (Athens, 1981).
The question of whether these itinerant portrait-makers in rural America were "folk
artists" or not is a hotly debated topic among art historians and folklorists. I found
the vast literature on folk artists to be useful for its thorough scholarship on the great
number of individuals traveling through the countryside and painting likenesses in
this period. See Beatrix T. Rumford, et., *American Folk Paintings and Drawings
from the Abby Aldrich Rockefeller Folk Art Center* (Boston 1981) for its valuable introduction which places the artists in their proper context and contains biographical
sketches on particular portraitists. See also Jean Lipman and Tom Armstrong, eds.,
American Folk Painters of Three Centuries (New York, 1980); and Ellen Miles, ed.,
Portrait Painting in America: The Nineteenth Century (New York, 1976).

[3] For Chandler, see Nina Fletcher Little, "Winthrop Chandler" in Lipman, ed.,
American Folk Painters, pp. 26-34; Nina Little, "Winthrop Chandler," *Art in
America* XXXV (April, 1947), entire issue.

4 *Massachusetts Spy,* August 19, 1790; Little, *Art in America,* pp. 77-79.

5 Chester Harding, *My Egotistigraphy* (Cambridge, 1886), pp. 10-12, 17-18. Autobiographies like *Barnum's Own Story* (New York, 1927) attest to the entrepreneurial bent of these itinerant Yankees. The traveling "pedlar" stories of Seba Smith and T.C. Haliburton, "The Clock Maker," contain some valuable social history about nascent capitalism in the nineteenth century countryside. See Walter Blair, *Native American Humor* (New York, 1937); Richardson Wright, *Hawkers and Walkers in Early America* (Philadelphia, 1927); and Jay Dolan, *The Yankee Peddlers of Early America* (New York, 1964).

6 Harding, *Egotistigraphy,* pp. 21-26; James Guild, "Journal, *Proceedings of the Vermont Historical Society,* V, 3 (1937), pp. 267-268.

7 John Neal, "American Painters and Painting," *The Yankee: and Boston Literary Gazette,* I. (1829), p. 45. Neal wrote about his discovery of a new visual sense in his autobiography, *Wandering Recollections of a Somewhat Busy Life* (Boston, 1868), p. 108. Harding recounted his instruction by "one of the primitive sort," *Egotistigraphy,* pp. 26-28.

8 Chris Bailey, *Two Hundred Years of American Clocks and Watches* (Englewood Cliffs, N.J., 1975), pp. 54-60; John T. Kenney, *The Hitchcock Chair* (Rutland, Vermont, 1971). I examine this cultural revolution in my project, "Artisan-Entrepreneurs and the Transformation of the Rural North, 1760-1860," which looks at several crafts and craftsmen—chair-makers, clock-makers, booksellers, and portrait-painters.

9 Rufus Porter, *A Select Collection* ... (Concord, N.H., 1825), pp. iii-iv; see Jean Lipman, *Rufus Porter, A Yankee Pioneer* (New York, 1969, rev. ed. 1980) for analysis of Porter's varied career and also "Rufus Porter, Founder of the Scientific American," *Scientific American,* September 6, 1884, for the details of Porter's early life. Artisan-inventors of ante-bellum America are discussed by Brooke Hindle, *Emulation and Invention* (New York, 1981); Eugene S. Ferguson, "The Mind's Eye: Nonverbal Thought in Technology," *Science,* CXCVII (August, 1977), p. 827-36; Otto Mayr and Robert C. Post, eds., *Yankee Enterprise* (Washington, D.C., 1981); Anthony F.C. Wallace, *Rockdale* (New York, 1980); and Merrit Roe Smith, *Harpers Ferry Armory and the New Technology* (Ithaca, 1977).

10 *Scientific American;* advertisement in Lipman, *Porter,* p. 5; Rumford, *Portraits,* pp. 169-72, for details of Porter's production of portraits. One prodigious silhouette-maker claimed a lifetime total of 30,000 likenesses (Rumford, p. 107). See Alice Carrick, *Shades of Our Ancestors* (New York, 1928) on silhouettists.

11 See Lipman, *Porter,* pp. 89-158 on his farmhouse frescoes; also his own series of articles on "The Art of Painting," published in 1847 in *Scientific American.* David Pye, *The Nature and Art of Workmanship* (Cambridge, 1968) suggests a general theory of design, based on his own construction of objects, which is consistent with his account of the enthusiasm which greeted the introduction of standardized products during the early days of industrialization. For contemporary accounts start with Horace Bushnell, "The Age of Homespun," *Work and Play* (New York, 1864), originally delivered at the Litchfield County Centennial in 1847.

12 For Field see Mary Black, "Rediscovery: Erastus Salisbury Field," *American Art Journal,* LIX (Jan-Feb 1966), p. 50; also Rumford, *Portraits,* pp. 93-99; Black, *Erastus Field, 1805-1900* (Williamsburg, 1963); Black "Erastus Field," in Lipman, ed., *American Folk Painters,* pp. 74-80.

13 Field quoted in Mary Black, "Rediscovery," *American Art Journal,* LIX (Jan-Feb 1966), p. 50.

14 Rumford, *Portraits,* pp. 93-99.

15 Black, "Field," *Folk Painters,* p. 77; Laura C. Luckey, "Family Portraits in the Museum of Fine Arts, Boston," *Antiques* CX (November, 1976), p. 1008.

16 On the early history of photograhy see Robert Taft, *Photography and the American Scene* (New York, 1938); William F. Robinson, *A Certain Slant of Light: The First*

Hundred Years of New England Photography (New York, 1980); Floyd and Marion Rinhart, *The American Daguerrotype* (Athens, 1981); and for an excellent case study of the reception of the new technology by local entrepreneurs, Margaret Denton Smith and Mary Louise Tucker, *Photography in New Orleans* (Baton Rouge, 1982).

17 On Robert Peckham: Stephen Farnum Peckham, *Peckham Genealogy* (New York, 1922), pp. 267-69, 315-17; William S. Heywood, *History of Westminster, Massachusetts* (Lowell, 1876), pp. 821-822; and Dale T. Johnson, "Deacon Robert Peckham," *American Art Journal*, XI (January, 1979), pp. 27-36.

18 Peckham, *Peckham*, pp. 267-68; Johnson, "Peckham," 27-28.

19 Johnson, "Peckham," p. 29; on the Adams family, see Haywood, *History of Westminster*, pp. 514, 632.

20 Some of these Peckham portraits are unsigned. They have been attributed by Dale Johnson, "Peckham" to Robert Peckham of Westminster. I have found the argument that all these paintings of children from the 1840's are by the same hand convincing. See Johnson for biographical information about the sitters.

21 Inez and Marshall McClintock, *Toys in America* (Washington, D.C., 1961), pp. 147-51.

22 The historical literature on the "consumer revolution" involved in industrialization is a recent and expanding one, mostly European. See Neil McKendrick, John Brewer and J.H. Plumb, *The Birth of a Consumer Society: The Commercialization of Eighteenth Century England* (Bloomington, 1982); Stuart and Elizabeth Ewen, *Channels of Desire: Mass Images and the Shaping of American Consciousness* (New York, 1982); Michael B. Miller, *The Bon Marche: Bourgeois Culture and the Department Store, 1869-1982* (Princeton, 1981); and Rosalind H. Williams, *Dream Worlds: Mass Consumption in Late Nineteenth-Century France* (Berkeley, 1982). For the anthropologist's view see Mary Douglas and Baron Isherwood, *The World of Goods* (New York, 1979). Contemporary sociologists have studied the place of objects in the home: see Mihaly Csikszentymihalyi and Eugene Rochberg-Hatton, *The Meaning of Things: Domestic Things and Self* (Cambridge, 1981).

23 *Greenfield Gazette*, June 9, 1900, quoted in Black, *Erastus Field*, n.p.

Hard Times and Happy Days: The Visual Iconography of Depression America

WILLIAM M. STOTT

A car pulled off the road and a woman got out. The migrant couple stopped walking westward toward a better life and waited to see what she wanted. She was a small woman, Dorothea Lange, and she came toward them limping slightly, smiling a crooked smile. Her clothes were dark like theirs and, like the migrant woman, she wore pants. She also wore a black beret.

No doubt the couple hoped she was going to help them—at least give them a lift, since to see the billboard (which was why she stopped), Lange also had to be going towards Los Angeles on Route 66 that cool, high-pressure day two months after President Roosevelt had told the nation one-third its people were ill-housed, ill-clothed, ill-fed. The migrants had no house, of course; they had abandoned one behind them—a shack, we imagine, in a state we have come to think of as Oklahoma, though it could have been Texas, Arkansas, Kansas, Iowa, Missouri, or half a dozen others. But their clothes were still new enough not to have lost their color, and the couple was too burly for one of Lange's haunted close-ups. She had stopped because they were *there*, near the marvelous billboard.

They were amenable to have their picture taken in the way the lady wanted. She told them just to walk—no, wait, not yet, she wasn't ready yet. And she backed up in the car (it would seem: tiremarks are visible in the picture's foreground) until the composition was right and the billboard's lower edge set up a line that, continued, bisected the picture and the migrants. Even then there was a wait because Lange was working with a hand-held view camera, which meant she held the camera low, looking down into it as though panning for gold, and she needed to have the camera high to raise the horizon and get the broad expanse of earth she wanted. She may have stood on the car bumper, even on a fender. The migrants were waiting all this time, shifting foot to foot, uncertain whether to drop their gear and how to make it look like they were walking (when we first saw the picture they seemed to be walking; when we look again we see they aren't: they are performing). The picture done, Lange (we like to think) gave them a lift toward the California town where they, or their offspring, voted for Reagan in the 1960's.

Dorothea Lange, "Toward Los Angeles, California, March, 1937,"
(Farm Security Administration).

Lange's message in "Toward Los Angeles, California. March, 1937," as in most of her Depression pictures, was Hardship, the staple of thirties' documentary. Here, as usual, she showed people suffering (the migrants) and—this was unusual—also showed the insensitive, well-off folk overlooking, in both senses of the word, the suffering (the chubby rich man riding in the billboard). She could have shown hardship without setting up the picture so elaborately, but, as often in her best work, she wanted her message intensified, magnified.

The way she magnified the hardship was to add to the documentary style in which she worked the graphic vocabulary of another style. This style, the other central style in thirties iconography, goes by several names. In Europe it is called Futurism, Constructivism, de Stijl, Suprematism, Art Deco, New Objectivity. In the United States it is called some of these things and Purism and Streamlining.

The goal of documentary is to show experience as complicated, rough, sad, "raw," and true. The object of streamlining is to show experience smoothed, simplified, "clean lined" (an early synonym for streamlining), heavily patterned, and fabulous—better than life. Lange, who had been a portrait photographer and a member of the reality-is-beautiful f64 school, chose in this picture to monumentalize the migrants by standing them at the center of a radically simple—streamlined!—pattern made by a triangle and an oblong. She set them in an enormous funnel, with road, road shoulder, road shoulder mound, and telephone poles steeply thrusting toward one point, and made them the fulcrum of this wedge into the picture and counterbalanced its inward movement with the oblong billboard floating (so it seems) perfectly horizontal to the picture plane and cutting everything in half: picture, migrants, and thrust toward the horizon. The streamlined frame Lange gives the migrants emphasizes their importance and immobility. They stand at the center of the camera's parallax and obscure its vanishing point; without them, the picture would be one of unimpeded, empty force.

The sources of American streamlining are many and well worth attention we can't give them here. They certainly include the European arts that provoked the names mentioned earlier and the imaginative icon that stood behind these arts: the Machine, especially the automobile, airplane, radio, and electric generator and powerlines; the innovations of the Bauhaus, some of which got to America before the first big exhibition devoted to Bauhaus art (at the Museum of Modern Art in 1938); Nazi propaganda style; Soviet propaganda style; Picasso's joyous Mediterranean god and goddess graphics of the late 1920's, the work of such American Purists as Charles Sheeler, Charles Demuth, Georgia O'Keeffe, Ralston Crawford, Rockwell Kent; and, to a degree not yet appreciated, the work of the American Scene painters: particularly Thomas Hart Benton with his nervous curve of beauty and Grant Wood with his tidy landscapes.

The point to be emphasized here, though, is that streamlining, which now strikes our taste as glib and cornball, was the prestige style of the 1930's. It was considered beautiful. Svelte. Orderly. As Jeffrey Meikle shows in *Twentieth Century Limited: Industrial Design in America, 1925-1939,* it was the style business-America called upon to overcome the Depression by selling the public products redesigned—often in plastic—in the streamlined mode.

The Southern Pacific billboard shows us a little of what business America was selling in the thirties. The emphasis is on the comfort both of well-designed transport and (implicitly) of the affluence that makes such transport possible. "Relax" is what the leaning, aerodynamic letters tell the motorists hurrying past in their cars; and the cherubic businessman on the streamlined train is relaxed indeed. (The fact that he wears a suit while napping testifies to the formality of the decade's public imagery.) The theme of comfort is carried through in the main text where the man's head becomes a sort of comma after "NEXT TIME" and before "TRY THE TRAIN," encouraging from us readers a pause, a drowsy sigh of contentment.

Lange is of course making fun of the billboard and insensitive ad-America. We are meant to be contemptuous of fatheads who ride ignorant of those who walk. The picture's moral heart is with the migrants walking in the dust. But Lange uses the streamlined visual style of ad-America to add force to her condemnation of the economic values of those who paid for the billboard and those—the two-thirds of the nation decently housed, clothed, and fed—to whom the billboard was addressed.

A great deal of thirties imagery does what Lange's picture does: combines "documentary" and "streamlined" styles—the rough and the smooth, raw and cooked, grim and colorful, real and fabulous. Consider *The Wizard of Oz,* one of the decade's central films, and its offsetting of hardscrabble black-and-white Kansas—presented visually as Dust Bowl Oklahoma—with the luscious, pastel Land of Oz, where the landscape comes from Grant Wood and the buildings in Oz's city are streamlined versions of Southern California stucco.

Lange and the other documentary photographers of the period meant to document life as it was, yet much of the work by many of them —Walker Evans, Russell Lee, Margaret Bourke-White—shows the Purist influence. In the decade's iconography, I suggest, the tendency toward documentary "realism" fought the tendency toward pretty streamlined make-believe. And generally lost.

Consider the Hollywood films of the period. Consider the network radio product.

Or consider—and this is where we will end— *Life* magazine.

When *Life* began in late 1936, publisher Henry Luce boasted that its goals were "To see life; to see the world; to eyewitness great events; to watch the faces of the poor," and so forth. The magazine had a success unprecedented in American journalism and certainly could have followed this documentary bent. It seldom did. During its first three or four years, its articles treating American life grew increasingly soft, pretty, bizarre. By the early 1940's, *Life*'s America often seemed a place as fabulous as the land over the rainbow.

To capture this America in pictures, *Life* used large, slow cameras and film, supplemental lighting, and, where possible, studio setups. It very seldom used the 35mm camera, though this camera made possible split-second documentation of actuality without setups or extra lighting. *Life* didn't use 35mm images to document American life because they were grainy and slightly blurred.

To be sure, such images did appear in *Life*—but in "The Week's Events" section at the front of the magazine when the subject was Europe and, especially, the impending or current war. *Life* had to run grainy images from Europe because those were the sort available. European journals were generally printed on lower quality paper than American ones and were accustomed to less sharp images. They had made the 35mm camera the standard instrument for their press photography. In addition, pictures from Europe usually came by telegraph, further reducing their sharpness. The resulting grim, shaggy images felt right for reporting war and life in Europe under the terror. But wrong for America.

Thus *Life* in the late 1930's and throughout the war was in a real sense two magazines. The front of the magazine reported recent hard news, largely the foreign war, in rough, documentary images. The back of the book, where *Life* spent its big money and attention, showed a glossy, sanitized, joyful, streamlined America, frozen in bright light, and often (especially the ads) in color. This America—like Hollywood's or Norman Rockwell's or Madison Avenue's—was comfortingly better than life.

Life and other visual media suggest that by the late 1930's, certainly by Pearl Harbor, the American people had reevaluated the documentary style of the thirties and judged it appropriate for foreigners and hideously unAmerican activities like war, but too rough to use on the folks back home.

Part II

The Industrial City

Program

The Industrial City

April 29-30, 1983

SESSION I

Teaching Urban History
Chair: Michael H. Ebner, Lake Forest College

Eric E. Lampard, State University of New York at Stony Brook
"Urbanization of Population and Mutation of Cities in the Industrializing Era: An Ecological Framework"

Comment: Michael Frisch, State University of New York at Buffalo
            Francis R. Walsh, University of Lowell

SESSION II

Preserving the Industrial City
Chair: David Gillespie, National Trust for Historic Preservation

Panel: Kenneth T. Jackson, Columbia University
        Ian Menzies, Boston *Globe*
        David Sekers, Quarry Bank Mill
        Sam Bass Warner, Jr., Boston University

SESSION III

The Urban Industrial Community, Part I
Chair: Ellen Fitzpatrick, Wellesley College

John Bodnar, Indiana University
"The European Origins of American Immigrants"

Susan E. Hirsch, Northwestern University
"Job Segregation and the Replication of Local Social Hierarchies"

Francis G. Couvares, Clark University
"The Remaking of Urban Culture in 19th and 20th Century America"

SESSION IV

The Urban Industrial Community, Part II
Commentary
Chair: Paul Hudon, Museum of American Textile History
        Stephan Thernstrom, Harvard University
        Virginia Yans-McLaughlin, Rutgers University

SESSION V
Technology and the City
Chair: Heather A. Huyck, National Park Service

Sam Bass Warner, Jr., Boston University
"Technology and Its Impact on Urban Culture"

Comment: Ruth Schwartz Cowan, State University of New York at Stony Brook

SESSION VI

Presenting Urban History to the Public: Lowell National Historical Park

Discussion of Lowell National Historical Park programs

Mutations of Cities in the Industrializing Era: An Ecological Perspective on Urbanization in the United States

ERIC E. LAMPARD

"It will become...clearer in time that the theory of urban growth is a special case of the theory 'of organization."

Richard L. Meier (1962)

The focus of this paper is on interrelations between urbanization and changes in the social functions and morphologies of cities during industrialization. It treats urbanization as a (macro) process of population concentration that, if sustained, brings a majority of a population into "cities." Cities—points of concentration or peaks of relative population density—are viewed as (micro) processes of human interactions in which residents *inter alia* "learn" to adapt their physical and social environments in ways that sustain the (macro) process of concentration. The unprecedented urbanization of population since the late 18th century in parts of Europe and North America is seen not only as a *condition* of the industrialization of production and distribution but also, through the concomitant building and reorganization of the urban "artifact" under market aegis, as *itself* a major vehicle for capital formation and economic development. After a substantial majority of a growing population has come to live and work in urban areas, the momentum of concentration subsides and social-economic change proceeds without much benefit from further increments to numbers or proportions of urban population. Meanwhile, relaxation of centripetal tendencies among population and productive activities within the extended urban areas of the present century prompts a devolution of the metropolitan form of settlement into multi-centered "urban fields" in which older central cities experience deconcentration and deterioration of core areas.

Human Ecosystems: A Framework

For present purposes a territorially-based human population is considered as an ecological system. The growth and redistribution of a population in space depend upon its sustenance activities, consumption or saving of its product, on net investment, and upon the character of its collective and private organizations (insofar as these become differentiated and interact in the course of time). Human ecosystems, like those of other species, are dependent on the biosphere for all the biochemical life processes. Their population members derive energy from the natural environment, convert and excrete it (in part) in the course of their daily metabolism. But human populations may also "learn by doing" and hence their eco-systems are at once cultural-social and biological, and for their members symbolic as well as metabolic, in character. Social adaptation takes place continually and cumulatively as members of a population respond to their ambient settings selectively in the sense of perceiving, interpreting, and intermittently reacting to "information" derived from their social and physical environments.[1]

A population embodies these learned capabilities in its technological repertory and organizational behavior. *Organization* is the critical ecological parameter since only by division of labor and social transactions do members of a population acquire and institutionalize the capacity for functional differentiation (including the necessary means for integrating a structural "whole" out of more or less specialized "parts"). Increases or decreases in human populations are distributed spatially in close relation to the varieties of social environment (including relations with other peoples) that they are collectively able to interpose and maintain *between* themselves and the underlying regimen of nature. Migratory populations with no fixed abode may maintain their eco-system (and their numbers) by moving themselves and their effects from one physical milieu to another roughly similar milieu with only limited artifactual or other environmental modification at any time. Settled agricultural populations, on the other hand, may be able to augment their numbers and lands by elaborating their social organization or installing more productive modes of husbandry (even preserving the fertility of the soil). Any considerable expansion of a population or territory, nevertheless, is likely to entail alterations in the relative sizes and proportions of eco-system components that will require compensatory adjustments in organization—in mediating and coordinating functions—to conserve the system's working structure. In default of morphological adaptation, the population of an "overgrown" system may find its expansive activities lack coherence and subject to diminishing returns except as they revert to some more manageable scale.

A human eco-system is composed of smaller and variously interacting "subsystems" whose salient characteristics at any time derive from their interrelations with the larger system in which they are nested. Since late neolithic times, villages, hamlets, manors, and the like have furnished the basic territorial units for organizing rural-agricultural populations into larger aggregations *via* "central place systems." Such subsystems constitute elemental "communities" of activity and interest for their residents. Although comparatively self-sufficient and independent with respect to their customary means of life support, the local communities are integrated steplike, *via* administrative and market nodes, into regional systems or subsystems that may, in turn, provide the structural components for "national" or "international" political aggregations focusing on royal or imperial capitals: the "head-quarters".[2] During urbanization, the predominantly rural populations migrate increasingly to towns and other locally-bounded work concentrations to form more differentiated and specialized subsystems whose mutual interaction and resulting inter-*dependency* sum to an evolving "system of cities." The migrations of country people to the towns differ from inter-rural and nomadic migrations in that the former are moving to predominantly artifactual and built environments and becoming involved in novel sets of social relations. A system of cities resembles a classical central place structure in that it also is integrated through networks of local and regional linkages on a more or less hierarchical size scale, although the functional bases for the location and size of many agglomerations in an urbanizing system (the volume and variety of their transactions) differ radically from those of the smaller and more "independent" central places of traditional, even commercialized, agricultural societies. The larger aggregations of cities—whether national or transnational "super-systems"—are, like their components, an outgrowth of the population's acquired capacity for maintaining itself and enhancing its survival chances by constructing more elaborate social-artifactual environments, subject to the limits imposed at any time by its organizing competence.

Within a context of human ecology, the focus on urbanization as population concentration furnishes useful macro-and micro-frameworks for exploring certain problems in the history of cities and societies. Viewed from the vantage point of today's highly urbanized, low fertility, and high per capita income populations of western Europe, North America, Australia, or Japan, the urban transformation of society has proceeded through three analytically distinctive phases:

1) from initially *low levels* and *low* (sometimes negative) *rates* of net concentration extending almost universally over long periods of time (except on a very restricted local basis)

2) through an intermediate, comparatively brief, transitional phase of *higher rates* and *rising levels* of net concentration getting underway (in the first instances) from the later 18th or early 19th centuries A.D. and, if sustained, continuing into the 20th century with majorities of a growing population coming to live and work in "cities"

3) until entering, more recently, on a phase of more or less stationary *high* (or slowly falling) *levels* and *low* (even negative) *rates* of net concentration, with a few instances to date of net deconcentration and incipient urban decline.

Urbanization: A Macroframework

In light of this compressed natural history of rates and levels of net concentration, the three phases might be dubbed respectively: 1) *pre-urbanization* ca. 5-15 per cent concentration; 2) *urbanization* ca. 20-80 per cent concentration; and 3) *post-urbanization* ca. 80 ± per cent concentration. Increases in rates and magnitudes of concentration, the multiplication of points of concentration, and the eventuality that a majority of an enlarged population becomes domiciled in such concentrations, are defining characteristics of the societal process of urbanization. These demographic phenomena—the implied natural increases and net migrations—provide a formal description *ceteris paribus* of the process of urbanization which varies in historical detail, of course, from region to region as well as over time. "Explanations" for such phenomena—when, for instance, the rate of population concentration in a territory is faster than its rate of population increase—are to be found in the changing technological and organizational capacities of the population with respect to its social and physical environments: in short, in the parameters of the human eco-system. The human eco-systems of North America (or elsewhere) are ultimately reducible to the *populations* themselves, e.g. differences in adaptation among various indigenous "Indian" populations and alien Europeans of the 16th and 17th centuries. While such a reduction might be fairly obvious in regard, say, to social *organizaion* or in the cultural domain of *technology* and practical arts, it holds no less for the *environment* insofar as the characteristics and capacities of a population at any time (including relations with other peoples) largely determine which of nature's properties is potentially a resource or asset. Adoption of plants long domesticated to the Atlantic seaboard by "Indian" peoples facilitated the seizure and occupancy of lands by organized bands of English, Dutch, and French invaders early in the 17th century.

The three phases of urbanization and the ensuing transformation of the population's residential distribution between country and town are well illustrated in the history of the Anglo-American colonies which became the United States. The early stockade settlements of the 17th century contained substantial proportions of the settler populations, but as the conquest and occupation proceeded, concentrations of any magnitude were confined to port towns of four or five English (and one French) mainland provinces. Levels of concentration tended to decline, however, during the early 18th century when population was able to spread itself over the more accessible and fertile territories of the interior. From the 1760's concentration was again marked in Massachusetts, Rhode Island, southern New York, and eastern Pennsylvania, although the high levels which had obtained in parts of the narrow coastal belt of the early 1700's were not restored before the 1780's in Massachusetts, early 1800's in Rhode Island, and not before the second quarter of the 19th century in the larger expanses of Pennsylvania and New York State. Despite the disruption of commerce and communications attendant on the War of Independence, concentration gathered momentum in the new nation and by 1790 almost half of the enlarged urban population of 201,000 (then around five percent of the enumerated total) resided outside the five large Atlantic seaports; for all the decline of Newport, Rhode Island was the most urbanized state at the first federal census with 19.0 per cent of its people resident in incorporated centers with >2,500 inhabitants. Indeed, over the second half of the 18th century through 1810, the numbers of smaller clusters, 2,500-7,999, had doubled and redoubled, while their aggregate population had grown at a faster rate than that of the emergent cities, >8,000. Only in the latter year, in fact, did the share of total population in the larger centers recover the level of ca. 1730.₃ After further dislocations during the second war with the mother country, 1812-15, urbanization slowly recovered again nationally, but rapidly in southern New England and, somewhat surprisingly perhaps, in the sparsely settled area of Louisiana in the southwest. From the 1820's urbanization was itself a dynamic current in the redistribution of population westward which, in conjunction with the rising export trade in cotton and the reorganization of industrial manufactures in New England, helped change the volume, composition, and directions of national output. Table 1 presents the urban transformation of the U.S. population under a variety of measures.

Over the century after 1820 population concentration required the construction and cumulative "improvement" of hundreds and thousands of square miles of urban artifact across the land (dwellings, workplaces, public buildings, streets, sewers, bridges, transport installations, street illumination, communications facilities, and other social overhead). People coming to live and work in such protean settings learned new ways of doing familiar things and often discovered new things to do. Innumerable products and services were introduced to the urban market place during the 19th and 20th centuries which had been unknown or unneeded by earlier generations residing in country or town. As a rising proportion of the increased national population experienced the changing conditions of town life and livelihood, an urbanized eco-system took place, in both spatial and temporal senses, across the continent. The growing weight and work of the urban numbers in the whole was making "the difference" insofar as the "growth" involved not simply more of the same but *development* and *structural change.* Under 19th-century conditions, urbanization of population proved to be "an open-ended, information-generating process."⁴

Once a substantial majority had come to live and work in census urban places, ca. 1910-1930, however, the momentum of concentration slackened markedly and subsequent urbanization had a diminishing

Table 1

The Urbanization of U.S. Population, 1790-1980

Decade	Urban Population Increase (000's) %>2,500 ΔU/U	Per Cent Urban of U.S. Population Increase ΔU/U ÷ ΔP/P	Urbanization of Population Δ(U/P) %-point	Growth of Urban Share of U.S. Population Δ(U/P) ÷ U/P	Level of Urbanization U/P %
					(5.1)
1790-1800	120	59.9	8.7	1.0	19.6	6.1
1800-1810	203	63.0	10.5	1.2	19.7	7.3
1810-1820	168	31.9	7.0	-0.1	-1.4	7.2
1820-1830	434	62.6	13.4	1.6	22.2	8.8
1830-1840	718	63.7	17.1	2.0	22.7	10.8
1840-1850	1,699	92.1	27.7	4.5	41.7	15.3
1850-1860	2,673	75.4	32.4	4.5	29.4	19.8
1860-1870	3,685	59.3	51.8	5.9	29.8	25.7
1870-1880	4,228	42.7	36.4	2.5	9.7	28.2
1880-1890	7,976	56.5	62.4	6.9	24.4	35.1
1890-1900	8,054	36.4	61.7	4.6	6.0	39.7
1900-1910	11,839	39.3	74.1	6.0	15.1	45.7
1910-1920	12,159	29.0	88.5	5.5	12.0	51.2
1920-1930	14,797	27.3	86.7	5.0	9.8	56.2
1930-1940	5,469	7.9	61.5	0.3	0.5	56.5
1940-1950+	14,503	19.5	76.2	2.5	4.4	59.0+
					(64.0)+
1950+-1960	28,422	29.3	101.5	5.9	9.2	69.9
1960-1970	24,056	19.2	100.7	3.6	5.2	73.5
1970-1980	17,640	11.8	75.7	0.2	0.3	73.7

+ Urban population, 1790-1950 is population resident in incorporated places >2,500. Urban population, 1950-1980 (lower panel) is population resident in incorporated and unincorporated places >2,500. For full statement, see U.S. Bureau of the Census, *Historical Statistics of the U.S.*, *Colonial Times to 1970* (Washington D.C., 1975), Pt. 1, Notes A 43-72, and 1980 U.S. Census. NB:1950 lower panel includes Alaska and Hawaii; also 1960-1980. U/P 1790 = 5.1 per cent.

impact on social and economic change.. Increases in urban population and built area continued along metropolitan lines, nevertheless, especially after World War II, although the rate of increase in the urban share of all U.S. population had dwindled in the intervening decades. By the mid-1960's, more people lived in the suburban and satellite rings of census metropolitan areas in the aggregate than in their central cities, although for two decades after midcentury the urban areas nationwide had absorbed more than the total increase in U.S. population, with the result that actual numbers of rural population fell until the surprising reversal of the early 1970's. During that decade nonmetropolitan population grew faster than metropolitan population for the first time since the census recognized the metropolitan phenomenon early in this century. Likewise, the net increase of country dwellers exceeded that for any decade since the 1870's, and the shift of more than 17 million people into census urban places represented the lowest *positive* decadal increase in the urban share of U.S. population in the nation's history (lower even than the 5.4 million increment in the depressed 1930's).[5] For the moment, at least, with less than three-quarters of population resident in urban areas, the urbanization of the United States had ground to a halt.

Urbanization: A Microframework

It is not only during this most recent phase of posturbanization that the concentration process (or its abatement) has had implications for "cities." A primary postulate of ecological thinking holds that tendencies prevailing in the actions of the larger population will be concentrated and, in all likelihood, intensified within the more constricted spaces of the nodes (e.g. functional specialization, incidences of literacy, of poverty, epidemic, etc.). Similar interaction serves to transmit urban tendencies out among the population at large albeit with their impacts diminishing over distance. Changes in the volumes and velocities of concentration since the early 1700's, say, not only increased the numbers and augmented the size range of densely populated agglomerations but, as in the larger society, eventually altered their structural-organizational forms. Each of the earlier phases in this long run rural-to-urban shift had a particular significance for the internal order of cities in its own time that was registered *inter alia* in a characteristic social and physical morphology. With the growth and redistribution of population and the cultivation of novel organizational and technological competencies among its members, the "city" underwent a metamorphosis that altered its size, shape, and to some degree, its nature and role as a *form* of human settlement.

This is where the interests and findings of historians of urbanization may intersect with those of some historians of cities. The points of concentration (peaks of relative density) are the urban areas or "cities" studied, among others, by urban historians. Each city is an accommodation *over time* of the macro-tendencies of its society insofar as the latter mold the form and character of a settlement to the *particular* features of its site (including the more random contingencies of local events and personalities). A city's situation in the larger system broadly shapes the life chances of its residents, their culture and condition, as long as they occupy a niche within its bounds. The historian of a city faces the almost insuperable task—given his or her materials and training—of rendering the general into the circumstantial, as it were, of performing a poetic miracle by transmuting a world into a grain of sand. Since our muse is Clio (not Calliope or Euterpe) we approach the particular schematically and empirically by exploring possible connections between the urbanization of population and mutations of the cities.

1) *Preurbanization* is associated with the organization of compact and typically *micro-differentiated* urban space extending anywhere from a few hundred to a few thousand acres and containing upwards of a few thousand to a few score thousand inhabitants. Such centers may grow in population through the repletion of their inner spaces or in area by the accretion of "outer" or extra-mural space. This expansion will generally involve no critical adjustment to either the inherited physical form or the social order of the city which alternately extends or contracts its corporate reach in cellular fashion (with lengthy intervals of apparent morphostasis). Although any, even lower order, central places might suffer from an external breakdown of the system, internal dysfunction is more likely to be a consequence of local famine, epidemic, civil or fiscal disorder than of marginal increases (decreases) in population or territory.

2) *Urbanization* is marked by the enlargement of *micro*-into *meso-differentiated* urban space over areas anywhere from half a dozen to a hundred or more square miles, with net concentrations containing up to several hundred thousand inhabitants. This unprecedented extension and agglomeration during the 19th century, unlike the earlier cellular growth of even great cities, takes the form of increased specialization and articulation of people and places along primarily functional (and correlative social) lines. Extension of the built area in course of urbanization entails a notable scale shift in the organization of urban space whereby: 1) the most intensive differentiation of activities, niches, and land uses takes place toward the center of the agglomeration, and is accompanied by 2) the more or less continuous "development" of fringe lands for various classes of residential and related land uses. By the early 20th century, the larger cities relax into a more decentralized *macro-metropolitan* form of urban differentiation—Patrick Geddes's "conurbation" or R.D. McKenzie's "cluster or constellation of centers"—in which a wider spectrum of productive (as well as domestic) activity gravitates to satellite towns and other "ring" locations.[6]

3) *Posturbanization* sets in at a more advanced phase with the devolution of macro-differentiated space into the late 20th-century "urban field," now extending over many hundreds, even thousands, of square miles and embracing hundreds of thousands, even millions, of inhabitants. This increasingly *eccentric* mode of settlement has been described as a "polycentric" urban field in which the highly differentiated ("polynucleated") central business district inherited from the older "central" city is, according to J.D. Kasarda, "just one specialized node in a multi-nodal, multi-connected ecological field of interdependent activity centers." Thus, *centripetal* movement and "centrality"—timeless features of the historic city and until recently defining characteristics of U.S. Census standard metropolitan statistical areas—are waning attributes of social organization and spatial orientation in highly urbanized eco-systems: a prelude to de-urbanization. The incipient shift in focus and seemingly boundless scale of late 20th-century settlement patterns might correspond in name, if not precise structure, to "the nonplace urban realm" forecast by prescient planners in the early 1960's.[7]

Besides increasing the numbers and size ranges of "cities," the growth and concentration of population since the 18th century—in broad synchronism with the "S" curve of the demographic transition—had the following (overly schematized) impacts on the morphologies of urbanized areas:

Period	Urbanization Phase	Approx. U/P Level	Morphological Tendency (typical built areas, U.S.)
-18thC.	Preurbanization	5-15% of slow-growing populations	"Traditional" cellular organization of microdifferentiated urban space. (2-4 sq. m.)
18th-20thC.	Urbanization	20-75% of faster-growing populations	Extension and reorganization of urban space through meso-differentiation to macro-metropolitan scale. (5-50 : 50-150 sq. m.)
Late 20thC.	Posturbanization	80% ± of slow-growing populations	Devolution of macro-metropolitan scale of differentiation into more extended polycentric urban field. (200 + —10,000 sq. m.)

Mutations of Cities During Urbanization:

If the unfolding city is in each case a particular accommodation of site characteristics and contingencies to predominant tendencies of the larger eco-system, it is in the *general* features of cities—especially cities of comparable size and function in any period—that relations to the process of urbanization will be most discernible.

1) *Preurbanization and Micro-Urban Organization:*

European city growth through early modern times was largely confined to royal capitals and major seaports with little or no net urbanization. The compact and comparatively undifferentiated built areas of even sizable towns rarely extended over a surface of more than one or two square miles. More typical of 17th-century towns proper (excluding suburbs) were areas of from a quarter to three-quarters of a square mile. Even by the later 18th century, few places had expanded the built-up parts of their formal territories beyond two or three square miles; apart from such agglomerative spots as London or Paris, it was easy to traverse their entire length or breadth on foot or by horse in little more than half an hour.

Between Europe's late "Middle Ages" and the early 18th century, the corporate areas of towns were enlarged somewhat more slowly than the net numbers of their residents, although both had usually spread well beyond their remaining walls. Observable increases in superficial density and numbers of persons per dwelling in many towns reflected this discrepancy but there was no parallel trend in numbers per town household. Both large and small towns benefited from net migration at various times as well as from a resilient surplus of births over deaths. Natural increase was usually modest, however, owing to the high mortality of town populations where crude death rates of from 35 to 50 per thousand per year were commonplace facts. In periods of famine, plague or other epidemic, in the aftermath of war, the surplus might dissolve altogether into substantial deficits, and recovery might depend on the age and sex structures of survivors as well as net in-migration. Even quite small towns depended on migrants if, as in the 18th century, they were to achieve a rapid increase of their labor force, but barring a local catastrophe, stable or slowly-growing towns could get by for lengthy periods on a local surplus of baptisms over burials supplemented only by a selected admission of "strangers."

There is always difficulty, to be sure, in distinguishing functional from corporate areas, actual inhabitants from legal residents. There was almost always an amount of suburban settlement which commonly, though by no means certainly, fell within the jurisdiction of the town. A town's legal residents, their dependents and servants, for example, may include those dwelling *ante civitatem* or *extra muros,* and the latter in some instances appear to have outnumbered those residing *intra muros.* There were usually several categories of autochthonous "nonresidents" and "foreigners" also present in a large town, its suburbs, outskirts, or other enclave who should properly be included in its functional population: denizens of a *voorstad, sobbergho, faubourg,* even of the *casale* or *banlieu* in certain instances. Those residing/working in functionally-related ring areas were probably an essential part of a town's "geo-social" space long before horse-drawn omnibuses, tramcars, or steam railways in the second quarter of the 19th century. Meanwhile, modes of transport and communications were confined to pedestrian or equestrian means and their vehicular counterparts, sometimes supplemented by barges or river boats. Communications within towns, as well as over long distances, depended on oral and, increasingly, written language forms that both necessitated physical contact and placed a premium on literacy among laity.

The crowding of many thousands of people into such confining places allowed for no more than micro-differentiation of town space.[8] At the same time, confinement eased the integration of various orders of citizenry whether on functional or wholly customary lines. Numbers of residents per acre furnish a rough indication of prevailing density; numbers per room or dwelling, per household, by parish ward or other subdistrict would, of course, be more revealing of actual living conditions, but they are no more readily available or easily determined than, for example, what part of a population present in a locality is properly assignable to the town on a daily or other periodic basis. Nevertheless, despite the constriction of urban space, conditions of diversity prevailed *within* towns at any time as well as among them. Mean or affluent streets and quarters were almost always present; likewise precincts and alleys given over to particular trades, industries, or nationalities whose several fortunes might follow divergent temporal paths. Richer and poorer elements among town residents, sometimes linked in patronage or cliental relations, appear to have commingled during their daily rounds, with lower orders and deviant sorts as likely to be located in cramped and deteriorating "old quarters" as on the outskirts.

As at any other time in urban history, density of settlement might vary from one neighborhood to the next. Those towns which did experience sustained increases in numbers also appear to have enlarged their corporate bounds or to have extended their built areas within an existing domain. While two and three story buildings everywhere made up the majority of structures for private or public use, four and five stories were not uncommon from the later 16th century, indicating not only mounting population pressures on town space but also changes in the domestic and social arrangements of townspeople. Almost without exception, however, residential densities appear to have been higher during the 18th than in previous centuries, although the heavy crowding in 18th-century Grenobles, Breslau, Bordeaux centre, or Leipzig was certainly not typical.

Increases in numbers per town dwelling are also evident over these same centuries. Evidences for numbers of persons per household or *menage* are harder to come by than for dwellings (except on a case basis where wills and other testamentary records abound). Town households seem to have been somewhat smaller on average than those of rural areas, although differences in numbers between wealthier rural households and those of the agricultural proletariat were closely paralleled in several regions by their urban counterparts. Not surprisingly, perhaps, the lowest household densities were found in a town's "poorer quarters." This circumstance arose not so much because the lower orders were unable to support larger families but rather from the greater incidence among them of unattached men and women, widows, female heads of household, and women taxables. Such "deviant" households, moreover, were often located near the centers of town (especially in manufacturing districts), while ampler households were to be found in the more affluent quarters, in districts with large numbers of servants or hired hands, and still farther out in the less congested suburbs. Again, contrary to conventional wisdom, the perimeters of compact towns in northern and western Europe were frequently occupied by higher orders in the community, if not always by its wealthiest ones.

Renaissance perceptions in print did not always translate into practice. Only in "planned" capitals of princely states, diocesan seats, and "new town" plantings in conquered areas such as the Americas might governmental and religious edifices or mansions of the elite maintain (or usurp) a hold on the town centers. The larger urban mosaic was *already* in place: with its vested rights of way and established daily round (marked since 1500 by the striking of tower clocks), with its civic ceremonies, seasonal rituals, and recurrent flurries in the market place. Town design was there too; but it was a form unfolding in the rub and scuff of centuries, not one springing from the artful geometry of a planner's brain. All this is not to slight effective management, for example, of vital coastal resources by some of the Mediterranean and northern city states. Long before the 16th century, town fathers had indeed undertaken large works of port improvement and even general oversight of town extension, but their projects were responses to the exigencies of commerce and conflict, not to blueprints of political science. Unless imposed from outside, town order had usually grown—like language—in a vernacular mold.

From the 16th and 17th centuries new states and old towns entered upon their fruitful, if unequal, partnership in pursuit of profit and power. The tempo and articulation of activities in the larger and more influential nodes were shaped during that "mercantile" era by the mutually confirming, if subsequently contradictory, tendencies of Renaissance statecraft: absolutism and wealth-getting, fortification and finance, militarism and monopoly. The custom of the community lapsed and conditional rights of user held decreasing sway over allodial town lands. While subject to sovereign command in *l'etat bien police,* the uses of urban space were affected more immediately by local competition and expectations of "rent productivity" or capital gain: except where proprietors or estate managers adhered to some traditional, less "rational" canon, such as the endowment of special dwellings, hospitals, schools, asylums, convents, and the like.

Between 1530 and 1590 the population of Seville increased from 49,000 to more than 90,000, registering the shift from the slow-growing Andalusian center of the 13th-century *reconquista* into "not a city but a world," the focus of the *carrera de Indias*. Even before the flood of 16th-century wealth had transformed "the new Babylonia" into the largest concentration of the Spanish kingdoms, its earlier expansion had covered over the original districts granted by Ferdinand III to his crusading knights and had quite disrupted the orderly allocation of streets and alleys to particular crafts and professions. The local water supply had been augmented by large supplies brought in from three or four leagues hence by underground conduits, surface pipes, and an aqueduct to be "distributed to the churches, monasteries, plazas, streets and houses that contain[ed] fountains and water spouts."[9] The building boom affected every *barrio* inside and outside the walls of a city that had become "in all respects, a house of trade." It extended across the new Triana bridge constructed by the municipality as part of its "improvement plan" to catch up with the vast private and charitable real estate developments of the late 16th century. The municipality expanded its street paving program (prompted much earlier by the Catholic king); it filled in swamps and stagnant lagoons, built a park, and renovated the Moorish public baths but failed to clear up the mountains of accumulated trash or to clean up the rampant corruption of its officers and institutions. Meanwhile, with the Lonja (Exchange) finally constructed "to end the desecration of the Cathedral by merchants and bankers," the commercial district had spread from the vicinity of las Gradas and the Alcazar through a maze of streets and alleys to the Calle de la Sierpe. The Plaza de San Francisco became the new administrative and civic center adjacent to the great Casa de Contratacion, the Mint, the Custom House, and to the wharves and warehouses along the Guadalquivir whither came the loot of the Indies. The "power of gold" had turned merchants and commoners into *hidalgos* and nobles, and the latter into merchant venturers. The enoblement of the rich, as Braudel has shown, was already commonplace in the cities of early modern Europe, but in Seville, at least, the *embourgeoisement* of nobility could also occur.[10]

At the other end of Europe Amsterdam had come into existence in the early 13th century when the Counts of Holland built a sea dyke and a sluice dam where the small Amstel river emptied into a bay of the Ij. Not until 1342 were the first defensive "ditches" dug on either side of the river to enclose the settlement in an area—below sea level—of 617 acres. A second line of ditches was constructed in 1383 about 55 yards farther out and the four now converged in a crescent at the south, while sluice gates connected them separately in the north to the Ij. Houses and commercial buildings were constructed on deep wooden piles along the banks of the river and canals reflecting the prosperity enjoyed by the port as a member of the Hanseatic League. A series of new moats was built in 1442 on the east and west sides of town, and a large quarter was annexed on its south side where the first substantial fortifications and some buildings for religious orders were erected; a specialized manufacturing and shipbuilding district emerged on Wallion Island. In the late 1500's population increased rapidly with the influx of refugees, especially after the Spaniards had captured the city's great rival, Antwerp, in 1576 and Amsterdam had joined with the United Provinces. A much greater depth of bastioned walls was built in 1593, and a double barrage was constructed in the Ij to shelter the growing merchant fleet.[11] It was the city's Chamber of Commerce which, through its financing of an English navigator's voyage to find a northeast passage to the orient in 1609, established claim to the land where in 1626 another of its companies founded a New Amsterdam.

In 1610, with an estimated population of about 100,000, the municipality of Amsterdam introduced its "master plan" which envisaged a threefold expansion of its territory (including reclamations) to 2.8 square miles—possibly the largest single extension to date of any European town. The "plan of three rings"—completion of which took more than a century—involved a sequence of encircling canals with new fortifications to begin along southern portions of the outermost Singelgracht, while the inner canals were extended to link an enlarged water front to the city's core. On its western side a spacious artisanal and industrial area was laid out (the later Jordaan) with worker dwellings built close in to the new woolen factories, tanneries, velvet shop, and a dye mill (completed in 1650). The projected fortification was completed in a vast crescent with 27 bastions by 1663, when the city covered 3.09 square miles and contained a population of about 200,000. After 1667 a reserved park and garden area—the Plantage—was located on the northeast side, although parts of it were later sold off for a fashionable residential quarter laid out on the grid plan—befitting the financial and commercial capital of northern Europe. While the municipality controlled the placement of the canals and the layout and supervision of the land sales, private capital undertook the "development" of the three island rings between the waterways, one result of which was a lack of conformity between the street plan of the industrial west side and that along the canals themselves. Some minor reclamations and harbor improvements eventually spread Amsterdam's urban space over 3.3 square miles within boundaries that endured until the mid-19th century, when the population approached a quarter of a million.[12]

Between the monopoly of Seville and the competitive aggrandizement of Amsterdam, 17th-century France furnishes an example of port construction as a national enterprise. Just as modern economists insist that the only basis for higher consumption and improved welfare services is "sustained growth," so 17th-century policy scientists declared population and production to be the only enduring basis for the military power that would, in turn, enhance the wealth and glory of a monarch, the embodiment of his nation. As far back as 1517, Francis I had become involved in the creation of Le Havre de Grace; Henry IV accomplished major works of social and political renovation in Paris; frontier and prestige projects were carried through in whole or part at Charleville, Nancy, and Richelieu; Colbert began the "modernization" of medieval Marseilles; and still later the Intendant Tourny rebuilt the squalid jumble of Bordeaux centre along Baroque lines of efficiency and beauty. But the grand project under Louis XIII and Louis XIV between 1630 and 1670 resulted in the promotion of four diverse coastal sites into major maritime assets: the spacious, land-locked haven at Brest was initially developed under Richelieu into a formidable Atlantic naval base and arsenal; Lorient, also in Brittany, as an entrepot and East India Company port; Rochefort on the Charente developed under Colbert and fortified by Vauban as a naval arsenal on the central Biscay coast; and Sete, the least successful of the bases, located on the Gulf of Lions in Languedoc. Each concentration was intended to endow a particular place as a nursery for technical labor skills and as a spur to local resource development, although all remained essentially "metropolitan colonies recognizably dependent in purpose and fortune upon the French state."[13]

Other ambitious state-building ventures to foster the sinews of power and wealth by port development and urban renewal were the Dutch—as distinct from Italianate-French—inspired architectural and engineering works carried out by Christian IV around his several Scandinavian lands. The medieval "Merchants' haven," Copenhagen—with its arsenal and Borsen located on Slotsholmen as the nucleus of a revitalized city, the new Christianshaven (1617), and the Nyboder workers' quarters (1627)—was especially famous and, for Denmark at least, quite effective. The rebuilding of Goteborg (founded 1603-07) by Gustavus II and Oxenstierna as a "Venice of the North," after its destruction by the Danes in the Kalmar War, was a less spectacular achievement at the time, perhaps; but the Dutch model of canalized river axis, grid layout, central market square, with semicircular fortifications based on the river, furnished a well-designed infrastructure for a site that was to become Sweden's second city and greatest port.[14] Dutch-style expansions projected by local elites in Hamburg and Bremen, moreover, indicate that great expectations of business enterprise, other things being equal, did not require a despotic state framework before corporate investors could recognize the benefits that a well-endowed urban port facility might bestow. A port city, in addition to its role as administrative and market center, might become a social engine for generating wealth.

Already present in many of these late renaissance and early baroque town projects was the modern enthusiasm for "growth poles." Such artfully contrived settings were expected to attract migrants and money in ways that would nourish innovations in trade and transport, the mechanic arts, the strategies of seapower, while all the time serving as persuasive advertisements for law and order. They were an expression likewise of the principle of acquisitive rationality—the spirit of enterprise—applied to the reorganization of collective life by a "national" bourgeoisie which revealed its heightened perception of the spatial discontinuities that inhere in social organization. Nevertheless, such works—as in the case of the Goteborg-Stockholm navigation scheme—often overreached themselves. Adequate technical, financial, and bureaucratic resources were not available, and since other things were decidedly *unequal,* extant means were as likely to be squandered in the dynastic and sectarian struggles which characterized the welding of diverse peoples and places into "nation" states as in augmenting their production *per se.*

For all the planning and public works, the 17th century passed in Europe with no more than a dozen additional concentrations of 10,000 or more residents, and with the built areas of most cities at its close barely more extended than in the early 16th century. Only a handful of state populations were a matter of four or five percentage points more urbanized in 1700 than a hundred years before—England and Wales, Spain, and Denmark—while others, such as the Low Countries or France were virtually unchanged or, as in the cases of the Italian peninsula and possibly the Germanies, slightly less urbanized than in 1600. Notwithstanding the unprecedented transfer of resources from outside Europa *via* Seville or Lisbon, and their leavening effects on production in certain other parts of western Europe, the promise of the early 1500's for the growth of cities and urban populations had simply not been realized; the question of urbanization, of course, had never even been raised. Given the limits of technology and organization with respect to transport and communications in enabling populations to surmount recurrent crises of subsistence and epidemic, or to cope with man-made devastations of the environment, most energies were consumed in sustaining population numbers, in establishing and securing state systems, and in embellishing their capitals and ocean ports. No productive tendencies among the populations had meanwhile gathered sufficient momentum to prevail over structural rigidities in the ecosystem which inhibited economic development and still circumscribed economic or demographic change. The inherited urban structures were not yet fully open to the ethos, let alone the practices, of individual enrichment at any level of society, while collective national projects usually failed to generate the impetus expected from them.

Neither the promptings of state building nor the constraint of local customs, however, did much to curb the acquisitive impulse for profit or plunder. All but vestiges of corporate town autonomy waned in western Europe from the later 1600's under the enlivening prospect of personal gain upon a wider stage of operations except, to be sure, in hard times when local interests both artisanal and mercantile might again seek to revive the parochial exclusiveness and protectionism of an earlier day. Whatever "design" had belonged to town order was rapidly overlaid by 1700 when fashionable architects were already shaping the details of each commission into its immediate surroundings—according to the private "needs" and resources of their wealthier or more powerful clients. What redeemed the early modern city of size or pretension was its essentially pedestrian scale and cellular structure: even when immured behind costly defenses or gilded over with the extravagances of kingly or capitalist baroque. It was still physically self-contained and comprehensible, although its citizens—no matter now internally divided from each other—found themselves collectively tying into a more competitive environment and becoming more perplexed by an equation linking the welfare of communities and nations to unfettered exchange.[15]

The exertions necessary to solve that equation institutionally during the 18th century were to undo townsmen's economic and psychological defenses and render even their physical bastions obsolete. Eventually the town would be denatured as a corporation in all but a diminished municipal sense. Meanwhile, town dwellers as functional subsystems exhibited a wider range of compositional, distributional, and size attributes within larger provincial or national systems. Most observable differences—allowing for local materials and building styles—seem readily explicable in terms of primary functions and circumstances: notably a town's nodal and productive roles within its broader system and its more or less recent experience of epidemic disease or wartime dislocation. Already in the 17th century some of the most populous places, especially those with an extended territorial base, were developing a perceptible degree of functional "districting" that went beyond the formal divisions and social zones of previous centuries. Yet, with the exception again of royal capitals, Atlantic seaports, and a few large industrial/marketing centers, the social heterogeneity and economic diversity of town life and livelihood postulated no urgent grounds for the articulation of town space. In late 16th-century London, nevertheless, where population grew from about 50,000 towards 100,000 over the near half century of Elizabeth's reign, some noteworthy clusters of manufactures and commerce were observed, for example, by John Stow, within the 1.05 square mile expanse of the city proper.[16]

London was probably the fastest growing agglomeration in Europe during the 17th century, and by its third quarter, more than half a million people were concentrated in a built area which of necessity had spread well beyond the city's historic 672 acres. Meanwhile the clustering of particular mercantile and artisanal pursuits at different points about the Royal Exchange in late-Tudor/early-Stuart times prefigured a substantial accession to urban form: the "polynuclear central business district."[17] Except for some incipient clumping of specialized functions within the great commercial ports of Antwerp and Amsterdam, none of the ten or dozen largest continental centers (with 100,000 or more residents) had yet undergone this critical mutation. There were pressures of population and activities, to be sure, on some Iberian cities; and by the early 1600's, some informally—as well as formally—variegated social landscapes marked at least another 18 or more places of 50,000 inhabitants or more, but nothing on the scale or pattern of central London. By the early 1700's, nevertheless, the crowding of people in the micro-spaces of quite small cities was clearly registered by rising superficial densities and suburban extensions in both Europe and America. Many of these smaller places—especially ports and new manufacturing clusters—were now growing markedly more from net migration than from local natural increase and, as a consequence, tended to have younger, more productive and reproductive populations than most of the established regional centers or older market towns.

These same centuries also witnessed the planting of embryonic European towns in uncongenial New World environments. Sixteenth-century Spanish town mutants adapted the social instruments of the *Reconquista* to the task of subduing Indian America. Of many stockaded ports founded by French, English, and Dutch invaders of North America during the 17th century, only four or five had grown into substantial small-town settlements by the early 1700's. Boston was the sole English entrepot until the more rapid growth of Philadelphia and New York City during the second quarter of the 18th century. The high birth rates accomplished by Philadelphians around mid-century, in contrast to Boston, were a partial consequence of migration and the youthfulness of its population (the indentured servant market centered there). Compared with most European cities, both Boston and Philadelphia enjoyed low residential densities before and after the War of Independence (as did New York City for a brief period after the war), but working settlements already extended beyond the existing town limits. By 1800 some proto-nucleation among commercial functions was taking place on certain streets when overall densities were no more than 25 per acre in Boston, about 28 in Philadelphia proper, and somewhat greater in New York where the major portion of the inhabitants was still concentrated in the southernmost wards (which occupied a mere fraction of the city's 21.9 square mile expanse, roughly coextensive with Manhattan Island). If the availability of land in Anglo-America had not produced a distinctive urban settlement pattern nor permitted the municipal bounds or built areas of port towns to be notably larger (Boston 1.5 square miles, Philadelphia 2.3 square miles, Norfolk 1.3 square miles) than those of typical European counterparts, (1) their populations ca. 1800 were still somewhat smaller, (2) their residential densities much lower, and (3) the amounts of space allocated to public streets and circulatory movement relative to building cover munificent by European standards. Thus there appears to have been ample room on town lots for repletion by additional structures, workplaces, and dwellings, although the expansion of early 19th-century ports was already marked by the invasion of outer wards and much spilling over into neighboring jurisdictions.[18] If there were declines in residential numbers of some innermost precincts of American port cities by the 1830's, it is as much testimony to the conversion of "central" space (as in European cities) to more specialized commercial, financial, or manufacturing uses as it is to reductions in overall densities by peripheral spread.

2) *Urbanization and Mesourban Organization*

Urbanization takes place *only* when the rate of increase of a region's urban population exceeds that of its rural—and hence total—population in any period. During the 16th and 17th centuries levels of urbanization had been raised a few percentage points in the Iberian Peninsula and British Isles; but elsewhere, notwithstanding ambitious public works or the growth of port cities and capitals, the levels remained stable or even fell somewhat, as in Italy and the Low Countries. The gathering concentration of the later 18th century likewise sustained urbanization only in Britain, France, and certain parts of the northeastern U.S., for the contemporary surges in Denmark and Italy had lost their momentum again by 1800. Meanwhile, other countries such as Belgium, the Netherlands, Switzerland, Saxony, or Prussia seem not to have experienced much net urbanization before the 19th-century's second quarter.[19]

Acceleration of the urbanizing process owed little at first to technologies and organization of communications or transport. Increases in rates and resultant levels of urbanization from the late 18th century took the form of (1) multiplication of small concentrations, especially at sites which developed a water-powered manufacturing base, and (2) increases in populations and built-areas of medium-sized centers ranging upwards from 20,000 to 99,000 inhabitants. By midcentury the two-or-three-square-mile large cities from 1800 spread their boundaries to areas from five to ten square miles or more; while the new concentrations of specialized manufactures in some cases enlarged their earlier village proportions over territories anywhere from two or three up to five or eight square miles, at which time they were incorporated as "cities" or "boroughs."[20] As rapidly as some towns had managed to stretch their municipal power over newly urbanized space, both residential and commercial developments still proceeded beyond their legal reach. On the fringes of expanding centers, villages and hamlets often resisted the encroachments of their more sizable neighbors and occasionally adopted political or other measures of their own to maintain their "independence" and distinctive social milieu. The historical-institutional situations governing the acquisition and development of fringe lands by private or public agencies—like the capacities of local governments to annex and absorb peripheral territories—varied among regions and countries. Neither "rational" market forces nor technological "imperatives" could readily dislodge embedded "misallocations" of resources arising, say, from the rejection of real estate developers' or railway promoters' highest bids.[21] Nevertheless, regardless of imperfections in the working of local land markets, competitive pressures on existing urban space would sooner or later tend to drive up the price of land and related costs of doing business in a town's central district or other choice site. As a corollary, any delay in opening up peripheral lands to development would tend to reduce the moderating effect that new subdivisions and "improvements" might be expected to have on unearned and other incremental values at the center.

The larger American (and even British) towns seem to have expanded their official territories—as well as populations—before midcentury to a greater extent than did their counterparts in continental Europe. They were likewise, and here the British were usually in the vanguard, the concentrations that developed more specialized, and hence more differentiated, manufacturing districts, as well as more socially-variegated and spatially-separated residential turfs. Both British and American centers, followed more closely in this regard by larger European cities, also evolved more articulated financial, wholesaling, and shopping districts: the pinnacles of land values, the ultimate in capitalizing urban space. The polynucleation of a "central business district"—sometimes quite "off center" where a prominent topographical feature or established civic edifice obtruded—originated in a desire to conduct at a most conveniently accessible point those activities which were peculiarly "linked by competition and complementarity": subject, of course, to constraints represented by site rents and property tax assessments. Other mutations—wrought in the competition for space among different types of manufacture, transport, or residence—indicated the accretion of new modes of production and work organization superseding the close-in artisanal retailing clusters of an earlier day. Residential differentiation, meanwhile, attested the enduring restraint on working people, especially casual laborers, to live near their jobs as well as the freedom of wealthier folk to walk or ride to their place of work.[22]

During the second quarter of the 19th century, the intrusion of railroad stations and freight yards on cheaper peripheral lands led to the formation of secondary centers of manufacture and warehousing that eased congestion somewhat in older riverside wharfage and harbor districts. The introduction of horse-drawn short stages and omnibus routes tied these newly differentiated clusters of workplaces and dwellings into the older core *via* residential and commercial streets, bestowing a firmer arterial structure thereby on the burgeoening urban space. In smaller towns, moreover, with the advent of railway tracks the business center itself might gravitate four or five blocks over toward the station away from its earlier locus along the river or canal bank. Nevertheless, the physical impacts of steamboats and locomotives apart, there were no transport innovations with the power to enhance local circulation, although the building of additional bridges might at almost any time precipitate new town salients and bring on a localized flurry of construction. Inasmuch as early applicatons of electromagnetic telegraphy were also directed towards long-distance communication—usually in conjunction with the organization of railroad operations—the internal reordering of cities went forward on a larger scale *within* the historic time-space limits imposed by pedestrian and equestrian means.[23]

By midcentury the areal specialization of land uses in response to functional differentiation and competition for place had not gone very far. Moreover, urbanized areas were constructed piecemeal more or less on demand and, notwithstanding the confidence of later Chicago sociologists that "forces at work within the limits of the urban community...tend to bring about an orderly grouping of its population and institutions," there remained numerous irregularities and "disorderly" niches within blocks, neighborhoods, and districts—as even a casual reference to 19th-century street directories reveals. Indeed, the fact that particular trades and industries, occupations, nationalities, sects, or "classes" were becoming more localized *within* the population expanse of a growing city does not mean that the resulting "localities" and "districts" were *internally* homogeneous, uniform, or exclusive.[24] Under the impetus of urbanization, nevertheless, the multiplication of activities and progressive specialization of functional or social attachments and affinities was taking place with greater rapidity in towns altogether smaller in size relative to their standing or rank in the hierarchically-extended city system. In this respect, at least, the vicinities of a Main Street or Market Street in the "downtown" sections of quite modest 19th-century industrial towns had come to resemble 17th-century Cheapside and Cornhill in the metropolitan City of London.

The concentration and crowding of population continued along the same lines and with much the same motivations throughout the latter half of the century. Six places with 10,000 or more residents in the United States of 1800, for example, had become 62 by midcentury (six with more than 100,000) and 440 by the century's close (38 with more than 100,000). Already by 1870 more people resided in census urban places than had inhabited the entire republic only half a century before. Horse-drawn public vehicles which had augmented pedestrian and private circulation during the century's second quarter were in turn supplemented and, in part, supplanted by horse-drawn street railways, elevated steam trains, cable cars, and like innovations during its third quarter. Municipal boundaries were pushed outwards by local authorities under various state provisions, peripheral communities were annexed, and the incorporated territories of the largest agglomerations distended over areas up to 100 and more square miles of highly capitalized urban space, much of it in the form of less congested residential development.[25] At the same time, some localities would seek to separate and preserve themselves politically from parent communities which appeared to stand in the projected path of annexations and consolidations; a few other enclaves succeeded even in detaching themselves legally from the tentacular embrace of their cities.

The unfolding of immense built areas in the later 19th century prompted novel ventures in residential structures and living arrangements. In a conscious effort to reduce monotony and remedy squalor, "improved" modes of multiple dwelling house were adopted in the U.S. (and Britain) from the continent, although the single-family town house—whether detached or in rows—remained the ideal in both countries. In 1864 Frank Leslie's *Illustrated* referred to large multi-storied "French Flats" or *appartements* as "First Class Tenement Houses" in contrast to the earlier "court houses,'"rookeries," and other squalid multiple-family dwellings of the poor such as the notorious Five Points tenements in lower Manhattan. Outside of Manhattan and a few central blocks in other large cities, however, apartment houses or "flathouses" never did attain the wide acceptance granted by almost all classes of urban population in Paris, in Vienna, or Berlin. Even without the costly "safety elevators" or "lifts" which had been installed in a variety of commercial buildings since the Haughwout in 1857, it was still true, as Friedrich Ratzel, the geographer, noted with reference to Manhattan at the time of his 1873 visit, that multi-room apartments on a single floor or a large structure represented a belated effort to achieve a more "efficient" use of "the land and capital available for building" and were, perhaps, the only way to avoid "retreating" from areas of business altogether. Nevertheless, the growing range of domiciliary means and ends in large cities—ranging from cellars and attics, single-room lodgings, and old-style boarding houses through two and three-decker row houses, detached single and two family dwellings, mansions, large flats, and huge five or six-storied "tenement" or apartment blocks—permitted the rapidly increasing numbers of urbanites to divide and distance themselves from each other along broad income and class lines to a degree that would have been impracticable in smaller towns either then or in the past.[26] The continuing reorganization of places of business and residence upon a larger meso-urban scale contributed, in conjunction with the more abundant locational options available to manufactures and commerce, to the heightened segmentation and enhanced financial yield of more specialized urban properties.

Clearly, the construction and reconstruction of urban artifacts on the installment plan resulted in a marked variability of residential densities and nonresidential land uses around the extended cities. If average densities per acre in the U.S., outside of a few congested areas, were appreciably lower than in most continental European cities—owing to comparative absence of socio-economic obstacles to land purchase, the rising incidence of home ownership, and exemption from obstructive military works—the average number of persons per census dwelling in the 28 largest U.S. cities of 1890, 7.4, was above that for an equivalent range of large cities in England and Wales, while public standards for sanitation and sewage disposal remained considerably lower. But the average number of tenements per dwelling, the proportions of families and individuals in any given number of rooms, like the percentages of owner occupied tenements, etc., varied within and among U.S. cities: for example, from New York City's 18.5 persons per dwelling in 1890, 9.8 in Brooklyn, 8.6 in the "spread city" of Chicago, 7.4 in St. Louis, to 6.0 in Baltimore and only 5.6 in Philadelphia. By the English statutory definition of "overcrowding" (more than two persons per room), however, only the "slum" population of New York's lower East Side—among the four major cities studied by the U.S. Commissioner of Labor in 1893—exceeded the levels of overcrowding reported from London's borough of Finsbury or from Tyneside. Nevertheless, whereas overall densities and numbers of "overcrowded" persons were falling in London and most U.S., as well as English, cities those in Manhattan continued to increase, and in 1905 some 12 city blocks on the same lower East Side were reporting from 1,000 to 1,400 persons per acre. The range and intensity of residential differences within old New York surpassed those of any other U.S. city, but the miracle was that, both before and after the great political consolidation of 1898, New York City did not exhibit the highest crude mortality among the cities.[27] Crude mortality was in fact declining in most cities over the closing decades of the century. The effects of improved diet, high pressure water supplies, better sewage treatment, and other environmental ameliorations (including rapid transit service) were especially felt between 1895 and 1905, although chronic infant mortality (as distinct from mortality of children under 5 years) exacted its grim toll on urban life well into the years after World War I.

3) *Macro-Metropolitan Organization of the Urban Habitat*

With the rapid electrification of streetcars in the U.S. during the 1890's the larger agglomerations (and newer medium-sized ones) had already crossed the threshold into the era of macro-organized urban space. The introduction of more or less "open access" rapid transit service at street level had effectively doubled the distance that might be traveled in a given time over that attainable by horse-drawn vehicles except, of course, through the most congested tracts of the "downtown." The first city and suburban telephone connections had been inaugurated in Boston and New Haven in 1877-78 at about the time when the new carbon arc street lamp promised to turn the city night into "eternal day." Local and long distance commercial telephone service became widespread in the 1880's well before the electrification of street and elevated railways or the later distribution of purchased electric power to widely dispersed industrial users.[28] The reduced time and cost involved in traversing *long distances* which had been such a conspicuous feature of advances in inter-local transport and communications since the second quarter of the 19th century were at last being matched and magnified in effect within the lesser ambit of intra-local transactions.

The particular effect of this time-space "convergence" upon the local scene was not so much the resulting size, transactional density, or social heterogeneity of urban populations, nor even the enlargement of their daily circulation, as the scale of functional and affiliational segmentation of people and properties within their dilated areas. Between the tenacious enclaves of rich and poor households fringing parts of the expanded business districts (now larger than the area of most cities ca. (1800) and the retreating elites of the outermost suburbs dwelt the masses of lower and middling strata in a variegated mosaic of workplaces, commercial and residential thoroughfares, parks and cemeteries, in ethnic neighborhoods or "sides of town" laid out fairly uniformly in streets of one and two family "homes." Residential land uses (including contiguous public facilities, rights of way, and private services) had meanwhile come to occupy from half to two-thirds of a large city's incorporated area—which had commonly undergone a four to six-fold expansion during the decades 1850-1910 overspreading the surrounding countryside and engulfing its communities. Once population concentration and the invention of more lucrative land uses had compelled *horizontal* and, with centrally located commercial skyscrapers and residential high-rise from the 1880's, *vertical* extension of the built area, technical and financial constraints upon construction and communications more effectively governed the rate of peripheral "development" and the capitalization of incremental urban land.[29]

The spread of concentrated populations beyond their cities' existing perimeters is, to be sure, the classic mode of urban growth. Awareness of the discrepance between a city's official boundaries and its ecological field goes back at least to early 19th-century descriptions of Philadelphia and its suburbs. It was foremost in the mind of Andrew H. Green in recommending a "municipal union" of New York City, Brooklyn, and adjacent Westchester for capital spending purposes in the late 1860's and early 70's, and it is not surprising that the same divergence was apparent to the Bostonian, Sylvester Baxter, in the early 1890's when he called for recognition of "the true boundaries" of a city based on the "geosocial life" of its metropolitan population. Somewhat belatedly, the 13th U.S. Census in 1910 identified some 25 "metropolitan districts" (misleadingly characterized as "cities and suburbs") containing central or twin cities with 200,000 or more inhabitants and ranging in population and area from Portland, Oregon, with 215,048 residents spread over 67.2 square miles (47.3 sq. m. city proper) to New York-Newark, N.J., with a 956.5 square mile base (299 sq. m. NYC) for its 6,474,568 inhabitants, 73 per cent of whom lived in New York City. In 16 of the districts, moreover, the "suburban" ring population exceeded 10 per cent of the metropolitan total, peaking in the Boston district where 55 per cent were credited to the functionally related ring area outside the 39 square miles of the central city.[30]

By and large informed opinion in the U.S., as well as in Europe, had welcomed this "suburban trend" as the most "natural" and effective remedy for the physical and moral "problems" afflicting the great cities. Circulatory congestion, human and industrial pollution, squalid housing, malnutrition and morbidity, criminality and vice could be left behind as more people—including many even among the less affluent—were removed *via* rapid transit to lower density suburbs or satellite towns. While population filtered outward and "upward" into less crowded domiciles, more "professional" and honest engineers and administrators would be empowered to devote resources and expertise to solving "problems" which had hitherto been exacerbated by the sheer crush of life and work in the core areas. This optimistic vision of "city and suburb" as a new order in space and time—the suburbs for domesticity and child rearing, the core for production and commerce—was the ultimate in functional and social segmentation: as if the ecosystem had achieved some final "steady state." It would vouchsafe growing numbers of urbanites the best of both worlds, while ameliorating conditions for all. As Adna F. Weber had affirmed at the close of the century: "the rise of the suburbs...furnishes the solid basis for hope that the evils of city life so far as they result from overcrowding may be in large part removed."[31]

The suburban solution did not necessarily entail a withdrawal from the political jurisdiction of the city. It was a social and economic rather than a political answer to the Social Question. Streetcar operators and building contractors motivated by profit expectations would bring about an actual decrease in overcrowded persons with little recourse to city planning let alone "municipal socialism." The orderly reduction in crowding and congestion through "voluntary" decentralization of residence—with, at most, a little nudging from Frankfurt-style zoning—excited virtually no misgiving among urban reformers at the time. To be sure, a few planners, or rather would-be planners, of the City Beautiful era, had gone beyond routine traffic engineering concerns to voice doubts about the withdrawal of so many customers from primary "downtown" shopping districts. Unless street transportation and public circulation to and from central areas were improved, argued such protagonists as Daniel H. Burnham and John Nolen in their presentations to businessmen clients and civic groups, many retail activities and personal services would be obliged to pursue their retreating patrons to the outskirts. While some public health officials and political economists, influenced by British and German examples, had long recommended the displacement of noxious manufactures, labor-intensive sweated trades, and even branches of heavier industry from what were by now "inner areas" in order to reduce air and water pollution, ease pressures on central space, and ameliorate both job and home conditions for low paid workers, other experts noted that there was as yet no very evident tendency for manufactures to scatter. As Adna F. Weber put it: "the transference of manufacturing industries to the suburbs...cannot be forced; it must wait upon economic forces." Compared with the conventional wisdom prevailing on both sides of the Atlantic, Ebenezer Howard's *Tomorrow: A Peaceful Path to Reform* (1898) displayed a singular grasp of what "economic forces" were already doing to the vitality of urbanized areas that seems remarkably prescient. For him the crowded industrial cities "have done their work" and are disintegrating in a "railway chaos."[32] What forms of urban settlement could be devised for the future that might preserve a viable city center but allow "new wealth forms to be created?"

And there was the rub. What was to hold at the center? With the annular enlargements of urban space, the accessibility of cheaper peripheral land, lower rents and taxes, more flexible and graduated power sources, availability of railway sidings and spur lines, and instant communications, the decisive "advantage" of an inner location for many kinds of enterprise (as well as selected classes of residence) was eroded over the early decades of this century. Mounting recourse to the automobile for commercial and personal transport after World War I—not so much for the journey to work as yet—modified the arterial traffic patterns that had persisted from the mid 19th century through the short-lived era of profitable rapid public transit in metropolitan areas early in the 20th century. The lateral mobility of the motor car on public streets outside the core brought more metropolitan territory into the city's daily orbit, especially where state and local governments hastened to invest the proceeds from a gasoline tax and licensing revenues in the construction of circular roads and belt-line highways. Some exuberant members of the recently organized city planning profession predicted that electric power transmission and the internal combustion engine would soon arrest the process of formless peripheral spread and "reunite" town and country in the fruitful intercourse of "true regionalism." Within the decade the "natural" solutions to the inherited problems of congestion and overcrowding were being recycled by the next generation of reformers as the emergent "problems of metropolitan areas in the automobile age." "True regionalism" was becoming lost in what R.D. McKenzie called the division of "the entire territory of the continental United States" into "a comparatively small number of supercities...becoming more nearly uniform in their economic and institutional structure."[33]

By 1929—before the onset of the calamitous Depression—up to 80 per cent of the extended territories of many U.S. cities was allocated to residential and related public service uses with less than 20 per cent of developed land used for private industrial and commercial activities. Before the collapse of the 1920's construction boom, 85 per cent of all urban residences were single family dwellings, and nearly two-thirds of urban families lived in such structures. No longer the distinctive trait of rural America, nonfarm home ownership *via* short term mortgage conveyance had risen among native and foreign-born alike from about a third of all units in the late 1880's to about 40 per cent by the end of World War I. The incidence of home ownership was particularly high in the younger agglomerations of the Middle and Far Wests ranging from almost 45 per cent in Los Angeles and 41 per cent in Detroit down to 17 per cent in Boston and less than 12 per cent in greater New York (a minuscule 2.9 per cent in the American-style "rental barracks city" of Manhattan) by 1910. There was still a majority of renters, of course, in all major U.S. cities, but those high proportions—low by the standards of other urbanizing nations—were lowered still further when renters became the special target of the real estate industry's "Own Your Own Home" suburban building drive in the prosperous mid-20's. At the time of the 1929 "Crash" some 46 per cent of all nonfarm housing units were "owner occupied," although proportions of tenants rose again in most parts of the country down through World War II.[34]

The impacts of peripheral building developments on the morphology of urbanized areas became marked countrywide during the 1920's. From the close of World War I the *aggregate* population of the suburban and satellite ring areas of the nation's metropolitan districts (97 by the definition of 1950) was growing at a substantially faster rate than that of their "central cities," while many of the older and large cities of the Northeast, and some in the older Middle West likewise, were politically unable to annex greater portions of their extended urban areas. Fifteen cities with populations of 50,000 or more actually registered numerical declines during the 1920's and many others barely held their own. Such were the changing contours of the macro-metropolitan urban areas the better part of a decade *before* the federal government moved directly into the affairs of cities in 1934 with the hasty introduction of publicly-financed mortgage insurance and long-term amortized mortgages to bail out the construction and mortgage lending industries and preserve depression-stricken America as a property-owning democracy of cities and suburbs as well as of farms.

By the second quarter of the 20th century almost every road was leading out from the city. As A.N. Whitehead saw it in 1933: "the reasons for this concentration are largely disappearing...the reasons for the choice of sites for cities are also altering...Almost every reason for the growth of cities, concurrently with civilization, has been profoundly modified."[35] For several decades manufactures as well as retail and personal services had been gravitating beyond the city's limits to the outer rings of suburbs and satellite towns—much as Ebenezer Howard had predicted. With gains in real personal income per capita (no longer closely associated with incremental urbanization), as well as advances in transport and communications, the agglomerative city was "coming apart" economically and financially in ways less striking but more fundamental perhaps than the social-political disarray that had sparked the countervailing tendencies of administrative centralization in the "progressive years" before the first World War. The underlying centrifugal currents, hitherto moderated if never wholly contained by competitive demands for "access," now reinforced the peripheral drift.

Population went on increasing within most city jurisdictions, however, despite the outward surge. City governments in many parts of the country were able to annex some of their peripheral subdivisions. Of 93 large cities with 100,000 or more residents in 1930, 54 had annexed additional areas during the decade 1910-1920, while only three had actually lost territory; 49 of these large cities annexed further territory during the 1920's. Nevertheless, the faster increase of populations and, to a lesser extent, of employment opportunities in the ring areas of metropolitan districts after 1920 persisted down through World War II despite the wider swath of territories annexed by central cities countrywide. Some 59 cities with 50,000 or more inhabitants—at least 35 of them "central cities"—experienced a net loss of population during the 1930's; 23 continued or commenced to lose population in the 1940's, while another 14 had not yet recovered their 1930 numbers by 1950 notwithstanding wartime "full employment" and heavy migration from parts of the rural South. Local property taxes also took a beating during the depression years but continued to yield the bulk of revenues necessary to keep the city functioning and sustain the partnership in city government of local office holders and organized interests. The possible consequences of this net displacement of jobs as well as people for the economic vitality of older central cities were only dimly understood in the late 1920's when two decades of depression and war, 1930-1953, diverted public attention to the more momentous political questions of economic and military survival. The ominous spread of physical and social blight, depressed industries, and urban decline could meanwhile be attributed almost wholly to circumstances rather than secular tendencies of society.

Thus the early warning signals that "market forces," in cooperation with municipal governments, were becoming unable to renew substantial segments of the urban core by redevelopment or replacement were misinterpreted or slighted outright.[36]

By the 1920's the central cores of older macro-metropolitan areas were ceasing to be "self-renewing" zones of enterprise. In early volumes of the *Regional Survey of New York and Its Environs* appearing in 1928, the land economist, Robert Murray Haig, had documented not only the substantial loss of different categories of manufacture to satellite locations but also some of the deleterious consequences of this shift on parts of New York City. Although the separation of means of communication from transportation would allow the "managerial function" to be exercised from centrally located office buildings which facilitated face-to-face conferences among executive specialists, factories and warehouses would be located elsewhere. Thus New York, like a few other highly capitalized centers, was beginning to experience what was already widely noted in older "one industry" towns from Lowell and Nashua in New England across New York and New Jersey to Pennsylvania and eastern Ohio: the emergence of blighted zones larger in acreage and involving more varied land uses than in the late 19th-century "slums" studied by the U.S. Commissioner of Labor in 1893. The "slums," moreover, whether large tenements or simply run-down multi-family dwellings, had provided low-income housing *otherwise unavailable*, had made money for their owners (sometimes co-residents), and had helped buttress central land values. While housing reformers had sought to improve such structures by restrictive legislation and local regulation, no one had abandoned them until some higher yielding improvement actually displaced them from the site—not an easy succession since well-managed slum properties might yield handsome returns during periods of rapid concentration. The effect of residential and business withdrawals from "downtown" districts in the 1920's—as R.D. McKenzie reported in *Recent Social Trends* with a dramatic incidence of declining land values between about 20th and 78th Streets along Cleveland's Euclid Avenue—had been "to hasten the obsolescence of much of the older pattern of the city." If anything, the motor roads recently built by state and local governments had aggravated conditions since blight and deterioration were not so much the causes of households and jobs departing the inner cities as their consequence. Meantime, congestion persisted in adjacent parts of "the downtown" and had in certain respects been intensified by the real estate and mortgage lending industries' inability to promote revitalization of the blighted tracts. Even before the Wall St. "Crash" in October, 1929, money-lending and other commercial interests could not always afford to renew such districts and neighborhoods as readily as they had been willing to do only a few years earlier, since, apart from large unit office space, fancy apartment houses, and luxury hotels, "these areas are in competition with newer subdivisions which offer a more inviting field for private enterprise." In 1925 Clarence Stein had already characterized some of the older and more bloated concentrations as "Dinosaur Cities."[37]

As the great property boom faded in the later 1920's the costs of replacing, even of rehabilitating, many obsolete or blighted premises were exceeding the likelihood of their profitable current use. With the deepening depression after 1929, property and land values (not to mention their fanciful tax assessments) could not be deflated fast enough to make redevelopment attractive to investors not withstanding the sharp fall in interest rates. Depression enlarged the areas of central decay without altogether arresting the macro-metropolitan spread (underwritten after 1933 by U.S. government support for home ownership and new construction which met federal standards).[38]

The New Deal understood little about urbanization of the economy and less about the possible relation between them. Although the National Resources Committee published in June 1938 what the Secretary of the Interior, Harold L. Ickes, claimed to be "the first major national study of cities," its report broke little new economic ground. *Our Cities, Their Role in the National Economy* did indeed recognize that cities were "one of the fundamental supports...of the Nation's economy" but chose, nevertheless, to feature the city as "one of the primary problems" of that economy. It went on in the familiar tradition of American social science to dwell upon "the problems of cities" and offered some eleven recommendations toward their solution. While *Our Cities* deplored the "uncontrolled subdivision and speculative practices" which had so recently fed "the most fantastic real estate boom" and pointed, in light of metropolitan problems, to urban public finance as "another emerging problem of vast proportions," it failed—despite a section headed "the process of urbanization -underlying forces..."—to explore relations between urbanization and economic change in any systematic manner. Even when noting the "most dramatic inequalities of income and wealth" among city dwellers, for example, the report ignored possible connections between this prosaic finding and the instabilities that inhered in industrial development and periodically manifested themselves *inter alia* in the form of fluctuations in urban construction. Neither the New Deal nor its research agencies confronted the changing role of cities in the capitalist economy, although by 1940 some of its planners—particularly those associated with the National Resources Planning Board and the "Keynesian" economist Alvin Hansen—saw urban renewal as an area in which "compensatory spending" by federal authorities would likely stimulate an otherwise "stagnant" private investment sector.[39] In the same year the Urban Land Institute—research arm of the National Association of Real Estate Boards—published studies of "what decentralization is doing to our cities" and followed up with "an outline for a legislative program to rebuild our cities." So domesticated had these "radical" ideas become between the sharp recession of 1937-38 and the attack on Pearl Harbor that such foundation-media pillars as the Twentieth Century Fund and *Fortune* magazine got into the act of promoting federal aids in support of local governmental acquisition and private renewal of land in blighted zones and of "freeing" land in redevelopment areas from inflated assessments which discouraged venture capital.[40] In any event, the unprecedented federal spending on World War II not only restored aggregate demand to full employment *plus* levels but actuated a whole gamut of structural changes in production which made postwar federal involvement in city building politically unnecessary and ideologically suspect.

This is not the place to rehearse the details of what happened to the "rebuilding" of U.S. cities or, more significant perhaps, what did not happen. Since the Housing Act of 1937 no more than about eight square miles distributed over 86 cities (involving a mere 70,000 dwelling units) had actually been cleared by 1953 out of hundreds of square miles of blight and rot gathering countrywide. In Detroit alone there were some 63 square miles of blight involving housing that had been built without plan or regulation during the automobile industry's growth boom, 1916-29. Nationwide, the Advisory Committee on Government Housing Policies and Programs discovered five million housing units unsalvageable and a further 15 million structures in need of immediate rehabilitation. Between the end of World War II and Eisenhower's last year in office some 23 million new housing units had been built—nearly 40 per cent of the entire housing stock of 58 million units—mostly on newly converted and subdivided land. More than two-thirds of those units stood on land which in 1960 had not yet been annexed by central cities. "Free enterprise" had been constructing its "cities" elsewhere—under a variety of federal supports including FHA insured mortgages, Farm Home and Veterans' Administration programs—rather than in the slum areas or urban blighted zones. In 1965 had come the long awaited federal Department of Housing and Urban Development and in 1968 the final report of the National Commission on Urban Problems, *Building the American City,* by which time the extent of one or another form of federal involvement meant that about 77 per cent of the nation's 70 million housing units (1970) were nominally subject to terms of Title VIII of the Fair Housing Act of 1968. Clearly, federal subsidy of "downtown" renewal under local government auspices and subvention of scattered fringe developments on "pragmatic" grounds had gone far beyond anything envisaged by "radicals" before World War II, whereas public housing had been accorded no more than token provision. During the 1970's came general revenue sharing by the federal government to enlarge public spending by those in control of state administrations. There were likewise huge increases in loans and loan guarantees exceeding half a trillion dollars under the federal government's own programs by 1979. When the President's first National Urban Policy Report appeared in that year, it was apparent that much of federal (and state) expenditure in and around cities bore no relation to any coherent "national urban policy" since none existed except in a rhetorical sense.[41] Meanwhile, the media's "Urban Crisis" of the 1960's had come and gone and the 1980 federal census confirmed that "the Exploding Metropolis" of the 1950's was no longer a bang but a whimper.

By 1982 the policy scientists could finally report to the President that the city was "the problem" not "the solution." Their bottom lines revealed the city to be too expensive, hence it had become "expendable." Public policy needed to be more "people oriented" and less "place oriented." Both population and private resources were accordingly to be encouraged to flow from the urban core (especially in the older Northeast) to the suburbs and to what might be regarded perhaps as the nation's outer ring: the mythic "sunbelt." But there were still too many private resources, not to mention voting people, tied up in and around the older urban centers for the Congress to buy such nostrums unreservedly, even though their content represented little more than a logical, spatial, extension of the convenient wisdom lying back of the celebrated Moynihan "Memorandum for the President" ca. 1969.[42] Not surprisingly, perhaps, a great deal of what the "urban experts" were recommending for the 1980's had already happened. Moreover, efforts to reduce the prodigious federal deficits by further cuts in domestic spending would accomplish much the same end without the necessity for "controversial" legislation. Let the case of Phoenix, Arizona, illustrate the point. Although Phoenix reputedly rose upon the ruins of an old Indian civilization in the late 1860's (in the manner of Whittier's "city lots...staked for sale - Above old Indian graves"), it had not risen very high two decades later when it became the territorial capital with a population of about 4,000. Like Houston and Los Angeles, among other prominent beneficiaries of early 20th-century federal legislation and largesse, Phoenix became the marketing center for a rich agricultural valley after completion of the federally financed Roosevelt Dam on the Salt River in 1911. Yet as late as 1950, Phoenix, with a population no greater than 105,000, formed the 17 square mile "central city" of a standard metropolitan area extending over 9,223 square miles but containing only 329,000 inhabitants. At midcentury Phoenix was equal in area and population to Lowell, Massachusetts, with its urbanized area of 17 square miles (city, 13 sq. m.) and population 107,000. The population of the entire Phoenix SMA was scarcely larger than that of Jersey City (13 sq. m.), which together with Newark (439,000 on 24 sq. m.), made up 5.8 per cent of the New York-N.E. New Jersey SMA population of 12,831,000 crowded on to 3,936 square miles. Over the ensuing three decades, Phoenix annexed an additional 312 square miles (an area larger than New York City had assembled in three and a half centuries), but the census population of the 329 square mile city in 1980 was only 765,000 (little more than a tenth of shrinking New York), while its SMSA now covering 9,155 square miles contained barely a million and a half people.

Vast social and economic changes have swept across the United States since the recovery of the 1940's. Demographic changes likewise did not halt with the end of the postwar "baby boom" in the late 1950's. Phoenix again, with its World War II airfields, its flourishing postwar electronics research and production, its data processing activities, aircraft, fabricated metals and machinery, as well as more traditional textile and apparel industries, has been a Mecca for migrants. The numbers of city dwellers countrywide have gone on rising through the third quarter of this century but the numbers coming to live and work in the suburban and satellite communities of metropolitan areas have increased at a much faster rate. In spite of annexation of scattered fringe territories by city governments, especially in southern and western states, more people lived in the outer rings of the 240-odd metropolitan areas by 1970 than in *all* of their central cities. By that date more than half the national housing stock had been built since the bombs fell on Hiroshima and Nagasaki, with some two-thirds of the increase on newly developed ring acreage.[43] More real gross national product had been put on in the thirty years after Pearl Harbor than in the previous three hundred, and President Nixon was proudly hailing the advent of the trillion dollar economy.

The deep social changes manifested in these spatial and structural tendencies of population and production were not much affected—let alone effected—by the momentum (or measure) of ubranization. Neither economic nor demographic developments received much leverage in recent decades from net concentration or resultant increases in the urban share of U.S. population. To be sure, census urban population in the 50 states rose by 42 million between 1960 and 1980, but only one in four of that increment could be credited to the central cities of SMSAs which had meanwhile climbed in number from 212 to 318 and had *doubled* their expanse to 16 per cent of total U.S. land area. The share of central city in all urban population had fallen in the interim from 46.2 to 40.7 per cent.[44] The 42 million urban increment, moreover, represented a gain of but 3.8 percentage points in the urban share of national population—only 0.2 ponts of which had occurred during the 1970's: the smallest positive decadal rural-to-urban shift in the nation's history (see Table 1).

Clearly, once a substantial majority of a population has come to reside in urbanized areas, the pool of residual country folk is likely to dwindle. Thereafter, the urbanites can only redistribute themselves among cities or leave town altogether. The growth of urban population in southern and western states and the surge of rural nonfarm residents since 1970 suggests that both possibilities are taking place, although scarcely three-quarters of U.S. population was either urbanized or metropolitanized.

The metropolitanization of the southern and western rims, like earlier deconcentration from cities beyond their metropolitan bounds in northeastern and northcentral states, reveals the tendency for urbanized populations to evolve new ecological forms for working and living. For all the well-advertised "growth" of the relatively undeveloped and "redeveloping" regions—and even that petered out during the sharp recession of 1981-82—such areas, with the exception of the Pacific coastal states, were mostly catching up with the national average in respect to levels of urbanization, labor force structures, per capita personal incomes, etc. by capitalizing their physical (and human) resources, not unlike "frontier" territories and urban fringe areas throughout the 19th century. The recently developing regions, however, do not have to recapitulate the historical ontogeny of either economic or urban development, but as in the case of Phoenix, may move directly into advanced decentralizing forms of macro-metropolitan organization or follow the manner of Nassau-Suffolk Counties on Long Island into a sprawling, centerless, "autopia." Since midcentury, if not before, newly urbanizing areas have been expanding across the countryside for much the same reasons as people relocated their productive activities around the older macro-metropolitan areas, namely the loss of favorable externalities and other advantages formerly accruing to "centrality" and "access." Many such places have not yet evolved a "central city" of 50,000 or more residents and may lack other physical attributes or social amenities typical of "city life," yet they already contain anywhere from 100,000 to 200,000 inhabitants who exhibit "a high degree of economic and social integration" among their small town and village clusters. Benton Harbor, Michigan; Sharon, Pennsylvania; Jacksonville, North Carolina; and Yuba City, California, for example, were credited with fewer than 20,000 residents in 1980 (the first two were actually losing population); they are nevertheless to give their names to new "metropolitan statistical areas" once the U.S. Office of Management and Budget has eliminated the minimum "central city" population requirement of >50,000 (their metropolitan populations were respectively in thousands: 171, 128, 112, and 101). Many minor cities have recently become submerged by their outlying settlements, but whereas eligibility for metropolitan status was hitherto determined by size of "central city," the size and density of settlements *outside* the nominal nucleus will henceforth confer the metropolitan cachet.[45] At the other macro extreme of metropolitan spread likewise, the merging of SMSAs into "consolidated metropolitan statistical areas" since the

1960 Census has shown that belts of urbanized settlement, such as that stretching from S.W. Connecticut across southern New York State into N.E. New Jersey, constitute an evolving form of multi-centered "functional entity," albeit one still falling short in built expanse and population of the much touted "megalopolis" announced by the Twentieth Century Fund in 1961. But, whether in the newer, centerless, low density form (be it new growth or detached from an existing SMSA) or the consolidated, multi-centered, macro-metropolitan form, the *extended urban field* (not the compact agglomeration or even the "monocentered metropolis") is becoming the late 20th-century mutation of "the city."

Across much of the United States the macro-metropolitan area is already devolving into what sociologists have denominated a "multinodal, multi-connected, ecological field of interdependent activity centers." Population and employments have been clustering out around federally-subsidized peripheral airports or dispersing along extra-metropolitan stretches of the vast federally subsidized inter-metropolitan-inter-regional highway system—"the Interstate"—built as part of the nation's "defence" posture since the mid-1950's and by now falling into substantial disrepair—like the old inter-city railway network it displaced. Even a "boom-town" like Atlanta, Georgia, for long the media's symbol of the latest "New South," must now combine with its six surrounding counties in order to attract capital toward its supra-metropolitan space.[46] The 1980 Census indicated for the first time since the "metropolitan" concept was introduced in 1910 that *non-metropolitan* population is now growing faster than metropolitan and that, notwithstanding the third largest decadal urban increment in the nation's history and with barely three-quarters of U.S. population resident in census urban territory, the process of urbanization has dwindled to nothing.

4) *Urbanization as Capital Formation: Human and Material*

The urbanization of the eco-system in the U.S. was no mere side effect of "industrialization" or "westward movement." Except at the very beginning, it was not a by-product of something else; it was never an extrinsic happening. Likewise, cities of the 19th century were not costly and grotesque center stages on which to play out the programmed melodrama of what—since World War II—has been labelled "economic growth." Neither profit making nor "problems" were ever incidental to living in such places. In the U.S., as elsewhere, population concentration in the form of increasing numbers and sizes of agglomerations was both a condition and contributory cause of what we conventionally and loosely call "industrialization." No country industrialized its economy in the 19th and early 20th century modes, not even Switzerland, without a concomitant *shift* of its growing population into compact, built-up settlements, and none, with the doubtful exception of the Netherlands, ever induced a majority of its people into urban settlements without a concomitant industrialization of its labor force and output. The building and operation of towns, the servicing of their residents and facilities, and the linking of their activities into "systems of cities" regionally and nationally, were in themselves crucial components of the 19th-century "growth" process which may be viewed as the profitable and accumulative substitution of "capital" for other factors in any output. The concentrations of people performing productive and consumptive roles were not just *where* the action was but in growing part *what* it was. They formed settings in which the course of subsequent innovation was largely motivated and molded. Under 19th-century competitive conditions, urban activities and opportunities became primary movers of a self-transforming process in which—somewhat ironically—farming, once the chief occupation and support of the population, became virtually the nation's largest single category of industry (albeit government subsidized) but by 1980 employed less than three per cent of its civilian work force and produced but 2.5 per cent of current national income. Urbanization was thus a powerful vehicle of resource mobilization in whose absence social and economic changes would not have gone so fast or so far, let alone in the direction historically taken.[47]

How did uncontrived 19th-century urbanization—in contradistinction, say, to planned 17th-century city building—become a mainspring and mold of social change? Concentration represented a reordering and focusing of human energies that, if sustained, shaped the pace, content, and direction of total activities toward further agglomeration: more of the the incremental labor force, capital endowment, and materials input gravitated to the production *of* cities and production *in* cities. The marginal product of labor outside of agriculture—which, to be sure, is not identical with labor in cities—was notably higher than that in agriculture early in the 19th century. Income per worker outside of farming in the U.S. ranged on average, with regional variations, from two to two-and-a-half times income per farm worker (in current prices) over the last two-thirds of the century albeit with no consistent trend. As recently as 1970 productivity per worker still increased marginally with size of metropolitan population. Thus, as nonfarm activities unfolded in and around the populous districts, towns and cities embodied a growing share of the capital stock and were the locus of productivity increments in most branches of industry and trade. Outside of highly specialized centers of manufacture such as Lowell, the economies of scale came not so much "internally" to larger plants and firms but rather "externally" in the Marshallian sense, i.e. "internally" to the agglomeration or its local industries and, of course, to the water and rail corridors along which greater volumes of freight moved between them. Such discrete spatial-structural "advantages" to urban producers, almost without regard to technique or firm size, reinforced concentration which further reduced the relative freight factor in unit prices of the commodities moving along the main-traveled routes. Other routes and inaccessible areas were placed at a comparative "disadvantage."[48]

"What was at first an effect of economic causes, has in its turn become a cause" wrote A.F. Weber of the concentration of workers in towns. The mutually confirming transactions of enterprisers and workers, whatever their differences over conditions of work and wages, had fostered a social milieu in the larger port cities and new manufacturing towns that, under competitive conditions, proved singularly conducive to technical and organizational change. The spectacular economic rents gained by innovators excited emulation and, when competition prevailed, prompted the diffusion and "using up" of the novel processes and products *via* the wider system of cities at some more normal or "going" rate of profit. The progressive specialization and differentiation of activities in this protean learning environment would, moreover, reveal which among the novel ventures had passed the critical market test; but of those departures which had been abandoned or aborted for lack of returns, few traces remained—unless taken up later by some local authority, charitable society, or other nonmarket agency. Thus, in contrast to the seemingly stable and durable mold of most agrarian societies, or to the lively urban capitalism of early modern Europe, population concentration constituted a dynamic and increasingly disruptive experience for those individuals and households engulfed by its streams. For society, prolonged oncentration served to amplify other, reciprocal deviations from prevailing distributions and structures—going beyond mere quantitative increases in population or product—to effect a transformation of the ecosystem: *via* redistribution of population, structural differentiation of activities, and reorganization of functional interdependence. So far from counteracting all deviations from existing modes of behavior, competitive striving in agglomerative settings had the effect of *selectively augmenting* (rather than diminishing) technical and other departures and hence of *maintaining* the "advantage" of concentrated over dispersed activities *at* any time and, within the evolving system of cities, *over* time. In this sense, the future unfolded in "cities," and as a progressive learning experience, the momentum of urbanization—while it lasted—helped counter any inherent tendency toward diminishing returns and system entropy.[49]

The concentration of activities in space and the heightened contest for place at the vertex of their interaction imparted a characteristic structure to 19th-century urban land values. Since centric sites proffered their occupants access to the highest potential volume of clientele (or other select concourse), and insofar as "centrality" was a limited or "scarce" attribute at any time, the hub of activities almost always became the most sought after and costliest space in town. The price (or rental) of land rose gradually from outer and comparatively inaccessible fringe developments—with only occasional intermediate foothills or subcenters—towards a steep upward gradient at the core. The changing contours of urban land values under the impacts of local concentration and multiplying land uses reflected the bidding up of purchase prices (and site rentals) by those in a position to enlarge their net incomes from the "uses" they might make of a site. Peak central areas in large cities acquired the most highly capitalized "values" and the capital improvements on such sites were to enable their owners (or lessees) to utilize them in the most profitable ways. Hence the continuous sifting and sorting of land uses by the real estate market to uphold and, if possible, elevate the structure of property values. Land uses either yielded the returns necessary to maintain their site occupancies or they must shortly give place to other improvements which could. The assessed valuations of land and buildings for purposes of local property taxation meanwhile added direct political coercion to that already exercised by all too "personal" market forces: landlords, competitors, creditors, and collectors. By the same token, if a comparable or otherwise satisfactory net yield might be expected from the same activity carried on at an eccentric site of lower rental and tax valuation, there would be little or no financial incentive for an entrepreneur to cling to a central location for the conduct of his business. An owner-occupier, on the other hand, might convert himself into a landlord and rent to other more adept tenants, or simply sell out for capital gain and relocate his business with the proceeds at some suitably cheaper site. Similarly, a lessee might seek a lower-priced lease to carry on his activity elsewhere in town. Sustained concentration in and around the growing settlements of the mid 19th century also affected the values of peripheral lands; owners of outlying tracts must either raise their expected returns by adopting more lucrative modes of farming made possible by local markets, or in due course, convert their land to still higher yielding nonfarm uses: subdivision, housing developments, a whole succession of investments and improvements.[50]

Investments in the development and improvement of urban land by commercial and residential building, transport facilities, public utilities, and other social overhead installations were among the major components of 19th-century capital accumulation in the United States and other urbanizing countries. Attention has understandably been focused by national income accountants on the magnitudes of "value added" to materials-inputs by manufacture, agriculture, or mining (and on the volumes of employment generated in these same commodity sectors), but the student of urbanization cannot fail to note that the bulk of gross capital formed in the 19th-century U.S. nevertheless took the form of new capital construction: the building and linking of cities into regional, inter-regional, and ultimately nationwide networks. In pre-Civil War decades construction already absorbed two-thirds and more of net investment—in canals, railroads, housing, plant, public utilities, and other nonresidential buildings. Without this larger dimension of construction (the "services" of which contributed vast externalities to other sectors), the demand for savings would have been substantially lower since no more than five to nine per cent of net investment at the time was going into producers' durable goods purchased by manufacturing, mining concerns, or farmers, and barely a fifth even into business inventory changes. For much of the century, in fact, the measured productivity of investment was highest in some of the urban public utilities. Even late in the century, when more numerous and comparatively short-lived producers' durable goods had assumed a larger share of net investment (upwards of a fifth) and of capital formation (an eighth), the more slowly depreciating and relatively more costly construction sector still represented half of U.S. net investment and more than two-thirds of real net capital formation.[51] As it was, the relative price of capital fell by half in the later 19th century (only to rise again more gradually from the 1920's).

From the 1870's urban residential building regularly formed about half of net construction capital and was again, particularly in its suburban form, much the most buoyant component of construction after World War II (around 60 per cent during the "baby boom" years). Nevertheless, it is government that has become the dynamic capital-forming sector during this century, and it now seems scarcely credible that until the later 1890's all government (up to 90 per cent state and local before 1933) should have originated only four or five per cent of net domestic capital formation in peacetime.[52] To be sure, the recent rise of governmental capital spending with its outlays for extended urban-suburban infrastructure and highway building began to offset the perceptibly shrinking share of business and farming capital, while within the market sector, the declining shares of railroads (before World War I) and manufactures reflected the expansion of "service" industries. Even with the direct federal share of increased capital outlays by governments mounting spectacularly and, apparently, irreversibly from the early 1930's, state and local expenditure—particularly in metropolitan areas—still constitutes two-thirds of the public sector.

Accumulations of capital in the myriad forms represented by the building and linking of cities into larger transactional systems not only yielded scale economies in moving goods and information and critical externalities from the specialization of occupations and localities, but also contributed to the rising productivity of land uses in city *and* country. Quite apart from the feats of technical and organizational "progress" which had paid off in larger interregional markets for particular products or services, the rising "artificiality" of the built environment reduced the lingering seasonality among manufactures even as advances in interior (as well as outdoor) illumination prolonged daylight into the hours of darkness. Urbanization meanwhile had concentrated unprecedented numbers and proportions of population into these protean social/physical settings where rates of natural increase, the surpluses of births over deaths, were comparatively low. Nevertheless, by market evaluations, the marginal productivity of workers in such heavily capitalized environments was persistently higher on average than elsewhere. Indeed, the higher incomes per worker (likewise the returns to capital in urban land and improvements) *had* to be sustained if workers and funds were to be attracted from their existing locations at home or abroad.[53] In turn, the removal of people from the countrysides and the creation of remote markets for greater portions of farm output fostered improved labor productivity—through mechanization and other means—among those who remained upon the land. By the second quarter of this century, the use of chemicals and other "knowledge" inputs had even raised productivity *per acre* on the farm diminishing the demand for labor still further in all but a few seasonal hand-picked crops.

The urbanization of the ecosystem in North America was not, of course, an upward and onward tendency without perturbation or instability. Indeed, the interactive processes of population concentration and urban capital formation were alike leading variables in both short-term fluctuations in levels of business and in longer run "swings" in the rates of change in resources' supply. While the potential size of labor and capital flows at any time was primarily governed by supply conditions (existing stocks or capacity), the actual composition and rates of such flows were largely determined by demand considerations, with both supply and demand levels reflecting changes in relative prices. Throughout the 19th century, output was in fact alternately overshooting and undershooting aggregate demand levels to beget the familiar, albeit nonetheless painful, ups and downs of the business-inventory cycle. There were as a consequence substantial longer-term movements on the supply side in the creation of *new* productive capacity or, more specifically, in the rates at which firms produced such incremental resources: additional or novel plant, equipment, storage facilities, energy, and other materials necessary for enlarging output and income *in the future*. Hence the long swing movements in commodity output, private and public capital goods production, etc., which, together with services, formed the bulk of the incremental "economic growth" measured in national income and product accounts.[54]

The supply of labor in general, and of particular types of labor, also varied over these same long swings in the rates of producing other resources. Rates of migration to cities, whether from the countrysides or overseas, were especially sensitive to these alternating surges and slackenings in the output of other resources, just as they were, in lesser degree, to secular trends in the relative prices of capital (downward in the later 19th and early 20th centuries) *and* labor (broadly upward over the same span despite the waves of immigration). Migration from near and far increased when the growth of output accelerated and retarded when that growth subsided or turned negative. Obviously, local natural increase could not supply additional working population at anything like the same rate as migration even when more women or younger children were attracted into the work force. Similarly, when new building lagged the current demand for additional dwelling space (as it might well do during rapid in-migration), vacancy rates for housing would decline and rent levels rise until the construction of additional accommodation once more surpassed the level of demand or otherwise eased, at which point vacancy rates might again be expected to increase and rent levels/housing prices fall, etc., thereby damping down the rate of construction.[55] These longer run movements, distressing enough in their own way to people whose expectations were disappointed, also had repercussions on the demand for "development" land and building sites as well as for construction materials, fixtures, and labor and, not least, for the funds to finance such structures. Changes in the marriage rate and the formation of new households by city-born people, as well as by migrants, generated whole sequences of "urban household demand" for shelter, furnishings, food, fuels, clothing among other domestic paraphernalia, and a widening range of personal services particularly responsive to rising incomes. It is significant in this regard, perhaps, that the migration and concentration of people and funds facilitated more rapid adjustments locally than would otherwise have been the case. Given the declining rate of population increase, the comparative lack of technological progress in the building industry, and the exclusion of most consumer durables from the standard capital accounts, it is remarkable that the share of households in net domestic capital formation (in 1929 prices) fell only from about a third or so in the post Civil War decades to about a quarter during the upturn of the "baby boom" years after World War II.[56]

In 19th-century U.S. construction "swings"—peaking in the early 1850's and early 70's—*nonresidential* building in the aggregate (and likewise total construction) moved in close association with *residential* building, although the latter tended to lag the former until around 1890 by periods of anywhere up to two years. From before the turn of the century, however, nonresidential building (including public overhead) tended to lag and residential to lead in the construction cycle, especially towards the peaks before World War I and again in the mid-1920's. Industrial building, meanwhile, which conformed in the aggregate to the shorter rhythms of the business cycle, was sometimes offset in decline by public construction (school building was probably the least irregular component in the public sector). Over time, the enhanced employment opportunities in and around cities stimulated demand for housing, with attendant facilities and services, while all the expenditures for dwellings, household items, and related services were fed back by multiplier effects *via* markets to buttress broader upswings in business activity, entry of new firms, more nonresidential building, utilities, public goods, and other concentration-sensitive forms of capital. Thus, responses to improvement of the general business climate lead households and firms to what R.A. Easterlin calls "long term commitments" which serve to sustain expenditures over periods notably longer than the average business cycle. But unless these commitments are further augmented, exhaustion of the time-lagged, supportive, outlays involved will eventually lead to a slowdown in rates of growth of new capacity (with equivalent interactions among the pertinent variables except that *declining* rates of increase are now substituted for the formerly rising rates).

Process and product innovations probably followed much the same periodic course down into the early 20th century. Within the U.S., technological inventions—as indicated by fluctuations in the numbers of patents per 100,000 of state populations—vary directly with the business cycle and among the states according to their respective levels of urbanization at any time (at least, outside the South). Robert Higgs has argued that the kinds of information about production processes and market prospects needed for producing patentable inventions were much more readily and, hence, cheaply available to interested parties in 19th century urban settings than in any other contemporary ambiance. The generally close correlations between levels of urbanization and inventiveness among state populations, and with levels of per capita personal income by states, held down through the early 20th century, but weakened notably from the 1920's.[58] Similarly, the periodic alternations of rising and falling rates of increase in the supply of productive resources characteristic of the 19th and early 20th centuries seem to have become overlaid by the massive impacts of subsequent warfare and depression. Technological innovation—so essential in industrial society for capitalizing a future—no longer has much association with incremental urbanization and increasingly depends on budgetary allocations by governments and corporations for *institutionalized* "Research & Development."[59] Meanwhile, the loss of momentum of population concentration generally and the relaxation of centripetal inducements locally have conjoined to pose a "problem" for local governments and their city-bound business and labor clients of contriving something profitable (or otherwise "worthwhile") to do with inner-city land—particularly in peak central districts created by investors in the course of their intensive differentiation and reordering of specialized land uses during the meso- and early macro-phases of urban development.

Compact urban habitats can no longer be built or renovated at cut-rate prices. Such a form of human settlement is in decreasing demand and seems to be "unfundable" when, as in the late 20th century, more or less extensive urban fields with no well-defined core are becoming the mode in high-income countries. Under conditions of market oligopoly and public "economic management," cities are not the "natural" nurseries of capitalizable inventions, and private enterprises have largely abandoned their *quondam* role—even with tax abatements and outright subsidy—of building and renewing the urban artifact.[60] To be sure, urbanization goes on in late developing regions and accommodates increasing numbers of people in the macro-metropolitan mode. Profitable speculation continues to attract domestic and foreign funds to bright-light hotel, amusement, and large-unit office districts of midtown Manhattan, Dallas, and a few other glass-aluminum citadels, but elsewhere—and especially in older centers of manufacture—it is the taxpayer alone or in "partnership" who underwrites the quasi-philanthropic enterprise of conserving inner cities in the wake of private disinvestment and partial abandonment.[61] The industrial revolution in manufacture first gathered momentum outside the microspaces of market towns, port cities, and grand capitals of Europe during the 18th century. To augment production and productivity, the concentrations of manufacturing population mostly built and extended their own 19th century meso- and macro-environments and constructed appropriately mechanized linkages between them with but modest subventions from public authorities. During the second and third quarters of this century as manufacturing employment contracted, the cities disgorged many of their most productive activities to satellites in macro-metropolitan ring areas or out along the newly-built "interstate" motorways—drawing population in their train. More recently, as the vicious circle of decline reinforces decline, much wholesale trading has also decamped leaving only selected financial, educational, health-related "professional," and local government among job-creating "services" as the sheet anchor holding other things in place. See Table 2.

To the extent that space-time convergence—the "annihilation of distance"—represented an abrogation of effort-time constraints on communication even more than on transportation, no very stable territorial basis for reordering the human ecosystem has emerged. Boundaries of "community" locally and nationally have been demolished—much as old town walls and frontier fortresses in their day—by the contemporary scale of spatial reorganization, further devitalizing any contributory sense of place. Local activities and parochial interests have been integrated with, and dominated by, collective national and transnational agencies. Private capital seeps away from the shrinking central city and its productions into more enticing courses that by means of the much advertised paraphernalia of "high technology'' can be profitably pursued almost without regard to place or social setting—provided global economic order and financial stability can be secured. Whatever may be the fate of industrial capitalism or any other—state or corporate—that supersedes it, the productivity of the human ecosystem will be even less dependent on building or renewing cities and, as the latter dissolve into more extended urban fields, will receive less stimulus from them.

Table 2

Changes in Major Employment Sectors of Selected Central Cities, By Regions, U.S., 1958-1972
(000's)

Central City	Employment					Net Shift 1958-72 in 5 Sectors:	
	Manufactures	Wholesale Trade	Retail Trade	Selected Services	Local Government	Net Shift (5 Sectors) 000's	Net Per Cent Shift of 1972 Employment
Boston	-27.2	-9.1	-14.6	+19.9	+4.0	-27.0	-11.1
Providence	-9.9	-1.1	-5.8	+1.7	-0.4	-15.5	-19.2
Buffalo	-17.6	-4.9	-10.3	+4.1	+3.2	-25.5	-17.0
Rochester	-3.6	-0.6	-4.0	+3.0	+2.4	-2.8	-2.0
New York City	-138.5	-42.1	-31.4	+72.9	+126.7	-12.4	-0.6
Jersey City	-9.6	-0.6	-0.7	+1.5	-1.8	-11.2	-17.9
Newark	-31.3	-5.6	-12.1	+1.2	+1.8	-46.0	-30.3
Pittsburgh	-2.3	-9.7	-12.1	+6.0	-0.4	-18.5	-11.1
Philadelphia	-84.0	-13.8	-16.4	+16.3	+6.0	-91.9	-17.0
Baltimore	-20.5	-2.1	-16.1	+5.6	+13.0	-20.9	-7.7
Washington, D.C.	-1.4	-4.7	-9.1	+20.4	+25.2	+30.4	+19.2
Cleveland	-43.6	-10.5	-20.5	+5.9	-1.0	-69.7	-21.8
Cincinnati	-8.1	-1.0	-6.9	+31.3	+5.4	+20.7	+12.9
Detroit	-24.0	-12.1	-31.7	-0.6	+0.6	-66.6	-15.8
Chicago	-104.3	-31.1	-32.0	+32.9	+7.8	-126.7	-12.0
Milwaukee	-17.0	-6.5	-5.6	+8.1	+5.0	-16.0	-7.3
St. Louis	-38.6	-11.1	-22.6	+5.1	+1.1	-66.1	-24.2
Minneapolis	-0.5	-4.8	-4.6	+9.2	+0.4	-0.3	-0.2
St. Paul	+9.4	-0.8	-1.6	+5.5	-1.7	+10.8	+12.4
Kansas City	+4.2	-3.1	-0.4	+12.7	+0.9	+14.3	+10.2
Louisville	+4.5	+0.6	-1.5	+4.0	+0.4	+8.0	+7.2
New Orleans	-0.5	-2.4	-3.9	+10.2	+1.9	+5.3	+4.6
San Francisco	-11.9	-11.6	+0.7	+21.5	+5.4	+4.1	+2.1
Oakland	-7.9	-0.9	-4.5	+5.6	+0.8	-6.9	-8.3
Los Angeles	-7.3	-1.7	+22.7	+57.5	+8.2	+79.4	+12.7

Sources: U.S. Bureau of the Census, Census of Manufacturing, of Wholesale Trade, of Retail Trade, and of Selected Services, 1958, and 1972; Census of Government, 1958, "Compendium of Public Employment," vol. 2, no. 2; and Census of Government, 1972, "Employment of Major Governments," vol. 3, no. 1.; Committee for Economic Development, An Approach to Federal Urban Policy (New York, 1977).

NB: No adjustments made for changes in central city boundaries.

NOTES

1 Ecosystems are the prevalent processes and forms of human adaptation. Adaptation implies a variability of population response to a given environmental stimulus (physical or social). Symbols are signs which convey more or less publicly shared meanings and facilitate the communication involved in human transactions. The classic "book of hypotheses" in the study of human ecology remains Amos H. Hawley, *Human Ecology: A Theory of Community Structure* (New York, 1950). E.E. Lampard, "Historical Aspects of Urbanization," *The Study of Urbanization*, P.M. Hauser and L.F. Schnore eds. (New York, 1965), pp. 519-54, treats human ecological systems as sets of transactional structures that conserve population numbers. Ecological theory, however, postulates no universal or normative principle of conservation other than population survival through collective adaptation. Humans may collectively maintain or increase their numbers and/or their symbolic effects but the varied patterns of their organizations and settlements defy even a minimal "least effort" principle let alone the normative preoccupation with minimizing costs and maximizing (or satisfying) returns in the use of factor services assumed more or less throughout this paper. Nevertheless, contingent structures of human interdependence are inherently "political" or directive. The dependence which stems from functional differentiation (and resultant stratification) among population members (individuals, families, "communities") gives rise to the ecological phenomenon of *dominance*. Dominance is the special attribute of those integral niches (roles) which variously determine "the conditions necessary to the functioning of other units" (Hawley, p. 221). Performance of such influential roles—beyond the formal exercise of religio-political authority—assures the organized population its routine sustenance and security: human and mechanical energy sources, information, credit, and other vital circulations.

2 Population members relate to each other in two critical ways: (1) *functional* relations are the symbiotic dependencies resulting from specializations of time and effort in the social division of labor; (2) *affinitive* relations are commensal dependencies that are not (or are no longer) grounded in functional interdependence but in some voluntary association, like interest, common characteristic, or predicated identity. Groupings of functionally related people are designated *corporate* units; groupings by elective or predicated affinity comprise *categoric* units. Individual population members variously adhere to both corporate and categoric units throughout their lives. The family is at once a congeries of both relationships comprising people differing in age and sex, with lateral as well as filial linkages, dwelling in more or less close residence, and performing mutually supportive functions. Likewise production units contain internally specialized roles but with some common interest or identity perhaps in the performance of their corporate unit in output, sales, etc. *vis a vis* other units. Localized groupings of individuals, families, and production units constitute corporate units of a *territorial* kind and, as spatially—or otherwise—discrete populations, form internally differentiated "communities" infused with a more or less strong sense of identity in competitive or complementary relations to other variously differentiated communities. Thus conjoint operation of functional and affinitive relations—the warp and woof of the social fabric—enhances a population's productivity and cohesion. The same operation, however, may also generate self-conscious, even opposing, categorical units within corporate units: social classes, occupational or voluntary associations, clubs, genders, sects, ethnicities, regions, etc., thereby creating tensions and conflicts within and among families, firms, communities, nations.

3 E.E. Lampard, "Urbanization," *Encyclopedia of American Economic History*, G. Porter, ed. (New York, 1980), 1039, Table 6, for estimates of colonial urbanization.

4 E.E. Lampard, "The Evolving System of Cities in the United States," *Issues in Urban Economics*, H.S. Perloff and L. Wingo, eds. (Baltimore, 1968), 98-100, on cybernetic notions of *morphogenesis*.

5   While emphasizing the declining rate of increase in the urban share of U.S. popula-
    tion, it is noteworthy that the increase of 70.4 million urban residents between 1950
    and 1980 represented an increment greater than the entire urban increase between
    1790 and the early 1930's.
6   Patrick Geddes, *Cities in Evolution* (rev. ed. New York, 1950), chapt. 2. Geddes also
    used the term "house-province." The original and, for historians, more useful edi-
    tion appeared in 1915. R.D. McKenzie, *The Metropolitan Community* (New York,
    1933), chapt. 23.
7   J.D. Kasarda, "The Implications of Contemporary Distribution Trends for National
    Urban Policy," *Social Science Quarterly,* 61 (Dec., 1980), 373-400; M.M. Webber,
    "The Urban Place and the Nonplace Urban Realm," *Explorations into Urban Struc-
    ture,* Webber, ed. (Philadelphia, 1964), 79-153; Katharine L. Bradbury *et al., Urban
    Decline and the Future of American Cities* (Washington, D.C., 1982), 193-201, on
    trends relevant to the future of urban areas.
8   Based on data from sources in R. Mols, *Introduction a la demographie historique
    des villes d'Europe du XIVe au XVIIIe siecle* (3 vols., Louvain, 1954-56), III, Appen-
    dix Tables, 1, 2, 3, 4. Also, E.E. Lampard, "The Nature of Urbanization," *The Pursuit
    of Urban History,* D. Fraser and A. Sutcliffe, eds. (London, 1983), n. 32.
9   Pedro de Medina, *Libro de grandezas y cosas memorables de Espana,* 1548, fol. li,
    cited by Ruth Pike, *Enterprise and Adventure: The Genoese in Seville and the Open-
    ing of the New World* (Ithaca, N.Y., 1966), 28. On the rivalry of Seville and Cadiz for
    the American trade, A. Girard, *La rivalite commerciale et maritime entre Seville et
    Cadix jusqu'a la fin du XVIIIe siecle* (Paris, 1932).
10 F. Braudel, *La Mediterranee et le monde mediterraneen a l'epoque de Philippe II*
    (Paris, 1949), 619; Pike, *op. cit.,* 37-9.
11 J.F. Hazewinkel, "Le Developpement d'Amsterdam," *Annales de Geographie,* 35
    (1926), 322-29; Violet Barbour, *Capitalism in Amsterdam in the 17th Century*
    (Baltimore, 1950); J.G. van Dillen, *Van rijkdom en regenten* (The Hague, 1950); H.
    Soly, *Urbanisme en kapitalisme te Antwerpen in de 16de ceuw (Brussels, 1977).*
12 Hazewinkel, *loc. cit.* On the emergence of a short-lived nonhierarchical "system of
    cities" in the second half of the 17th century: Jan de Vries, "Barges and Capitalism,"
    AAG *Bijdragen 21* (Wageningen, 1978), 347-54; Johann de Vries, *Amsterdam-
    Rotterdam, Rivaliteit in economisch-historisch perspectief* (Bussum, 1965).
13 J.W. Konvitz, *Cities and the Sea: Port City Planning in Early Modern Europe*
    (Baltimore, 1978), 140; P. Lavedan, *Histoire de l'urbanisme, Renaissance et temps
    modernes* (Paris, 1941), 220-24; M. L'Heritier, "L'Urbanisme au XVIIIe siecle. Les
    idees du Marquis de Tourny," *La Vie Urbaine,* 3 (1921), 47-83. The municipal and
    mercantile-directed growth of Amsterdam and Antwerp differs markedly in motiva-
    tion and effectiveness from the state-sponsored promotions in France or Scan-
    dinavia.
14 E.A. Gutkind, *Urban Development in the Alpine and Scandinavian Countries* (New
    York, 1965), 308-21, 417-21; R.E. Dickinson, *The West European City* (London,
    1951), 438-45.
15 E.E. Lampard, "The Nature of Urbanization," *Pursuit of Urban History,* 16-20; Jan
    de Vries, "Patterns of Urbanization in Pre-industrial Europe, 1500-1800," *Patterns of
    European Urbanization since 1500,* H. Schmal, ed. (London, 1981), 79-108: con-
    cludes that changing relationships between "cities and the rest of society and the
    changing internal structure of the urban system" between 1500 and 1800
    represented "the destruction of an old urban structure and its replacement by a new
    one, but...the constituent cities of these two structures remained the same....The
    histories of individual cities during these three centuries are largely concerned with
    their search for a place in a new urban environment."
16 John Stow, *A Survey of London, Written in the Year 1598* (1603), (Ed. C.L.
    Kingsford, 2 Vols., London, 1908), I, 272-92, 346. On population pressure and Lon-
    don's water supply, 16-17; II, 369 for the theater "district" in Southwark.

[17] On the mercer Sir Thomas Gresham's building of the Royal Exchange in 1567 after the fashion of the antwerp *beurs*: Stow, *Survey of London,* I, 193; N.G. Brett-James, *The Growth of Stuart London* (London, 1935); M.J. Bowden, "Growth of the Central Districts in Large Cities," *The New Urban History,* L.F. Schnore, ed. (Princeton, 1975), 78-83.

[18] R.M. Morse, "A Prolegomenon to Latin American Urban History," *Hispanic American Historical Review,* 52 (August, 1972), 359-94; E.E. Lampard, "Urbanization of the United States: The Capitalization and Decapitalization of Place," *Villes en mutation XIXe-XXe siecles* (10e Colloque International: Credit Communal de Belgique, Brussels, 1982), 147-64. The comparatively low residential densities of Anglo-American port cities in the 18th century did not mean that such places were exempt from the filth and disease which characterized most European cities. From the early 17th century, magistrates sought to prohibit human and industrial pollution and 18th century municipalities not only adopted ordinances to counter such abuses but fostered improved drainage, rudimentary street cleaning, well protection, and sewage removal.

[19] Lampard, "Nature of Urbanization," *Pursuit of Urban History,* 19, Table 1.2; H.A. Diederiks, "Patterns of Urban Growth since 1500, mainly in Western Europe," *Patterns of European Urbanization since 1500,* 3-29. Improvements in Dutch farm output and exports early in the 19th century contributed after 1825 to modest increases in textile and food manufacturing and a revival of urban construction: J.M.M. de Meere, *Economische Ontwikkeling en levensstandaard in Nederland in de eerste helft van de negentiende eeuw* (The Hague, 1982).

[20] Lampard, "Nature of Urbanization," *Pursuit of Urban History,* 21-2, 33-6. Table 1.4 on official territories of cities. Net increases in numbers of towns in England and Wales by size groups, 1700-1800: $>100,000 = 0$; 20-$99,999 = 12$; 10-$19,999 = 26$; $>9,999 = 94$. But of 13 towns $>20,000$ (excluding London) only 5, apart from ocean ports, had been notably affected by recent manufacturing developments whereas approximately 19 of 34 towns, 10-19,999, were centers of the new manufactures. For a contemporary explanation of the growth of towns, $>10,000$, in the U.S., 1830-40, see J. Chickering, "Cities and Towns in the U.S.. Increase of the Thirty Six Principal Cities and Towns," *Hunt's Merchants' Magazine,* 10 (May, 1844), 461-64. Mobile, Ala.; Allegheny, Pa.; and Lowell, Mass. were the outstanding growth concentrations of the decade. Lowell at the time of its incorporation in 1836 enclosed 5.09 sq. m.; Utica, N.Y. 5.38 sq. m. in 1832. With the notable exceptions of New Orleans, San Antonio, and New York City, the legal areas of virtually all U.S. cities around 1840 were under 10 sq. m., but the built areas of Philadelphia, Boston, Cincinnati, Pittsburgh, and even New York City (if we include Brooklyn and Jersey City) already merged with contiguous towns. We cannot infer, however, that growth of population in counties around such cities was necessarily or even primarily "metropolitan" spillover in the integral sense of the modern census SMSA. On the other hand, people may move into parts of such counties from elsewhere because local work opportunities are enhanced by the proximity of a town or village to the nearby metropolis.

[21] Differences between the legal-institutional conditions affecting peripheral land purchases by private developers (as well as public acquisitions) in, for example, Prussia, England & Wales, Scotland, or the U.S. account in part for different rates of urban development; likewise political-legal procedures for annexation or consolidation of territories.

[22] F. Vigier, *Change and Apathy: Liverpool and Manchester during the Industrial Revolution* (Cambridge, Mass., 1970), 49-53, 67-70, 102, 132-42, 198-99, and land use figures; Lampard, "Urbanization of the U.S.," *Villes en mutation,* 164-79. On the dynamics of the "Growth of Central Districts," Bowden, *The New Urban History,* Schnore ed. 89-107, with special reference to San Francisco after 1850. On residence and workplace, see especially T. Hershberg, ed. *Philadelphia* (New York, 1981), Pt. 2, "Space."

23 One important adaptation of telegraphic communications to urban uses was the central fire alarm system, such as the one installed in Boston City Hall in 1852.
24 The point is not so much that Robert E. Park and his Chicago colleagues were incorrect as that their description and measures of "orderly grouping" of social characteristics were incomplete or, more likely, misunderstood: some trades and industries, occupations, national or racial categories, etc. became more "grouped" than others, but few "local habitats" were exclusive of all categories other than the one used to identify the habitat. Obviously, the same holds for land uses as "commercial," "residential," "industrial," etc., where, for example, living, fabricating, and selling retail might all take place on the same city lot. Numerical indices of separation and the simpler modes of mapping, while intended to be figurative, have contributed to the notion of *homogeneous* districting of social phenomena. See, E.E. Lampard, "Some Aspects of Urban Social Structure and Morphology in the Historical Development of Cities in the U.S.," *Cahiers Bruxellois,* 22 (1977), 103-11, and Table VI.
25 Between 1840 and 1850 population in the recently annexed territories, 3.49 sq. m., around Cleveland, Ohio, grew far more rapidly than in the original city of 1840, 1.89 sq. m., and by the later date contained more residents than had the city of 1840; likewise St. Louis over the same decade, where the population of the 13.06 sq. m. annexation had by 1850 surpassed that of the old city (0.72 sq. m.) of 1840 and 1850. The faster growth of peripheral populations in annexed areas was common over midcentury decades when original cities had incorporated such microspaces. Boston was a notable exception until the 26.02 sq. m. annexations of the 1870's were added to the 7.88 sq. m. annexations of the 1860's. On the political areas and urban land areas of major U.S. cities, see contributions of Calvin Schmid and E.M. Fisher to R.D. McKenzie, *The Metropolitan Community* (New York, 1933), 191-212, for later 19th and early 20th centuries. The complex social and individual factors affecting migration patterns to industrial-urban concentrations are brilliantly traced for the Pawtucket-Providence "ring area" by J. Modell, "Mobility and Industrialization: Countryside and City in Nineteenth-Century Rhode Island," *Essays from the Lowell Conference on Industrial History, 1980 and 1981,* R. Weible, ed. (Lowell, 1981), 86-109.
26 *Frank Leslie's Illustrated,* 9 (March 10, 1860), 224; "Family-Houses for People of Small Incomes," *New York Times,* Oct. 19, 1866; "The New Homes of New York," *Scribner's Monthly,* 3 (March, 1874); "Houses on the European Plan," *Real Estate Record and Builders' Guide,* 5 (March 26, 1870), 1; "Some Apartment Houses in Chicago," *Architectural Record,* 30 (Feb., 1907). The cast-iron front E.V. Haughwout Building erected on lower Broadway at Broome St. in 1857 contained the first safety elevator with an automatic brake (E.G. Otis) which facilitated passage to the four floors above ground level. The *New York Tribune Monthly,* March, 1896, 35, comments on the many high "flathouses" put up in the late 1880's "in which children are not wanted." On the other hand, the older dingier schools below 14th St. were so crowded that some 28,825 children could not be accommodated and half-day classes were commonplace; these children included many Negroes who were not admitted to schools in their own neighborhoods: *ibid.,* 48, 51, 59. North of 57th St. newer and more spacious "uptown" schools even had playgrounds: City Superintendent [of Schools], *Report,* 1896, 142; F. Ratzel, *Stadte und Culturbilder aus Nordamerika,* (2 Vols., Leipzig, 1876), 7. A. Sutcliffe, ed. *Multi-Storey Living: The British Working-Class Experience* (London, 1974), 14-5, shows that by 1911 structurally separate blocks of flats constituted only 3.4 per cent of all structurally separate dwellings in England & Wales, but 17.8 per cent in London.
27 *7th Special Report* of the [U.S.] Commissioner of Labor, "The Slums of Baltimore, Chicago, New York, and Philadelphia" (Washington, D.C., 1894), 84-93; E.E. Lampard, "The Urbanizing World," *The Victorian City,* H.J. Dyos and M. Wolff, eds. (2 Vols. London, 1973) I, 19-27. Persons per dwelling in 1910: Manhattan 30.9 (New York City 15.6); Boston 9.1; Chicago 8.9; St. Louis 6.5; Baltimore 5.5; Philadelphia

5.2, 13th U.S. Census, *Population 1910*, I (Washington, D.C. 1912), 73-5. T.C. Clarke, "Rapid Transit in Cities," *Scribner's Monthly*, 11 (May, 1892).

28 The shift from site-generated electric power to power purchased from utilities only gathered momentum in the second decade of this century, but the switch to electricity as the preferred source of power for mechanical drive rested on the earlier (1890's) adaptation of alternating current and the polyphase induction motor: W.D. Devine, Jr., "From Shafts to Wires: Historical Perspectives in Electrification," *Journal of Economic History*, 43 (June, 1983), 347-72. Notwithstanding the soaring increases in per capita energy consumption in the U.S., the more efficient use of energy per unit of output as well as rising productivity in manufactures contributed to a *falling* energy-GNP ratio from the early 1920's: S.H. Schurr and B.C. Netschert *et al.*, *Energy in the American Economy 1850-1975* (Baltimore, 1960), 155-71; S.H. Aronson, "Bell's Electrical Try...The Sociology of Early Telephone Usage," "The Social Impact of the Telephone, I. de S. Pool, ed. (Cambridge, Mass., 1977), 23.

29 The legendary skyscrapers were mainly Italianate towers placed (or added) on to five or six story horizontal neoclassical block structures. Fear of fire probably delayed the use of interior iron framing until fire-proof tile casing in the early 1870's, but not before the mid-1880's was it possible to free the masonry walls and partitions from any bearing function. By the early 1890's some 12 and 15 story buildings were constructed, and in 1894 a braced and riveted steel skeleton enabled the American Surety Building in New York to reach 20 stories: C. Condit, *American Building* (Chicago, 1968), 114-30. W. Weisman, "New York and the Problem of the First Skyscraper," *Journal of the Society of Architectural Historians*, 12 (March 1953), 13-21. Electric-powered elevators replaced steam and hydraulic lifts from the early 1890's, but for all the skyscraper mystique, New York's "artificial mountain range" remained essentially a horizontal massif rather than a line of matterhorns until the later 1920's.

30 David Bowen, *A History of Philadelphia, with a notice of villages in the vicinity* (Philadelphia, 1839); Andrew H. Green, *Public Improvements in the City of New York, etc.* (New York: Dept. of Finance, Sept. 20, 1874), 4-23; S. Baxter, "A Study for a Federalized Metropolis Comprising the City of Boston and Surrounding Cities and Towns," Boston, 1891; also *Report to the Board of Metropolitan Park Commissioners* (Boston, 1893), 12, 71-5; 13th Census of the U.S. *Population 1910*, I, Washington, D.C., 1912), 73.

31 A.F. Weber, *The Growth of Cities in the Nineteenth Century* (New York, 1899), 475. A less roseate view of the suburban trend had been stated in 1884 by Benson J. Lossing, eighty years before "the Urban Crisis" of the 1960's: "New York, unfortunately, is becoming in a large degree a city of two conspicuous classes, the rich and the poor. The great middle classes, which constitute the bone and sinew of the social structure, have been squeezed out as it were, by the continually increasing pressure of the burden of the cost of living in the city. They constitute the great bulk of the suburban dwellers to whom the elevated railroad system is an inestimable boon." *History of New York City* (2 Vols. New York, 1884), II, 865.

32 Weber, *Growth of Cities*, 473, but see 202-09. Howard's tract was reissued with minor revisions in 1902 as *Garden Cities of Tomorrow*. Howard's proposal, *pace Fabian News*, Dec. 1898, was intended to preserve the economic base of the city by altering the patterns of its peripheral growth and not a plan "to pull them all down and substitute garden cities...."

33 *Survey Graphic*, 54 (May 1,,1925). R.D. McKenzie, "Metropolitan Communities," *Recent Social Trends in the U.S.* (2 Vols. New York, 1933), I, 493-94, concludes that the "city-regionalism" of the metropolitan districts, although "a product of contact and division of labor," was nevertheless leading to the deterioration of parts of the "large city" and "extensive exploitation of new urban territory." In his monograph, *The Metropolitan Community*, McKenzie argues that the automobile (unlike the railroad or street railway) had brought the city and its "surrounding territory within a common transportation system...and has introduced a type of local community entirely without precedent in history" (p. 6). The resulting "rearrangement of populations

and institutions" had become "the communal unit of local relations throughout the entire nation" and was not confined to the vicinity of "great cities."

[34] Homer Hoyt, *The Structure and Growth of Residential Neighborhoods in American Cities* (Washington, D.C., 1939) sought to determine principles affecting historical changes in urban housing values. But see Roger Simon, *The City-Building Process: Housing and Services in New Milwaukee Neighborhoods, 1880-1910,* (American Philosophical Society Transactions, 68, Pt. 5, 1978), esp. 6-8, 53-7; H. Bartholomew, *Urban Land Uses* (Harvard City Planning Studies No. 4: Cambridge, Mass., 1932). J.H. Niedercorn and E.F.R. Hearle, "Recent Land-Use Trends in Forty-eight Large American Cities," *Land Economics,* 40 (Feb. 1964), indicate about 21% of land is "undeveloped" and more than 2% "underwater." 13th Census of the U.S. *Population 1910,* I, 1313. *Historical Statistics of the U.S.: Colonial Times to 1957* (Washington, D.C., 1960), Ser. N 143-146.

[35] A.N. Whitehead, *Adventures of Ideas* (Cambridge, 1933), 120-122: "the inseparable accompaniment" of cities and civilization had been affected by "the trend of technology" with respect to long-distance power transmission, telephonic and cinematic communications, the airplane and automobile. The cities were undergoing "transformation" and as the age of steam, iron, and textiles passed away "we are faced with a fluid, shifting situation in the immediate future."

[36] McKenzie, *Metropolitan Community,* 191-98. Losses of city populations are from U.S. census reports and are not adjusted for annexations, hence the incidence of loss is understated. "The financial and physical plight of the cities was not generally realized by the general public or even by municipal officials until the advent of the Depression": Henry S. Churchill, *The City is the People* (New York, 1945), Chapt. 5. The early 1930's witnessed over a thousand municipal defaults on some $2.6 billions of indebtedness surpassing by far the previous record "harvest" incurred after 1893: E.E. Lampard, "Survival of Industrial Cities: Comment," *Modern Industrial Cities,* B.M. Stave, ed. (Beverly Hills, 1981), 277.

[37] Committee on the Regional Plan of New York, *Regional Survey of New York and Its Environs* (New York, 1928), Vols. IA, IB, on centrifugal tendencies among manufacturing industries. R.M. Haig, "Towards an Understanding of the Metropolis," *Quarterly Journal of Economics,* 40 (May, 1926), 426-28. But Thomas Adams, director of plans and surveys for the Regional Plan, saw this efferent tendency of manufactures (and other activities) as an opportunity to create new subcenters and satellite communities; meanwhile he sought "adequate measures to restrain the improper use of unhealthy or deteriorated structures of the city": *Planning the New York Region* (New York, 1926), 62; McKenzie, "Metropolitan Communities," *Recent Social Trends,* I, Table 8, Fig. 2, 494-96; C.S. Stein, "Dinosaur Cities," *Survey Graphic,* 7 (May 1925).

[38] On urban land and real property values as "the economic topography of the city," see Rowland Bibbins's analyses of assessed valuations in 15 large cities, 1901-25: McKenzie, *Metropolitan Community,* 226-39. "A Census of Skyscrapers," *American City,* 41 (Sept. 1929), 130, reported altogether 377 buildings with 21 or more stories located in 74 cities, >100,000. The February, 1943 *Bulletin* of the Urban Land Institute reported some 500 skyscrapers with 21 or more stories and claimed that none had been financially successful. On the inefficiency and extra burden on municipal finances resulting from excessive or "premature" peripheral subdivision, see P.H. Cornick, "Problems Created by Premature Subdivision of Lands in Selected Metropolitan Areas," Division of State Planning, Albany N.Y., 1938; New Jersey State Board of Planning, *Premature Land Subdivision. A Luxury* (Trenton, 1941); F. Dodd McHugh, "Cost of Public Services in Residential Areas," American Society of Civil Engineers, *Transactions,* 107 (1942). "Almost all FHA developments, whether for sale or rent,...were suburban or peripheral since they had to be on cheap land. This...added to the trend towards decentralization, and...did much to increase blight and to further endanger the value of mortgages in the older parts of cities.": H.S. Churchill, *The City is People,* Chapt. 5.

[39] National Resources Committee, *Our Cities, Their Role in the National Economy* (Washington, D.C., 1937). Also, Marion Clawson, *New Deal Planning: The National Resources Planning Board* (Baltimore, 1981), esp. 158-86, on urban-related federal research.

[40] Urban Land Institute, *Decentralization: What Is It Doing to Our Cities?* (Chicago, 1940); *Idem, Outline for a Legislative Program to Rebuild Our Cities* (Washington, D.C., 1942). See also, Urban Land Institute, *Proposals for Downtown Louisville* and *Proposals for Downtown Milwaukee;* Guy Greer and Alvin Hansen, "Urban Redevelopment and Housing," National Planning Association, *Pamphlet No. 10* (Washington, D.C., 1941); and particularly *idem,* "Toward Full Use of Our Resources," *Fortune,* November 1942. Also Hansen in the *National Municipal Review,* Feb. 1943, on the need for political action "to squeeze out quickly the whole of the excess of valuation...so a fresh start can be made." But land value expectations as well as taxes helped undermine the "inner cities." Even the U.S. Housing Authority undertaking token "slum clearance" after 1937 chose in most instances to build on vacant or semivacant peripheral sites; otherwise, as in New York City, it had to construct high-density projects in order to "take up" land costs.

[41] E.E. Lampard, "Urbanization in the U.S.," *Villes en mutation,* 190-91; R. Hansen, *The Evolution of National Urban Policy, 1970-1980: Lessons from the Past* (Washington, D.C., 1982); U.S. Department of Housing and Urban Development, *The President's National Urban Policy, 1980* (Washington, D.C. 1980). An estimated 18 per cent of the federal fiscal 1979 budget was to be spent in "central cities" of metropolitan areas: Anthony Downs, "Urban Policy," *Setting National Priorities: The 1979 Budget,* J.A. Pechman, ed. (Washington, D.C., 1979), 182-87.

[42] Two HUD officials disputed the report of the President's Commission for a National Agenda for the Eighties, *Urban America in the Eighties: Perspectives and Prospects* (Washington, D.C., 1980), by insisting that the Carter Administration had sought to "balance" the "people-oriented" and "place-oriented" programs since 1978. In addition to helping people help themselves, they pointed to a vigorous response to "strategic public and private-sector help" in Boston and Pittsburgh and concluded: "Merely to go with the market tide...would reflect premature submission to the new conventional wisdom that cities' decline is immutable and that the Government is impotent.": R.C. Embry, Jr. and M. Kaplan, "U.S. Cities in the 80's,"*New York Times,* 21 Jan. 1981. On the same point, Katharine L. Bradbury *et al., Urban Decline and the Future of American Cities* (Washington, D.C., 1982), 18-9, argue that "to assume market forces by themselves will lead to an ideal outcome, even in terms of pure economic efficiency, is to ignore the many elements of externalities and other 'market failures' inherent in urban areas." The "strategic public-private partnership" policy for economic revitalization is likewise no sure thing although it is politically more digestible; see the hedged conclusion of the Committee on National Urban Policy, *Rethinking Urban Policy: Urban Development in an Advanced Economy* (National Research Council: Washington, D.C., 1983), 158-70. Even the Committee for Economic Development, *Public-Private Partnership: An Opportunity for Urban Communities* (Washington, D.C., 1982), stipulates necessary (albeit not sufficient) civic cultural and political conditions for partnership ventures. See also, R. Fosler and R. Berger, eds. *Public and Private Cooperation in American Cities: Seven Case Studies* (Lexington, Mass., 1982). On David Rockefeller's efforts since 1977 to form an effective coalition of "business and civic leaders" for New York City, see *New York Times,* Feb. 4, 1983, B3. But "The American Way of Public Subsidy for Private Enterprise" under federal auspices goes back to housing and other urban policies of the 1930's and 40's, H.S. Churchill, *The City is the People,* 126-29, and may work this time around. For the larger metropolitan context of the Moynihan "Memorandum," see W. Lilley III, "Housing Report," *National Journal,* Oct. 17, 1970, 2251-62.

[43] P.M. Hauser, *Population Perspectives* (New Brunswick, 1960), 93-130; Marion Clawson, *Suburban Land Conversion in the United States: An Economic and*

Governmental Process (Baltimore, 1971), 189-307, on metropolitan patterns of land use; 342-76, on "planned modification of the suburban land conversion process." But see, M.M. Gaffney, "Urban Expansion—Will It Ever Stop?", *Yearbook of Agriculture 1958* (U.S. Dept. of Agriculture: Washington, D.C., 1958), 503-22. In the 1920's "metropolitan government" was thought to be a solution *inter alia* to problems of peripheral land conversion: P. Studenski *et al.*, *The Government of Metropolitan Areas* (National Municipal League: New York, 1930), and T.H. Reed in McKenzie, *Metropolitan Community*, 303-10. For divergent patterns of socioeconomic status distributions within postwar SMSAs, L.F. Schnore, ed. *The Urban Scene: Human Ecology and Demography* (New York, 1965), 132-83, 203-41; E.E. Lampard, "Urbanization," *Encyclopedia of American Economic History*, III, Table 3, 1032.

44 Calculations based on U.S. Census data for SMSAs and urban population since 1960.

Changing Central City Shares of Total SMSA Population, By Regions, 1900-73
(1.00 = SMSA Population)

Region	SMSAs	Included	1900	1930	1960	1970	1973
Northeast +	(18)	Mean	0.59	0.56	0.41	0.36	0.34
		S	(0.14)	(0.15)	(0.13)	(0.13)	(0.12)
South +	(27)	Mean	0.43	0.62	0.59	0.60	0.61
		S	(0.22)	(0.13)	(0.14)	(0.17)	(0.19)
Midwest	(22)	Mean	0.53	0.67	0.52	0.48	0.45
		S	(0.17)	(0.11)	(0.11)	(0.13)	(0.14)
West	(18)	Mean	0.51	0.61	0.51	0.49	0.47
		S	(0.19)	(0.14)	(0.15)	(0.17)	(0.18)

Northeast includes New England and Middle Atlantic +
South includes South Atlantic +, East South Central, and West South Central
Midwest includes East North Central and West North Central
West includes Mountain and Pacific
+ Middle Atlantic includes, South Atlantic excludes: Del., Md., and D.C.
S = standard deviation. Central City share includes annexed populations.

Source: data from Advisory Commission on Intergovernmental Relations, *Trends in Metropolitan America* (Washington, D.C., 1977).

45 U.S. Bureau of the Census, *Statistical Abstracts of the U.S., 1982-83* (Washington, D.C., 1983), Appendix II, "Metropolitan Area Concepts and Components," 895-96; U.S. Office of Management and Budget, *Metropolitan Statistical Areas 1983* (Washington, D.C., 1983), 2; *New York Times,* July 8, 1893, where one business statistician described the abandonment of the minimum central city size requirement as the "most far-reaching [change] since the Government began designating metropolitan areas in 1910." Indeed, it might be called a *contradiction* of that designation as understood historically. The corruption of the notion of a dominant central city closely integrated with contiguous counties (towns in New England) was already evident in the case of Nassau-Suffolk, N.Y. SMSA before 1973, and the need "to please the state Congressional delegations" is clearly present in the 1983 changes, but for other inconsistencies, see Ira Rosenwaike, "A Critical Examination of the Designation of SMSAs," *Social Forces,* 48 (March, 1970), 322-33.

46 *New York Times,* April 28, 1983, on the Metropolitan Atlanta Council for Economic Development's attempt to compete for investment with centers such as Dallas, Tex., and Raleigh-Durham-Chapel Hill, N.C. The Dallas-Fort Worth area has recently surpassed Houston as the leading "employment center" in Texas, but despite that state's continued population growth, the "Texas economy seems exempt from recovery": *ibid.,* Aug. 6, 1983. Yet Texas unemployment remained lower than "all nine other major industrial states except Massachusetts."

47 Concentration reduces total effort-time expended in *x* interactions among *y* population members compared with that spent on equivalent interactions in a dispersed mode of settlement organization (hypothesis). As resulting density of *y* increases,

ceteris paribus less of y's effort-time need be used in effecting x interactions (i.e. the marginal energy "cost" of surmounting spatial frictions among y members decreases to some congestion limit). If y contrives something "worthwhile" to do with the effort-time its concentration has collectively "created" (net of that used in reproduction and sustenance tasks), it can proceed to additional and/or novel $(x + n)$ interactions in whatever balance of effort-time is potentially available after concentration. Whether, and how much of, these socially-acquired resources ("saving") can be appropriated by individuals, families, or other y agencies for discretionary use depends on the socially-instituted behaviors for allocating effort-time savings. Such net gain accrues to y existentially from ecological reorganization apart from the "external" or "internal" saving that may be derived from, say, functional specialization of effort-time and ensuing transactions under reciprocal or redistributive norms, "price" bargaining, or other exchange ratios: e.g. the space (land) cost saving to y members and community from a structure of space (land) "prices" competitively ordering classes of use within the y agglomeration. Much of this "external" saving from concentration is also social (if not strictly ecological) in that it is not the exclusive outcome of y members' labor service skills or investments (unit "internal" saving). Clearly, much ecological-social resource potential is foregone if y population, regardless of other possible "benefits" from nonhierarchical, nondominant, relationships, organizes in self-supporting communities uniformly distributed across country at minimum distances of 16 miles from each other as, for example, in Robert Owen, *The Book of the New Moral World* (London, 1949), 63. Competitive interaction *among* systemically differentiated concentrations of activities (esp. manufactures) sustains the self-motivating, information-generating feed back of demand upon supply—the cumulative causation—which fosters innovation *inter alia* in process and product lines and reorders population in diverse agglomerations of variable size and interactive density. See, Hawley, *Human Ecology,* 100-02; L.F. Schnore, "Social Morphology and Human Ecology," *American Journal of Sociology,* 63 (May, 1958), 620-34; E. Durkheim, "Note sur la morphologie sociale," *L'Annee sociologique,* o.s., 2 (1897-98), 520-21.

48 R.A. Easterlin, "Interregional Differences in Per Capita Income, Population, and Total Income, 1940-1950," *Trends in the American Economy in the 19th Century,* W.N. Parker, ed. (Princeton, 1960), Appendix A, Table A-1; L. Sveikauskas, "The Productivity of Cities," *Quarterly Journal of Economics,* 89 (1975); H.S. Perloff *et al, Regions, Resources, and Economic Growth* (Baltimore, 1960); Lampard, "Evolving System of Cities," *Issues in Urban Economics,* 82-92; and A.R. Pred, *Urban Growth and the Circulation of Information: The U.S. System of Cities 1790-1840* (Cambridge, Mass., 1973).

49 Weber, *Growth of Cities,* 209-10; E.E. Lampard, "Urbanization and Social Change," 7th International Economic History Congress, *Proceedings,* M.W. Flinn, ed. (Edinburgh, 1978), II, 533-40. "The primary tasks of the urban environment during the period of economic development is to redeploy the factors of production *in such a fashion* that overall output continues to increase": Meier, *Communications Theory of Urban Growth,* 155, italics added.

50 Based on the "need for direct face-to-fact contact," Meier, *op. cit.,* 64-6, "...we may attribute the daily migration to the center of the city, with everybody who is anybody on hand at the same time...as an attempt...to maximize the transaction rate." R.M. Hurd, *The Principles of City Land Values* (New York, 1903), 56-88, saw the intensively commercial-industrial core as a congeries of more or less specialized districts comprising their own symbiotic sets of competitive, complementary, and supportive activities. J. Rannells, *The Core of the City* (New York, 1956), 17-30, 51-61. On the relative values of farm land and buildings in selected urban fringe areas compared with their respective state average values, 1850-1950, see Lampard, "The Urbanization of the U.S.," *Villes en mutation,* Table 2, 171.

51 S. Kuznets, *Capital in the American Economy: Its Formation and Financing* (Princeton, 1961), 142-74; L. Grebler *et al.; Capital Formation in Residential Real*

Estate (Princeton, 1956); M. Abramovitz, *Evidences of Long Swings in Aggregate Construction Since the Civil War* (New York, 1964), 10-17; M. Gottlieb, *Long Swings in Urban Development* (New York, 1976), 137-90.

52 Kuznets, *Capital in the American Economy*, 167-69, Table 18, 327; L.E. Davis, "Saving and Investment," *Encyclopedia of American Economic History*, I, 183-201. Although the proportion of municipal income of large cities devoted to capital investments probably declined from about 30 to 20 per cent over the latter half of the 19th century, R. Goldsmith, *A Study of Saving in the U.S.* (3 vols. Princeton, 1955), estimates that local governments saved nine times as much in the aggregate, 1897-1906, as state governments.

53 E.E. Lampard, "Historical Contours of Contemporary Urban Society," *Journal of Contemporary History*, 4 (July, 1969), 12-14. Average income levels in the U.S. by states are historically associated with state levels of urbanization (and attendant economies of agglomeration, higher levels of capital per worker, and of value added by manufacture). Urbanization, in turn, is a function of higher income levels and of proportions of the work force in manufactures: Perloff *et al.*, *Regions, Resources, and Economic Growth*, 184-90, 274-83, 589-607. In the late 19th and early 20th centuries levels of state urbanization helped determine state levels of per capita incomes and *vice versa*. Both per capita incomes by states and shares of state work force in manufacturing exert significant *positive* effects on state levels of urbanization while *pari passu* urbanization levels have significant effects on income levels until the 1920's—less so ca. 1900 or among southern states. Had the generally favorable income differential outside of farming and most other rural occupations not persisted, migration to towns would have waned: Lampard, "Urbanization," *Encyclopedia of American Economic History*, III, 1044. That it did not come to a halt reflects the ability of urban populations to capitalize inventions: R. Higgs, "Urbanization and Inventiveness in the U.S., 1870-1920," *New Urban History*, Schnore, ed. 247-59. Also, H.A. Simon, "Effects of Increased Productivity upon the Ratio of Urban to Rural Population," *Econometrica*, 15 (Jan. 1947), 31-42.

55 S. Kuznets, "Long Swings in the Growth of Population and in Related Economic Variables," American Philosophical Society, *Proceedings*, 102 (Feb., 1958), 25-52. For a distinctive view of "long swings" as a form of development (and as therefore inseparable from development) and hence subject to distortion by standard techniques adopted for eliminating influences of both long and short-term cycles, Gottlieb, *Long Swings in Urban Development*, 5-7, 33-7; R.C. Bird *et al.*, "Kuznets Cycles in Growth Rates, The Meaning," *International Economic Review*, (May 1965). For other critical citations, see Lampard, "Nature of Urbanization," *Pursuit of Urban History*, n. 28, 31.

55 A.K. Cairncross concludes that the building cycle is "little more than a migration cycle in disguise," cited by Gottlieb, *Long Swings in Urban Development*, 130, and chapt. 5, *passim*.

56 Kuznets, *Capital in the American Economy*, 178; R.A. Eastelin, *Population, Labor Force, and Long Swings in Economic Growth: The American Experience* (New York, 1968).

57 Gottlieb, *Long Swings in Urban Development*, 191-219.

58 Higgs, "Urbanization and Inventiveness," *New Urban History*, 247-51, 258-9, "because urbanization encouraged greater inventiveness, it produced a *feedback effect* on growth by promoting more rapid technological progress."

59 Lampard, "Nature of Urbanization," *Pursuit of Urban History*, 32-3, n. 31. The contention that post-1920's surges in investment and capital formation occur in very different political-institutional settings from earlier "long swings" is buttressed, provisionally at least, by Gottlieb, *op. cit.*, 36-7: "the feedback processes between construction and the total economy and between residential building and real estate markets had altered in so many fundamental respects that...it seemed worthwhile to drop...the thirty years after the Great Depression trough (1933)." See also, M. Abramovitz, "The Passing of the Kuznets Cycle," *Economica*, 35 (Nov., 1968),

350-54. The fact that scientific and technical research into physical and social environments involves huge budgets does not mean that only large corporations and government agencies "do" the inventing. Small firms—often breakaways or spin-offs from large ones—working on contracts or grants produce many capitalizable novelties in electronics, genetics, urbanology, etc. Such Research and Development networks and funding sources are the formal cognitive counterparts perhaps of the informal, competitive industrial-urban environments in which countless 19th-century inventor/entrepreneurs empirically, cumulatively, and often serendipitously, developed their "better mousetraps." But see A.P. Usher, *A History of Mechanical Inventions* (2nd ed. Cambridge, Mass., 1954), 1-83.

60 Historically, there is a tendency to run down almost all urban capital goods since replacement does not notably increase a locality's money income, and thus, according to canons of financial orthodoxy, the capacity to pay for physical renovation (even in parts of the private sector) must be in doubt. For example, from 1889 to 1968 the annual *average* amount of replacement investment in the U.S. housing stock (the current dollar value of the *excess* of units constructed over net increases in numbers of households in a period expressed as a fraction of the capital value of the housing stock at the time of investment) is about one-third of 1% "which implies a replacement cycle for U.S. dwellings of 300 years": W.F. Smith, *Urban Development* (Berkeley & Los Angeles, 1975), 296-301. The excess of housing unit starts over new households turned negative at roughly 20 year intervals reflecting the impacts of severe recessions and wars.

61 In the absence of the net population growth of contiguous urbanized areas and concurrent annexation (% increase in central cities' incorporated *areas*), the thirty largest cities (as of 1970) would have lost *on average* 62% of their population since 1950: R.D. Norton, *City Life Cycles and American Urban Policy* (Academic Press, 1979). See also Bradbury *et al.*, *Urban Decline and the Future of American Cities*, 84-7, where for 120 large central cities *on average*, annexations of *population*, 1960-70, "more than offset the underlying rate of suburbanization" but, 1970-75, only recaptured about 60% of local suburbanization. Suburbanization has slowed markedly since the 1950's and in the 1970's SMSA population countrywide for the first time grew more slowly than non-SMSA population. There is no evidence that the long-run disjunction between urbanization and economic development in the U.S., which we date from about the 1920's, has been halted, nor can the tendencies of one recent decade be accorded the status of an "historical turning point;" but the short-period synchronic analysis of Bradbury *et al.*, 68-83, properly emphasizes the divergent "experience of individual areas" within "national historical trends" based upon "local attributes" which are said to affect recent locational choices by households and firms. The attributes are identified as disamenity avoidance, tax avoidance, positive attraction, economic evolution, biased federal policies, and demographic trends. Nevertheless, there is a marked historical-regional pattern to the distribution of 121 growing, stagnant, and declining central cities within growing (+) or declining (+) SMSAs in the U.S. as of 1970.

Population Changes of Central Cities in their SMSAs, U.S., by Region, 1970-1975

Cities	SMSA	New England	Middle Atlantic	Great Lakes	Plains	South -east	South -west	Mountain	Far West
Growing	+ SMSA	1	0	1	3	17	11	1	10
	+ SMSA	3	6	9	2	6	3	2	1
Stagnant	-SMSA	3	3	1	2	1	0	0	1
	+ SMSA	1	3	5	3	5	0	0	2
Declining	-SMSA	1	4	7	1	1	0	0	1

NB: All growing cities are in growing SMSAs (1975 boundaries)

Source: K.L. Bradbury *et al.*, *Urban Decline* (Washington, D.C., 1982), 4-8; Regions from H.S. Perloff *et al.*, *Regions, Resources, and Economic Growth* (Baltimore, 1960), 4-8.

See also E.S. Dunn, Jr., *The Development of the U.S. Urban System* (Baltimore, 1980).

Comment: Exorcising the Demons

FRANCIS R. WALSH

I was happy to accept the invitation to comment on Professor Lampard's paper since it gives me a chance to exorcise some demons that have vexed me since I first began to teach urban history in 1970. Professor Lampard doesn't know it, but it has been his articles and papers which have been appearing with great regularity for some twenty years calling for a conceptual framework for the study of urban history that set those demons loose.

As you probably know, Professor Lampard has been challenging those people who call themselves urban historians to distinguish what is generically urban history from what is incidentally urban history: "to explain something in history that cannot be explained by recourse to other frames of reference." His talk today has provided a model which one could use to develop one type of urban history course.

Professor Lampard once said that Clio's house has many mansions. Based on an informal survey of urban history courses that I have conducted, I must say that there seems to be a different type of urban history course going on in each of the rooms of the urban mansion.

First, let me say something about how I became involved in teaching urban history and then a word about those demons that I see emanating from Professor Lampard's work. Shortly after finishing my dissertation I was asked to fill in for someone who was scheduled to teach an urban history course at Boston University, but who had to change his plans. I accepted the invitation, although I had never taken an urban history course. Nevertheless, I felt I was eminently qualified. After all, my research interests were in ethnic history; many ethnics had lived in the city; I lived in a city; what could be simpler? Moreover, I was also interested in social history, and this seemed a golden opportunity to develop that material. All one had to do was to simply snip off those parts of social history that fell beyond the city limits, and the rest was urban history. Roy Lubove has described this approach to urban history as one that turns the city into a kind of historical variety store.[1]

I remember that period very clearly. I made a list of topics that seemed to belong in an urban history course: urban politics, immigration, social mobility, etc. Soon a mass of articles and books began to accumulate on my desk which would form the basis of my lectures—a well-stocked variety store indeed.

Before preparing the actual classroom presentations, I read several historiographical articles on the nature of urban history. The ones that always stand out in my memory were three by Professor Lampard: "American Historians and the Study of Urbanization"; "Urbanization and Social Change"; and "The Dimensions of Urban History."[2] The last article hit with special force since it not only appeared while I was preparing my course, but also expressed little sympathy for the type of course I had decided to develop.

At that point I began to remove those books and articles from my desk which fell into Professor Lampard's category of "incidental urban history." By the time I was finished, all that was left was a book by Sam Warner and Lampard's three articles.

Needless to say, I made it through that first course. Since that time I have become comfortable with a more eclectic approach to teaching urban history: one that pays a good deal of attention to Professor Lampard's ecological concerns, but one that often strays into areas on his proscribed list. Let me hasten to add that I do not wish to portray Professor Lamprd as some sort of modern-day Savonarola, intent on purifying the profession. On the contrary, his criticism of the field has always been couched in gentle terms. But it always seemed to me that just when I was feeling satisfied with my course, a new paper of his would be delivered, or a new article would appear calling for a more carefully delineated conceptual focus.

Nevertheless, I do think that a successful urban history course for undergraduates requires a number of different approaches in order to obtain the fullest historical explanation of the subject. Everyone who teaches urban history recognizes the need for an interdisciplinary orientation. But I also believe that there is a need to draw upon a variety of different approaches within the field of urban history: everything from an ecological framework through urban impact studies, city building, comparative studies, and urban problems, to name a few.

Urban history must be one of the most self-conscious of the subdisciplines of history. Witness the considerable amount of time devoted to the debate over whether the "new urban history" was really urban history at all. Yet, despite all of the space devoted to defining urban history, the field still lacks anything that could be called a consensus, and that may not be a disadvantage. Most of us can accept the thesis that the central issue of urban history is the spatial distribution of people, institutions, activities, and artifacts.[3] How one organizes a course around that theme, however, varies widely. One has only to look at the various textbooks in the field, or read Bruce Stave's interviews with urban historians in the various issues of the *Journal of Urban History* to realize how many different approaches do exist.

One personal positive result of this continuing controversy is that it has long since relieved me of my early fear, sparked by Professor Lampard's articles, that my course was incidentally rather than generically urban history. After all, who among us would want to teach an incidental course in anything? In fact, I now envision a sort of composite

Clio-Diogenes-like figure traveling from one campus to another in a vain search for an honest urban history course.

Since the topic of this session is "teaching urban history," I thought it might be useful to say something about the urban history course that I teach. Hopefully, as Mark Twain once said about classical music: "it's a lot better than it sounds."

It is a two-semester course for undergraduates, and of the one-hundred-and-fifty or so who enroll in a given year, only a handful are history majors. The course is organized topically rather than chronologically with most of the topics directed toward presenting an historical perspective on current urban issues. The organization of the course reflects in part the fact that I began teaching it when the urban crisis was a popular issue. I have stayed with this approach because it seems the best way to show students how the present is conditioned by the past. If nothing else, it seems to me that an urban history course should demonstrate how our present urban infrastructure and built environment have evolved over time.

One of the arguments usually raised against a problems or issues approach to the teaching of urban history is the danger of forcing material from the past into a contemporary mold. One of the major safeguards against truncating aspects of the urban past in search of relevance is the fact that one of the major goals of the course is to help students realize that what we call a city today and what they called a city in the eighteenth century or the nineteenth century are all different entities with different organizing principles, different spatial arrangements, and different purposes. Consequently, although the course does focus on urban issues in a historical perspective, room has been made to show how the city itself developed and evolved over time.

Let me cite a few examples from my course. I have found a film, "The City and the Self," which is designed for social psychology courses, a useful way to begin the course.[4] It deals with the nature of city life and its impact on behavior. Much of the film consists of a series of experiments testing the generalizations raised by Louis Wirth in his article, "The City as a Way of Life."[5]

The film has the advantage of raising a number of urban issues in a short space of time, issues that can best be understood within an historical framework. One of the issues touched upon in the film, for example, is people's unwillingness to take responsibility for their environment. One explanation offered by the film's narrator for this indifference is that we have handed over responsibilities for the city's condition to specialists: the fire department, the police, sanitation workers, etc., and we are protected and estranged from our environment through the same process. The film also presents a largely negative view of the city: suspicion, alienation, hostility characterize the actions of most of its inhabitants. All of this presents a useful jumping-off point for a number of topics covered in the first semester of my course: the nature of colonial cities; demographic changes in the nineteenth century; changing attitudes toward the city; and the development of city services.

I will give just one example of how a particular topic, urban transportation, can draw on a variety of urban history approaches. One objective of this unit is to demonstrate to students, as Professor Lampard has shown in his paper today, how changes in transportation systems helped to transform the walking city of the eighteenth century into the spread-out settlements of today, and how those changes in turn led to specialized areas of the city as well as affecting the distribution of population along class and racial lines.

A second goal is to show how the solutions of one era can give rise to the problems of a succeeding generation. It is difficult for students caught up with current environmental concerns to realize that the automobile was once welcomed by environmentalists of an earlier era who were concerned with pollution of a more tangible nature that fouled the city's streets. For those of us who do a lot of city driving an article in an 1899 issue of *Scientific American* heralding the automobile as a solution to "the nervousness, distraction, and strain of modern metropolitan life" reads more like science fiction than a piece of scientific analysis.[6]

An excursion into comparative urban history at that point is valuable as a means of comparing and contrasting American and European transportation systems. One effect of this approach is to put to rest the oversimplification that it was the government's favoritism combined with the neglect of public transportation that led to the automotive revolution in the United States. Europe, where vehicle ownership and operation have been heavily taxed and where roads and parking have been neglected at least until the 1960's, has experienced its own love affair with the automobile.

Finally, the unit concludes with an analysis of proposed solutions to our current transportation problems. Much of the discussion in the press has focused on the development of mass transit systems, a solution which fails to take into consideration the changes that have occurred in the pattern of the metropolitan population distribution since the late nineteenth century. In analyzing this problem, students can appreciate the changes in the ecology of cities—that we cannot reinvent a nineteenth century urban transportation system for a city in the late twentieth century. Richard Shackson, for example, has argued that comprehensive coverage of metropolitan regions by mass transit can save energy as long as the systems are designed to provide no more than ten to fifteen percent of all rides to and within the city, as opposed to the six percent carried by public transportation today. Shackson maintains that any increase in the supply of mass transit beyond that point would be energy inefficient because it would be serving low density areas with a resulting poor load factor.[7]

I have found it useful to conclude my course with a unit on the history of urban planning. One of the disadvantages of following a topical approach to urban history as I do is that there is a tendency to fragment history into artificial units. Finishing with planning can pull all of the various strands together.

I have found it especially valuable to look at the history of comprehensive town planning from Pullman through Howard's garden cities, Radburn, the Greenbelt communities, and Columbia, Maryland. The British historian S.G. Checkland once wrote that while serving on the development corporation for a planned town, he came to "really understand how multiple the interrelations that compose the town really are, and how subtle the patterns they form can often be."[8] It is that kind of appreciation that a survey of urban planning can hopefully instill in the student.

However one teaches a course in urban history, I think we all owe a debt of gratitude to Professor Lampard for making us think a little harder about what we are doing.

Notes

[1]   Roy Lubove, "The Urbanization Process: An Approach to Historical Research," *Journal of the American Institute of Planners* (June, 1967), p. 33.
[2]   Eric Lampard, "American Historians and the Study of Urbanization," *American Historical Review*, 67 (1961), pp. 49-61; Lampard, "Urbanization and Social Change: On Broadening the Scope and Relevance of Urban History" in *The Historian and the City*, eds. Oscar Handlin and John Burchard (Cambridge, Mass., 1963); Lampard, "The Dimensions of Urban History: A Footnote to the 'Urban Crisis'," *Pacific Historical Review*, 39 (Aug., 1970), pp. 261-278.
[3]   John B. Sharpless and Sam Bass Warner, Jr., "Urban History," *American Behavioral Scientist*, 21 (Nov./Dec., 1977), p. 225.
[4]   "The City and the Self," produced by Stanley Milgram, Time-Life Films.
[5]   Louis Wirth, "Urbanism as a Way of Life," *American Journal of Sociology* XLIV (July, 1938), pp. 1-24.
[6]   Thomas Conyngton, "Motor Carriages and Street Paving," *Scientific America Supplement*, 48 (July 1, 1899).
[7]   Quoted in Mark S. Foster, "The Automobile in the Urban Environment: Planning for a Energy-Short Future," *The Public Historian*, 3 (Fall, 1981), p. 27.
[8]   S.G. Checkland, "Toward a Definition of Urban History," in *The Study of Urban History*, H.J. Dyos, ed. (New York, 1968).

Comment: The Ground Zero Paradox

MICHAEL FRISCH

I am afraid I cannot respond very directly to Professor Lampard's rich and interesting paper, having received my copy only hours before coming here to Lowell. Since I am thus in more or less the same position as my audience, it might be more useful for me to suggest something of a context for appreciating his remarks, and their relevance to the more particular challenges spotlighted in our session's title, "Teaching Urban History."

I'll begin with an anecdote of a very recent vintage. Yesterday afternoon, I participated in a rally on our campus marking the culmination of Nuclear-Awareness Week. Improbable as it may seem, the rally provided an apt metaphorical expression of the challenges of teaching urban history and the particular place of Eric Lampard's imposing work in it over the years. Perhaps the connection was forged only by my concern over whether his paper would arrive before my airplane was scheduled to depart, but I will share it with you in any event.

The rally featured a large mock-up of a missile, standing at the "ground-zero" center of concentric circles marked on the campus plaza in colored crepe. Drums beat out an ominous countdown, after which a physics professor took the microphone to dramatize the awful tangibility of a nuclear explosion by detailing its "history," millisecond by millisecond, from the initial blast.

He described the first force of the explosion and the birth of the awesome fireball. But when he began to use the surrounding buildings to help people grasp the stunningly total and instantaneous destructiveness, his sermon suddenly went off track. "In a microfraction of a second the entire administration building melts and is vaporized," he intoned solemnly. This news brought cheers from a few students. He went on: "The Library disappears into the fireball ..." The cheering spread, and then grew more general as he stubbornly proceeded to detail the sequence of campus buildings engulfed in the Holocaust. When he pronounced, at the 1.2 second mark, the total incineration of the entire campus, extending as far as the hideous Marriott Inn standing at its edge across a sea of parking lots, general jubilation prevailed. The demonstration, I'm sorry to say, never quite recovered its seriousness after that, and its grave point was probably not carried home by anyone who had not brought it in with them at the start.

Perhaps because my mind was already on our upcoming conference, all this suggested to me the paradox that in teaching urban history as well, our attempts to concretize the most general truths about the cities and urbanization can founder, just as the looming presence of an all-too-tangible new campus actually deflected our students from reflecting on the very nuclear terror its putative destruction was supposed to illustrate. Yet the dilemma is that if we don't try to make that connection, the deeper or broader points may seem to many only abstractions and intellectual constructs, with little graspable reality in day-to-day application.

I don't think many of us who have been challenged and stimulated over the years by Eric Lampard's writings can claim to have resolved this tension in dealing with his work, in bringing down to the earth of successful teaching the ecological insights and the focus on urbanization as a societal process that he shows us—and he has done so again today—to be essential. More than we might wish, we may have often felt—at least I have—like that physics professor colleague, preaching at ground zero while the audience misses, or more accurately evades, the real point.

At least it can be said that these dilemmas are somewhat inherent in the problem at hand. Students often come to urban affairs or urban history courses with a hunger for "relevance" that actually obscures the deeper structures and broader processes at the core of the problems concerning them; the most central insights and tools are hence almost by definition the hardest to teach. I would say that the central pedagogic challenge in urban history is to break through this impasse.

To this end, let me share some guidelines that have helped me in my own teaching, a broad framework that has helped me to help students explore the connection between illustration and underlying structure, between event and theme, between context and construct in urban history. I'm sure most of this audience has wrestled with similar challenges, so I offer this less as a prescription than as a ground for broader discussion of methods for bringing Lampardian wisdom—or any other kind—into our classrooms. Let me present these as a series of propositions that more or less build sequentially.

1. The first theme is the simplest yet the most elusive: that cities, the elements composing them, and the processes of urbanization they reflect, are historical. Things have not always been as they are, things have not always happened in the same way, or had the same meaning. The terms, categories, and processes familiar to students express a particular conjunction, a particular mix of general and contingent. The point of studying urban history is thus not so much to know "what happened" as to gain understanding into "how things change or why they don't"—not a bad definition for a history course, I think.

2. The second requirement is some sort of abstracted model for examining the process of urbanization and the structure of cities. This can help make clear "how things work," especially by untangling for

analysis the complicated linkages between dimensions of urban structure and experience. The challenge and opportunity of an urban historical approach is to make such models tools for exploring a complicated reality rather than an end in themselves, taxonomic labelling exercises that often strike students—not incorrectly—as sterile abstractions uncomfortably distant from reality.

It has always seemed to me important to stress the complex interface of these two themes—the contingency of historical context and circumstance, and the particular nature and contraints of urban form and dynamics. I organize much of my urban history survey course, for instance, around the twin poles of a broad narrative chronology of American economic, social, and political history, on the one hand, and on the other a generalized model adapted in part from Charles Tilly's wonderful but little known "text," *An Urban World*. We look at cities and urbanization in terms of a triangle whose points represent space, people, and activities, and whose sides represent the interlocked dimensions these define: social ecology, economic geography, and socio-political organization and activity. The course uses this model to explore the linkages of independent and dependent variability in the urban system and in the urbanization process: changes in each dimension are examined historically, and their causes and consequences in the others traced through.

When this works well (an occasional result) students come away with an analytic ability to look at any situation—historical or contemporary—with an eye to identifying the forces in motion, the structures affected, and possible directions of change in the context. To measure this, I've occasionally employed final exam questions involving no history at all, but rather speculations on the future: I asked one group, for instance, to hypothesize a dramatic increase in world food prices—similar to the oil crisis of 1973-74—and to examine what the urban consequences would be in all dimensions, the policy issues raised, and the possible choices presented. Those students who understood both the linkages of the urban system and the contingency of larger historical forces and contexts had a lot of fun with this; those who still understood cities in static terms and history in terms of "what happened" had considerably more difficulty.

3. If such an approach to urban historicality is not to resolve down to an oversimplified and immobilizing kind of developmental determinism, however finely traced through, it must have one other central dimension as well: I have come to find it important to stress the political dimension of urban history far more than has been fashionable in recent years. By this I don't mean simply the history of bosses, reformers, and the like—what I have called elsewhere the recurring case of Plunkitt v. Steffens. Rather, I refer to the basic truth that at any moment, whatever the constellation of long-range forces and structural inhibitions, there are still choices that must be and are

made, contingent on the distribution, organization, and struggle for power. What are they? Who makes them—where, how, and why? Which choices are made? Which avoided? Which ignored?

Students are initially comfortable reading and talking about "politics," but I think it is a more demanding task to help them learn to evaluate, in any given context, the tension between choice and constraint, the potential latitude for conscious change and the way this is mediated culturally and politically. I've found readings from, and about, a book like Caro's *The Power Broker,* for example, especially helpful for grounding such discussion: obviously the automobile in all its manifestations would have had an incalculable impact on modern urbanity had Robert Moses never lived; just as manifestly, this one man and the forces he commanded made an enormous difference in institutionalizing certain values, responses, and physical forms—often after bitterly fought battles against advocates of other equally visible, equally viable choices.

In sum, then, to help bring Lampardian insights into the classroom and to make them maximally usable in the broadest sense, I have found it helpful to focus, in both the history and the urbanology, on Change, Contingence and Constraint, and Choice. If anything, this has been underscored by every darkening indicator of the current urban fiscal crisis and the more particular crisis of the northeastern industrial cities. There is a fine appropriateness to discussing such themes here in Lowell, where we celebrate the drawing of both historical understanding and contemporary vitality from the archeological remains of dead industry. There is also poignancy, especially for one coming from a city where Bethlehem Steel has recently announced its intentions to destroy 17,000 jobs and much of a community; Buffalo stands on the brink of the past tense from which Lowell has begun its dramatic escape-via-historical commemoration, and the wounds are perhaps too fresh to permit much comforting historical perspective.

That very immediacy, however, reinforces the points I've been making. The current crisis has produced a dramatic imbalance in political discourse, and not only in Buffalo. The death of the industrial cities has been prematurely, casually, and incorrectly assumed to be a structural imperative of modern life, while the complexities of the fiscal crisis have seemingly displaced substantive political choice and conflict in many cities. Now more than ever we need to find ways of joining the powerful insights contained in Eric Lampard's paper, and all of his work, to a heightened awareness of our latitude—and responsibility—for change at this exciting juncture of historic transformation. We stand at a kind of urban ground zero, and ought to aim—unlike my colleague who sought to frighten his audience and succeeded only in amusing them—rather at empowering our students, so that they can imagine turning the force of historical insight to contemporary advantage.

The European Origins of American Immigrants

JOHN BODNAR

The movement of nearly forty million people from Europe to America in the century prior to 1930 remains a momentous historical event whose dimensions and implications continue to evoke conflicting historical interpretations. It is not for lack of trying that scholars have yet been unable to agree on even the most fundamental aspect of this movement of people: exactly who left Europe and what was the purpose in leaving. For over three decades the answers have poured forth. The classic statement of Oscar Handlin left an impression of desperate people leaving an impoverished world and arriving in urban America barely clinging to existence. Handlin's immigrants were tradition-bound peasants who did not flee until their world had been destroyed by the forces of industrialization and commercial agriculture which drove them off the land. Handlin's views were embellished by the work of Brinley Thomas who saw immigrants as "victims" crossing the Atlantic only in response to the flow of capital. Investment in the American economy led to expanded job opportunities which in turn stimulated a westward flow of migrants.

The assault on the early interpretations of immigrant origins and objectives has taken two distinctly different forms. One line of scholarship maintained that immigrants were certainly poor but luckily possessed strong cultural traits which continued to shape their behavior and objectives in America; immigrant life was far from the disorganized struggle portrayed by Handlin. More recently a widespread image of immigrants as modern achievers intent upon social advancement and improvement has occupied historical attention. In this view the process of industrialization and agricultural change in Europe was not conceived as a threat to peasants and their culture. The new view saw peasants emancipated by the transformation of their rural homelands and quickly seizing upon new opportunities to climb higher in the social structure by moving to America. Timothy Smith, a leading spokesman of this school, even saw in the pervasive religious intensification among immigrants an inherent attempt to mobilize themselves on an ethno-religious basis to seek social and political advancement. To some extent scholarly studies of social mobility have produced some evidence of immigrant gains in America and have consequently reinforced the impression of the aspiring immigrant.[1]

At the center of this dispute is a precise understanding of the world the emigrant has left. Most historians would agree that vast changes were affecting the immigrant homeland. But divergent opinions emerge in our understanding of how emigrants responded to these changes and how that response influenced the decision to emigrate. Some would describe the response as a desperate abandonment of a declining rural order; others would emphasize a determined attempt to preserve traditional life in the face of increasing change. Still others would argue that the response of old world peasants to encroaching modernization was a decision to instantly accept the promises of a new order and pursue them. It is the intent of this essay to clear a path amidst the web of conflicting interpretations and abundant scholarship, provide a clearer picture of the events taking place in rural Europe in the century of massive emigration after 1830, and show how those events shaped the nature of American immigration.

If immigrants were drawn by the promise of America or driven away from lands of poverty, then we could expect to see them coming from nearly every region of Europe where economies compared unfavorably with that of the United States. A growing body of historical information, however, suggests that emigration was usually restricted to specific counties or locales and was not a random movement following the direction of capital investment.

The evidence on regional-specific emigrant streams comes from a wide array of European countries. In western Europe Scotland was a good case. Areas of severe economic depression, such as the Highlands, did not participate in the exodus as much as the Lowlands. Generally Lowland emigration outnumbered the Highland exodus by a ratio of 17 to 1. Movement from nearby England and Wales was not as intense as that from Scotland but still displayed some regional variations. Agricultural counties near London had their emigrants absorbed by that city but in rural areas further away, such as Sussex and Cornwall, emigration rates to America were very high. Even in Ireland, whose emigrants at times came closest to matching a flight from poverty model, emigration was least likely to occur from the poorest and most densely populated areas in the west and considerably more likely to take place from regions with slightly better economic conditions, such as Ulster, Leinster, and Connaught. Even during the 1846-1854 famine emigration the heaviest flows were more from the central and eastern mountains than the impoverished west.[2]

German emigration also displayed some of the regional variation characteristic of other lands. In its early phases it centered in the southwest, especially during the heavy years of the 1850's. Twenty years later it emanated primarily from the eastern and northeastern regions. The early dominance of the southwest took place especially in Baden and Wurttemberg where growing numbers of weavers went bankrupt and farming land was increasingly subdivided.

Sweden demonstrated characteristics similar to Germany. A regional structure was evident with direct correlations existing between high emigration rates, distance from large cities, and small amounts of arable land. Southern Sweden was strongly represented as was the city of Stockholm. It was rural Jonkoping County that supplied large amounts of newcomers to Chicago between 1860 and 1880: in regions adjacent to Stockholm, Uppsala, and Gothenburg emigration levels were very low. Neighboring Finland did not differ greatly, with emigration strongest from the rural provinces of Kuopio, Turku, and Pori. In Denmark those leaving came largely from the southern portion of the country especially the island of Bornholm. Even among the Dutch, whose rates of emigration were comparatively low, regional differences were marked.[4]

The eastern part of the European continent proved no exception to the pattern of regional variation. Austria-Hungary, which was a hardy producer of emigrants, sent very few from Lower and Upper Austria. But in Galicia and Bukovina emigration to America was very heavy. In general the inclination to migrate was greater in northeast Hungary than in districts close to Budapest. Most of the Magyar emigration, in fact, flowed from counties north of the Tisza River, many of which now lie in Slovakia or the Ukraine. Galicia had the highest rates of people leaving in both relative and absolute terms with fully 10 percent of the population emigrating between 1880 and 1910.[5]

Elsewhere in eastern and southern Europe regional patterns continued. Thus, the rate from Lower Carniola was twice the rate for the whole of Slovenia. Lika-Krbava stood out has a heavy center of Croation emigration. Congress Poland revealed emigration to be highest from certain districts such as Kaliz, Kiecle, and Piotrkow. In Italy the rate of emigration in the 1880's was 0.6 percent per 1,000 population but it was 2 percent from Lucca and 2.2 percent from Palermo.[6]

Emigrants not only came from specific regions but generally emanated from a particular position in the European social structure. Indications exist that those departing were not coming from the depths of their respective society but occupied positions somewhere in the middle to lower middle levels of their homeland's social structure. It was seldom the poorest who left; they could rarely afford it. In Italy the average yearly wages in Abruzzi and Molise and Calabria were well above those in Tuscany and Lombardy and yet the emigration was considerably heavier from the former provinces than the latter. In the Irish counties of Tipperary, Waterford, and Kilkenny, where rates of poverty and landlessness were highest, emigration was weakest. Even in such emigration centers as Galicia, more departed from the western areas even though its per capita income was among the highest.[7]

Germany was a clear case of emigrants originating from lower-middle levels of rural society. In the 1830-1845 period in southwestern Germany mostly small farmers and independent artisans left. Lower orders of farmhands and apprentices were unable to muster sufficient resources to cross the Atlantic and large estate owners enjoyed a measure of economic stability. As northeastern Germany replaced the southwest as a leading center of emigration by 1853 a greater proportion of those departing were individuals from lower social categories, especially the propertyless and the unmarried, but not those in the most dreadful economic state.[8]

The structure of emigration from Great Britain exhibited remarkable similarities to the German pattern. During the three decades prior to the 1850's, the lower middle class landowners and artisans from rural regions were most likely to leave. In Wales prior to 1850 it was also small farmers and laborers who had not yet reached the "stage of destitution" who generally departed. As time passed after the 1850's, the social status of most emigrants declined somewhat into the ranks of the landless but not to the bottom of the most impoverished. Those in the highest levels of society, of course, seldom left at all.[9]

Throughout much of the rest of Europe the trend continued wherever and whenever emigration took place. Sweden witnessed the movement of small farmers and skilled workers, especially lumbermen who saw their forest holdings being absorbed by timber companies.[10] While the numbers of landless and day laborers composed larger portions of the exodus from eastern Europe than in the western countries, the movement still consisted largely of the middle and lower-middle peasants. In northern Hungary and Slovakia small land holders departed along with day laborers, miners, and cottiers. In Croatia almost one-half of those leaving were independent farmers. Skilled workers actually predominated in Bohemia. Even among east European Jews evidence exists that those in the lowest stratum of society were too poor to emigrate. In Galicia the poorest Jews took road-building jobs and transported wood because they could not afford to leave. In Poland many moved to urban factory jobs.[11] Finally, as suggested above, in Italy as well, those with a "stake in society" were more likely to leave than day laborers. In one study of Sicilin passports between 1901 and 1914, 54 percent of departing males were in skilled trades or mercantile operations.[12]

The evidence that emigrants were coming primarily from the lower-middle ranges of society is strengthened by scattered indications that those leaving tended to be more literate than those who moved only short distances or did not move at all. Among Swedes the greater the illiteracy the shorter the distance the migrant moved. In Hungary 41 percent of the entire population was illiterate and yet among Slovaks who emigrated the rate was only 22 percent and only 11.4 percent among departing Magyars. Studies of Irish newcomers to Canada confirm the trend. While about 54 percent of the inhabitants of Ireland in the 1840's could neither read nor write, the figure was only 20 percent in a Canadian sample of 1861.[13]

If emigrants were leaving specific regions and particular social categories, they must have been sharing a common experience which caused them to consider emigration as an alternative life course. The tendency, expecially by American scholars, to deal with the entire process of immigration in separate units such as the ethnic group, however, has obscured important features which most emigrants faced at one time or another that lent a degree of similarity to the entire experience. A survey of the regions of high emigration underscores that commonality shaped the experience of most American immigrants between 1830 and 1930.

As industrialization proceeded across Europe internal demands increased in particularly fertile areas to maximize the efficiency of agricultural production in order to take advantage of the demands of growing urban markets. For commercial agriculture to succeed, however, land owners needed greater tracts of land, sufficient capital, improved technology, and better methods of crop and livestock production. In their pursuit of increased land holdings and improved rates of productivity, the landed elites began to drive small owners and landless but aspiring farmers from their regions. Indeed, much of the impetus for the emancipation of serfs stemmed from these large owners who saw the traditional array of peasant-noble rights and obligations as an obstacle to improved agriculture. Not surprisingly, emancipation seldom led to the destruction of large estates even where widespread parcelization of land took place. In Hungary, after emancipation, 53 percent of the land remained in the hands of large owners. By 1900 only 30 percent of the Hungarian peasantry owned enough land to assure an independent existence.[14] In Prussia after emancipation large owners were so successful in acquiring estates sufficient for commercial production that fully 80 percent of the agricultural population of Prussia were wage earners working for large estates or migrating to industrial jobs in Silesia.[15] Italian peasants fared little better as agriculture became increasingly commercial throughout the nineteenth century. An 1806 law encouraged the division of public lands among serfs but it was rarely enforced. In a familiar pattern groups of large estate owners, possessing greater leverage with the state, were able to expand while small independent owners and the "contadini" obtained inferior land because they lacked capital needed for improvements or sold out to wealthier owners all together. In Sicily a preoccupation with the export of wheat benefited large owners but made it difficult for smaller holdings to survive.[16]

Because commercial agriculture could only proceed in fertile areas it was inevitable that small and aspiring holders who could not gain adequate land in such regions would emigrate. Thus, newcomers to America were most likely to come from fertile areas such as the Scottish lowlands and vast grain producing regions such as East Elbia in

Germany, the Tiza plain in Hungary, Lower Carniola, and Sicily. In Romania emigrants tended to come from fertile plains rather than mountainous areas, and in the Balkans where the land was either mountainous or underdeveloped agriculturally, emigration rates were always comparatively low. Serbs who came to America for instance originated from farming areas of Croatia and not Serbia proper.

In some respects Ireland's agricultural history would appear to stand as an exception to the rest of Europe. Due to political domination by England, Irish agriculture was not entirely free to modernize. Large amounts of land were in the hands of middlemen who subdivided their plots and rented or sold for short term gains. By the 1840's about one-half the holdings in Ireland were below the minimum needed to maintain a sufficient income—usually about five acres. Even the process of agricultural improvement and consolidation which occurred in Germany and Austria-Hungary, for instance, was generally retarded. Some commercialization did take place but not on a scale with other countries. In fact, the British Corn Laws in the 1840's which ended preferential treatment for Irish grain in British markets resulted in a decrease in the amount of tilled land in Ireland. A consequence of less land in tillage was a drop in the demand for rural labor. When this decline combined with the over-division of Irish holdings and the fact that domestic industrial development was severely arrested by Britain and a lack of domestic coal and iron, the rural Irish were ready for emigration. The potato famine only accelerated a process which would have taken place anyhow.[18]

In nearby Great Britain, agricultural development was much closer to that of the rest of Europe rather than Ireland, with a steady movement taking place toward holdings large enough to make scientific farming practicable. New techniques improved agricultural efficiency to the point where the demand for agricultural labor was decreased. In the lowlands of Scotland the process was particularly pronounced. Improvements were introduced into Scottish agriculture almost continuously after 1775. The acreage under plow was always being extended and the yield per acre doubled during the nineteenth century. Livestock yielded a much larger proportion of farm income. Whereas small families had viewed five to fifteen acres as a desirable minimum for survival, profit-oriented commercial farmers now sought at least seventy acres and some reached six-hundred acres and did not hesitate to evict tenants to obtain it. On these larger tracts gradually appeared the use of more than one plow team and even threshing machines.

Individuals living in fertile areas and facing the introduction of commercial agriculture had several options. They could retaliate against the forces of modernization and change and attempt to retain their traditional patterns of life, including farming for self-sufficiency rather than profit.Some could attempt to adjust to new conditions and gain the necessary expertise and capital to launch commercial agricultural ventures of their own. Finally, migration to a nearby industrial area or abroad was a possibility. All three options were actually chosen at one time or another. Whatever alterntive was selected, however, it was usually carefully considered. Indeed, emigration may have been weighed more fully as a choice than all others.

Without question the response of rural dwellers could frequently be reactionary and something less than realistic. As peasant society produced more and more for a national and export economy, it became more intimately aware not only of alternative economic futures but also of the outlines of its unique past. Historians who have emphasized the upward aspirations of peasants in lands undergoing transition have overlooked the point that they were equally as likely to rivet their attention upon the glories of a past and a heritage which now seemed threatened and in need of enrichment.[20]

In Hungarian villages the complexity of the peasant response to the urban industrial system can be seen most clearly. Growing trade contacts brought new goods to villages, for instance, and peasants began to decorate their homes with greater variety. In fact, interest in decorative arts actually intensified. Yet costumes continued to be made in a common peasant fashion ignoring differences in social rank and strata. Despite growing differences in economic functions, the desire to retain a "peasant way of life" was widespread. In fact, most "peasant styles" of dress, as they are known in the twentieth century, appeared precisely when peasants began to interact increasingly with urban people. Peasants—and the nationalist leaders who discovered them by the late nineteenth century—began to drift away from an earlier trend of adopting the music and language of the upper-classes and initiated a quest for a more authentic and peasant-based folk. In everyday life trends toward patterns of the gentry now gave way to "peasant" look.[21]

The pattern was repeated elsewhere in Europe. In Vierlanden near Hamburg rural folk art began to grow more "rustic" and manifest an anti-urban bias.[22] In Morovia and Slovakia folk costumes became more elaborate and colorful in a defiant gesture toward urban functionalism. This self-awareness was especially marked in towns near expanding cities such as Bratislava and Brno. Ornamentation on costumes increased. On hunting costumes so many decorations were added that men could no longer hunt in them. Specific occupational groups began to elaborate on their traditional costume design. Millers in Moravia, for instance, wore close-fitting blue breeches. Even religious and ethnic attachments were expressed more strongly in dress, especially among minorities such as Germans in Czech-dominated villages or Slovaks in Magyar towns. Italian village peasants sought a mythical past without exploitative landlords and hungry mouths to feed. In the village of Nissoria a movement was begun to change the patron saint of eight centuries from one who had been identified with petty nobility to St. Joseph, who was seen as a special protector of laborers. Elsewhere revolts against church authorities who sought to switch festivals from traditional dates of celebration occurred.[23]

In many instances the flourishing of peasant art, culture, and costume by the late nineteenth century was not simply an expression of growing peasant self-awareness; it also represented a growing integration into the national state especially in areas such as Germany, Italy, and Hungary. Rising elites who saw their futures tied to the state sought to exploit traditional peasant cultures in strengthening their particular conception of nationalism. Dance masters and composers in Budapest, for instance, sought peasant dance and musical forms as a basis for mobilizing nationalist sentiment and in the process hoped to draw peasants into their movement. In fact, nationalist sentiment was becoming so strong in Hungary that the Hungarian government did not become very concerned about emigration until Magyars—who took longer to move away from their psychological moorings than other groups—began to leave.[24]

But the image of the reactionary peasant must not be carried too far. More common was a much more pragmatic and calculating reaction on the part of peasants; emigration was a concept derived from this prevailing pragmatism. In many areas large numbers of agricultural workers and other toilers formed organizations to further the aims of workers and provide for a modest amount of economic security. In Bosnia-Herzegovina the Association of Skilled Workers and Day Laborers was formed. Mutual-aid societies proliferated in the premigration world. After emancipation peasants were often forced to make redemptive payments, improve their farms, and buy or rent land. Drawn increasingly into a cash economy, peasants lacked the qualifications and connections to acquire much capital on their own and thus founded credit unions and cooperatives. By 1914 in Denmark most of the rural population belonged to one of these associations. Germany had over 1,000 credit groups by 1883 and over 23,000 by 1910. Hungary had 2,830 credit associations in 1903. In Slovenia peasant loan cooperations had 165,000 members by 1910 and attempted to generate not only funds for capitalistic development but consciously sought to prevent the acquisition of Slovenian real estate by non-Slovene capital as well.[25]

In Slovakia, Hungary, Croatia, and elsewhere increased drinking, wife-beating, and sexual offenses were reported as older institutions and mores were challenged. But such "breakdown" was not normal. Among the South Slavs, for instance, a peasant movement led by Anton and Stjepan Radic sought to restore the interdependence of the rapidly disappearing zadruga with newly established cooperatives. The fact that they also sought to preserve peasant architecture, folk dances, and costumes did not mean they were totally unaware of new economic demands.[26] In Russian Poland the peasant bank had loaned enough money by 1901 to enable peasants to acquire five percent of the entire amount of land owned by the peasant class. In Romania even shepherds formed mutual benefit societies which offered loans and death benefits by the 1890's.[27]

Jews in eastern Europe, incresingly restricted in their economic activities and prevented from attending many universities, sought learning and economic equality with non-Jews. Some Jewish leaders called for adaptation through a modernization of Jewish customs. Young Jews were attracted to Vilna and other cities where they studied religion less and the gospel of socialism more in an attempt to improve the lot of the working classes.[28]

Realistic attempts to deal with a new economic order not only characterized the activities of those who remained in the homeland and sought to adjust, but also those who decided upon emigration. Italians, for instance, were especially adept at considering the implications of moving. Emigration was heavy in rainy years which usually led to poor harvests. A warm spring which boded well for the winter wheat crop kept many in their villages. They knew an abundant harvest could lead to greater farm employment at home. In the 1880's the residents of one village learned that Pennsylvania coal miners were getting nearly two dollars a day and quickly estimated that in two years they could save enough to return to Italy and purchase sufficient land to support a family. Even among those who stayed the dream of returning home to establish independent farms persisted.[29]

Some sociologists have described peasants as inhabitants of a culture of poverty which favored immediate gratification over forced savings. But no such culture characterized most emigrants to America who were making realistic decisions about familial and individual survival.

The theme of peasant realism is underscored significantly when one considers that in every area of heavy emigration people were leaving in the midst of a labor shortage on nearby large estates. But calculating peasants knew that work on these estates was only seasonal and still not as well paying as industrial pursuits. Often labor had to be imported into these regions at the very time individuals were moving somewhere else. Scotland was a good example of an area where agricultural wages were rising because large owners had to bid higher for the local supply of workers which was shrinking. Large farms in Scotland began to import Irish laborers.[30] In Elbia large landowners lobbied for policies which would lead to a large supply of cheap labor. In Austria-Hungary estate owners were continually complaining about a dearth of labor even though their own practices of adopting more machinery and devoting more land to commercial crops were driving away the native supply of toilers. One great estate owner in Bukovina complained that all his peasants had emigrated and "we sit here com-

pletely without workers and must spend a lot of money to bring people from Russia and Rumania." Indeed, labor shortages prevailed in
Bohemia, Moravia, and Upper and Lower Austria.[31]

Those that could work, of course, often benefited from the wage increase. In Germany between 1850 and 1913 the wages of agricultural
labor rose 127 percent even as thousands emigrated. In Kalisz,
Suwalki, and Plock, three centers of Polish emigration to America,
wage scales rose continuously for men and women. In Kalisz the scale
for a day's wage was double that for the rest of the country. A Polish
villge study found that in the village of Maszkienice the day's wage for
a field worker increased 80 percent and that of threshers 125 percent
between 1899 and 1911.[32] The point was that emigrants were consciously rejecting abundant work opportunities on nearby estates in
order to get longer term, higher paying positions in the industrial
economy. This was done, however, not to simply pursue "a better
life" in America but usually to gain resources sufficient for meeting the
economic realities of their places and times; more income promised an
ability to purchase the greater amounts of land needed to survive in
commercial agriculture.

Two final factors seem to strengthen the impression of the emigrant
as rational rather than disillusioned or aspiring. In nearly every instance where emigration emerged, and due in part to the labor shortages it created, some attempt was made by local governments to arrest the tide. Decisions had to be made consciously in the face of existing regulations and prohibitions. Furthermore, tremendous
amounts of emigrants moved only on a temporary basis and returned
whenever they could to launch their own agricultural endeavors.

Since emigration in one sense represented a loss of an essentially
young and productive sector of the population, governments in the
emigrants' homeland often opposed the exodus. Italian Catholic
publications publicly censured those who left for neglecting their
duties to their families and their land. In Great Britain mercantilists opposed emigrant departures because they felt it was a drain upon national strength. The conservative gentry in Russian Poland were
unreservedly opposed to peasants leaving since they wanted to retain
a surplus labor supply in rural areas. In Galicia the Austrian government supported the gentry's opposition to emigration. In 1868 the
Galician Sejm abolished restraints on the free disposition of land in
part to prevent peasants from sinking into a landless proletariat which
might be more inclined to leave. The minority which correctly argued
that parcelization would actually encourage emigration was ignored.[33]

But homeland governments did not persist in attempting to prohibit
something as uncontrollable as massive population movements. They
often saw benefits to be derived from the emigration of their citizens
and sometimes moved to encourage it. As the nineteenth century pro-

gressed in Great Britain mercantilists gradually dropped their earlier opposition and began to see emigration as an outlet for overpopulation, a means of reducing the burden of caring for the poor (even though the poorest seldom emigrated), and a safety valve for popular discontent. Emigration was also viewed as a safety valve by some in Austria and Denmark and as a means to help liquidate debts and tax liabilities since migrants sent money home. Despite opposition from the landed gentry and even the military establishment who feared a loss of manpower, commercial transportation interests often stood to profit from migration streams. Social liberals even argued on behalf of the peasant's right to emigrate to improve his standard of living.[34] Understandably, when governments realized they could not totally control the exodus and that they were often caught between opposite political factions they moved to regulate the process in order to avoid a loss of influence altogether. Thus, the Croation government established a foundation to which all emigrants paid a fee before they left. Collected funds were used to assist penniless Croats in America return home. Various emigrant aid societies were established by concerned governments and citizens. The Polish Emigration Society, headquartered in Cracow in 1907, sought primarily to assist all Poles in need beyond the borders of the Austro-Hungarian Empire. Hungary sought to profit from the emigrant traffic by contracting with the Cunard shipping lines to pick up emigrants at the port of Fiume. The advantage for Hungary would be that her emigrants would avoid German ports and keep expenditures within the economy of the empire.[35]

No aspect of the entire immigration process revealed so much about the predisposition to use industrial wages to improve or maintain status in the rural world as did the act of return migration. Because everyone did not or was unable to return did not mean that nearly everyone originally held such a hope. The only major exceptions seem to have been those who had worked as craftsmen or those who ventured to America before 1860 with sufficient capital to initiate farming enterprises in the new world. Even among Jews, long thought to be among the most permanent of newcomers, recent evidence suggests a return rate of about 20 percent. While estimates vary, return rates usually ranged from 25 to 60 percent, although most records on immigration are somewhat imprecise. Hvidt found about 30 percent of the Danes returning, and the German figure was between 35 and 40 percent. About four of every ten Greeks returned and the Polish figure was only slightly below that. The most likely of all to return were those from central and southern Italy (56 percent) and northeast Hungary. Magyar rates have been estimated at 64 percent and those of Slovaks at 59 percent.[36]

Like emigration itself, however, the return movement was diverse and composed of various sectors of immigrant society, and it was stimulated by several motives. Finnish farmers with wives, and presumably with more of a chance to sustain themselves in farming, were considerably more likely to return than landless laborers. A sample of returning Finns listed homesickness and family obligations such as farm responsibilities as the leading factors. Unemployment was always a significant but not a primary cause of return, although a sharp upturn in the return of Finns and others was noticed after 1929.[37] Furthermore, the Hungarian government supported an extensive program of "American Action," which used financial inducements to gain control over immigrant churches and newspapers in America in order to maintain a desire on the part of emigrants to return with their American earnings and blunt disaffection from the cause of Hungarian nationalism. Their efforts were rewarded: one study of a Hungarian village found more than 50 percent of those who had gone to America to have returned within three to five years. Even among those who stayed, many continued to buy land in Hungary. "We'll only stay in America and work hard until we have [enough money for] twenty acres, and then we'll go home," one Hungarian recalled. In Italy remigration was less frequent in the north than in the south. While southerners tended to return to their villages seasonally or within three to five years, those in the north often stayed away longer and did not necessarily return to the villages they left. In part this can be attributed to the fact that more land was available for sale in the south than in the north. Where emigrants left regions of large holdings where parcelization was not as extensive, return migration rates were generally lower. This was not only true for northern Italy but for similar regions such as Austria and Prussia.[39]

European immigrants to industrial America have acquired numerous labels. But a close analysis of their backgrounds suggest that previous descriptions of impoverished peasants fleeing the ruins of agricultural Europe or eager entrepreneurs seeking to exploit the riches of a new urban-industrial order are somewhat less than accurate. Emigrants did not flee randomly but considered carefully options available to them in fluid economic circumstances. Most were confronted with the challenge of commercial agriculture. Where this challenge was absent few emigrants to America could be found.

Located in the middle to lower-middle sectors of their homeland's social structure, emigrants were seldom the poorest. Carefully weighing the advantages of overseas work against the demands for labor on local estates, they decided that they could maximize their income in the short run through emigration to areas which paid industrial wages. But their decision did not mean they sought dramatic improvement in their lives; nor did it mean they were abandoning an older form of life. The intensifiaction of traditional religious and cultural values in their homeland served as powerful reminders that many steadfastly rejected change. But emigrants wanted the best of both worlds. Life on the land was still desirable, but new economic realities could not be ignored. Credit associations and agricultural improvement societies all underscore the duality of peasant thought and the central fact that emigrants moved to modern America generally to return with accumulated wages to resume life where they had left it in their changing homelands. Immigrants were pragmatic people without grand illusions. In America as in Europe they took what was available. Those who continually tried to alter their pragmatism—priests, proselytizers, labor leaders, socialists, and Americanizers—would, like the historians who have studied them, only learn this gradually.

NOTES

1   See Oscar Handlin, *The Uprooted* (Boston: Little Brown, 1951), pp. 21-37; Marcus Lee Hansen, *The Atlantic Migration, 1607-1860* (Cambridge: Harvard Univ. Press, 1940). For views of immigrant cultural persistence see especially Herbert Gans, *The Urban Villagers* (Glencoe, Ill., 1962); Rudolph Vecoli, "The Contadini in Chicago: A Critique of the Uprooted," *Journal of American History*, LI (Dec., 1964); Vecoli, "Prelates and Peasants: Italian Immigrants and the Catholic Church," *Journal of Social History* 2 (1969), pp. 227-33. Newer views of immigrants acquiring higher, new aspirations in their homelands and bringing them to America are found in Timothy L. Smith, "Religion and Ethnicity in America," *American Historical Review*, 83 (Dec., 1978), pp. 1155-1185; John Briggs, *An Italian Passage* (New Haven, Ct.: Yale Univ. Press, 1978); Josef Barton, *Peasants and Strangers: Italians, Rumanians, and Slovaks in the American City*, (Cambridge, Mass.: Harvard Univ. Press, 1975). Recent mobility studies which tend to partially sustain the impression of the striving and often successful immigrant include Thomas Kessner, *The Golden Door and Jewish Immigrant Mobility in New York, 1880-1915.* (New York: Oxford Univ. Press, 1977; Kathleen Conzen, *Immigrant Milwaukee, 1836-1880; Accommodation and Community in a Frontier City* (Cambridge, Mass.: Harvard Univ. Press, 1976); John Bodnar, Roger Simon, and Michael Weber, *Lives of Their Own: Blacks, Italians, and Poles in Pittsburgh* (Urbana, Ill.: Univ. of Illinois Press, 1982).
2   Maldwyn A. Jones, "The Background to Emigration from Great Britain in the Nineteenth Century," *Perspectives in American History*, VII (1973), 47, 83; Malcom Gray, "The Scottish Emigration: The Social Impact of Agrarian Change in the Rural Lowlands, 1775-1875," *Ibid*, 97-73; Howard L. Malchow, *Population Pressures: Emigration and Government in Late Nineteenth Century Britain* (Palo Alto, Cal.: Sposs Inc., 1979); Gino German: "Migration and Acculturation," in *Handbook for Social Research in Urban Areas*, Ed. by Philip Hauser (Paris, 1964), pp. 159-78; Lynn Hollen Lees, *Exiles of Erin: Irish Migrants in Victorian London* (Ithaca, N.Y.: Cornell Univ. Press, 1979), pp. 22-24; R.C. Taylor, "Migration and Motivation," in *Migration*, Ed. by J.A. Jackson (Cambridge, Eng.: Cambridge Univ. Press, 1969), p. 132; Barbara L. Solow, *The Land Question and the Irish Economy, 1870-1903* (Cambridge, Mass.: Harvard Univ. Press, 1971); Oliver MacDonagh, "The Irish Famine Emigration to the United States," *Perspectives in American History*, X (1976), 418-30.
3   Mack Walker, *Germany and the Emigration, 1816-1885* (Cambridge: Harvard Univ. Press, 1964), pp. 44-47; Wolfgang Kollmann and Peter Marschalck, "German Emigration to the United States," *Perspectives in American History*, VII (1973), 531-39; Kristian Hvidt, *Flight to America: The Social Background of 300,000 Danish*

Emigrants (New York: Academic Press, 1975), p. 14.

4 See Struve Lindmark, *Swedish America, 1914-1932* (Uppsala, 1971), pp. 17-27; Ulf Beijbom, *Swedes in Chicago: A Demographic and Social Study of the 1846-1880 Immigration* (Stockholm: Laromedelsforlagen and the Chicago Historical Society, 1971), pp. 134-55; Harald Hunblom and Hans Norman, *From Sweeden to America: A History of the Migration* (Minneapolis: Univ. of Minnesota Press and ACTA UNIVERSITATIS UPSALIENSIS, 1976), pp. 136-40. Despite their rural image, by 1910 over 60 percent of all Swedes in America were city dwellers; see Beijbom, *Swedes in Chicago*, p. 11. Keijo Virtanen, *Settlement or Return: Finnish Emigrants, 1860-1930, in the International Overseas Return Migration Movement* (Helsinki: Finnish Historical Society, 1979), pp. 24-100; see also A. William Hoglund, *Finnish Immigrants in America* (Madison, Wis.: Univ. of Wisconsin Press, 1960). Hvidt, *Flight to America*, pp. 40-69. Yda Saueressig-Schreuder and Robert Swierenga, "Catholic Emigration from the Southern Provinces of the Netherlands in the Nineteenth Century," (Voorburg: Interuniversity Demographic Institute, 1982), pp. 1-18; Robert P. Swieringa, "Dutch Immigrant Demography, 1820-1880," *Journal of Family History*, 5 (Winter, 1980), p. 390-405;Swieringa, "Dutch International Migration and Occupational Change: A Structural Analysis of Multinational Linked Files," unpublished paper delivered at the Social Science History Association Conference, Bloomington, Indiana, Nov., 1982. Little discussion is provided for France since its emigration was very low, due primarily to a rise in agricultural production that kept ahead of a slower, growing population. See David Grigg, *Population Growth and Agrarian Change: A Historical Perspective* (Cambridge: Cambridge Univ. Press, 1980), p. 201.

5 Tibor Kolossa, "The Social Structure of the Peasant Class in Austria-Hungary: Statistical Sources and Methods of Research," *East European Quarterly* (1979), III, pp. 430-32; Paula Kaye Benkart, "Religion, Family, and Community Among Hungarians Migrating to American Cities, 1880-1930," (unpublished Ph.D. dissertation, The Johns Hopkins University, 1975), pp. 10-11; Julianna Puskas, *Kivandorlo Magyarok Az Egyesult Allamokba, 1880-1940*, pp. 56-70. Istvan Raxz, *A Paraszti Migracio es Politikai Megitelese Magyarorszagon*, 1849-1914 (Budapest: Akademiai Kiado, 1980), pp. 111-15, provides details on Zemplin County. Johann Chmelar, "The Austrian Emigration, 1900-1914," *Perspectives in American History*, VII (1973) pp. 318-30; Franciszek Bujak, *Galicya* (2 vols; Lwow: Nakladem Ksiegarn H. Altenberga, 1908-1910), II, p. 270, for a discussion of limited industrial employment within Galicia. For examples of extreme parcelization and even contractual obligations to the land in Romania see Daniel Chirot, *Social Change in a Peripheral Society: The Creation of a Balkan Colony* (New York: Academic Press, 1976), pp. 136-47.

6 Chmelar, "The Austrian Emigration, 1900-1914," pp. 333-34; Frances Kraljic, "Croatian Migration to and from the United States Between 1900 and 1914," (unpublished Ph.D. dissertation, New York University, 1975), pp. 19-31; Toussaint Hocevar, *The Structure of the Slovenian Economy, 1848-1963* (New York Studia Slovenica, 1965), pp. 83-85; Ivan Cizmic, *Iseljenistvo i Suvremena Ekonomska Emigracija a Prodruja Karlovca* (Zagreb: Matica Hrvatska, 1973), pp. 17-30; Branko Mita Colakovic, *Yugaslav Migrations to America*, (San Francisco: R&E, 1973) pp. 24-56; Mark Stolarik, "Immigration and Urbanization: the Slovak Experience, 1870-1918," (unpublished Ph.D. dissertation, Univ. of Minnesota, 1974) pp. 3-30; "Slovenska do USA a jeho pribeh az do roku 1918, jeho priciny a Nisledky," in Josef Polisensky, ed., *Zaciatk Ceskej a Slovense j emigracie do USA* (Bratislava, 1970), pp. 54-55; Celina Bobinska and Andrezej Pilch, *Employment Seeking Emigration of the Pole World Wide XIX and XX Century* (Krakow, 1975) pp. 39-79; Witold Kula, Nine Assorodobraj-Kula and Marian Kula, eds., *Listy Emigrantowz Brazylili Stanow Zjed Noezonych, 1890-91* (Warsaw, 1973) pp. 241-330; Bodnar, Simon, and Weber, *Lives of Their Own: Black, Italians, and Poles in Pittsburgh*, p. 35; T. Lindsay Baker, *The First Polish Americans* (College Station, Texas: Texas A&M Press, 1979), pp. 8-25.

The growing literature in Polish emigration is summarized in Irena Paczynska and Andrzej Pilch, eds. *Materialty do, bibliografiidziejow emigracji oraz Skupisik Polonijnych w Amerike Polnocnej in Poludniowej w XIX i XX Wicku* (Krakow: Jagiellonia University, 1979).

7 Barton, *Peasants and Strangers*, p. 30; Charlotte Erickson, ed., *Emigration From Europe, 1815-1914: Select Documents* (London: Adams and Black, 1976), p. 93; Chmelar, "The Austrian Emigration, 1900-1914," pp. 318-30; Bujak, *Galicya; Chirot, Social Change in a Peripheral Society: The Creation of a Balkan Colony*, pp. 136-47; Lees, *Exiles of Erin*, pp. 25-39; MacDonagh, "The Irish Famine Emigration to the United States," pp. 418-25.

8 Walker, *Germany and the Emigration, 1816-1885*, pp. 163-66; Kollmann and Marschalck, "German Emigration to the United States," pp. 541-45.

9 Conway, "The Welsh Emigration to the United States," pp. 200-210; Jones, "The *Background to Emigration from Great Britain in the Nineteenth Century,"pp. 83-87;* Erickson, *Invisible Immigrants: The Adaptation of English and Scottish Immigrants in Nineteenth Century America* (Coral Gables, Fla.: Univ. of Miami Press, 1972), pp. 24-34, 232-39; Berthoff, *British Immigrants in Industrial America*, pp. 11-19. See also J.H.M. Lazlett, "The Independent Collier: Some Recent Studies of Nineteenth Century Coal Mining Communities in Britain and the United States," *International Labor and Working Class History*, (Spring, 1982), No. 21, pp. 18-27, who saw some Welsh miners emigrating partially to preserve an agrarian way of life. Grigg, *Population Growth and Agrarian Change: A Historical Perspective* (Cambridge, Eng.: At the University Press, 1980), p. 187. See N.H. Carrier and J.R. Jeffrey, *External Migration: A Study of the Available Statistics, 1815-1950* (London, 1953).

10 Beijbom, *Swedes in Chicago: A Demographic and Social Study of the 1816-1880 Immigration*, p. 39, 167; Runblom and Norman, *From Sweden to America: A History of the Migration*, pp. 132-43.

11 Barton, *Peasants and Strangers*, pp. 36-39; Stolarik, "Immigration and Urbanization: The Slovak Experience, 1870-1918," p. 14; Frantisek Bielik and Ela Rakos, *Slovenska Vystahovalectvo Dokumenty, I, do roku, 1918* (3 vols; Bratislava: Slovenska Akademia Vied., 1969) I, pp. 30-40; Puskas, *Kivandorlo Magyarok Az Egyesult Allamokba, 1880-1940*, p. 26; Benkart, "Religion, Family, and Community Among Hungarians Migrating to American Cities, 1880-1930," p. 27; Kraljic, "Croatian Migration To and From the United States Between 1900 and 1914," p. 34; Chmelar, "The Austrian Emigration, 1900-1914," p. 337; Puskas, "The Conflicts of Adaptation of the Hungarian Emigrants in America," unpublished paper delivered at United States-Hungarian Conference on Industrialization, Budapest, Aug. 23-25, 1982, p. 7; A. Klima, "Agrarian Class Structure and Economic Development in Pre-Industrial Bohemia," *Past and Present*, 85 (1979), pp. 421-32. A fairly complete breakdown of the occupational status of Hungarian emigrants is found in Racz, *A Para s zti Migracio es Politikai Megitelese Magyarorszagon*, p. 85.; Simon Kuznets, "Immigration of Russian Jews to the United States: Background and Structure," *Perspectives in American History* IX (1975), 35-105; Moses Rischin, *The Promised City: New York's Jews, 1870-1940* (New York: Harper and Row, 1962), p. 20; Chmelar, "The Austrian Emigration, 1900-1914," p. 341; Franciszck Bujak, *Limanowa: Miasteczko Powiatowe w Zachodniej Galicyi Stan Spolecnzy I Gospodarczy* (Krakow: G. Gebethner I Spolka, 1902), pp. 42-47.

12 John W. Briggs, *An Italian Passage: Immigrants to Three American Cities, 1890-1930* (New Haven: Yale University Press, 1978), pp. 2-12.

13 Barbara A. Anderson, "Internal Migration in Modernizing Society: The Case of Late Nineteenth Century European Russia," (unpublished Ph.D. dissertation, Princeton Univ., 1973), pp. 35-38. I would like to thank Professor Ben Eklof for this reference. Puskas, *Kivndorlo Magyarok Az Egyesult Allamokba, 1880-1940*, pp. 47-72; Benkart, "Religion, Family and Community Among Hungarians Migrating to American Cities," p. 32; Sune Akerman, "Swedish Migration and Social Mobility: The

Tale of Three Cities," *Social Science History*, I (Winter, 1977), pp. 178-209. Harvey J. Graff, *The Literacy Myth: Literacy and Social Structure in the Nineteenth Century City* (New York: Academic Press, 1979), p. 65; Dino Cinel, *From Italy to San Francico* (Stanford, Cal.: Stanford Univ. Press, 1982), p. 23; Richard A. Easterlin, et. al., *Immigration* (Cambridge, Mass.: Harvard Univ. Press, 1982), pp. 8-9

14 Jerome Blum, *The End of the Old Order in Rural Europe* (Princeton, N.J.: Princeton Univ. Press, 1978), pp. 113, 376-404; Grigg, *Population Growth and Agrarian Change: A Historical Perspective*, pp. 30-32. See Alexander Gershenkrom, "Agrarian Policies and Industrialization, Russia, 1861-1917," in *Cambridge Economic History of Europe*, (6 vols; Cambridge, Eng.: At the University Press, 1965), VI, pp. 750-54; Stefan Kieniewicz, *The Emancipation of the Polish Peasantry* (Chicago: Univ. of Chicago Press, 1969), pp. 180-81; Blum, *The End of the Old Order in Rural Europe*, pp. 410-18; Benkart, "Religion, Family and Community Among Hungarians Migrating to American Cities, 1880-1930, " p. 28; Ivan T. Berend and Gyorgy Ranki, *Economic Development in East-Central Europe in the Nineteenth and Twentieth Centuries* (New York: Columbia Univ. Press, 1974), pp. 28-41; Joseph Held, *The Modernization of Agriculture: Rural Transformation in Hungary, 1848-1975* (New York: Columbia Univ. Press, 1980), pp. 22-50; Erickson, ed., *Emigration from Europe, 1815-1914*, pp. 80-81; Geoffrey Drage, *Austria-Hungary* (London: Murray, 1909), p. 314; Puskas, *Kivandorlo Magyarok Az Egyezult Allamokba, 1881-1940*, pp. 30-60. I am also indebted to Professor Charles Jelavich for helping me to understand Austria-Hungary.

15 Kieniewics, *The Emancipation of the Polish Peasantry*, pp. 190-94; Bodnar, Simon, and Weber, *Lives of Their Own*, p. 38.

16 Jane Schneider and Peter Schneider, *Culture and Political Economy in Western Sicily* (New York: Academic Press, 1976), pp. 4-8, 115-25; Rudolph Vecoli, "Chicago's Italians Prior to World War I," (unpublished Ph.D. dissertation, Univ. of Wisconsin, 1963), pp. 102-06.

17 Kollman and Marschalck, "German Emigration to the United States," pp. 526-27; Walker, *Germany and the Emigration*, pp. 76-78; Michael Mitterauer and Reinhard Sieder, *The European Family: Patriarchy to Partnership from the Middle Ages to the Present* (Chicago: Univ. of Chicago Press, 1982), pp. 145-46; David Chirot, *Social Change in a Peripheral Society: The Creation of a Balkan Colony*, p. 137.

18 Oliver MacDonagh, "The Irish Famine Emigration to the United States," *Perspectives in American History*, X (1976), pp. 358-78; Kennedy, *The Irish: Emmigration, Marriage and Fertility*, pp. 89-93.

19 Jones, "The Background to Emigration from Great Britain in the Nineteenth Century," p. 8; Malcom Gray, "Scottish Emigration: The Social Impact of Agrarian Change in the Rural Lowlands, 1775-1875," *Perspectives in American History*, VII (1973), pp. 124-35.

20 Benkhart, "Religion, Family and Community Among Hungarians Migrating to American Cities," pp. 9-10; Tomas Hofer, "Changes in the Style of Folk Art and Various Branches of Folklore in Hungary During the Nineteenth Century," *ACTA Ethnographica Academiae Scientiarum Hungaricae* 29 (1980), p. 153; Karoly Voros, "A Parasztsas Va Itozasa a XIX Szazadbam," *Ethnographia*, LXXXVII, 143.

21 Tomas Hofer, "Changes in the Style of Folk Art and Various Branches of Folklore in Hungary During the Nineteenth Century—An Interpretation," pp. 154-56.

22 See Ulrich Bauche, *Lan d tischler, Tischlerwerk und Intarsienkunst in den Vierlanden* (Hamburg, 1965), *passim*.

23 Petr Bogatyrev, *The Function of Folk Costume in Moravian Slovakia* (The Hague: Mouton, 1971), pp. 46-56; Linda Degh, *Folktales and Society*, (Bloomington: Indiana Univ. Press, 1969), pp. 20-25; Hofer, "Peasant Expressive Culture, 1800-1914: Tendencies of Separation and Mergence," (unpublished paper delivered at Conference in Industrialization in Hungary and the United States, Budapest, Aug. 23-26, 1982). For the Irish religious upsurge of the nineteenth century see Emmet Larkin,

"The Devotional Revolution in Ireland, 1850-75," *American Historical Review* 77 (June, 1972), pp. 625-52.

24 Hofer, "Changes in the Style of Folk Art and Various Branches of Folklore in Hungary During the Nineteenth Century," Puskas, *Kivandorlo Magyarok Az Egyesult Allamokba, 1880-1940,* pp. 46-77.

25 Peter Sugar, *Industrialization of Bosnia-Hercegovina, 1875-1918,* (Seattle: Univ. of Washington Press, 1963), *passim*. Blum, *The End of the Old Order in Rural Europe,* pp. 432-37; Drage, *Austria-Hungary,* pp. 316-17; Hocevar, *The Structure of the Slovenian Economy,* pp. 58-59, 63-68.

26 See Dinko Tomasic, "Personality Development in the Zadruga Society," *Psychiatry,* V (May, 1948), pp. 229-61.

27 Wladyslaw Rusinski, "The Role of the Peasantry of Poznan in the Formation of the Non-Agricultural Labor Market," *East European Quarterly,* III (1970), pp. 509-24; Barton, *Peasants and Strangers,* pp. 68-69.

28 Rischin, *The Promised City,* pp. 35-42.

29 Rudolph Bell, *Fate and Honor, Family and Village,* (Chicago: Univ. of Chicago Press, 1974), pp. 179-88; Vecoli, "Chicago's Italians Prior to World War I," p. 84; Cenel, "The Seasonal Emigrations of Italians in the Nineteenth Century," *Journal of Ethnic Studies* 10 (Spring, 1982), 47-48; Fejos Zoltan, *Kivandorlas Amerikaba A Zemplen Kozepso Videkerol* (Miskolc, Hungary, 1980), pp. 298-307, reports of Hungarians who emigrated over ten times to improve their farm or acquire one.

30 Blum, *The End of the Old Order in Rural Europe,* p. 439; Gray, "Scottish Emigration: The Social Impact of Agrarian Change in the Rural Lowlands," pp. 153-57.

31 Gray, "Scottish Emigration: The Social Impact of Agrarian Change in the Rural Lowlands," pp. 156-57; Drage, *Austria-Hungry,* p. 312; Chmelar, "The Austrian Emigration, 1900-1914," pp. 332-57; Hocevar, *The Structure of the Slovenian Economy,* pp. 55-83.

32 Blum, *The End of the Old Order in Rural Europe,* p. 439; Benjamin Murdzek, *Emigration in Polish Social-Political Thought, 1817-1914* (New York: Columbia Univ. Press, 1977), pp. 156-57.

33 Cinel, "The Seasonal Emigration of Italians in the Nineteenth Century: From Internal to International Destinations," p. 47; Jones, "The Background to Emigration From Great Britain in the Nineteenth Century," pp. 8-9; Murdzek, *Emmigration in Polish Social-Political Thought,* pp. 60-79.

34 Jones, "The Background to Emigration from Great Britain in the Nineteenth Century," pp. 8-9; Chmelar, "The Austrian Emigration," pp. 284-85, 338; Hvidz, *Flight to America,* pp. 17-21.

35 Chmelar, "The Austrian Emigration," p. 335; Cizmic, *Iseljenistvo i Suvremana Ekonomska Emigracija a Prodrucja Karlovca (Zagreb: Matica Hrvatsra, 1973),* pp. 300-10.

36 Hvidt, *Flight to America,* p. 187; Kraljic, "Croatian Migration to and from the United States Between 1900 and 1914," p. 165; Chmelar, "The Austrian Emigration, 1900-1914," p. 335; Betty'Boyd Caroli, *Italian Repatriation from the United States, 1900-1914* (New York Center for Migration Studies, 1973). On Jews see Jonathan D. Sarna, "The Myth of No Return: Jewish Return Migration to Eastern Europe, 1881-1914," *American Jewish History,* LXXI (Dec., 1981), pp. 256-68.

37 Virtanen, *Settlement or Return: Finnish Emmigrants in the International Overseas Return Migration Movement,* pp. 93, 108, 175-76.

38 Puskas, "The Conflicts of Adaptation of the Hungarian Emmigrants in America," unpublished paper presented to U.S.-Hungarian Conference on Industrialization, Budapest, Aug. 23-25, 1982, pp. 3-5.

39 Cinel, *From Italy to San Francisco,* pp. 57, 65-83.

Job Segregation and the Replication of Local Social Hierarchies

SUSAN E. HIRSCH and JANICE L. REIFF

American industrial cities were a focal point for individuals' aspirations for change. Seeking material improvement, immigrants from other countries and Black migrants from rural areas moved to America's industrial cities in huge numbers. For Blacks, women, and young people in general, the search for new work opportunities was often but one aspect of their aspirations for change, but it was a crucial one. The conjunction of people and city was not a matching of individual talents and aspirations with a wide range of jobs and opportunities for mobility, however, but the segregation of jobs and opportunities for advancement by ethnic, racial, and sexual criteria. The competition among individuals for jobs was mediated by their membership in ethnic and racial groups, which were stratified in local social hierarchies by differential power, wealth, and prestige. In turn, patterns of job segregation provided a bulwark against change in local social hierarchies. Conflicts over jobs were endemic and reflected the competition of ethnic and racial groups and the continued resistance of the most oppressed.[1]

Job segregation has been a complex and changing phenomenon, however. Both Blacks and women have experienced structural inequality, the systematic denial of opportunities in entire industries on the national level, throughout this century. Prior to World War I, Black men found few openings in factory labor, but by the 1940's most worked at industrial jobs. Since 1900, 60 percent or more of all employed women have worked in occupations in which women predominated. Now, however, clerical work rather than domestic service is the major employment of women. Patterns of segregation may change, but segregation itself may be maintained.[2] For some groups, however, segregation has lessened, as for the Japanese in California who are no longer concentrated in food production, processing, and distribution as they were before World War II.[3]

Despite the persistent denial to women and Blacks of opportunities for the best jobs, the patterns of segregation produced by the interaction of racial and sexual criteria, as well as their longevity, have varied by region, city, and firm. Large numbers of Black men were steelworkers and miners in Alabama before they were hired for such jobs in Pennsylvania. During World War I, Black women moved into industrial jobs in some cities but not in Chicago. The Ford Motor Company hired large numbers of Black workers long before other Detroit automakers did.[4] Regional differences in the ratio of Black to White median income have resulted in part from the regional differences in patterns of job segregation. Between 1949 and 1972 the income gap between White and Black males was consistently and significantly greater in the South than in other regions. The income gap for Black and White females was also consistently greater in the South than elsewhere, but the differential between the South and other regions was greater for women than for men.[5]

The contrasting experiences of Asians on the East and West Coasts suggest the importance of local social hierarchies in creating some of these differences in patterns of job segregation. Up through the 1940's, White hostility against the Chinese and Japanese was stronger in the West than in the East. The Japanese were concentrated in small ethnic businesses in the West, while in the East they were occupationally more urban and more diverse. Even in 1960, more Japanese were professionals in the East than in the West, while in the latter a higher percentage were in labor and service occupations than elsewhere.[6] Whether these patterns are attributable directly to different degrees of White racism in different regions or whether they reflect the varying numbers of Asians on the East and West coasts is unclear. Some scholars suggest that Blacks and Asians have found better opportunities where their numbers were small and their presence incited less fear among Whites. This might be true for wage work, but entrepreneurs and many professionals need large numbers of their own group to prosper.[7] The question of numbers also complicates the issue of whether the North or the South provided greater opportunities for Black workers at comparable levels of development, and whether differences are related to degrees of White racism.

Regional and city-level variations in patterns of job segregation were even more pronounced for White ethnic groups. At the beginning of this century, Italians found many more opportunities for white collar work in New York than Pittsburgh and more opportunities for skilled work in both than in Steelton, Pennsylvania.[8] In Buffalo, Italian women did homework or agricultural/cannery labor, while in New York City they flocked into garment factories.[9] There was some evidence of generalized ethnic clustering in different industries, such as the Polish concentration in iron and steel making in the North, but most of these concentrations dissolved, albeit at varying rates for different groups, over the course of this century.[10] All large firms and industries hired workers from a wide variety of European national groups, and the composition of a firm's labor force was likely to shift as new groups moved into the city. Much ethnic clustering seems to have been structural in origin—the conjunction of people, place, and time. This was particularly likely where foremen controlled hiring and gave preference to members of their own ethnic or kin groups. Whichever group arrived first was likely to stay and enlarge its role in the industry.[11] For European immigrants and their children, job segregation seems to have been a qualitatively different experience than for Blacks. Although most male immigrants first took unskilled jobs, opportunities for advancement were not systematically denied them or their sons.[12] So too, the extent of job segregation experienced by ethnic women never approached that experienced by Black women.[13] Scholars do not agree, as yet, whether the experience of immigrants from Latin America is more comparable to that of Blacks or European immigrants, or is a third phenomenon altogether.

There are now many studies of particular cities which describe the local patterns of ethnic and racial job segregation or occupational stratification. They relate these patterns to the local social hierarchy via such issues as neighborhood segregation, political power, and the elaboration of subcultures through institutional development. Some analyze the effect of these patterns on working class unity and the class struggle at the local level.[14] There is as yet no bridge between these case studies, which often suggest very different generalizations, and the studies from national aggregates. Not only is a comparative perspective necessary, but cases which are comparable and reflect the wide range of forces affecting job segregation must be found.[15] Until then the implications of the regional and city-level variations in patterns of job segregation remain unclear. Nor can it be established whether ethnic job segregation was of a national order or a local phenomenon. Without a better understanding of the mechanisms which support job segregation for different groups, effective policy to achieve equity cannot be made.

Despite the importance of job segregation, scholars have given it much less attention than it deserves. Much of the research on the relationship between employment and social hierarchies is focused on rates of mobility between strata of occupations or comparative income levels.[16] Neither type of study addresses the underlying phenomenon of job segregation, although mobility studies sometimes include information about such employment patterns. In part, the lack of attention derives from lack of access to company records. Aggregate statistics compiled by government bureaus reveal large-scale patterns, but they are inadequate for understanding the mechanisms creating and supporting job segregation or the forces that change those patterns. Even if patterns of job segregation extend industry-wide, their basis lies at the firm level in an accretion of thousands of individual decisions to hire or fire, to apply for work or quit.

In the nineteenth century, patterns of job segregation fractured along the lines of separate craft-based industries, such as the German domination of brewing.[17] But in the twentieth century segregation patterns often appeared within the largest firms and industries rather than between them. The largest corporations sponsored the expansion of management control over production processes and work habits that entailed the classification of jobs, the specification of their contents, and the elaboration of avenues of mobility or job ladders. Complex and hierarchical job structures, governed at least in part by stated rules, laid the foundation for the development of internal labor markets within large firms. Entry was most common at the bottom, and on-the-job training opportunities allowed for mobility within the firm. By the early twentieth century many of the best jobs in America—defined by steady employment, competitive wages, and some opportunity for advancement—were in these large, bureaucratically organized firms.[18] Who could get a job in these firms, who could get onto the best job ladders, and who could stay on them and rise became important issues not only for individuals, but also for group relations. Local social hierarchies were reflected in job structures as in the steel industry in Pittsburgh. In 1906, 85 percent of Slavic workers had unskilled positions in steelmaking, two-thirds of English-speaking Europeans had semiskilled or skilled jobs, and over three-quarters of native Whites had semiskilled or skilled jobs.[19] Groups also might be segregated by department within firms, if departments varied greatly in desirability. As increasing numbers of large companies had operations in more than one location, any differences in patterns of job segregation between the locations may have reflected the strength of local social hierarchies.

To understand the impact of local social hierarchies on patterns of job segregation we need to see how the many factors that can affect job segregation are related to local social hierarchies. Employers can create, maintain, or change patterns of job segregation, and public policy places the main effort to eliminate job segregation on them. Employers may base their actions on preferences for racism, sexism, or ethnic prejudice or on their beliefs, correct or incorrect, about the skills and aptitudes of different groups. Whether these preferences accord with local social hierarchies may depend on the level at which hiring policy is made. Where foremen were given a free hand, ethnic clustering in jobs and departments was common. When companies have made affirmative action plans, they have often forced change in local operations that runs counter to the wishes of the most powerful local groups.[20]

Employers have had other reasons than preference for manipulating patterns of job segregation, however. In their attempts to extend their control over workers and the work process and to undercut unionization employers have had two options: hiring workers from different groups, mixing individuals they hope will be hostile to each other, or hiring an entirely new, and perhaps more tractable, labor force from a previously excluded group. Thus Blacks entered the steel and meat packing industries of the North first as strike breakers and then remained as permanent employees in racially mixed work forces.[21] Those groups on the bottom of local social hierarchies are always potentially available for use in undercutting better situated groups because of their underemployment. The underemployment of Blacks has been so severe nationally that they constitute a reserve army of labor in most regions, and Black gains have always been made in times and places of full employment.[22] When employers introduce new technologies they may also change patterns of job segregation to counter worker resistance to new methods. Slavs entered the steel industry in Pennsylvania as massive deskilling occurred, and women's entrance into clerical work occurred in the context of the introduction of new office machines.[23]

Scholars have noted, however, that workers as well as employers can influence patterns of job segregation. Local ethnic and racial divisions may affect the latter through the actions of workers themselves. Workers can implement their preferences for racism, sexism, or ethnic prejudices through a variety of spontaneous actions. Acceptance or rejection by co-workers, for instance, can facilitate or block an individual's success once hired. Worker turnover, absenteeism, or refusal to cooperate can pressure an employer to maintain a pattern of job segregation.[24] Through unionization workers consciously can create, maintain, or destroy patterns of job segregation by collective bargaining or job actions. Most unions in the South were racially segregated and sought to limit the employment of Blacks, while in the North some were not. In New Orleans, the longshoremen had two segregated unions that cooperated to some extent, but White workers monopolized the easiest work and got the steadiest employment. In New York, where work gangs were divided by ethnicity as well as race, the longshoremen's union and most of its locals were mixed racially. But union work rules and entrance requirements also can exclude entire groups without being overtly discriminatory.[25] Employers have usually justified their discriminatory policies as attempts to appease the prejudices of their workers. But in many cases employers effected changes with little difficulty despite the wishes of their workers.[26] The relative importance of employer actions or worker actions in creating, maintaining, or changing patterns of job segregation is unclear. Blacks, for instance, have found no greater opportunities in general in non-unionized firms than in unionized ones.[27] Workers' preferences might differ by city or region, but their impact on local patterns of job segregation is not yet established.

Ethnic and racial groups may also have different cultural preferences for types of work that might affect patterns of job segregation. Carolyn

Golab maintains that Poles settled in Pennsylvania outside Philadelphia while Jews and Italians sought out Philadelphia because of their preferences for cetain types of work.[28] Swedish and Irish women were much more likely to engage in domestic service than Jews or Italians in part because such employment was a common experience for women in their homelands. Married Black women were more likely to be employed than married Italian women at comparable levels of husband's income. There is no evidence, however, of cultural preference keeping Blacks from applying for specific jobs, although there is evidence that they can become discouraged workers and seek employment only where they expect to be accepted.[29]

Questions of cultural preference are complicated, however, by the issue of opportunities. The work alternatives available in a city or neighborhood also affect who actually applies for any particular job. City-level differences in the employment patterns of any group may exist because workers take the jobs available despite cultural preferences for work that is not attainable. At least some of the ethnic clustering seen in the early part of this century was a function of the development of new opportunities in specific localities. Jewish domination of the garment industry rested not solely on the basis that many Jews brought tailoring experience with them to New York City, but that most Jews settled in New York and large numbers were recruited by co-religionists into the burgeoning industry.[30]

Patterns of job segregation also may differ by city because of local demographic structures. Which groups are present locally determines the nature of group competition and it is possible that a group might be better situated in one city than another.[31] The age structure of each group determines the possible contribution it can made to the labor force. To the extent that most immigrant groups have much higher ratios of adults to children, they contribute disproportionately to the labor force. Patterns of neighborhood segregation may also affect job segregation to the extent that public transportation or automobile ownership is limited.[32]

Structural considerations may go beyond the question of who is available to that of the skills of potential employees. Some scholars have maintained that patterns of job segregation are related to the qualifications of workers, their endowments of human capital, which might vary by ethnic or racial group or by sex. Regional and urban differences in the availability of schooling or training to specific groups could promote differences in patterns of job segregation. School expenditures for Blacks compared with those for Whites, for instance, were proportionately much lower in the South than in the North.[33] To the extent that many of the human capital studies blame the victim, the useful information that may be derived from this avenue of investigation often is overlooked.

By themselves, however, human capital models have not been conspicuously accurate in predicting results in contemporary situations, and they are difficult to specify in ways which take cognizance of the real requirements of jobs. Years of schooling is the most common proxy for human capital, and even in contemporary society where credentialing is a way of life, it is a poor predictor of mobility or income for Blacks and women.[34] On the other hand, the inability to speak or write English was a significant impediment to most immigrants in obtaining corporate white-collar jobs. In the twentieth century, standards of schooling have been important for managerial positions above the foreman level, and any investigation of job segregation in those strata would need to consider schooling and literacy criteria. For clerical positions, English literacy was an important barrier for immigrants, but schooling requirements were not inordinate. With the deskilling of clerical work that began in the early twentieth century an eighth-grade education with perhaps a year of high school or private commercial courses met the requirements for most jobs, except that of secretary.[35] Certainly in some cities, large numbers of the children of immigrants and of young Blacks met those criteria.

The importance of human capital considerations for production jobs seems much less likely, however.[36] The entire thrust of twentieth-century industrial engineering has been to negate the need for extensive skills or schooling and to create mechanisms for on-the-job training. The expansion of unskilled entry-level positions assured that most people, regardless of race, ethnicity, or sex, could meet entry requirements. The ease with which employers could break strikes by importing new workers from groups previously excluded from employment in those industries suggests the limited utility of the human capital approach. Nor was the inability to speak English, much less read or write it, necessarily a significant impediment to successful performance of many production jobs.

The complexity of the phenomenon of job segregation complicates any research strategy to understand the mechanisms which sustain or change it. Coping concurrently with employer actions, worker actions, worker attributes, and local demographic and economic structures is beyond the scope of all but the largest projects. Much of the disagreement in the literature on job segregation, especially that on White ethnics, may stem from the inability to consider the complete range of pertinent variables. One avenue for limiting the range of variables without ignoring them is a case study of a large firm with comparable operations in multiple locations. If employer policies and actions, job structures, and the like are similar, then the variable elements are reduced to worker actions and attributes and local demographic and economic structures. The extent of variation in patterns of job segregation from one location to another will reveal the strength of local factors; the impact of local social hierarchies can be disentangled from that of structural considerations. The limiting factor to such a research strategy most often has been lack of access to company records. Without concrete knowledge of management policies, individual worker job histories, and workers' shop level and organizational activities, no advance over aggregate methods is made. Fortunately, after the Pullman Company, the operating division of the railroad sleeping car service, went out of business in 1969, instead of destroying the files of its industrial relations department and its employee records, it donated them to the Newberry Library. Manuscript material is rich on company policies and strategies and includes evidence of workers' social organizations and union activities. From the quantitative records it is possible to reconstruct patterns of job segregation at fixed points in time and promotional ladders to measure "opportunity."[37] These records supplemented by oral history interviews can be used to analyze the effect of local social hierarchies on patterns of job segregation.

The Pullman Company is a particularly apt one for such a comparison of cities and groups. It was one of the largest corporations in the United States during the first half of this century with operations throughout the country, and it was also the largest single employer of Black Americans for most of that time.[38] Centralization and bureaucratization were prominent characteristics of its management style. The monopoly mentality of the directors extended to internal operations, and in the early years of this century an industrial relations department was responsible for creating the system of record keeping, minister uniform employee policies for the entire company.[39] This department was responsible for creating the system of record keeing, implemented nationwide, that forms the core of the data available. The Company kept a file on each employee, including basic demographic information, data on previous experience and literacy, and a complete job history specifying job classifications, rates of pay, layoffs, terminations, and the like. Upon the creation of company unions for different groups of workers in the 1930's, representatives of management and workers negotiated national contracts that were binding on operations in all locations.[40] Such centralization continued after 1947 when the Company was sold by court order to a consortium of railroads, and the AFL railroad unions became the representatives of all the unionized workers.

Some of the most complete employee records are for the repair shop workers, and the occupational structure of the repair shops makes them excellent cases for a study of job segregation. In order to operate sleeping cars nationwide, the Pullman Company located six repair shops for routine maintenance and large-scale repairs of equipment at Chicago, Illinois; Buffalo, New York; Wilmington, Delaware;

Atlanta, Georgia; St. Louis, Missouri; and Richmond, California. These shops, ranging in size from 431 employees to 2236 in 1936, replicated the Pullman manufacturing facilities: virtually every skill or piece of equipment used in building a car was necessary for repairing it.[41] The relative size of departments was probably not the same in the shops as in the manufacturing plants, however (there were probably more painters in the shops than the factories, for instance). The shops' labor forces included managers, clerical staff, foreman and work leaders, watchmen and service workers, laborers, and large numbers of the skilled and semiskilled: wood workers, steel and iron workers, brass and tin workers, upholsterers, painters, glaziers, and electricians, among others. The shops were not organized primarily along traditional craft lines, however, as the Company began to restructure jobs prior to World War I. Laborers and helpers rather than mechanics did much of the work and the position of helper-apprentice allowed unskilled workers to become mechanics within three years.[42] Technology and job structures were similar in all the repair shops because all the equipment was from the same source, the Pullman manufacturing division. Because the Company was able to keep AFL craft unions out of the repair shops and because the company union for the repair shops was organized like an industrial union, the bureaucratic job structures were maintained until 1947. Thereafter the Company was in the midst of a twenty-year decline. Atlanta was the first repair shop to close, in 1954, while Chicago, in 1969 was the last.

Over the course of the twentieth century the work forces of the repair shops included Whites and Blacks, native born and immigrants, women and men. By the 1920's the labor force of the Chicago repair shop included men from every ethnic group in the city, as well as Black men and White women.[43] Although the Company seems not to have had any exclusionary policy for ethnic groups, after 1904 it did not allow foremen to hire.[44] Thus ethnically dominated departments were probably less likely to occur in the repair shops than in the facilities of some other firms. The Company did encourage hiring of kin, which might increase ethnic clustering. But, at least in Chicago, kin often worked in different parts of the Company—the car works, the repair shop, the yards, the central office, etc.

The Company did have policies on Black and women workers, however. Until World War I the Company used Blacks primarily as porters, maids, laundresses, and car cleaners. Prior to the War, there were no Blacks in the Chicago repair shop, but during the Railroad Shopmen's Strike of 1922, the Company hired Black men in large numbers as strikebreakers. The Company used this opportunity to break the remaining craft traditions in the shop and reclassify jobs. In the next few years the Company hired more Black men in the Chicago shop, but many stayed only a short time.[45] Some left the shop for the potentially more lucrative position of porter. Others learned skills through the helper-apprentice positions and became mechanics.[46] The Chicago shop force remained integrated thereafter. The Company may have disregarded local social hierarchies and used Blacks, or other groups, in a similar fashion in the other shops.

At the beginning of this century, the Company carefully delineated women's work. It had begun slowly to allow White women into clerical positions at the Chicago headquarters, but summarily fired all of them in 1902 to make way for young men.[47] By the next decade, the Company was once more opening clerical positions to White women, but only the unmarried. Women were fired when they married until policy changed in the mid 1920's.[48] The Pullman Company also employed women in "traditional" jobs, as seamstresses, laundresses, and maids. In the Chicago repair shop, the seamstresses were all White, but unlike the clerical workers, many were widows, and women were not fired when they married. Perhaps because of the Company's policy of hiring kin, perhaps because women usually worked where their relatives did, at least one-third of the seamstresses had kin working for the Company.[49] Until the late 1940's Black women found no jobs in the Chicago shop, although they worked for the Company elsewhere in the Chicago area as maids, laundresses, and car cleaners. During both World Wars, the government pressured the Company to expand employment opportunities for women. The Company's response was sluggish, and at least in Chicago, there was no lasting effect on the sexual division of labor in the shop.[50] Greater change might have occurred in other shops, however.

Within these known parameters of Company policy, the extent of local variations in patterns of job segregation reveals the importance of local worker-associated factors. To specify these a combination of approaches is necessary. Government statistics provide city-wide and neighborhood-level demographic profiles; they can be used to specify employment opportunities and the relative importance of the Pullman Company as a local employer. Unemployment statistics help assess the constraints on group advancement. For all the cities, except Richmond, previous scholarship provides information about local social hierarchies, especially concerning the issues of political power and social prestige. The Company's manuscript materials supplemented by interviews with surviving employees reveal worker social organizations and union activities.

The repair shops spanned the continent facilitating examination of major regional issues. The Jim Crow social norms of the South, for instance, appeared in the company union of the repair shops. Atlanta and St. Louis each had segregated locals for Whites and Blacks, while the other repair shops had single integrated locals.[51] The Company might have hired both Whites and Blacks, but Southern social norms found some expression in the shops. It will be important to see if Blacks found similar job opportunities in the Atlanta and St. Louis shops, and how these patterns compared with those in the other shops.

The six locations also represent important types of American industrial cities. City scale, economic structure, and growth rate all affect the development of local social hierarchies and the nature of competition between groups. St. Louis and Buffalo were major regional metropolises with strong manufacturing sectors that originated in the nineteenth century. (See Table I.) Employment opportunities differed greatly in each, however, especially for women. St. Louis was a center of boot and shoe and men's clothing manufacture, providing many opportunities for women that were absent in Buffalo, which was dominated by foundries, automobile production, and railroad car construction.[52] Both St. Louis and Buffalo experienced moderate growth and extensive suburbanization during this century. The suburbanization of jobs and people altered the neighborhoods around the Pullman shops, and St. Louis, with a much larger Black population, experienced massive White flight as well.[53]

Wilmington was a prominent manufacturing center in the nineteenth century, but it was never a major metropolis. By 1900 it was in economic decline, and very slow growth has accompanied its more recent transformation to a corporate headquarters. Manufacturing and railroad workers found shrinking opportunities and overcrowding of the labor market throughout this century. Perhaps this explains the failure of the Wilmington shop force to support the Pullman strike of 1894.[54] In Richmond, by contrast, opportunity was abundant for those who settled it before 1930 or during World War II. Richmond was founded in 1900 as an industrial suburb of San Francisco, a creature of modern railroading and manufacturing. Alongside the giants—Santa Fe, Standard Oil, Ford, and Kaiser-Bechtel—Pullman was a small employer.[55] Women may have made greater inroads into the Pullman shop force there than elsewhere, however, because as a center of defense production during World War II, Richmond was one of the places in which women made their greatest advances in heavy industry and skilled work.

Atlanta has never been an industrial city. It was a rail center and regional wholesaling city which experienced rapid growth as the Southeast began to develop. Employment opportunities, expecially in manufacturing, were new and developing throughout this century, though not at the rate of Richmond.[56] The sixth Pullman repair shop opened there in 1926 at the peak of Company and railroad prosperity.

The Chicago shop was located in the far south side manufacturing district, isolated from the downtown and much of the rest of the city. This internal industrial satellite, not Chicago itself, was the effective

Table I

Population Characteristics of Six Cities [a]

	1910			1950		
	Total	% for bn white	% black	Total	% for bn white	% black
Atlanta	154,839	2.8	33.5	331,314	1.3	36.6
Buffalo	423,715	28.0	0.4	580,132	12.1	6.3
Chicago	2,185,283	35.7	2.0	3,620,962	14.5	13.5
Richmond	6,802	b	b	99,545	19.3	13.4
St. Louis	687,029	18.3	6.4	856,796	4.9	17.9
Wilmington	87,411	15.6	10.4	110,356	6.1	15.6

a. Source: US Censuses of 1910, 1950
b. Data unavailable in published sources.

community for the shop. Unlike the situation in Richmond, however, the Pullman Company was a major employer in the area. The repair shop was just south of the Pullman car manufacturing plant and the famous planned Company town. The region around it included major steel plants, the International Harvester works, and miles of worker housing. It was a viable place of residence and employment until the 1960's.

The six cities also differed significantly in their demographic profiles so that the effect of group size, composition, and succession on job segregation can be investigated. The foreign-born and their children dominated Chicago and Buffalo in the beginning of this century, while Blacks were virtually invisible. (See Table I.) Similarly the Chicago shop force was heavily foreign-born and all White. In the next decades, the Black population of Chicago grew to be a substantial minority in the city, but in Buffalo Blacks were still a small group. The integration of the Chicago shop coincided with the increase in the Black population there. In both St. Louis and Wilmington the foreign-born outnumbered Blacks in 1910, but native-born Whites were the dominant group in each city, and the Black minorities were larger than those in Chicago and Buffalo. The Black populations of both St. Louis and Wilmington became more sizeable in the next forty years, while the importance of the foreign-born decreased, as it did virtually everywhere. Atlanta's population was about one-third Black throughout the first half of this century, while its foreign-born population was always exceptionally small. Although White racism was similarly effective in segregating the Company union in Atlanta and St. Louis, the differences between each in population composition may have led to very different patterns of job holding at the shops. Richmond's rapidly growing population came to include sizeable numbers of Blacks and Mexicans. Since the Pullman Company had a large work force in Mexico itself, Mexican immigrants may have had greater access to employment in the Richmond repair shop than in other local establishments.

The ethnic composition of the cities varied significantly, so that issues of competition and status between different ethnic groups can be explored. In 1910, Germans were the largest group in Buffalo, Chicago, and St. Louis, but in Atlanta, Russians—primarily Jews—predominated. (See Table II.) In Wilmington, the Irish, Russians, and Italians all outnumbered the Germans in 1910. In the next decades, the ethnic mix of all the cities changed significantly. Poles and Italians became the most numerous groups in Buffalo, while Poles, Russians, and other Slavs came to outnumber Germans in Chicago. Germans continued to be a major group in St. Louis, joined by Slavs and Italians.

Several hypotheses and specific issues about which to investigate their validity seem appropriate from preliminary work in the Pullman

Table II

Predominant Ethnic Groups in Five Cities[a]

1910

	Germany	Ireland	Canada	Aust.-Hun.	Russia	Italy
Atlanta	16.2				29.8	
Buffalo	36.9		14.7		15.7	
Chicago	23.3			16.9	12.3	
St. Louis	37.8				23.1	
Wilmington		23.0				16.7

1950

	Germany	Aust.-Hun.	Poland	Russia	Italy
Atlanta	10.1		10.2	18.9	21.0
Buffalo			21.8	14.5	15.0
Chicago	19.4	13.2	17.9		
St. Louis		20.1			
Wilmington	b	b	b	b	b

a. Source: US Censuses of 1910, 1950
b. Data unavailable in published sources.

manuscripts and the employment records for the Chicago shop. First, within the ranks of production workers, ethnic segregation was probably minimal, a product of neither employer nor worker preferences as much as local structural conditions. Extensive skill degradation and the creation of ladders of on-the-job training negated the possible effects of "ethnic skills" or group variations in human capital. Timing of arrival might have induced ethnic clustering, however. The Pullman Company began to replace wood cars with steel ones after 1910, and the ethnicity of Pullman's steelworkers may well have reflected the groups seeking new employment opportunities between 1910 and 1920. Since the ethnic composition of the cities varied, the ethnicity of Pullman's steelworkers may have varied likewise. Second, as ethnic occupational segregation was probably minimal and did not have a cultural basis, it did not weaken significantly work group solidarity or class organization. In Chicago, ethnic solidarity did not extend to foremen, since they could not hire, and complaints of foremen's tyranny were general. The strike unity of 1922 was maintained across ethnic lines.[57] This suggests that ethnic divisions which were not bolstered by job segregation did not weaken working class struggles.

Job segregation for Blacks seems to have been very much a consequence of employer actions, in that the proclivities of White workers for racism could be overcome anytime it was in the Company's interests prior to 1947. Much of the time, however, the Company seems to have perceived no compelling interest, and thus local and worker-associated factors could affect patterns of job holding for Blacks. First, certain structural conditions could have been important. For instance, more Blacks may have sought jobs in the shops in the 1930's as porters' tip income declined or in cities where porter jobs were not available because those cities were not district headquarters. In cities without adequate public transportation, neighborhood segregation might have limited the number of Black job seekers. In Chicago, however, although the neighborhoods around the shop remained all White and hostile enclaves until the 1940's, Black workers could take the Illinois Central directly from Black neighborhoods to the door of the Pullman Car Works and walk on Pullman property to the repair shops. [58]

Second, the segregation of the company union in the South suggests that job segregation may have been more intense there than in the North because of the depth of White racism. Blacks may have been more heavily concentrated in unskilled positions, denied access to helper-apprentice jobs, more subject to layoffs or less sheltered during plant closings. The Company policy of giving employment preference elsewhere to workers whose shops closed may not have been applied equally to Blacks and Whites in all cities.

Third, the direct effect of racial competition should appear forcefully around issues of unionization. The Pullman Company used its company union to keep the AFL shopcraft unions at bay, but certain shops evidenced greater restiveness at times than others. In 1937 a CIO challenge was almost successful in Chicago, though apparently of negligible strength elsewhere.[59] It seems likely that where job competition between Whites and Blacks was strongest, the challenges to the company union might also have been strongest. Where the company union was seen as encouraging job segregation Blacks might have been attracted to other organizations, but where, as in Chicago, the company union seems not to have encouraged job segregation, Whites may have been most active in seeking wider affiliations. When the AFL shopcraft unions became the workers' representatives in 1947, the new work rules imposed may have had important effects on patterns of segregation. To the extent that the old ladders of internal mobility were destroyed, Blacks may have found fewer opportunities in some shops than they had previously.

Although Company policies about women's employment were rigid, local, and worker-associated, factors may have influenced patterns of women's job holding in two ways. First, women shop workers may not have come from the same ethnic and racial groups as men in the shops, despite the tendency for American women of the nineteenth and early twentieth centuries to work with kin or neighbors. If one ethnic group's norms for women's work proscribed labor in such settings as the mixed and variegated repair shops, few women from that group might be found in the shops regardless of the presence of male workers from that group. The impact of local social hierarchies might also produce differences in women's and men's employment patterns, however. The focus on women's work as an extension of their family roles and as sharply bounded by group norms often overshadows the importance of monetary reward and better working conditions to women workers and their families. If the Pullman jobs for women were more desirable than other work available locally for women, but Pullman jobs for men were not similarly desirable, women from groups better placed in the local social hierarchy might monopolize Pullman jobs. At the Chicago shop in 1917, for instance, all the seamstresses regardless of age were native-born, although most men working in the shop were foreign-born.[60]

Second, local and worker-associated factors may have influenced the response to the new opportunities for women presented during World War II. Ethnic group norms may have inhibited some women from seeking "men's" work. On the other hand, local social hierarchies may have affected access to such employment, giving preference, for instance, to White women rather than Black.

A comparative analysis of Pullman shop workers should illuminate aspects of working class formation in American industrial cities. Regional variations in the extent of working class unity may well be

tied to the relationship between the composition of local social hierarchies and the extent of job segregation. In the absence of job segregation, ethnic and racial divisions may not seriously hamper unionization or even working class political activity stemming from economic
or work-related issues. Employers could play a crucial role in the competition between groups and hence in the development of local social
hierarchies. The extent to which the policies of large companies
violated or institutionalized ethnic or racial divisions within the working class may be an important determinant of the development of
working class consciousness.

NOTES

1   Harold M. Baron, "Racial Domination in Advanced Capitalism: A Theory of Na-
    tionalism and Divisions in the Labor Market," in Richard Edwards, et al., *Labor
    Market Segmentation* (Lexington, Mass.: D.C. Heath & Co., 1975), pp. 200-210;
    William M. Tuttle, Jr., *Race Riot* (New York: Atheneum, 1970), pp. 108-155; David
    Brody, *Steelworkers in America: The Nonunion Era* (New York: Harper and Row,
    1960), p. 121, 223-4, 267.
2   Valerie Kincaid Oppenheimer, *The Female Labor Force in the United States*
    (Westport, Conn.: Greenwood Press, 1976), p. 71; Sidney M. Peck, "The Economic
    Situation of Negro Labor," in Julius Jacobson, ed., *The Negro and the American
    Labor Movement* (Garden City, NY: Doubleday & Co., 1968), p. 213; Elyce J. Rotella,
    "Women's Labor Force Participation and the Growth of Clerical Employment in the
    United States, 1870-1930" (Ph.D. dissertation, University of Pennsylvania, 1977), pp.
    47-58; Allan H. Spear, *Black Chicago* (Chicago: University of Chicago Press, 1967),
    pp. 151-166; Stephen Thernstrom, *The Other Bostonians* (Cambridge, Mass.: Har-
    vard University Press, 1973), pp. 190-202.
3   John Modell, *The Economics and Politics of Racial Accommodation* (Urbana, Ill.:
    University of Illinois Press, 1977), pp. 94-172; John Modell & Edna Bonacich, *The
    Economic Basis of Ethnic Solidarity* (Berkeley, Ca.: University of California Press,
    1980), pp. 173-177.
4   Margaret Byington, *Homestead* (Pittsburgh, PA: University of Pittsburgh, 1974), pp.
    13-14; Maurine Greenwald, *Women, War and Work* (Westport, Conn.: Greenwood
    Press, 1980), p. 24; Herbert R. Northrup, "Blacks in the United Automobile Workers
    Union," p. 156, and Paul Worthman, "Black Workers and Labor Unions in Birm-
    ingham, Alabama, 1894-1919," pp. 46-47, in John H. Bracey, et al., eds., *Black
    Workers and Organized Labor* (Belmont, CA: Wadsworth Publishing Co., 1971).
5   Ann R. Horowitz, "The Patterns and Causes of Changes in White-Nonwhite Income
    Differences: 1947-1972," in George von Furstenberg, et al., eds., *Patterns of Racial
    Discrimination, Vol. II, (Lexington, Mass.: D.C. Heath, 1974)*, pp. 149-168.
6   Modell and Bonacich, pp. 173-177; Alexander Saxton, *The Indispensable Enemy*,
    (Berkeley, Ca.: University of California Press, 1971), chapter 12.
7   St. Clair Drake and Horace R. Cayton, *Black Metropolis*, Vol. I (New York: Harcourt,
    Brace & World, Inc., 1970), chapters 9, 11, 12; Modell and Bonacich, p. 182.
8   John Bodnar, Roger Simon, and Michael Weber, *Lives of Their Own* (Urbana, Ill.:
    University of Illinois Press, 1982), p. 145.
9   Miriam Cohen, "From Workshop to Office: Italian Women and Family Strategies in
    New York City, 1900-1950" (Ph.D. dissertation, University of Michigan, 1978), pp.
    79-80; Virginia Yans-McLaughlin, *Family and Community* (Ithaca, NY: Cornell
    University Press, 1971), pp. 52-53.

10 Bodnar, Simon, and Weber, pp. 60-63; Carolyn Golab, *Immigrant Destinations* (Philadelphia: Temple University Press, 1977), pp. 159-162; Thernstrom, pp. 130-142; Yans-McLaughlin, pp. 37-39.

11 John Bodnar, *Workers' World* (Baltimore, Md.: Johns Hopkins University Press, 1982), p. 171; Carl R. Graves, "Scientific Management and the Santa Fe Railway Shopmen of Topeka, Kansas, 1900-1925" (Ph.D. dissertation, Harvard University, 1980), p. 179; Tamara K. Hareven, "The Laborers of Manchester, New Hampshire, 1912-1922," *Labor History*, 16 (1975), pp. 256-257.

12 Josef J. Barton, *Peasants and Strangers* (Cambridge, Mass.: Harvard University Press, 1975), pp. 113-116; Thomas Kessner, *The Golden Door* (New York: Oxford University Press, 1977), pp. 44-70, 104-126; Thernstrom, pp. 142-144.

13 Barbara Klacynska, "Why Women Work: A Comparison of Various Groups—Philadelphia, 1910-1930," *Labor History*, 17 (1976), pp. 73-87; David Katzman, *Seven Days A Week* (New York: Oxford University Press, 1978), p. 293.

14 John T. Cumbler, *Working-Class Community in Industrial America*, (Westport, Conn.: Greenwood Press, 1979).

15 Harold Benenson, "Skill Degradation, Industrial Change and the Family and Community Bases of U.S. Working Class Response," presentation at the 7th Annual Social Science History Association meeting, 1982, p. 21.

16 Ronald Oaxaca, "Theory and Measurement in the Economics of Discrimination," in Leonard Hausman, et al., eds., *Equal Rights and Industrial Relations* (Madison, Wis.: Industrial Relations Research Association, 1977), pp. 1-30.

17 Clyde and Sally Griffen, *Natives and Newcomers* (Cambridge, Mass.: Harvard University Press, 1978), p. 169.

18 Richard Edwards, *Contested Terrain* (New York: Basic Books, 1979).

19 Byington, p. 40.

20 Hareven, pp. 256-257; William Harris, *The Harder We Run* (New York: Oxford University Press, 1982), p. 165.

21 Brody, pp. 254-255; Tuttle, pp. 116-119.

22 Harold M. Baron and Bennett Hymer, "The Negro Worker in the Chicago Labor Market," in Julius Jacobson, ed., *The Negro and the American Labor Movement*, pp. 258-259; Paul G. Schervish, "The Structure of Employment and Unemployment," in Ivar Berg, ed., *Sociological Perspectives on Labor Markets* (New York: Academic Press, 1981), pp. 153-186.

23 Brody, p. 96; Rotella, pp. 235, 251; Katherine Stone, "The Origins of Job Structures in the Steel Industry," in Edwards, et al., *Labor Market Segmentation*, pp. 27-84.

24 Duran Bell, Jr., "The Economic Bases of Employee Discrimination," in George von Furstenberg, et al., *Patterns of Racial Discrimination*, Vol. II, p. 122.

25 Horace Cayton and George S. Mitchell, "Blacks and Organized Labor in the Iron and Steel Industry, 1880-1939," in John H. Bracey, et al., eds., *Black Workers and Organized Labor*, pp. 132-154; Herbert Hill, "The Racial Practices of Organized Labor: The Contemporary Record," in Julius Jacobsen, ed., *The Negro and the American Labor Movement;* Sterling D. Spero and Abram L. Harris, "The Negro Longshoreman, 1870-1930, in Jacobsen, pp. 93-107.

26 Karen T. Anderson, "Last Hired, First Fired: Black Women Workers during World War II," *Journal of American History,* 69 (1982), p. 87; Northrup, p. 158.

27 Ray Marshall, "The Negro in the Southern Unions," in Julius Jacobson, ed., *The Negro and the American Labor Movement*, p. 143; Oaxaca, p. 27.

28 Golab, *op cit.*

29 Baron and Hymer, p. 265; Bodnar, Simon, and Weber, pp. 6-7; Katzman, pp. 67-69; Elizabeth Pleck, "A Mother's Wages: Income Earning among Married Italian and Black Women, 1896-1911," in Michael Gordon, ed., *The American Family in Social-Historical Perspective,* 2nd edition (New York: St. Martin's Press, 1978), p. 493.

30 Bodnar, Simon, and Weber, pp. 144-145; Moses Rischin, *The Promised City* (New York: Corinth Books, 1964), p. 61.

31 Thernstrom, pp. 251-253.

[32] John F. Kain, "Housing Segregation, Negro Employment, and Metropolitan Decentralization," *Quarterly Journal of Economics*, 82 (1968), pp. 175-197.

[33] Ivar Berg, et al., "Toward Model Specification ...," pp. 354-355; Paula England, Thesis: Issues and Prospects," in Ivar Berg, ed., *Sociological Perspectives on Labor Markets*, p. 357; Richard Freeman, "Alternatives Theories of Labor-Market Discrimination: Individual and Collective Behavior," p. 42, and Finis Welch, "Black-White Differences in Returns to Schooling," pp. 220-224 in George M. von Furstenberg, et al., eds., *Patterns of Racial Discrimination*, Vol. 11.

[34] Ivar Berg, et al., "Toward Model Specification ..." pp. 354-355; Paula England, "Assessing Trends in Occupational Sex Segregation, 1900-1976," in Ivar Berg, ed., *Sociological Perspectives on Labor Markets*, pp. 274-275; Lester Thurow, *Poverty and Discrimination* (Washington, D.C.: Brookings Institute, 1969), pp. 76-81.

[35] Susan Hirsch, "The Mutability of the Sexual Division of Labor: The Transformation of Clerical Work," Conference on Women's Wage Work, Northwestern University, 1981, pp. 6-7.

[36] Bodnar, pp. 170-174.

[37] Janice Reiff and Susan Hirsch, "Reconstructing Work Histories by Computer: The Pullman Shop Workers, 1890-1967," *Historical Methods*, 15 (1982), pp. 139-142.

[38] William Harris, *Keeping the Faith* (Urbana, Ill.: University of Illinois Press, 1977), p. 2.

[39] "500 Men Given Employment by the Pullman Co.," *Chicago Examiner*, Oct. 4, 1904, Pullman Scrapbooks A27, 1903-04.

[40] Minutes of Conference between Employee Association Representatives and Company Officials, July 15, 1936, p. 6, Box 39-260, Pullman Archives.

[41] Statement of Men Working at Repair Shops, Year 1936, Box 39-260, Pullman Archives.

[42] Susan Hirsch and Janice Reiff, "Common Sense Management, Scientific Management, and the Railway Strike of 1922," Social Science History Associaton, 1982, p. 23.

[43] *Ibid.*, Tables 2, 4, 5.

[44] "500 Men Given Employment ... "

[45] Hirsch and Reiff, "Common Sense ..." p. 23.

[46] Preliminary analysis of employment records reveals some mobility of Blacks through this avenue.

[47] Articles from *Chicago Chronicle, Chicago Interocean,* and *Chicago American,* February 12, 1902, in Pullman Scrapbooks, A26, 1902-03.

[48] Interview conducted in 1981 with employee of Pullman Company central office clerical staff from 1921 to 1967.

[49] Preliminary analysis of Chicago shop force of 1917.

[50] Hirsch and Reiff, "Common Sense ...," pp. 17, 23; General Letter to All Repair Shops from C.W. Pflager, Sept. 9, 1943, Box 39-260, Pullman Archives.

[51] Letter of Ben Lewis to H.R. Lary, July 7, 1937, Box 39-260, Pullman Archives.

[52] US Census of Manufactures, 1910.

[53] Timothy O'Leary, "Ethnicity in Defense of Class," (Ph.D. dissertation, Washington University, 1977), pp. 276-279.

[54] Carol Hoffecker, *Wilmington, Delaware, Portrait of an Industrial City, 1830-1910* (Charlottesville, Va.: University of Virginia Press, 1974).

[55] Joseph C. Whitnah, *A History of Richmond, California* (Richmond, Ca.: Chamber of Commerce, 1944).

[56] C.A. McMahan, *The People of Atlanta* (Athens, Ga.: University of Georgia Press, 1950), pp. 127-130.

[57] Hirsch and Reiff, "Common Sense ...," p. 21; see also Cumbler, pp. 36-52.

[58] Thomas Lee Philpott, *The Slum and the Ghetto* (New York: Oxford University Press, 1978), pp. 193-194.

[59] Typed notes of speech by Ben Lewis, attached to Repair Shop Agreement, Sept. 1, 1937, Box 39-260, Pullman Archives.

[60] Preliminary analysis of Chicago shop force of 1917.

The Remaking of Urban Culture in Late Nineteenth and Early Twentieth Century America

FRANCIS G. COUVARES

Is there such a thing as "urban culture?" As a social historian who has observed and participated in the search for class and ethnic conflict in American history, I pose the question here because increasingly I think that, first, the question will not go away and, second, the answer is yes.

Before proceeding to develop these thoughts, I want to consider a recent book that offers a resoundingly affirmative answer to the question, but does so in a way that can only make social historians uncomfortable and even peevish. In *City People: The Rise of Modern City Culture in Nineteenth-Century America,*[1] Gunther Barth brings to the study of apartment houses, newspapers, department stores, baseball parks, and vaudeville houses a kind of old-fashioned and smiling view of American history that most of us have properly abandoned or modified.

For Barth, new shared experiences of private and public leisure confirmed the "common humanity" of the urban polyglot, taught the rules of American success, and distributed the pleasures of consumption to all willing to work and pay for them. "Old urbanites, newcomers from the countryside, and immigrants from abroad," Barth announces, "relied on these novel social and economic devices in their search for privacy, identity, and happiness," a search which Barth has no doubt proved largely successful for the educable and assimilable urban masses.

Though we may recoil from such an interpretation, it would be a mistake, as Paul Johnson has recently noted in his review of the book, to dismiss either Barth's compelling description of that culture or his delineation of several of the crucial mechanisms that brought it into being. If we are willing to observe, with Johnson, that "the new urbanity transcended inequality and dramatized it at the same time,"[2] we can rescue Barth's perception from the interpretation that muddles it.

Why should we do so? Because without it, or something like it, we cannot explain the relatively successful incorporation of immigrant-stock, working-class people into American society in the twentieth century. Unless we can elaborate the ways in which the culture of the industrial city generated among such people shared commitments to

American society—or perhaps more accurately to some version of American nationality—we are tempted, on the one hand, to exaggerate the persistence and significance of parochial, especially ethnic loyalties or, on the other, to explain those shared commitments as demonstrations of capitalism's success in imposing "false consciousness" on the American masses. If, as I think, urban culture has been something other than either a smokescreen concealing a collection of ethnic and class subcultures, or a commercialized version of some "dominant" or "bourgeois" American culture, then the fact that the new-stock people "joined America" need not be denied or explained away. For the culture which mediated that juncture was, at least in some important ways, the creation of its customers and audiences, an outcome of the continuing interaction of such people with a variety of declining and emergent subcultural formations that contended for their loyalty and attention and that found some resolution in the common, commercial culture of the city.

Especially among social historians with a critical and oppositional attitude to modern American social and economic institutions, the tendency has been strong to avoid this conclusion in two ways. First, especially among historians of ethnicity, it is argued that the cultural incorporation to which Barth points did not in fact happen. Immigrants were not Americanized, homogenized, stripped of subcultural distinctiveness. Their families, kin networks, and communal institutions allowed them to resist cultural imperialism and to stubbornly create a pluralistic society. The impact of mass culture (and similarly of mass education) was, in this view, more superficial than Barth would have it, limited, as one recent student of Eastern European workers in Johnstown, Pennsylvania claims, "to largely external influences, leaving the more fundamental cultural values untouched."[3]

Second, historians who do credit the powerful hold of mass culture over twentieth century Americans are often inclined to interpret that hold as an imposition from above. Those influenced by Marxism and critical theory, though they recognize to a degree the complicity of audiences and customers in the process, nonetheless explain the triumph of mass culture in terms of the need of corporate and other organizational hierarchies to lull dissatisfied workers and to generate pliant consumers and clients. Thus, in a recent book by Stuart and Elizabeth Ewen, a perceptive account of how movies offered young working-class women models of personal liberation from restrictive behavioral norms is followed by the confident assertion that "the social order was able to utilize this new release for the construction of a new form of domination."[4]

To construct a more complex and nuanced story of the evolution of urban mass culture in the twentieth century—and it is only an exploratory beginning I offer here—it is necessary to locate the principal agents of cultural innovation and production in America's cities at the turn of the century. Relatively small entrepreneurs—the people whom Gareth Stedman Jones has called "merchants of leisure"[5]—were the middlemen of the evolving culture. Having emerged from the ranks of the retail trades, skilled labor, and even sometimes the immigrant-stock working class itself, these middlemen retained a sharp awareness of the tastes and inclinations of their plebeian clientele, even as they strove to defend themselves from respectable critics. Always their aim was to sell and to convince buyers to come again. In the process, these middlemen rushed to occupy if not a vacuum then a moonscape of fragmented and partial formations. For declining native craftsmen and rural migrants, for an increasingly diverse collection of recent immigrants, and even for middle-class citizens in search of post-Victorian models of public demeanor and personal expression, the middlemen provided whatever came to hand and to mind. The goods and services they sold, however benign, innocuous, or pernicious, can only through the most Manichaean of bifocals be seen as products of an American corporate or social elite intent on luring or indoctrinating the urban masses into "the American way." It is certainly true that, as the century advanced, the development of advertising and of great corporate networks of cultural production significantly increased the manipulative power of mass culture. But, as one historian of the British cinema has recently put it, the character of the new medium was "rather effortlessly determined by the collusion of *nouveau-riches* entrepreneurs and audiences, leaving cultural and political establishments to hoist themselves into a new age."[6] Well before "captains of consciousness" began seriously to shape the choices of their customers, the latter had already constituted themselves, with the aid of the merchants of leisure, into what Åsa Briggs has called "a vast new audience."[7]

What did those largely working-class and immigrant-stock buyers want and what did the merchants of leisure sell them? The second part of this question is easier to answer than the first: wants and desires are always difficult to assess, and the nature of a demand is not always easily inferred from the nature of that which is supplied to meet it. Yet, given the fluid character of the growing industrial metropolis and the close interaction of merchants and consumers of leisure, we may place more confidence in such inferences than we might in the case of contemporary cultural analysis.

In the first instance, the merchants sold a variety of simple pleasures whose appeal, especially to the sons and daughters of the immigrants, is relatively unmysterious. They offered cheap but fashionable clothing, especially for women, which could be purchased in palaces of consumption the very visiting of which gave pleasure; dance halls and amusement parks which gave young men and women not only the thrill of upbeat music and whirling rides but the chance to socialize with one another in an anonymous setting free of parental oversight; baseball parks which, even if visited rarely, taught young men, who played in the streets and followed the sport in the papers, not only the rules of the American game but also the perennial lessons of heroism, camaraderie, perhaps even of physical grace and beauty; and most important the movies which, since nickelodeon days, provided cheap thrills more than lessons in civility, and images of spunky, Chaplin-esque survive along with those of exotic romance and cowboy revenge.[8]

Movies won an immense following largely because they fed lower-class urbanites' hunger for liberation from the tedium of everyday life. Investigators for the Pittsburgh Survey in 1907 found themselves astonished by the "part these shows play in the life of the community." They found it less noteworthy that children were "always begging for five cents to go to the nickelodeon" than that men on their way from work, women out shopping, and whole families on Saturday nights regularly sought "a glimpse of the other side of life." Similarly, they noted working girls lined up outside downtown picture shows on Saturday nights, "hot and tired and irritable, but willing to wait" and "determined to be amused." New York social worker Mary K. Simkhovitch likewise noted in 1917 that "This great mechanical device has revolutionized the theatre for working people." And the *Survey* magazine observed that "in the tenement districts the motion picture has well nigh driven other forms of entertainment from the field." The same was true in Britain where, by World War I, the "cinema .. was manifestly *the* medium of the urban working masses."[9]

The appeal of the early movies is not hard to discern. They were cheap, of course, but more important, as Stuart and Elizabeth Ewen have put it, they "had not yet found a voice"[10] and therefore permitted audiences to populate the simple terrain of flickering images with personal meanings derived from everyday life. This was made easier by those movies that depicted urban, lower-class life, and in the early years there were many of these, especially comedies. Few reached the comedic heights of Chaplin or Sennett, but many portrayed heroes and heroines who achieved an absurd dignity in the face of hopeless odds and on the ruins of wrecked dreams.

In the first instance, the liberation that movies and other forms of mass culture promoted defined itself in personal rather than social or political terms. Speaking of second-generation working women in the 1920's, Leslie Tentler notes that the "gay sociability of adolescents in the industrial city," along with the heightened autonomy associated with the experience of wage earning, partially freed young women from the patriarchal restrictions of the family. Unlike the Ewens, who see such adolescent experiments as first steps toward a new form of domination, Tentler cautiously acknowledges that "whether the greater social freedom of adolescence represented a genuine break with the past ... is a complicated question."[11] With her we can recognize the partiality of the liberation offered by mass amusements without depicting them as part of an elite strategy to coopt working men and women into a culture of narcissism that subverted "truer" ethnic and class attachments. It can be argued, in fact, that the discrepency between commercially generated expectations of liberation and a structure of socio-economic opportunity that frustrated such expectations contributed to individual and collective protest. On the other hand, of course, that discrepency may have made the consoling, escapist, and compensation features of mass entertainments more compelling. It is probably safe to say that it did both. Having a good time reconciled people to inequality and tedium, but it also moved them to formulate demands for an "American standard of living" and to assert their right to the rough equality and social freedom they believed America stood for. It allowed them to do so, moreover, in a way that did not force them to choose between their specifically American ambitions and their commitments to the traditional subculture of their parents.[12]

It is here that I want to address the issue of so-called ethnic pluralism by returning to the question about what audiences wanted and what entrepreneurs sold them. A second answer to that question is that the latter gave the former a chance to become American without having to identify with their enemies. Mass culture offered the new urbanites a version of America which they could embrace, in sharp and often conscious contradistinction to that version which a particular group of bourgeois reformers sought to impose on them. Had those reformers been able to masquerade successfully as custodians of an official and seamless American culture, the children of immigrants would have been forced to grasp all the more tightly the traditions that their parents had bitterly defended and bestowed upon them. But the reformers were themselves parochials. Among the post-Victorian bourgeoisie "conspicuous consumption," "the strenuous life," and even libertine Bohemianism and modernism contended with new bureaucratic and organizational values.[13] With such bourgeois elements, reformers of the Anglo-Saxon pietist strain competed as often and as fiercely as with champions of more plebeian norms and values.

Given this state of cultural flux, immigrants and especially their children could explore the new delights of urban popular culture without having to scrutinize themselves excessively for signs of subcultural treason. Indeed, they could defend their new pleasures as they did the old satisfactions of ethnic culture—in much the same terms and against many of the same assailants.

This oppositional element in the growing appeal of mass entertainments can be exaggerated, but it should not be underestimated. As the Ewens have noted, the early movies "existed outside of the moral universe of correct and respectable middle-class society." According to Mack Sennett, they "reduced convention, dogma, stuffed shirts and Authority to nonsense and then blossomed into pandemonium."[14] The merchants of leisure no doubt knew that their fate was bound up with the opposition to Prohibition, Sabbatarianism, and other forms of cultural chauvinism, but whatever they intended, in simply doing their business they helped to line up a diverse though largely lower-class clientele against all those adversaries whom Sennett subsumed under the heading, "Authority." Audiences responded to images of rebellion against convention, which, however innocuous and apolitical, could not be drained entirely of political implication.

That implication was inevitable given the context of urban politics in the late nineteenth and early twentieth centuries. Probably no other cause impelled urbanites into politics more continuously than the need to defend themselves against cultural chauvinism. Nearly all immigrant-stock and working-class people could find common cause against enemies who threatened at the same time their Sunday religious parades, their Sunday beer, and their Sunday movies and baseball. It is thus not surprising that, until the New Deal, organized labor in Pennsylvania and many other industrial states fought as long and as hard against Prohibition and for Sunday baseball as it did for almost any other cause. Such cultural issues helped to cement the loyalty of most working-class and new-stock urbanites to political machines and eventually to the national Democratic party. These "urban liberal" coalitions, as John Buenker has labelled them, were not the building blocks of a working-class party. But they did bring more squarely into the forefront of American politics the values and interests of working-class urbanites who fought not only to create a more pluralistic and tolerant cultural consensus but also to create a labor movement and a welfare state.[15]

Like mass culture, that movement and that state have been interpreted as triumphs of conservatism, clever diversions into manageable channels of potentially more radical impulses. This is an argument to which I will return, but first I want to assert that, whatever interpretation we bring to those triumphs, we must also recognize that to a considerable extent they forged a greater trans-ethnic solidarity among working-class urbanites. As one recent British study of similar issues has noted, "twentieth century cultural forms expressed and helped to forge a greater cultural homogeneity within the working class, or at least helped to erode older forms of divisions."[16] In the United States they did both, despite greater ethnic fragmentation, partly because they accompanied and helped to justify labor and political agitation that put a similar premium on common interests and values.

By the 1920's the people who had grasped ethnicity as a crucial and often lone instrument of defense against economic and social insecurity increasingly grasped other instruments. Though the labor movement faced daunting odds, it nonetheless strove with some success to counteract capitalist power by building greater working-class solidarity across ethnic lines. As early as the first decade of the century, heterogeneous immigrant workers demonstrated—e.g., at McKees Rocks, Pennsylvania in 1909—that they could forge trans-ethnic solidarity and sustain tenacious strikes. At about the same time, a "new unionism" emerged among higher-skilled, old-stock workers who, under pressure from technological change and the Open Shop drive, came to embrace at least to a degree the principle of interskill and, perforce, trans-ethnic solidarity.[17]

At the same time, urban political machines responded, sometimes grudgingly, to demands from new-stock citizens for a "piece of the actio." Like the middlemen of culture, the middlemen of politics sensed the potential of new constituents to advance the fortunes of whoever patronized them. The partial success of socialists and progressives in attracting new voters made the decision to recruit them more than academic. In fighting off both class-based movements and reformers who promised better city services and an end to favoritism, machine politicians necessarily incorporated some of the policies of both while promoting ever more aggressively their reputation as the cultural defenders of the urban masses. However well they survived new political challenges, the middlemen of urban politics made a kind of "live and let live" cultural pluralism the *sine qua non* of that urban politics. Ironically, in doing so they helped to forge a more homogeneous, less fragmented political consciousness among their constituents. Inasmuch as the Democratic party absorbed those constituents, it promoted a version of American nationality defined in terms quite different from those of the chauvinistic promoters of "Americanization."[18]

Particularly in the 1920's this outcome was facilitated by an important political fact: most big cities had stopped expanding physically. Their tax bases having frozen or shrunken, urban politicians looked increasingly to the state for direct aid, subsidies, and new taxing powers. Fighting both for "home rule" and for greater leverage over state legislatures and executive bureaucracies, politicians such as Al Smith had to forge ever larger and more stable urban electoral majorities. And those majorities were indeed forged among urbanites who recognized their common political interests and who reacted predictably to increasingly bitter anti-urban diatribes from outstate politicians, rural fundamentalists, and other pretenders to the mantle of true Americanism. Because the latter tended to stereotype all urbanites as alien, perhaps dangerously radical, and certainly debased by both primitive old-world and trashy new-world culture, they accentuated the areas of commonality among the ethnically diverse urban population. Fighting for greater statewide political power against such anti-urban enemies gave ethnics a chance to defend their ethnicity *and* go beyond it at the same time.[19]

Meanwhile, fundamental socioeconomic changes were beginning to lessen the differences among new-stock Americans, albeit more slowly than Israel Zangwill imagined, and yet more significantly than his detractors allow. First, the consolidation and corporatization of American capitalism did something like what Karl Marx predicted it would. As Olivier Zunz argues in his new book on Detroit between 1880 and 1920, the "nineteenth century plural opportunity structure," which had allowed a modicum of security and mobility within ethnic enclaves, "gave way to a new, single opportunity structure, characterized ... by the centralization of control ... in the hands of relatively few, predominately native white American industrialists." Although Zunz recognizes that ethnic feeling remained strong and that a more homogeneous working class "had developed in Detroit before it recognized common concerns," he nonetheless shows that class became a more salient organizer of life at the same moment as "the traditional ethnic matrix for people's lives vanished."[20] Moreover, although the point has been too often overstated, the capitalist opportunity structure did allow immigrants and their children to realize real gains in income and living standards. Especially in the 1920's, real earning rose steadily, movement continued into skilled, retail, and white collar occupations, and immigrant children received more and more education. Beyond this, for many mass production workers corporate welfarism made the workplace safer and job security somewhat more likely than it had been.[21]

Of course, even after the ascendance of a more unitary opportunity structure and improvements in living standards, the ethnic matrix never faded away entirely; in some instances it remained largely intact. Ethnicity remained stronger among those workers who confronted circumstances that thwarted mobility, restrained growth in wages, or limited their ability to parlay economic gains into increased social and political power. For example, in industrial towns dominated by a single industry or by an exceptionally powerful and exclusive social elite, the realities of class could not as well express themselves in unionism or politics. Massive eruptions such as the 1919 steel strike showed the potential for trans-ethnic working-class consciousness, and World War I mobilization demonstrated the willingness of immigrants to develop a broader sense of American nationality. But in towns and cities dominated by Big Steel, repression and social exclusion drove workers back to traditional ethnic sources of support.[22] Furthermore, as John Bodnar has shown for Steelton, Pennsylvania in the 1920's, repression and exclusion also limited the tendency of immigrant children to mix socially and intermarry across ethnic lines. "Their integrative development being arrested," he notes, "the insulated world of the ethnic group afforded the same retreat for the second generation as it had for the first. Ethnicity was the answer of immigrants and their children to exclusion ..."[23]

Similarly, Ewa Morawska notes that tendencies toward interethnic mixing and the development of a sense of American nationality among second-generation workers in Johnstown, Pennsylvania were arrested by a hostile and repressive environment: "with the absence of unions and with the social exclusiveness of native Americans, until the late 1930's there were in Johnstown no institutions—clubs, halls, societies or recreational facilities—which could provide different groups in the city with opportunities for social and cultural integration. ... Even those second generation Eastern Europeans who were born and raised in Johnstown's mixed neighborhoods and who as children socialized 'with everybody,' by the age of 14-15 found themselves channeled into ethnic networks simply because there were no other ... cultural agencies of integration in the city."[24]

The negative character of both these explanations of ethnic persistence needs to be emphasized. Precisely because workers in Steelton and Johnstown were not permitted to follow up the logic of class and the logic of nationality, they reinforced the logic of ethnicity in their search for psychological and material security. In cities with a more complex socioeconomic structure, where mobility was greater, where unionism could less easily be contained, where employers could less readily exploit ethnic divisions, where social mixing proceeded more rapidly, and where new groups won greater power in political machines, the ethnic matrix loomed smaller on the social horizon. There the opportunity to carve out a specifically American identity loomed larger. Though some groups, such as the Poles,[25] appear to have seized the opportunity less readily and to have relied longer on traditional sources of support, most immigrant-stock people in the second and third generations found in unions, political machines, and the culture of the city ways to expand their opportunities and to reshape their sense of order and propriety beyond the received ways of family and ethnic group.

After World War I, interethnic integration was speeded by the cutting-off of immigration. Occurring at the same moment that an American-born generation was completing public schooling and coming to maturity in the city, the cutoff deprived ethnic communities of fresh infusions of old-country values *and* old-country marriage partners. The latter contributed to increasing rates of outmarriage among immigrant children. By 1930, 25 percent of all Italian men in Buffalo were marrying non-Italians, as were 7 percent of the women. In Cleveland, 39 percent of second generation Italian men married exogamously, as did 28 percent of Italian women; among Slovaks, outmarriage occurred almost half the time for men and more than half the time for women; Rumanians showed an even higher rate of outmarriage for men, 60 percent, and a fairly high rate for women, 28 percent.[26]

In the third and fourth generations, such intermarriage became the norm rather than the exception. By the 1960's, studies showed that a majority of Catholic ethnics, even the persistent Poles, chose marriage partners outside the ethnic group, and that even one of every three Jews was choosing an outsider spouse.[27] Such trends, which by and large confirm a Triple Melting Pot thesis, began in the industrial cities during the first three decades of the century and reflected the powerful integrative forces of American economic, social, and political institutions. They reflected the experience of collective struggles to build unions and urban political coalitions, struggles which came to partial fruition in the CIO and the New Deal and which took the children of immigrants well beyond the more confined world of their parents. Accompanying these trends and these struggles, reflecting and shaping them, a new popular culture took root among those children of immigrants impelled away from one world and toward another.

Finally, to return to the issue of false consciousness and cooptation, the new culture did reconcile the children of immigrants to America, but not to that version of America which most of their employers preferred. Though the prophets of consumerism may have been right in arguing that mass consumption would spur the economy and defuse social conflict, most businessmen and much of bourgeois America had to be dragged reluctantly into the world of mass unions, mass politics, and mass culture. Neither they nor the people with whom they contended found it easy to distinguish demands for greater pleasure from demands for greater power. And even after they learned to accommodate to and profit from such demands, they—and historians who have taken them at their word—exaggerated the conservative implications of new arrangements. Just as it is too easy and too simplistic to argue that the counterculture of the 1960's came to nothing more than granola bars and Jordache jeans, it is too easy to claim that the urban culture of the early twentieth century simply processed the new-stock working class into a mass of efficient and unrebellious consumers. That culture reinforced a kind of vernacular populism which could be employed in radical, conservative, or apolitical ways. In the TV age we may rightly concern ourselves with the disproportionate power of corporate and state elites to determine the character of our highly mediated culture, but we should avoid the temptation to ascribe to the technology or its managers too hegemonic a power. We should, like the sitdowners who danced to Benny Goodman within the walls of the auto plants they occupied, or the antiwar protesters who marched to the rhythm of rock and roll, remain alive to the unpredictable uses to which our highly mediated culture can be put.

NOTES

[1] New York, 1980.
[2] *Journal of Social History* 16 (Fall, 1982), pp. 145-146.
[3] Ewa Morawska, "The Internal Status Hierarchy in the East European Communities in Johnstown, PA 1890-1930s," *Journal of Social History* 16 (Fall, 1982), pp. 5-15.
[4] Stuart and Elizabeth Ewen, *Channels of Desire: Mass Images and the Shaping of American Consciousness* (New York, 1982), p. 105; also Stuart Ewen, *Captains of Consciousness: Advertising and the Social Roots of the Consumer Culture* (New York, 1976). See Christopher Lasch, *The Culture of Narcissism: American Life in An Age of Diminishing Expectations* (New York, 1979), for a perspective enriched by critical theory, but freed from many of its assumptions about elite manipulation of culture, in part because of a reliance on psychoanalytic theory. Michael R. Real, "Media Theory: Contributions to an Understanding of American Mass Communications," *American Quarterly* 32 (1980), pp. 238-258, is a useful survey of theories, including those derived from cultural anthropology, which to some extent I draw upon in this essay.
[5] Gareth Stedman Jones, "Class Expression Versus Social Control? A Critique of Recent Trends in the Social History of 'Leisure'," *History Workshop* 4 (Autumn, 1977), p. 163. See also my *The Remaking of Pittsburgh: Class and Culture in an Industrializing City, 1877-1919* (Albany, N.Y., 1984), Chap. 3, and "The Triumph of Commerce: Class Culture and Mass Culture in Pittsburgh," in M. Frisch and D. Walkowitz, eds., *Working Class America* (Urvana, Ill., 1983), pp. 123-152; and Neil Harris, "Four Stages of Cultural Growth: The American City," *Indiana Historical Society Lectures, 1971-1972: History and the Role of the City in American Life* (Indianapolis, 1972).
[6] Peter Stead, "The People and the Pictures. The British Working Class and Film in the 1930's," in N. Pronay and D.W. Spring, eds., *Propaganda, Politics, and Films, 1918-1945* (London, 1982), pp. 80-81.
[7] Asa Briggs, *Mass Entertainments: The Origins of a Modern Industry* (Adelaide, Australia, 1960), p. 18; also Couvares, "Triumph of Commerce," pp. 142-147.
[8] On department stores, in addition to Barth see Susan P. Benson, "The Customer Ain't God: The Work Culture of Department Store Saleswomen, 1890-1940," in Frisch and Walkowitz, *Working-Class America*, pp. 185-211, and Leslie W. Tentler, *Wage-Earning Women: Industrial Work and Family Life in the United States, 1900-1930* (New York, 1979), pp. 73-74, 97; on dance halls, see Lewis A. Erenberg, *Steppin' Out: New York Nightlife and the Transformation of American Culture, 1890-1930* (Westport, Conn., 1981); on amusement parks, see John Kasson, *Amusing the Million: Coney Island at the Turn of the Century* (New York, 1978); on movies, Robert Sklar, *Movie-Made America: A Cultural History of American Movies* (New York, 1975); on sports, Allen Guttman, *From Ritual to Record: The Nature of Modern Sports* (New York, 1977), which besides a brilliant explanation of the rise of baseball in America, also includes in its early chapters a fine survey of theories of the social function of sport.
[9] Introduction to Pronay and Spring, *Propaganda, Politics, and Film,* p. 17; S. and E. Ewen, *Channels of Desire,* pp. 86-87; Mary K. Simkhovitch, *The City Worker's World in America* (New York, 1917), p. 123; Couvares, "Triumph of Commerce," pp. 143-144; Virginia Yans-McLaughlin, *Family and Community: Italian Immigrants in Buffalo, 1880-1930* (Ithaca, NY, 1971), pp. 254-255.
[10] S. and E. Ewen, *Channels of Desire,* p. 87.
[11] Tentler, *Wage-Earning Women,* pp. 109-114, and also 71, 97.
[12] For several very different studies that treat new cultural forms as something other than cooptative, see Lizabeth A. Cohen, "Embellishing a Life of Labor: An Interpretation of the Material Culture of American Working-Class Homes, 1885-1915," in T. Schlereth, ed., *Material Culture Studies in America* (Nashville, 1982), pp. 289-305; William J. Baker, "The Making of a Working-Class Football Culture in Victorian England," *Journal of Social History* 13 (1979), pp. 241-251; Joseph Gusfield, "The

Sociological Reality of America: An Essay on Mass Culture," in H. Gans et al., *On the Making of Americans* (Philadelphia, 1979), pp. 41-62; and Natalie Z. Davis, "The History of Popular Culture," along with the essays that follow her introductory essay, in J. Beauroy et al., *The Wolf and the Lamb: Popular Culture in France from the Old Regime to the Twentieth Century* (Saratoga, Cal., 1976).

13 John Higham, "The Reorientation of American Culture in the 1890's," in *Writing American History* (Bloomington, Ind., 1970), pp. 73-102; Henry May, *The End of American Innocence: A Study of the First Years of Our Own Time, 1912-1917* (New York, 1964); Robert H. Weibe, *The Search for Order, 1877-1920* (New York, 1967), Chap. 6; Erenberg, *Steppin' Out;* and Couvares, "The Triumph of Commerce," pp. 127-130.

14 Quoted in S. and E. Ewen, *Channels of Desire,* p. 92.

15 John D. Buenker, *Urban Liberalism and Progressive Reform* j(New York, 1973); Bruce M. Stave, *The New Deal and the Last Hurah: Pittsburgh Machine Politics* (Pittsburgh, 1970); J. Thomas Jable, "Sport, Amusement, and Pennsylvania Blue Laws, 1682-1973," (Ph.D. diss., Pennsylvania State Univeristy, 1974), Chaps. 4-6; Edward P. Kantowicz, *Polish-American Politics in Chicago, 1888-1940* (Chicago, 1975).

16 Paul Wild, "Recreation in Rochdale, 1900-1940," in J. Clarke et al., *Working-Class Culture: Studies in History and Theory* (New York, 1979), p. 143.

17 David Brody, *Workers in Industrial America* (New York, 1980), Chap. 1; David Montgomery, *Workers' Control in America* (New York, 1979), Chap. 3; Gerald Rosenblum, *Immigrant Workers: Their Impact on American Labor Radicalism* (New York, 1973), Chaps. 4-7; see also Eugene M. Tobin, "Direct Action and Conscience: The 1913 Paterson Strike as an Example of the Relationship between Labor Radicals and Liberals," *Labor History* 20 (1979), pp. 73-88.

18 See footnote 14; also Michael Nash, *Conflict and Accommodation: Coal Miners, Steel Workers, and Socialism, 1890-1920* (Westport, Conn., 1982); Terrence J. McDonald, "Putting Politics Back into the History of the American City," review essay, *American Quarterly* 34 (1982), pp. 200-209; and David A. Hollinger, "Ethnic Diversity, Cosmopolitanism, and the Emergence of the American Liberal Intelligentsia," *American Quarterly* 28 (1975), pp. 133-151.

19 Buenker describes such struggles in several states, while Robert Caro in *The Power Broker: Robert Moses and the Fall of New York* (New York, 1974), Parts 3 and 4, brilliantly dissects the New York case; see also Loren Baritz, "The Culture of the Twenties," in S. Coben and L. Ratner, eds., *The Development of an American Culture,* 2nd Ed. (New York, 1983), pp. 181-214, on antiurbanism.

20 Olivier Zunz, *The Changing Face of Inequality: Urbanization, Industrial Development, and Immigration in Detroit, 1880-1920* (Chicago, 1982), pp. 401-402.

21 Brody, *Workers in Industrial American,* Chap. 2; Irving Bernstein, *The Lean Years: A History of the American Worker 1920-1933* (New York, 1966), pp. 63-74; also Thomas Kessner, *The Golden Door: Italian and Jewish Immigrant Mobility in New York City, 1880-1915* (New York, 1977).

22 David Brody, *Labor in Crisis: The Steel Strike of 1919* (New York, 1965).

23 John Bodnar, *Immigrants and Industrialization: Ethnicity in an American Mill Town, 1870-1940* (Pittsburgh, 1977), p. 144, and Chap. 7 generally.

24 Morawska, "Internal Status Hierarchy in East European Communities," p. 79.

25 Edward Kantowicz, "Polish Chicago: Survival through Solidarity," in M. Holli and P. Jones, eds., *The Ethnic Frontier* (Grand Rapids, 1977), pp. 179-209; Caroline Golab, "The Impact of the Industrialization Experience on the Immigrant Family: The Huddled Masses Reconsidered," in R. Ehrlich, ed., *Immigrants in Industrial America, 1850-1920* (Charlottesville, Va., 1977), pp. 1-32; Yans-McLaughlin, *Family and Community,* p. 257.

26 Josef J. Barton, *Peasants and Strangers: Italians, Rumanians, and Slovaks in an American City, 1890-1950* (Cambridge, 1975), pp. 163-166; Yans-McLaughlin, *Family and Community,* p. 257.

27 Stephen Steinberg, *The Ethnic Myth: Race, Ethnicity and Class in America* (Boston, 1981), pp. 68ff; Stephen Thernstrom, "Ethnic Groups in American History," in L. Liebman, ed., *Ethnic Relations in America* (Englewood Cliffs, NJ, 1982), p. 19; Philip Gleason, "American Identity and Americanization," in W. Petersen et al., *Concepts of Ethnicity* (Cambridge, 1982), pp. 57-143; James A. Crispino, *The Assimilation of Ethnic Groups: The Italian Case* (New York, 1980).

Comment

VIRGINIA YANS-McLAUGHLIN

I think it is fitting to think about this conference as a cultural event bringing together a group of people who care and think enough about American cities to live in, write about, and preserve them. Perhaps it is appropriate, then, to examine these three papers as cultural as well as historical texts; as cultural texts they convey a symbolic portrait of the American city which coexists with the historical interpretation. Examining these papers in this way, we can arrive at an understanding of the role of American cities in American cultural ideology—and historiography—and through an unraveling of this scheme arrive at an assessment of where urban historical methodology of the past fifteen years has taken us, if anywhere.

As I read these three papers, I could not help but place them within this broader context of cultural event and meaning. Fifteen years ago, a major conference on the Industrial City took place at Yale University, and the present conference agenda revealed many of the same actors would be present here. Also, roughly fifteen years ago several major re-evaluative articles appeared by present conference participants—Michael Frisch, Eric Lampard, Stephan Thernstrom, and Sam Bass Warner—which future generations will surely look to as gems of historiographical analysis.[1] The three papers we have before us emerge from this context; they are deeply related to the questions raised and traditions identified or established since.

In an article published in 1969 Michael Frisch offered some unusually sensitive insights upon urban historiography which are as relevant today as they were then. Frisch observed, first of all, the persisting interest of American urban historians in "the interrelationship of urbanization and American history in the broad sense of each ...." Noting their obstinate resistance to an analytic examination of urbanization *per se,* he added: "insofar as they have focused upon urbanization, ... [urban historians] have tended to define it, however informally, in terms which include a broad range of cultural and historical factors that theorists keep asking them to exclude." Put more concisely, "many of the most suggestive developments in urban history have come from works which either view urbanization and the city in broader contexts, or which handle broader societal themes within a specific urban context."[2] As examples, Frisch cited Thernstrom's *Poverty and Progress* (1964) and Robert Wiebe's *The Search for Order* (1967) as two emerging styles of urban historiography, the first representing an analysis of urban social structure, the second beginning at least to establish a much-needed analysis of the cultural component of the urbanization process. Both the structural and cultural analyses were, of course, tied to larger questions of American historiography—the nature of class and community in America. It is clear that Susan Hirsch's paper fits into the tradition established by Thernstrom's work, while Couvares follows the second. Insofar as it attempts to focus both upon the economic realities and culture of peasant life, John Bodnar's paper attempts a fusion of both traditions.

So fifteen years after Eric Lampard[3] and others entreated historians to focus more analytically upon the study of urbanization *per sé,* after millions in grant dollars have been spent on social mobility studies, after what Frisch called efforts to "almost surgically separate" the urban and national contexts, urban historians are still concerned, it seems to me, with issues related more to national consciousness and identity rather than specifically city-centered questions or even questions specifically related to urban development. They are concerned with the history of the American nation, not with a national history of American cities.

My curiosity was aroused as to just why these historians, who are, after all, quite a creative lot and open to admitting innovative techniques into the discipline, conceive their task as they do. And perhaps, after all, the only way to advance historical studies of the city is to explore the cultural significance and meaning behind why historians persist in perceiving their task as they do, despite admonitions to the contrary. I am intrigued with the possiblity of one explanation.

If historians are Americans with specialized training, they are still Americans. As such they have proven themselves to be as tantalized by, fascinated with, and preoccupied with symbols and myths that find less studied form in popular historical consciousness. The city itself—sometimes heavenly, sometimes hellish—does not occupy a steady state in that consciousness, but it does occupy a place. Those unaccustomed to thinking in terms of popular historical consciousness finding analogues in formal historical texts have only to think of the Christian and Messianic conceptions finding secular parallels in the Progressive view of history. At the very least "the city" provides a historical landscape for the acting out of significant aspects of America's mythical and symbolic past. Perhaps now that the nation of immigrants has matured to a nation of immigrants' descendants, it will come to occupy as significant a place in popular understanding of the formation of American culture and character as the frontier did. From the time of the Puritans to the days of the frontiersmen, America itself has symbolized a destination point on a journey and the possibility for redemption; the industrial city appears in modern historical iconography and in popular consciousness as a locus of economic achievement or political liberation for immigrant sojourners. In the current historiography, the traveling immigrant settles down in apparently volatile ethnic communities from which he struggles through self-improvement and popular entertainment to remove himself physically and psychologically.

Though perhaps it is more conventionally acknowledged in literary than social scientific discourse, the reproduction of popular symbolism in scholarly texts should not surprise us. The melting pot metaphor is probably the most obvious example of such a transformation of popular symbol into the professional scholarly literature, specifically that related to ethnicity and immigration. Let us not forget that Mark the Match Boy and Ragged Dick marched off the streets of America's cities into Horatio Alger novels and appeared in the scientifically controlled passages of Stephan Thernstrom's *Poverty and Progress.* John Bodnar's peasants and Susan Hirch's migrants are more calculatingly rational and more subject to the reality of economic circumstance than Ragged Dick ever was. But the same mythic assumptions motivate both historians' work, if only in their attempt to refute the standard mythology.

Francis Couvares' examination of popular culture, a clear descendant of several preceding generations of scholarship, still makes the assumption that American urban culture—whether controlled from above or influenced by its participant audiences—moves almost inevitably toward some trans-ethnic homogeneity. Paradoxically, although the sources of control focused upon differ, the hegemonic model which Couvares critiques offers a sketch of American culture equally as congruent with the homogenous cultural ideal. If he did not understand the methodology of these modern historians, Israel Zangwell would have been pleased with their interpretations.

I do not wish to imply that no difference exists between history making and myth making. But I think it worthwhile to point out that although their contextual uses and functions may vary, the parallel constructions do exist in popular and professional history. The existence of parallel symbolism in scientific and popular consciousness may explain the persisting resistance which American historians have to looking at the city in purely analytic terms. The city cannot be easily understood as a pure analytic category precisely because it has been designated as a central setting for the acting out of powerful American myths. These include the dream for economic achievement, the formation of a homogenous American culture or, conversely, the preservation of ethnic pluralism, an undefined class structure characterized not so much as being American as not being European because a Socialist revolution never occurred.

Lest I cause our three distinguished writers dismay by treating them only as story-tellers and not scientific practitioners of a craft, I would like to offer a few more conventional comments upon their presentations. Like Thernstrom before them, Bodnar and Hirsch locate the myths of achievement and America as a land of redemption within specific temporal and spatial confines. They use empirical data to sensitize us to the effect which time, location, region, sex, ethnicity, and race have upon fulfillment of success and formation of class structure and consciousness. In calling attention to the peculiarities of early twentieth-century industrial cities, cities with particular kinds of audiences and demands for local entertainment needs, cities which had not developed either the class practitioners or systems of delivery and control required for elite cultural domination, Couvares wisely cautions against the imposition of tidy theories upon the less consistent developing historical realities of popular culture. Both Couvares and Bodnar are particularly effective in displaying the interplay between structurally given conditions and the cultural interpretations of actors and participants in the events. Couvares' insistence that the captains of culture may have ultimately controlled the shape of popular culture as a product, but not its meaning for audiences, and Bodnar's demonstration that peasants interpreted economic change and immigration to America in their own ways each caution against the imposition of historical constructions—and myths—upon past city dwellers.

After my rather long digression from myth making to the making of history, my concluding questioning returns to issues raised by critics of urban historiography fifteen to twenty years ago. Are these papers, which I think are representative of much of the most recent significant work in urban history, telling us anything more about the history of American cities? What, in other words, is the state of the art? The focus upon social structure and cultural questions continues; but I think it operates in a more dialectical mode. And, for a variety of reasons I have not discussed, primarily having to do with developments in labor and working-class history and debates over the application of Gramscian theory to the American social context, these historians have presented us with a less crudely behavioristic model than pioneers such as Thernstrom could offer or quantifiers overwhelmed with statistical data cared to consider. Yet myths, metaphors, and icons still motivate this work. Instead of fighting this tendency as a methodological malady, perhaps it is time to accept it as a cultural fact.

NOTES

[1] Eric Lampard, "Urbanization and Social Change: On Broadening the Scope and Relevance of Urban History" in Oscar Handlin and John Burchard, *The Historian and the City* (Cambridge, Massachusetts, 1963); Warner, "If All the World Were Philadelphia: A Scaffolding for Urban History, *American Historical Review,* LXXIV, No. 1 (October, 1968), pp. 26-43; Thernstrom, "Reflections on the New Urban History," *Daedalus,* Vol. 100 (Spring, 1971), pp. 359-75.
[2] Michael Frisch, "American Urban History: Reflections on Recent Trends," *Annales,* (July, 1970).
[3] See Lampard cited above and "American Historians and the Study of Urbanization," *American Historical Review,* Vol. LXVII (October, 1961), pp. 49-61.

Technology and Its Impact on Urban Culture, 1889-1937

SAM BASS WARNER, JR.

This afternoon I want to take up my investigation of the relationship between technology and urban culture at the time when the city of Lowell and New England textiles had nothing fresh to teach to the rest of the world. In terms of technology I want to talk about some of the cultural consequences of electric power. My position in time will be that stage in physics and engineering which came after the mechanical equipment of Lowell and before our contemporary science and applications of low-power electricity, or electronics as we now call the field. My attention will focus particularly upon Stone & Webster, a Boston engineering, utility management, and investment firm, from the year of its founding in 1889 until its forced divestiture of its electric company holdings in 1937.

There are, to be sure, many ways to consider the changes in urban culture brought about by technological change. For instance, you can examine the use of new products, like electric washing machines or power saws, to estimate their use and thereby to try to guess at their social meanings and consequences. Or you might look for the new words and new symbols that spring up with the introduction of an invention, like the cluster of traveling images which the motor car stimulated (images from the old social and carriage parades, to picnics, racing, and adventure). Or you might choose to follow the path of innovation itself, hoping to pick up the trail of significant innovators and thereby to see how the innovators' outlook and situation influenced the use and further development of the new technology. The technique in this last method is to use innovator and innovation together as clues to technological influence on the larger society.

This last method will be my attack. I want briefly to review for you the historical process whereby new inventions in electric power were diffused through electrical engineering and utility construction by a Boston firm, Stone & Webster, and to relate how that institutional process of innovation affected our urban culture.

My story begins with the eighteen seventies and eighties, decades when many inventors attempted to turn the new physics of magnetism and electricity to practical purposes. The later division between high power and low power electricity had not yet severed the field so that telegraph, telephone, electric light, dynamo, transmission, and electric motor experiments all went forward simultaneously. The leading figure of the age, Thomas A. Edison (1847-1931), accordingly began with experiments in telegraphy and soon worked into all branches of electricity. Edison was fashioning his electric light bulbs in 1879 at the same time that Pacinotti in Italy, von Siemens in Germany, and Gramme in France were perfecting the dynamo to generate electric power. When in September 1882 the New York Edison Company started up its first central power station it was a steam driven dynamo making direct current for 400 lamps. At the same time many inventors experimented with electric locomotives, and by 1884 a practical electric car was running, albeit fitfully, in East Cleveland. Finally in 1887 Frank Sprague, a former Edison employee, combined all the latest improvements to establish a successful trolley car system in Richmond, Virginia.

Boston did not lag in all of this. The site of Alexander Graham Bell's inventions, it started up its own Edison Electric Illuminating Company in 1885, and nearby Lynn was the home of the Thompson-Houston Electric Company. This company joined with Sprague for the development of electric street railways, and soon came to be the heart of J.P. Morgan's General Electric Company. In addition to these businesses, the new technical college, Massachusetts Institute of Technology, added the major of electrical engineering to its civil and mechanical training.[1]

This climate of invention and progress attracted two young M.I.T. students, Charles A. Stone (1867-1941) and Edwin S. Webster (1867-1950). The two had met each other and become friends while taking the examinations for admission to Tech. Both were local boys. Stone had been born in Newton, the son of a wholesale butter merchant, and he received his education in the Newton public schools. Webster had been born in Roxbury, the son of a partner in the Boston banking firm of Kidder, Peabody & Company, and he was educated in private schools. At M.I.T. the two young men decided to take the brand-new major, electrical engineering, and as classmates they grew to be such fast friends that they were known to their fellow students as Stone & Webster. Today, they hold the distinction of being the only joint entry in the *Dictionary of American Biography*. For their senior paper they prepared a collaborative analysis of the efficiency of a Westinghouse alternating current generator.

Upon graduation in 1888 the two planned to set up as partners, but their senior professor, Charles R. Cross, discouraged them. He doubted there would be sufficient business to support one consulting electrical engineer, surely not two. So Stone spent the ensuing year at the Thompson Electric Welding Company in Lynn, and later worked for an electric motor company in Boston. Webster, for his part, toured Europe, and went to work at his father's investment bank, Kidder, Peabody & Company.[2]

The next year, however, in 1889, the year Henry M. Whitney undertook to electrify the street railways of Boston, the two young men decided to test the field. In November, 1889, they hired two small rooms on the top floor of 4 Post Office Square, and staffed the office with M.I.T. students. Uncertain of the outcome, neither of the two partners quit his job for a few months. The young men's announcement called attention to the rapid pace of electrical invention and offered their firm's services to test innovations for investors, to help inventors perfect their work, and to test electrical systems and equipment. They also stood ready to lay out wiring and to design small power plants. In short, as recent M.I.T. graduates, they stood prepared to bring all they had just learned in physics and electrical engineering to the world of practical application. As references they listed the President of M.I.T., their physics professor, and Webster's father.

Some of the new firm's first work consisted of testing the wiring, insulation, and appliances listed in the fire insurance underwriters' book of rules. They soon discovered that much of the fuse wire of the day did not melt under the loads it was rated for, so Stone and Webster began a regular testing and labeling of wire according to their own specifications. After half a dozen years of such work the insurance Underwriters Union established their own testing laboratories (1895), and Stone and Webster redirected their laboratory to electro-chemical explorations.[3]

The first big job came in 1890 as a referral from General Francis A. Walker, then president of M.I.T. The Warren Paper Company had surplus capacity at its Saccarappa Dam on the Presumpscot River (near Portland, Maine). There they wished to generate electric power and to transmit it to their Cumberland Mills, one mile away. At this time electric power transmission had yet to be mastered, but the young men succeeded with a 500-volt direct current system which worked, and which they later experimented with and improved. This initial job soon led to commissions to design and build more power stations, some of the earliest being two ordered by the Lowell, Lawrence, and Haverhill Street Railway.

Once underway, the firm of Stone & Webster quickly fell into its enduring role as a gathering point of new science and new industrial techniques, and as a broker that harnessed together the separate and unpredictable paces of science and investment capital. During the 1880's and 1890's modern science proved as unpredictable as always. Chemistry and electricity bounded forward with a rush of answerable research questions. Meanwhile American investment capital swung between a cautious risking only for what was known to be profitable and a wild chase for bonanza opportunities. In arbitrating among the scientific academy, the investor, and the operating corporation Stone and Webster not only made their personal fortunes, but they also played their role as makers of our modern culture. Their cultural force expressed itself directly through their electrical and industrial constructions. It also expressed itself indirectly through their contribution to the forming of new American institutions—the huge engineering firm, the privately owned public utility, and the private industrial corporation.

All the essential elements gathered together during the firm's first ten to fifteen years. The construction of new power plants and transmission systems followed along steadily from the first Warren Paper Company hydroelectric installation. Next, the collapse of many utilities during the depression of 1893-96 gave Stone & Webster their training and expertness in the evaluation of the engineering and management of electric, gas, and traction companies.

Since electric power was a new venture, investors in many cities had often been slow to come forward with sufficient capital. This capital shortage had been made up by the manufacturers of electrical equipment. Companies like Westinghouse and General Electric accepted stock as part payment for their supplies. Then when the panic of 1893 struck and the banks called in their notes, many new utilities failed. J.P. Morgan, father of the General Electric combination, immediately organized a syndicate of trustees to take over, manage, or dispose of the properties which owed large sums to General Electric. Stone & Webster, in turn were hired by Morgan to examine each utility, and soon this work became an important and enduring side of the firm's business. As an early partner, Russell Robb (b. 1864, M.I.T. 1888) put it: "Depression spurred this business .... Hundreds of examinations were made in these years by Stone & Webster and invaluable experience was accumulated .... All this work led, naturally, to the business side of the operation of properties, the preparing of plans for the reorganization of old companies, the organization of new companies, the building of properties, and the employment of Stone & Webster managers."[4]

Examination and reorganization immediately led to management itself. Small and middle-sized utilities could not support a staff of specialists, but through Stone & Webster, they could hire the services of a manager and a team of experts. The first such contract was written in 1895 for the Brockton (Massachusetts) Edison Illuminating Company, and management services soon became a hallmark of the firm.[5] It was a comfortable union of engineering and financial services, and it soon carried the partners by easy stages into the utility investment banking business. J.P. Morgan had offered the young men the Cumberland Electric Light & Power Company of Nashville, Tennessee for $60,000, and on his advice they borrowed enough money to purchase it. They operated it for a few years and then sold the company for $500,000. Soon thereafter they formed the Puget Sound Light & Power Company (Washington) and began forming, as well as operating, constructing, and assessing, power companies.[6]

Closer at hand, the New England paper business brought the young men further opportunities and useful connections. The new sulfite process for the manufacture of paper from wood pulp had been introduced into the United States at a Providence, Rhode Island mill in 1884. The mill superintendent was a young chemist, Arthur Dehon Little (1863-1935, M.I.T. 1885.). Two years later Little established his own chemical consulting firm in Boston and worked with Stone and Webster. Employing experiments from their Boston laboratory and tests at the Warren Paper Company's Cumberland mill, Stone & Webster set up their own chemical company and Arthur D. Little sat on its board of directors (Fort Hill Chemical Company). It was the beginning of a lifetime of collaboration among the three M.I.T. graduates.[7]

From such turn-of-the-century beginnings there emerged that common modern pattern of the double life—a family life which followed the conventions of its day, and a business life of revolutionary impact. In 1893 Edwin S. Webster married Jane dePeyster Hovey of Brookline (daughter of an editor of *The Boston Transcript*), and the couple had two daughters and one son. The son, Edwin S. Webster, Jr. (1899-1957, Harvard 1923) worked for a time at Stone & Webster's Boston office (1926-30), but rather followed his grandfather into Kidder, Peabody & Company. Webster, Sr., stayed in Boston where the engineering offices always remained. He raised his family in a large suburban house in Chestnut Hill, Brookline (307 Hammond St.), and later maintained a grand town house at 306 Dartmouth Street on the corner of Commonwealth Avenue, Boston, a country place at Beverly Cove on the North Shore, and another in Holderness, New Hampshire on Squam Lake, near the White Mountains. Webster joined the M.I.T. Corporation in 1910 and remained a permanent member and active alumnus. He also served for years as a trustee of the Boston Museum of Fine Arts, and for thirteen years as president of the Massachusetts Horticultural Society. As a Boston businessman he also sat on the board of directors of such local corporations as the United Fruit, Pacific Mills, and Ames Shovel & Tool Company. It was a life which moved from triumph in engineering and business to the fashions of a Boston gentleman: gardens, yachts, shooting, philanthropic committees, and corporate boards.[8]

His partner followed a similar path. Charles A. Stone married Miss Mary Adams Leonard of Hingham in 1902, and the couple had two daughters and two sons. The youngest boy, Whitney Stone (1908-1979, Harvard 1930), took an active part in the business, ultimately leading Stone & Webster into the oil, gas, and atomic power fields. For a time the young couple lived in a proper Boston Back Bay town house (234 Beacon Street), and Charles Stone followed the usual road of Boston clubs and boards. With his partner the two men became leaders in the move of M.I.T. from its first home in Copley

Square, Boston, across the Charles River to its present site in Cambridge. Indeed, Stone & Webster served as the chief engineers for the construction project (1913-15).

In 1915 in order to direct the securities business of Stone & Webster, and to serve as head of a private corporation formed to promote American exports, Charles A. Stone moved to New York City. There he quickly rose to be a major figure on Wall Street, serving as a director of the Federal Reserve Bank of New York (1919-23), and as a director of the International Acceptance Bank, the Bank of Manhattan, the International Mercantile Marine Company, and the Union Pacific Railroad. From this location he also secured a great many construction contracts from the New York-New Jersey-Pennsylvania region. An active club man, Stone belonged to twenty-three clubs. He also followed the then-popular English country-gentleman model of family life. He owned a town house on Fifth Avenue, New York City, and an estate in Locust Valley, Long Island. He purchased Thomas Jefferson's estate in Virginia, where he raised thoroughbred horses, and at his farm at Holderness, New Hampshire, he raised prize-winning Morgan horses and Welsh ponies.[9]

If growing wealth and success carried the young men towards conventional family and community roles, the expansion of their business pointed always toward novelty and change. Electricity proved to be one of those products which offered its best returns on a large scale, and as fast as high voltage and long distance transmission could be mastered, larger and larger power plants were demanded. Stone & Webster's early street railway and factory power plants soon grew to a succession of very large hydroelectric and steam generating projects.

The years 1909-13 carried the firm into the business of giant construction projects. The Pacific Light and Power Company ordered a series of three dams in the Sierra National Forest near Fresno, California, and a two-hundred-and seventy-five-mile transmission line to Los Angeles.[10] In Georgia the Columbus Power Company had the firm build a dam and power plant on the Chattahoochee River (Goat Island). A major consumer of this power, by the way, was the cluster of new cotton mills then opening in the region in competition with New England.[11] The largest project of the pre-war years, and the one that established Stone & Webster's reputation was the dam, lock, and power station at the Des Moines rapids of the Mississippi River, near Keokuk, Iowa. At the time of its completion in 1913 it was the world's largest power dam. The flow of the water exceeded that of the Nile at Aswan, and the five-thousand-foot dam created a lake fifty-five miles long that stretched north to Burlington, Iowa. To make the project profitable Stone & Webster had arranged to sell a third of the power on a regular basis to St. Louis, Missouri, one-hundred-and-thirty miles to the south.[12]

These successes with huge electric power installations brought Stone & Webster a continuing flow of commissions for hydroelectric works (Conowingo, Maryland and Pennsylvania, 1926-28, which generated more power than Muscle Shoals) and steam power stations (Charles L. Edgar Station, Boston Edison Company, Weymouth, Massachusetts, 1924), and in recent years this specialty has drawn the firm into atomic power plant design and construction.

The sheer magnitude of these works gives them their cultural impact and determines a great deal of their meaning. Electric power systems are but recent links in a long chain of modern foundations which made our metropolitan society viable. The chain began in the early nineteenth century with public water and sewer installations to which gas, telegraphs, street railways, steam railroads, telephones, electricity, and now freeways have been added in succession. The essential quality of all these systems is that they establish inadvertent communities. That is, they create networks of interdependencies among large numbers of scattered people who do not know each other or recognize their interdependence. They are to their own minds only a community of users, or rate payers. Yet when such systems break down users discover their helplessness, and from that shock they come to realize the vast compass of dependencies. Occasional severe droughts and pollution of water supplies, power blackouts, like that which hit New York in 1965, and recent accidents at atomic power stations have brought a partial public recognition of their inadvertent communities. Yet communities of inescapable significance though they may be, their centralized management, ubiquity, and few failures remove these communities from public awareness.

Therefore, although electric power, the great new source of energy, came to be developed on a vast scale by Stone & Webster and other firms, it was not developed as a conscious social product, nor as a system appropriate for public design. Contemporaries of Charles Stone and Edwin Webster immediately grasped the possibilities of cheap electric power generation and transmission soon after the success of Stone & Webster's Big Creek (California) project of 1913. Benton Mackaye in Massachusetts imagined electric power to be the tool which could make for an orderly dispersal of modern metropolitan populations, while Governor Gifford Pinchot of Pennsylvania thought he could rescue his state's encapsulated slums and empoverished mining towns by planning industrial dispersal through power location.[13] It is hard to imagine a new technology of greater cultural force and practical potential than electric power, yet it rarely (as with the Tennessee Valley Authority) has been the subject for conscious social planning. Instead electric power entered our society and extended through it by means of the incremental processes of private investment and market fashions.

The responsibility for this loss of opportunity rests primarily on the political and cultural climate into which electric power entered, and to which Stone & Webster catered during the years 1889 through 1937. It was a world which thought in terms of free markets and individual advantage. Therefore electric power, like streetcars or government itself, was regarded as a facilitator of private activity and not as an entity in itself. Even municipal socialists and those concerned with the economic and political concentration which such large corporate enterprises inevitably brought about thought only in·terms of rates, getting the power as cheaply and fairly as possible out to all consumers so that each could use it in his own way.[14]

Such thinking, whether socialist, trust busting, or private power defending, missed the possibilities for modern urban and ecological planning because it ignored the appearance of the inadvertent communities which electricity created. Such thinking also fastened a special set of values upon the construction projects and the men who built and operated them. Stone & Webster had by 1920 become one of the nation's largest electric power engineering firms; it was as well an operator and utility holding company, and as such it pressed the forefront of the new culture. By 1927 it had built ten percent of the nation's power facilities; it managed or owned 2.31 percent of that year's generated electricity.[15]

At Stone & Webster modern electrical engineering and modern business accounting met, and out of their union came our dominant twentieth century valuations of both public investment and private man. From the earliest years of the firm, accounting demanded the partners' closest attention. As consulting engineers their work went forward on a cost-plus basis, and therefore careful accounts had to be kept for the clients. Moreover, to succeed in the competition for business Stone & Webster had to complete its jobs on time and to bring them in close to their initial cost estimates.[16] Similarly, the management of gas works and street railways and electric companies for stock and bondholders required reliable accounting practices. Already in 1901 when the firm managed about a dozen properties, it established a uniform system of accounts for each of its clients.[17] The next year it commenced a series of reorganizations of its engineering operations with an eye to getting closer control over the costs of its construction projects.[18]

But Stone & Webster was more than an electrical engineering firm with some related business office where a lot of accountants were employed: its entire approach united the two arts. First as engineers exploring the possibilities of the application of the science of electricity, and then later as engineers helping to plan large capital investments, they were concerned with output per dollar, kilowatts per ton of coal, horsepowers per foot of dam, losses per mile of transmission. Whether in the optimistic early years (1887-1912), when costs of electricity fell from 25ᶜ to 10ᶜ a kilowatt hour, or in the discouraged Great Depression years, the drive of the firm and the industry concentrated upon reducing unit costs through ever larger production installations.[19] Stone & Webster's engineering designs for clients, its own management bookkeeping, its special statistical services which it created to monitor system performance, and its elaborate examinations for bondholders, bankruptcy trustees, and investment banking syndicates, all were directed toward this narrow goal of balancing capital investment with kilowatt output costs.

Such exactitude in calculations of goals and performance inevitably influenced the men and institutions that performed such tasks. Stone & Webster were no faddists caught up in the enthusiasms of the early twentieth century efficiency movement, but as the number of engineers grew from twenty, to two-hundred, to eight-hundred-and-fifty, all the modern organization's tests of billable output of staff teams came to be applied to the firm's employees.[20]

In the early years of the firm, the measure of man seemed to rest upon the simple propositions of college athletics. An employee was assumed to be a person who would respond favorably to a neat, clean, orderly setting, and who would accept such measures of productivity and personal evaluation as engineering and accounting conventions made possible. Within that context of safety, comfort, and measurement each worker was expected to be a manly competitor, a person who would find personal satisfaction and corporate reward by attempting to match or outdo his fellow employees.

"It ought to be stated right here, as a general principle," a Stone & Webster engineer wrote, "that any man who will allow another man under similar conditions to do more or better work than he does is not the man whom the superintendent wants as a foreman, or for that matter, in any capacity whatever."[21] A blunt voice of an earlier time before the elaboration of the technique and jargon of corporate personnel work, but the Stone & Webster field engineer gave an accurate description of the beginnings of modern measurement of employees in large organizations. Measurement to billable costs and the evaluation of white collar and supervisory workers by cost accounting should not be imagined to be a mere extension of the craft traditions of piece work. Here the worker himself often participates in the process of design of the task and often the design of the measurements as well. The result is that curious new culture of large-scale office work—an employee enmeshed in small and large networks, the acceptance of some degree of personal and group responsibility, clean comfortable surroundings, and a form of judging self-worth that rests upon the conventions of modern accounting and the firm's capital structure.

Now electric power companies, like railroads before them, and the military suppliers of our own day, have put out a lot of propaganda, even false and misleading advertising. Some power companies are alleged, like railroads, to have corrupted legislators, even purchased whole legislatures. But whatever injustices such activities may have wrought, they lack the significance of the impact of electric power directly and indirectly upon our culture. The most important direct consequence of electricity, of course, has been its addition of numerous very large inadvertent communities. Yet we Americans remain blind to the workings and possibilities of these communities.

Electric power was not hidden from us; indeed, we have been continuously urged to consume it. Nevertheless we are blind to it, as blind to it as the men who built and operated it because we all evaluate it in the same ways as the early engineers. We measure system efficiency by the narrow tests of capital costs and kilowatt output, and we measure the lives of those who work in the giant new offices and factories by equally narrow tests. Indeed the most perplexing inheritance we derived from the early twentieth century union of engineering and accounting is our strange fixity. We seem deeply absorbed in measuring everything, but we seem unable to carry on sustained public debate over what should be measured and how it should be weighed.

NOTES

1 William H. Blood, Jr., "The First Generation of Electricity," *Stone and Webster Public Service Journal*, 11 (November, 1912), pp. 321-23; John P. McKay, *Tramways and Trolleys, the Rise of Urban Mass Transit in Europe* (Princeton, 1976), pp. 36-51.

2 *Who's Who in New England, 1909; The Story of Stone & Webster, 1888-1932* (pamphlet, Company print, Boston, 1932); *Dictionary of American Biography*.

3 Russell Robb, "Early History of the Firm" *Public Service Journal*, 1 (August, 1907), pp. 4-5; L.B. Buchanan, "Stone and Webster's Laboratory," *Public Service Journal*, 1 (September, 1907), pp. 145-49.

4 Robb, "Early History of the Firm," *Public Service Journal*, 1 (July, 1907), p. 6.

5 "The Stone & Webster Organization," *Street Railway Journal*, 28 (July, 1906), pp. 27-31.

6 "Stone & Webster," *Fortune*, 11(November, 1930), p. 94.

7 L.B. Buchanan, "Stone & Webster in the Field of Electro-Chemistry," *Public Service Journal*, 1 (September, 1907), pp. 150-53; Arthur D. Little letter, *Public Service Journal*, 49 (July, 1932), p. 473; Arthur Dehon Little, *Who's Who in New England*, 1916.

8 *Who's Who in New England, 1916; Fortune* (November, 1930), p. 92; *New York Times*, obit, May 11, 1950; *Technology Review*, 52 (July, 1950), p. 523.

9 *Who's Who in New England*, 1916; *Fortune* (November, 1930), pp. 91-92; obit, *New York Times*, February 25, 1941; *Technology Review*, 43 (April 1, 1951), p. 263.

10 *Public Service Journal*, 11 (Sept., 1912), pp. 170-75.

11 *Public Service Journal*, 11 (July, 1912), pp. 7-11; 12 (January, 1913), p. 32.

12 *Public Service Journal*, 8 (April, 1911), p. 287; 8 (June, 1911), pp. 411-21.

13 *Survey Graphic* May, 1925, reprinted as *Planning the Fourth Migration: The Neglected Vision of the Regional Planning Association of America*, (Carl Sussman, ed., Cambridge, 1976); and Gifford Pinchot, "Giant Power," *Survey*, 51 (March 1, 1924), pp. 561-62.

[14] National Civic Federation, *Municipal and Private Operation of Utilities* (New York, 1907) 3 v.; *Public Service Journal,* 1 (September, 1907), pp. 145-46; Frederick P. Royce, "A Consideration of the Commissioner of Corporations on Water Power Development in the United States," 10 (May, 1912), pp. 335-44.

[15] "Tabulations of 15 Largest Public Utility Operators in the Country," July 1, 1928 memo in "Informative Data 1927-31," looseleaf notebook, Stone & Webster library, Boston, Mass.

[16] "Why Stone & Webster Does No Lump Sum Work," memo, January 1, 1929, "Informative Data 1927-31" notebook.

[17] "The Stone & Webster Organization," *Street Railway Journal,* 28 (July, 1906), pp. 27-29.

[18] Howard L. Rogers, "Stone & Webster Engineering Corporation," *Public Service Journal,* 1 (August, 1907), pp. 57-59.

[19] "Editorial Comment," *Public Service Journal,* 11 (October, 1912), p. 235; *Annual Report for 1933, Stone & Webster,* p. 10.

[20] Henry G. Bradlee, "Consideration of Certain Limitations of Scientific Engineering," *Public Service Journal,* 8 (May, 1911), pp. 334-37; "Size of Engineering Department," Memo, Sept. 1, 1927, Informative Data, 1927-31.

[21] "How to Increase the Efficiency of Retort House Foremen," *Public Service Journal,* 1 (August, 1907), p. 67.

Comment

RUTH SCHWARTZ COWAN

The hour is late, the room is warm, and only the *cognoscenti* are present; this is a fine moment to let our imaginations loose. Professor Warner has reminded us of the subtle ways in which the electrical network influences our lives, even though we (both as historians and as individuals) often forget that it is there. He has also suggested that the people who first established the network, such as Charles A. Stone and Edwin S. Webster, had a revolutionary impact on history (especially urban history) even though (in their private and personal lives) they were virtually models of conventionality. By taking flight into counterfactual history I would like to propose that Stone and Webster (and many others like them) were actually fairly conservative revolutionaries and that if their private lives had been something other than what they were, the electrical networks in which we are encased today would have altered our lives in ways which would have been so radical as to be scarcely imaginable.

Professor Warner tells us that in 1893 Webster married Jane dePeyster Hovey and that nine years later Stone married Mary Adams Leonard. Let us imagine, for a moment, what might have happened if those good ladies had (somewhat in the fashion of *The Graduate*) been spirited away from the altar, leaving Charlotte Perkins Gilman and Melusina Fay Peirce to stand in their places. The new brides would have been older than their respective spouses (Gilman by six years, Peirce by thirty) but since this is counterfactual history we need not worry. I have chosen Gilman and Peirce for this strange exercise because they were both passionate advocates of cooperative housekeeping.[1] Peirce had been the founder of the Cambridge Cooperative Housekeeping Society, which she organized in 1869, when Stone and Webster were only two years old, in the very same city in which they were later to attend college. This experiment (it was a consumer's cooperative) failed within a few months, but Peirce continued to write about the advantages of cooperative housekeeping throughout her long life, and in 1903 she even patented designs for the construction of apartment houses that would facilitate cooperative living. Gilman was somewhat less of an activist than Peirce, but in her influential books, *Women and Economics* (1898) and *The Home* (1903), she argued for the virtues of centralized housekeeping as well as childcare (although she believed that these should be undertaken as entrepreneurial rather than cooperative ventures). Subsequently in a

324 RUTH SCHWARTZ COWAN

novel, *What Diantha Did* (serialized in Gilman's magazine, *The Forerunner* in 1909 and 1910) she created a character, Diantha Bell, who succeeded at just such a venture, although when Gilman's disciple Harriet Rodman actually tried it a few years later in real-life New York the result was a failure. Peirce and Gilman were forceful and independent women; neither would have married the fledglings Stone and Webster if the two gentlemen had not been similarly convinced (counterfactually) of the great virtues of cooperative, or at the very least, communal housekeeping.

Having let our imaginations ramble to this extent we might just as well let them wander a bit farther, recalling as we do so, another M.I.T. alumnus, Gerard Swope (class of '95) who became the president of General Electric in 1922 and who thus also helped to shape the electrical network in which Professor Warner is interested.[2] Swope married a social worker, Mary Dayton Hill, in 1898. While allowing him his own choice in a spouse let us alter the facts of Swope's life to the extent of imagining what might have happened if he and his wife, instead of living in successively grander country estates, had remained residents of Hull House, which is where they had met and where they had lived during the first year of their marriage. Under the leadership of Jane Addams, Hull House advocated cooperative housekeeping not just for the residents of the settlement house, but also for the people the house was built to serve. By the end of the nineteenth century Hull House was operating a community day nursery, a public kitchen and a cooperative apartment house for young working women, as well as providing room, board, and laundering services for its staff and its volunteers. Swope must have admired what Addams was able to accomplish in this way because late in his life (long after retiring from G.E.) he became active in the movement to create cooperative housing in New York City, but he did not (except now, in our imaginations) choose communalism as a permanent life-style for himself.

But imagine what might have happened if he had! Swope would have realized that cooperative housekeeping requires huge refrigerators, locker-type freezers, central vacuum cleaners, enormous washing machines, industrial mangles, and twelve-burnered stoves; and thus, in 1923, when he began to include consumers' goods in G.E.'s manufacturing plans he might have scheduled these massive implements (rather than their miniscule cousins) for mass production and, hence, for lowered prices. At the same time he might have decided to devote General Electric's vast resources in advertising, marketing and public relations to the task of convincing other Americans that communal or cooperative kitchens were actually "better plans, for better living" than the private, single family dwellings to which they had previously been (well, at least some of them) accustomed. As the roaring 20's turned into the depressed 30's some

Americans, anxious to cut costs wherever they could, might actually have taken him up on it.

As it happens, in the period between 1900 and 1930 some Americans actually did try communal dining clubs, cooperative nursery schools, residential hotels, cooperative laundries, municipal heating plants and community freezers—bits and pieces of cooperative housekeeping—but the vast majority of these experiments failed within a few years.[4] But imagine what might have happened to them if they had been founded in cities in which Stone and Webster (our "counterfactual" Stone and Webster, that is) had been called in as consultants. Fervent believers in a bright future for cooperative housekeeping, Stone and Webster would have advised the owners of electrical utilities to design the grids that they were planning for new sections of the city on the assumption that cooking, refrigeration, and laundering (the prime household users of electrical energy) would be carried out, not in households, but in centrally located facilities. Stone and Webster might further have suggested that the utilities encourage the creation of such facilities by rate-structuring schemes that would make electricity (above the level needed for lighting and perhaps heating) expensive to householders and inexpensive to cooperatives. In such communities suburban developers might have had very good reasons for designing kitchenless houses; utility companies might have given up trying to convince every homeowner to buy a washing machine and a refrigerator; and nascent cooperative ventures might have found themselves in an encouraging economic environment rather than a hostile one.[5]

Imagine what might have happened then! The technological systems created in these counterfactual cities in the 1920's might have been extended to other cities in the 1930's, since they were clearly so advantageous in straitened economies. The postwar housing boom might have brought with it a Levittown that had communal kitchens and daycare centers, and a Crestwood Heights in which there was a communal laundry at the end of every cul-de-sac. In the sixties and seventies we might have been blessed with condominiums that had central vacuum cleaners and community kitchens where swimming pools ought to be. You and I might be going home this evening with the firm understanding (indeed, we might not even need to be thinking about it) that our dinners would be waiting for us when we got there, and our clean laundry as well.

Of course it is possible (unfortunately, probably likely) that even in my counterfactual world General Electric's mammoth appliances would have met the same fate as the Edsel and Stone and Webster would have been laughed out of Kansas City, Hoboken, and Poughkeepsie—but my point is, I hope, clear. The graduates of M.I.T. (and other similar institutions) had an important determining effect upon the shape of our cities and the conduct of our lives, unsung by

326 RUTH SCHWARTZ COWAN

historians (and sociologists) though they may be. These electrical engineers and management consultants and systems specialists carried their social assumptions along with them as they marched off to build our electrical grids, our roads and bridges and tunnels, our oil burner thermostats and our microwave ovens—and since those social assumptions were almost always conventional ones, the revolutions that they created were almost always conservative.

NOTES

[1] The description of Peirce and Gilman which follows is based upon, Dolores Hayden, *The Grand Domestic Revolution: A History of Feminist Designs for American Homes, Neighborhoods and Cities* (Cambridge, Mass., 1981), *passim.*
[2] On Swope see, David G. Loth, *Swope of G.E.* (New York, 1958).
[3] Hayden, *Grand Domestic Revolution*, pp. 164-170.
[4] For the reasons for their failure, see Ruth Schwartz Cowan, *More Work for Mother: The Ironies of Household Technology from the Open Hearth to the Microwave* (New York, 1983), Ch. 5.
[5] For an understanding of how electric grids are built and electrical rates are set, and how these affect urban history, see, Mark H. Rose and John Clark, "Light, Heat and Power: Energy Choices in Kansas City, Wichita and Denver, 1900-1935," *Journal of Urban History*, 5 (May, 1979), pp. 360-84; and Mark H. Rose, "Light and Heat in Denver and Kansas City: New Environments and the Social and Geographic Bases of Technological Innovation, 1900-1940" (forthcoming).

Authors

JOHN BODNAR is an Associate Professor of History at Indiana University. His research focuses on the relationship between industry and immigration; and his publicatons include *Immigration and Industrialization: Ethnicity in an American Mill Town* and *Workers' World: Kinship, Community, and Protest.*

RICHARD M. CANDEE teaches Preservation Management for Boston University's Historic Preservation Program. He has done museum and architectual consulting work for a host of clients throughout New England and is the author of numerous historical and architectural studies.

FRANCIS G. COUVARES is an Assistant Professor of History and American Studies at Amherst College. He is the author of several studies that examine the relationship between class, culture, and the city, including his *The Remaking of Pittsburgh: Class and Culture in an Industrializing City, 1877-1919.*

RUTH SCHWARTZ COWAN is an Associate Professor of History at the State University of New York at Stony Brook. A historian of science and technology, her most recent publication is *More Work for Mother: The Ironies of Household Technology from the Open Hearth to the Microwave.*

MICHAEL BREWSTER FOLSOM is the Director of the Charles River Museum of Industry in Waltham, Massachusetts. He has written on a wide range of topics; included among his publications is *The Philosophy of Manufactures: Early Debates Over Industrialization in the United States,* co-edited with Steven D. Lubar.

MICHAEL FRISCH teaches urban and social history at the State University of New York at Buffalo. His many published writings include *Town into City: Springfield, Massachusetts and The Meaning of Community, 1840-1880,* and *Working Class America: Essays on Labor, Community, and American Society,* co-edited with Daniel J. Walkowitz.

DAVID S. GROSS is an Associate Professor of English at the University of Oklahoma, where he received the University Regents' Award for Excellence in Teaching. He is the author of numerous articles on modern European and American literature and history and is presently working on studies of E.L. Doctorow and William Blake.

LAURENCE F. GROSS is the Curator at the Museum of American Textile History in North Andover, Massachusetts. He has extensive field experience studying American textile technology and has published a number of articles on American labor history and the history of technology.

PATRICIA HILLS is an Associate Professor of Art History at Boston University and Adjunct Curator of 18th and 19th Century American Art at New York's Whitney Museum. Publications include *The Painters' America: Rural and Urban Life, 1810-1910,* and the text of *The Working American,* a catalogue from the first major art exhibit organized by a labor union in the United States.

SUSAN E. HIRSCH teaches in the Economics Department at Northwestern University, where she is also Assistant Director of the Program on Women. Her work in the fields of American labor, urban, and women's history includes *Roots of the American Working Class: The Industrialization of Crafts in Newark, 1800-1860.*

DAVID P. JAFFEE teaches American material culture at Georgetown University and is working on an exhibition, "Everyday Life in Nineteenth-Century America," at the Smithsonian Institution's National Museum of American History. His research in cultural history focuses on rural art and country craft.

ERIC E. LAMPARD is a Professor of History at the State University of New York at Stony Brook. His many influential writings in the field of urban history have appeared in various publications during the past thirty years.

JANICE L. REIFF has worked as Co-Director of the Family and Community History Center at the Newberry Library and also teaches American social history and quantitative methods at Northwestern University and the University of Illinois, Chicago. She has written articles on urban, labor, and family history in *The Journal of Social History, The Journal of Urban History,* and elsewhere.

JOHN R. STILGOE, author of *Common Landscape of America, 1580 to 1845* and *Metropolitan Corridor: Railroads and the American Scene,* is a Professor of Visual and Environmental Studies and the History of Landscape at Harvard University; he is presently writing a book on the American response to ocean environments.

WILLIAM M. STOTT is Professor of English and Director of the American Studies Program at the University of Texas at Austin. His publications include *Documentary Expression and Thirties America* and the editing of Walker Evans photographs from the "Let Us Now Praise Famous Men" project.

CECELIA TICHI is a Professor in the English Department at Boston University. Her many writings on American literature include *New World, New Earth: Environmental Reform in American Literature from the Puritans through Whitman.*

FRANCIS R. WALSH is a Professor of History at the University of Lowell, where he has taught urban, social, and ethnic history for the past twenty years. His publications include articles on these subjects in a number of professional journals.

SAM BASS WARNER, JR., is William Edwards Huntington Professor of History and Social Science at Boston University. An acknowledged authority on urban history, Professor Warner's many writings include *Streetcar Suburbs, The Process of Growth in Boston, 1870-1900,* and *The Private City, Philadelphia in Three Periods of Its Growth.*

ROBERT WEIBLE is the Historian at Lowell National Historical Park, where his research relates to the park's interpretive planning and cultural resource management. He has served as Chairman of the Lowell Conference on Industrial History since 1980.

VIRGINIA YANS-McLAUGHLIN is an Associate Professor of History at Rutgers University. She has studied and written extensively about women's history, the family, ethnicity, and the city. Writings include her award-winning *Family and Community: Italian Immigrants in Buffalo, 1880-1930.*